Kennedy and the Promise of the Sixties

The book explores life in America during that brief promising moment in the early sixties when John F. Kennedy was president. Kennedy's Cold War frustrations in Cuba and Vietnam worried Americans. The 1962 Missile Crisis narrowly avoided a nuclear disaster. The civil rights movement gained momentum with student sit-ins, Freedom Rides, and crises in Mississippi and Alabama. Martin Luther King, Jr., emerged as a spokesman for nonviolent social change. The American family was undergoing rapid change. Betty Friedan launched the Women's Movement. The Beat authors Jack Kerouac and Allen Ginsberg gained respectability. Joan Baez and Bob Dylan revived folk music. Roy Lichtenstein and Andy Warhol produced Pop Art. Ginsberg, Aldous Huxley, Timothy Leary, and Ken Kesey began to promote psychedelic drugs.

The early sixties were a period of marked political, social, and cultural change. The old was swept away, and the United States began to become the country that it is today.

W. J. Rorabaugh has taught at the University of Washington in Seattle since 1976. He is the author of *The Alcoholic Republic* (1979), *The Craft Apprentice* (1986), and *Berkeley at War: The 1960s* (1989). Professor Rorabaugh has held fellowships from the National Endowment for the Humanities, the National Humanities Center, the Newberry Library, the Huntington Library, and the John F. Kennedy Library.

Kennedy and the Promise of the Sixties

W. J. RORABAUGH

University of Washington

CAMBRIDGE
UNIVERSITY PRESS

PUBLISHED BY THE PRESS SYNDICATE OF THE UNIVERSITY OF CAMBRIDGE
The Pitt Building, Trumpington Street, Cambridge, United Kingdom

CAMBRIDGE UNIVERSITY PRESS
The Edinburgh Building, Cambridge CB2 2RU, UK
40 West 20th Street, New York, NY 10011-4211, USA
477 Williamstown Road, Port Melbourne, VIC 3207, Australia
Ruiz de Alarcón 13, 28014 Madrid, Spain
Dock House, The Waterfront, Cape Town 8001, South Africa

http://www.cambridge.org

First published 2002

Printed in the United States of America

Typeface Sabon 10.5/15 pt.   *System* LATEX 2_ε [TB]

A catalog record for this book is available from the British Library.

Library of Congress Cataloging in Publication Data available

ISBN 0 521 81617 3 hardback

For Kurt and Gladys Lang

Contents

Introduction

It was a promising time. In January 1960 Americans were hopeful and optimistic. Having lived through the "fabulous fifties," they looked forward to the "soaring sixties," a phrase that evoked the coming of the space age. Enjoying peace abroad and prosperity at home, they envisioned a future national bounty that accommodated both private luxury and public expenditure. Americans expected fatter paychecks, suburban ranch houses, and color television. Families planned to explore faraway places, such as the new Disneyland theme park in California, in their 22-foot, gas-guzzling automobiles equipped with grand trunks and rocket-like tail fins, or they might travel abroad on Boeing's new commercial jet planes. Scientists might cure most illnesses, including cancer and heart disease, just as polio had been licked in the fifties. There was enormous confidence in government. Urban planners were preparing to demolish decayed neighborhoods in older cities to pave eight-lane freeways – 12 for the Dan Ryan Expressway in Chicago – and to build 20-story high-rise public housing for the poor. Unprecedented numbers of young people would be able to attend ever-expanding public colleges, and many of those who did not do so could obtain high-paying jobs in unionized industries.

Affluence made the sixties promising. Prosperity opened tantalizing possibilities for building anew, for curing injustice, and for remaking American society and culture. Harnessing change, however, required leaders capable of setting priorities and making choices. A youthful, dynamic, optimistic, and self-confident John Fitzgerald Kennedy offered to play that role. More than most political figures, he understood that the United States both faced difficult challenges and enjoyed unusual opportunities that rarely come to any nation. In 1960 he ran for president out of a strong conviction that he could seize the moment, shape the country, and change the world. Born to great wealth, superbly educated, and well-traveled, Kennedy had devoted his life to public service. Unlike many other politicians, he understood the United States and other countries from close personal observation. He also exuded the supreme self-confidence commonly found only in the upper class. Few doubted that patriotism and his perception of the national interest drove his ideas and plans. Serious, witty, demanding, inquiring, restless, and impatient, he spurred others to greater efforts as he sought to mold his country and its history. In no sense was he self-aggrandizing. Upbeat by nature, he was both a unique figure and a true representative of his times. Kennedy put such a stamp upon the early sixties that one can scarcely talk about those years without discussing him.

At the same time, the era was "promising" in two distinct ways. In one sense, the sixties, despite Cold War tensions, promised not only continued peace and prosperity, as we have suggested, but also new technology and major new government initiatives to improve the quality of life, as Kennedy advocated. In this sense, "promising" was about *fulfillment* of promises. In a second sense, however, "promising" meant that Americans sought more than could be obtained. They were hooked on hope. This second definition was about *making* promises, and it posed problems. The society ran the risk of becoming overextended in trying to carry out aspirations, or Americans might stumble by embracing unrealistic, exaggerated, or utopian schemes. Far too often, plans that were proposed in the sixties bore little relationship to goals that could actually be accomplished. In this "promising" time an aura of unreality sometimes prevailed, and the political, social, and cultural atmosphere too often bordered on euphoria. Not only was the increasing affluence of the fifties projected forward on a rising trajectory that admitted no possibility of a future slowdown, but the can-do spirit and exuberance with which Americans addressed all problems did not bode well when an issue arose, such as Vietnam, that called for a discerning eye to tell the difference between a situation that might be ameliorated and a difficulty that could not be solved. The coldly calculating Kennedy, had he lived, might have been able to tell the difference. Others failed to do so.

One problem with a "promising" time, in other words, is that hope will get so far ahead of experience that the gap will bring hope itself crashing to the ground. Some of the turmoil in the later sixties can be understood as the result of frustration that was derived from that kind of disappointment. In the early sixties the budding civil rights movement lived on hope, which enabled participants to make sacrifices and endure enormous hardships. The pinnacle of that movement's optimism came when Martin Luther King, Jr., gave his "I Have a Dream" speech at the March on Washington in August 1963, but that dazzling spectacle of affirmation did not explain how rights advocates ought to proceed in order to realize all their aspirations. The peace movement, too, enjoyed bouyancy in the early sixties, although supporters' optimism was rooted less in fact amid some of the Cold War's worst crises, including the Cuban Missile Crisis, than in a growing desire for peace. In an optimistic time, desire perhaps counted for more than did reason. In popular culture, folk musicians in the early sixties called for both peace and civil rights, but group singing did not create peace, even if it did generate solidarity among young Americans and put them in a frame of mind to make love rather than war, a fact that no one in power took into account when launching the Vietnam War in 1965.

Throughout American history intensely hopeful periods such as the Progressive Era, the New Deal, and the sixties have invariably, if not inevitably, ended in disappointment, as reformers have discovered that the political, social, or cultural changes which they tried to make were far more difficult to accomplish than they had expected. Here is the paradox: A general mood of optimism is necessary to launch any period of reform, but the prevalence of that very mood causes reformers to push for changes that go well beyond the society's capacity for change in a short period of time. In the early sixties gaps between hopes and realities were not always clear, since one characteristic of a "promising" time is that these discrepancies can be explained, even with little evidence, as problems about to be solved quickly. As the decade proceeded, however, and as promises remained unfulfilled, the discrepancies between aspirations and performance became more glaring, more painful, and more frustrating. Even before Kennedy's assassination in 1963, some Americans felt strong doubts about progress concerning peace and race. Rising doubts, which were an undercurrent rather than a main theme during the early sixties, are an enemy to any promising time.

Another trait of the early sixties concerns dark undercurrents. On the surface, Americans were eager to marshal resources and energy to address the hard problems of the Cold War and race relations. Although families were in crisis and women were beginning to question their role in society, the era's overall optimism obscured emerging difficulties about gender and sexuality. At the same time, American culture was also beginning to undergo major upheaval. Under the surface, however, Americans showed fear of nuclear war, anxiety about race relations, bewilderment over decomposition of the traditional family, and unease at unsettling cultural experimentation that threatened to dissolve longstanding mainstream mores. Respect for tradition, which had been strong in the fifties, rapidly eroded. At this deeper level the age was anything but "promising," and much of the emphasis on the country's bright future may have been an attempt to hide undercurrents of anxiety and doubt. Strident insistence upon a "promising" future inhibited discussion of darker truths that Americans wished to ignore. Incessant "promising" to solve problems, even when unrealistic, kept the focus optimistic and further obscured the society's dilemmas.

In the early sixties Americans preferred to ride on the surface, just like the California surfers in the Beach Boys' popular tunes. Although Kennedy's approach to the Cold War was not simpleminded, the administration rarely penetrated to the deepest levels of insight about the human condition. Perhaps the most important consequence of the Cuban Missile Crisis in 1962 was that it forced high officials to do a certain amount of soul-searching. The civil rights movement did reshape race relations, and Betty Friedan raised questions that started what was later to become the women's movement. The most profound challenges to superficial thinking, however, came in the cultural realm from a number of new practitioners. The Beat writers Jack Kerouac and Allen Ginsberg, both of whom gained increasing respectability in the early sixties, the great songwriter Bob Dylan, and the pop artists Roy Lichtenstein and Andy Warhol collectively destroyed an already decayed mainstream culture that was largely left over from the late nineteenth century. Dylan and Warhol, in particular, used irony, parody, and satire in new ways to juxtapose the overt surface against the culture's hidden underside. As we shall see, in the early sixties American culture, society, and politics showed many ambiguous qualities that suggest that the period was an in-between time that partook both of aspects that predominated in earlier years and of aspects that prevailed afterward.

Also evident in the early sixties are tensions between public expressions and private thoughts. While printed materials, including magazines and newspapers, provide a rough guide to the period, letters not intended for publication by both famous and ordinary people reveal more. Letters avoid the propagandistic excesses of the published word and better capture the period's flavor at a more introspective level. These private thoughts, which are quoted extensively in this book, both reinforce and somewhat alter our understanding of events. Letters show that Americans' two main concerns in the early sixties were the Cold War and race. At the time few were totally candid about either subject in public. In the case of the Cold War, public rhetoric, including Kennedy's, was tough. Private letters much more frequently expressed fear of nuclear war, which most people hesitated to state publicly. No one wanted to be called a communist sympathizer. In 1960, the era of Senator Joseph McCarthy's repression of dissent was a living memory. The difference between public expression and private thought about race is narrower and more subtle. While public talk about race often emphasized support for abstract rights in opaque ways, many white Americans' private views showed bewilderment about black demands as well as fear of an uncertain future in which race relations would have to change in ways that were yet to be worked out.

The relationship between private thought and public expression also underwent a significant transformation in these years. Elite control of culture declined, formal censorship began to collapse, and it became possible, even fashionable in avant-garde circles, to voice publicly what had previously been said only privately. Following the lead of *Playboy* magazine, entertainers such as Lenny Bruce discussed Sex on the public stage for the first time. As matters which had previously been private now became public, or as the distinction between that which was private and that which was public was increasingly blurred, the frankness and candor associated with private views began more and more to be heard in public settings. The Beat writers, avant-garde filmmakers, and pop artists attacked the hypocrisies that governed polite society, although a full flowering of this trend would not occur until the counterculture emerged in the later sixties. Stripping society of its protective armor, however, by giving public expression to private thought not only increased honesty, but it also coarsened discourse, offended many

Americans, and raised so much disharmony that it threatened the public cohesiveness necessary to see the era as a promising time.

These are the main themes in this book. As a larger goal, the book explores the intersection of politics, society, and culture during a relatively brief period marked by upheaval and significant change. At the political level, the book begins with Kennedy's remarkable, tone-setting election in 1960, moves through several Cold War crises, and ends with Kennedy's assassination in 1963. In the early sixties, however, politics was clearly less important than social and cultural upheaval. At the social level, the book considers the civil rights movement's explosive upsurge: the southern student sit-ins in 1960; the Freedom Rides of 1961; the white riot against James Meredith's admission to the University of Mississippi in 1962; and the March on Washington in 1963. In the early sixties families were also in crisis. The number of working women grew quickly, the first of the baby boomers born after 1945 became teenagers, sexual mores started to change, and Betty Friedan launched the women's movement. At the cultural level, changes were profound. In the fifties, the Beat writers had already attacked middle-class values. At the beginning of the sixties new folk musicians, including Bob Dylan, advocated social and political change, and pop artists redefined art in a way that announced the arrival of postmodernism. As early as 1960, a handful of visionaries that included Aldous Huxley, Allen Ginsberg, Timothy Leary, and Ken Kesey plotted to change the culture through psychedelic drugs.

Why should we examine the early sixties in so many different dimensions? Why should we look at this thin slice of time in such detail? First, the political, social, and cultural aspects during these years are interrelated in complex and fascinating ways. John Kennedy pledged to obtain better results in the Cold War with the Soviet Union. At the time, Americans perceived their country to be faring poorly. The Cold War required the United States to seek alliances with nonwhite nations, especially Japan, and civil rights leaders calculated, correctly, that they could gain federal support in their challenge to white supremacy. The rights movement not only presented ideals that encouraged others who felt dispossessed, including a number of women, to organize, but it also adopted new strategies and tactics that enabled the powerless to confront unjust power. This bottom-up, grassroots attack on the status quo is a key aspect of those years. At the same time, the cohesiveness of the Kennedy family and the public projection of that image appeared to offer reassurance about family as a source of stability at a time when many families faced redefinition, if not crisis. A waning white elite's stodgy, narrow definition of culture also came under attack. Cultural experimentation in the early sixties challenged traditional ideas about power, race, and gender. Indeed, without cultural change, social and political change might well have proved impossible at that time.

Second, this combination of cultural, social, and political change was greater than the sum of its parts. Not only did new literature, music, and art break down cultural barriers and open possibilities for further artistic exploration, but the very act of cultural reconceptualization encouraged Americans to liberate the *self* from social and political constraints. Similarly, civil rights activists found that their revivalistic movement was personally transformative. Although often initially drawn to action by idealism, most participants learned that a period of intense activism, sometimes risking jail or violence, left them emotionally exhausted. Accompanying the sense of burnout was a feeling of profound personal change: They felt their souls transformed and their values, having been sorely tested, affirmed by the testimony of their lives. They emerged stronger, shrewder, tougher, and more willing to challenge other forms of injustice. It is no accident that women active in civil rights later became prominent feminists. The Cold War, too, affected Americans emotionally. Both ordinary people and top administration officials who lived through the near-nuclear war of the Cuban Missile Crisis emerged determined to avoid further crises of that type. The will to resist war grew, as a burgeoning peace movement sought new ways to soften the conflict between the United States and the Soviet Union.

Third, this particular slice of time is a crucial formative period. Most accounts of the sixties have focused on the turmoil and tumult from 1964, beginning with the Free Speech Movement at the University of California, to 1969, when the Black Panthers swaggered and the Weather Underground raged violently in the streets. It is possible to argue that the sixties did not begin until 1965, when African Americans rioted in Watts and when large numbers of American combat troops were sent to Vietnam, and did not end until 1974, when Richard Nixon resigned, or even 1975, when the North Vietnamese marched into Saigon. Compared to the years between 1964 and 1969, the period from 1960 through 1963 has drawn much less attention. Today, many Americans believe that the United States during Kennedy's presidency was an idyllic society, some sort of Camelot. If only Kennedy had lived, runs this sentiment (it can hardly be called an argument), then the terrible violence and chaos of the late sixties would never have occurred. It is certainly true that Kennedy's death, as shown in this book, did jar the nation. A promising time ended, as the assassination in Dallas killed both a popular president and many of the hopes that he represented. At the very least, Kennedy's death proved sobering, and the years that followed lacked a certain joy and innocence that Americans had felt in the early sixties.

If it is easy, due to the assassination, to draw a distinction between the Kennedy years and the less promising time that followed, it is more difficult to fix precisely the beginning of the early sixties. One could start with Kennedy's inauguration in January 1961, when the new political administration began. On the other hand, Kennedy's rise from obscure contender to president-elect during 1960 also is part of the story. Kennedy was an underdog who won a narrow victory, a fact that deeply affected his presidency. The Cold War began more than a decade before Kennedy's election, and it lasted for a generation after his death, but critical crises occurred during the early sixties: The demoralizing Bay of Pigs invasion and the building of the Berlin Wall in 1961; the Cuban Missile Crisis in 1962; and the coup against Ngo Dinh Diem in Vietnam in 1963. By contrast, Eisenhower's presidency in the fifties was relatively tranquil. The civil rights movement can be traced to the bus boycott in Montgomery, Alabama, during 1955 and 1956, but although that event made Martin Luther King, Jr., famous, it did not spawn other large-scale demonstrations until southern black students began to protest against discrimination at lunch counters with sit-ins in early 1960. The movement then accelerated from 1961 to 1963. Changes in family life and culture, however, occurred more gradually.

One key to understanding the early sixties and how it differed markedly from the fifties is to think in terms of tone. Throughout the fifties a sort of conservatism and placidity predominated. Even though one can find contrary trends, as a number of astute historians have recently noted, advocates for change in those years, including the Beat writers, were often considered by mainstream Americans to be odd or offputting. In other words, while every decade has had its rebels, what sets the fifties apart from the sixties is that rebels in the fifties attracted few followers, because most Americans at that time prided themselves on conformity. Although conformity was always less widespread in practice during the fifties than the image of conformity would suggest, the country's atmosphere was not conducive to experimentation. McCarthyism cast a long shadow, and even in New York and San Francisco, the two cities at the heart of the fifties Beat subculture, the number of Beats was measured in the hundreds, not thousands, and harassment by police, thugs, media, and public opinion was constant. Only in the late fifties did the country begin to change. In an important development, censorship eased, and an establishment with waning power and self-confidence imposed fewer norms. Americans became more tolerant of difference, and restlessness amid the mainstream produced a rising interest in avant-garde experimentation.

The early sixties, then, is important because it was an in-between time, a short space lodged between a more conservative, cautious, and complacent era that preceded it and a more frenzied, often raucous, and even violent era that followed. It is easy, as scholars of the sixties know, to show the connections between the early sixties and the latter part of that decade. The saber-rattling of the Kennedy years, including the coup against Ngo Dinh Diem in Vietnam, encouraged the later American war in Vietnam. The civil rights movement, drained of its idealism, ended with demands for Black Power and urban riots. When one examines primary sources generated during the early sixties, however, one finds that these connections between the decade's earlier and later years, although real, are somewhat exaggerated. For example, when Students for a Democratic Society, which became a major antiwar organization late in the decade, drafted its crucial document, "The Port Huron Statement," in 1962, it had only about 500 paid members. At that same time a conservative group, Young Americans for Freedom, had 20,000 members. Scholars of the sixties give more importance to SDS than to YAF because SDS became the more significant organization during the course of the decade, but YAF counted for more in 1962. This book's intense exploration of the early sixties allows us to gauge more closely connections between the decade's earlier and later years.

At the same time, the fifties have thus far been insufficiently studied; to the extent that Americans in the early sixties continued to adhere to traditional values, many derived from pre–World War II culture, a close scrutiny of the early sixties will help shed light on customs that prevailed then but that were swept away during or after the upheavals of the later sixties. As suggested above, much change was already underway on a modest scale in the late fifties, so that the continuation of those trends and the acceleration of the rate of change were visible in the early sixties. Here again, private correspondence is valuable in suggesting the ambivalence that often surrounded change. Public expressions often either rigidly defended the status quo or trumpeted the new in hyped fashion. Private thoughts were more likely to express hesitation or ambivalence or to offer nuanced opinion about the meaning of new ideas and practices and how they related to other ongoing or new institutions or arrangements. A certain amount of puzzlement can be seen as matters were sorted out. In the end, cultures evolve and accrete. So do societies. And so do nonrevolutionary political entities. In the early sixties private letters often expressed surprise at innovations; change was occurring faster than many Americans could easily absorb, and letter writers frequently expressed apprehension or fear. Behind the glittering facade of Camelot as a promising time lurked an awful anxiety.

The more one thinks about the early sixties as a slice of time the more one is forced to focus on the curious figure of John Kennedy. As enigmatic a political personality as the United States has ever produced, he projected charm derived from a self-generated aura of mystery. When asked questions, Kennedy often replied with questions rather than with answers, preferred listening to talking, deflected the unwanted probe with quick wit, refused to make decisions that would disappoint some of his followers, and interposed himself between two people who disagreed with each other by leaving the impression with each that he agreed with that person. He was two-sided. Although these techniques along with his mastery of television guaranteed his popularity, which remained unusually high throughout his presidency, they did not enable him to accomplish much as president. To understand this preference for theatrical politics, we must remember that the early sixties was an in-between time partaking in part of the conservatism of the fifties and in part of the restlessness of the later sixties. Kennedy sensed this bifurcated mood and built his popularity upon it. Thus, he appealed to the country's already rising restless spirit by talking change, but, carefully watching how conservative southern Democrats reacted, he proved cautious by rarely engaging in action. The point of his televised political theater was to meld and reconcile those two halves while increasing his own celebrity.

In the end the early sixties, like any other era, has to be understood on its own terms. The years that preceded and followed were different, not only in tone, but in substance. This ambiguous, in-between quality is this short era's most important characteristic. Like all transitional periods, it truly did partake both of what had come before and of what would come after. Much of the anxiety expressed about both the Cold War and race was no doubt a misplaced psychological projection of a larger fear that all the old verities were crumbling. The cultural change was real, dramatic, and profound. People responded to this situation in quite different ways. Conservatives, in particular, felt threatened, believed that the country was changing beyond recognition, saw no way to rally the public to their side, and became helpless as they sank into insignificance. Despite the upsurge of the new Right, the early sixties was in no sense a conservative age. In this promising time, liberals responded to the perceived challenges by embracing change with enthusiasm, and because the problems looked like they could be solved, Americans as a whole during these years shifted from a more customary moderation toward liberalism. Boundless optimism and affluence helped sustain this outlook. Generational experience also played a role in this shift. Kennedy and other World War II veterans tended to have a more upbeat view about the future than did those Americans who had come of age before the war.

As in any other era where profound cultural changes take place, it was easier in the early sixties to see the breakup of the old order than to predict the complete shape of the new one. Many welcomed the decline of a stodgy elite culture, enforced by official censorship, that had predominated. The old order's destruction could be exciting, even exhilarating, particularly for creators of new literature, music, and art. At the same time, while such a cultural vacuum might enable visionaries to fantasize all sorts of tomorrows, which was another characteristic of the early sixties, the era's uncertain nature made it hard for anyone to plan for the prosaic future that was bound to follow upon the actual upheavals of the times. In other words, a certain yeastiness prevailed. The early sixties, however, offered other lessons. The Cuban Missile Crisis taught Americans and Russians that nuclear war was so dangerous that peaceful coexistence ought to be attempted. As the civil rights movement snowballed, it became clear that the racial crisis was going to be difficult to solve and that legalistic solutions, inevitably involving compromise, could not contain pent-up black energy. In 1963, the future of the women's movement was uncertain. In the long run, the political, social, and cultural changes that took place in the early sixties profoundly affected the way the United States evolved during the last third of the twentieth century.

Many people and institutions helped make this book possible. The project began with a generous Theodore C. Sorensen Fellowship from the John F. Kennedy Library. The University of Washington provided two paid leaves, support from the Keller Fund, and two excellent research assistants, David Faflik and Emily Graves. I profited from conversations about the period with Sydney Rome and Richard White. For hospitality, I am indebted to Jonathan Chu, Steven and Sheila Novak, Joseph and Cicely Ryshpan, Kent Wood and Teresa Lukas, and Mary Rorabaugh. Donald Critchlow, Susan Glenn, Richard Johnson, Richard Kirkendall, Phil Roberts, members of the History Research Group, and various press readers read part or all of the manuscript. I would also like to thank Lewis Bateman and Frank Smith at Cambridge University Press. Part of Chapter One includes some material from my article, "Moral Character, Policy Effectiveness, and the Presidency: The Case of JFK," *Journal of Policy History*, 10:4 (1998), 445–460. Copyright 1998 by The Pennsylvania State University. Reproduced by permission of the publisher.

Staff at the many archives where I examined manuscripts proved very helpful. Several people gave permission to use certain collections: Hugo L. Black, Jr., for his father's papers; William F. Buckley, Jr., for his papers; Anne Braden for the Carl and Anne Braden Papers; Betty Werlein Carter for the Hodding and Betty Werlein Carter Papers; and the NAACP National Office for the NAACP Papers.

For permission to quote from manuscript collections I would like to thank the University of California, Berkeley, Bancroft Library; University of California, Los Angeles, Special Collections; Columbia University, Rare Book and Manuscript Library; Cornell University, Rare and Manuscript Collections; Harvard University, Radcliffe Institute, Schlesinger Library; Lyndon B. Johnson Library; John F. Kennedy Library; Mississippi State University, Special Collections; University of Mississippi, Special Collections; University of North Carolina, Chapel Hill, Wilson Library, Southern Historical Collection; Princeton University, Seeley G. Mudd Manuscript Library; Franklin D. Roosevelt Library; Southern Illinois University, Morris Library, Special Collections; Stanford University, Hoover Institution Archives and Libraries Special Collections; Swarthmore College, Peace Collection; State Historical Society of Wisconsin; Yale University, Manuscripts and Archives.

For permission to quote specific items I am grateful to Mrs. Robert Amory for Robert Amory's oral history; Daniel Berrigan, S.J.; Hugo L. Black, Jr., for his father's papers; William F. Buckley, Jr.; Hodding Carter III for the Hodding and Betty Werlein Carter Papers; John Kenneth Galbraith; Bob Rosenthal and Harold Collen, respectively, for Allen and Louis Ginsberg items in the Allen Ginsberg Papers; Harold Ober Associates Incorporated for the John Bartlow Martin Papers; Matthew and Susanna Morgenthau for the Hans Morgenthau Papers; NAACP National Office; Walt Rostow; Arthur M. Schlesinger, Jr.; and Cathleen Douglas Stone.

W. J. R.
Seattle
January 2002

John Kennedy accepts the presidential nomination at the Democratic Convention, Los Angeles, July 15, 1960.

(Photo by Garry Winogrand. Seattle Art Museum. Purchased with funds from Pacific Northwest Bell, the Photography Council, the Polaroid Foundation, Mark Abrahamson, and the National Endowment for the Arts. 83.54.1

CHAPTER ONE

Kennedy

If John Fitzgerald Kennedy is intrinsically identified with the early 1960s, it is also true that those years are linked with Kennedy. In public memory, the man and the age are entwined and inseparable. However, in democratic societies, where custom, institutions, and public opinion both compel certain directions and inhibit others, leaders shape their times less than they, or we, like to admit. Yet, even in a democracy, a leader is not just a representative of the public will but a force for the projection, articulation, and refinement of that will. The best leaders express the aspirations of their age and, by using democratic means to forge political combinations, are able to implement some version of their own particular vision. For a brief period, John F. Kennedy tried to do so, and to understand the United States in the early sixties, one must come to terms with Kennedy, his character, and his often opaque politics. Kennedy's sudden rise to power itself reveals much about the times. At the beginning of 1960, half of Americans had never heard of the senator from Massachusetts. Before the year ended, he had won the nation's highest office. Along the way, he invented media-oriented, televisual, celebrity politics. His remarkable inaugural address in January 1961 impressed many people who had not voted for

1

him; he instantly gained 69 percent poll approval. Ratings throughout his presidency generally remained either at that level or higher. He became the most popular president since polling began in the 1930s.[1]

When Kennedy began his quest for the presidency in 1960, Americans sensed that they were entering a promising time. The country had settled into its post-World War II norm: unprecedented prosperity; the Cold War; a peacetime draft; technological innovation, including computers, which were already producing large corporate profits and layoffs due to automation among unionized blue-collar workers; permanent high income taxes – the top bracket remained 91 percent in 1960 – combined with massive government programs, including the new interstate highway system designed, in large part, to enable commuters to speed from the new suburbs to work downtown; and a commitment to schooling that would make the baby boomers the best educated generation in history. This drastic reorganization of American life during and after the war had caused little comment. Although World War II pushed young men forward with unusual speed, including the election of John Kennedy, Richard Nixon, and 67 other veterans to Congress in 1946, older conservatives who thought and acted in prewar patterns still ran key institutions in the fifties. There was nothing modern or reform-minded about the Federal Bureau of Investigation's J. Edgar Hoover (1895–1972; ruled 1924–1972), Selective Service's Lewis Hershey (1893–1977; r. 1940–1973), labor's George Meany (1894–1980; r. 1952–1979), or the Catholic church's Francis Cardinal Spellman (1889–1967; r. 1939–1967). Each held power for many years and would remain both entrenched and feared for a long time.[2]

During the fifties these grandees' enormous power along with the inevitable ossification of their respective institutions had provoked little comment. If Americans were tranquil and complacent, it was because the country was peaceful and prosperous. The standard of living, far above that of any other nation, was on its way to doubling in one generation. Despite automation, organized labor enjoyed steadily increasing real pay and benefits, unprecedented numbers of college graduates easily found good jobs, and corporate America, holding a near-monopoly on mass production of sophisticated goods for a global market, reaped record profits. This new wealth made Americans optimistic. "They are wonderfully confident...," observed the British journalist John Calmann in a letter to a friend. Millions bought increasing numbers of shiny, chrome-bumpered cars and watched television in their new suburban tract houses. By 1960, one-quarter of all American homes had been built in the past decade. Nothing symbolized the good life better than the backyard cookout, even if President Dwight Eisenhower had to grill his thick, succulent steaks on the White House roof. Sometimes the fifties were called the Great Barbecue.[3]

By the end of the fifties, however, some partygoers grew restless. "We maunder along," complained the historian Eric Goldman, "in a stupor of fat...." Many found Eisenhower's governance lethargic and lackadaisical. The philosopher Hannah Arendt privately declared Ike "senile," while Kennedy's young speechwriter Richard Goodwin considered the old president a "do-nothing." (One joke went: Q.: How does an Eisenhower doll work? A.: You wind it up, and it does nothing for eight years.) In a letter that expressed a frustration that was hard to state publicly, the liberal newspaper columnist Joe Alsop wrote that the federal government "resembles a dead whale upon a beach." In addition, many intellectuals, including Dwight Macdonald and John Kenneth Galbraith, found the crass consumerism of the fifties vapid. The twice-defeated Democratic presidential candidate, Adlai Stevenson, used a line written by Arthur Schlesinger, Jr., to attack "public squalor and private opulence." As Americans' bellies overfilled, their heads and hearts ached with emptiness. Eisenhower sensed this problem and ordered a panel to ponder the nation's goals. Another sign of restlessness in the late fifties came from African Americans, who began to protest discrimination more openly. Although the civil rights movement was small at the beginning of 1960, it served notice that not everyone had enjoyed the Great Barbecue.[4]

At the same time, America felt the press of children. Almost one-third of the country's 180 million people were baby boomers born after 1945. More were on the way, as the nation's population continued to grow, with only minor immigration, at the fastest rate in half a century. As dozens of children swarmed on every block, city and suburban schools overflowed. Educators struggled to cope and eyed the federal government as a source for new funds. In 1960, the oldest boomers were entering their teens with a hormonal surge that was about to inundate the country with youth music and their own version of popular culture. The country's institutions for handling adolescents, whether schools, churches, courts, or corporate employers, were stretched thin. In the five years after 1960, fast-growing California faced a 41 percent increase in the annual number of high school graduates. Where were they all to go? What were they to do? Neither businesses nor colleges appeared ready to handle the upsurge. Presidential hopeful John Kennedy's presentation of himself as a youthful candidate appealed to both youth-concerned adults and adolescents. Polls showed Kennedy ahead among those over age 18 but under 21 who, unfortunately for Kennedy, were not then eligible to vote.[5]

At a deeper level, the American problem was not about rapid population growth, suburbanization, unprecedented wealth, its maldistribution, nor Eisenhower's leadership. Intellectuals came closer to identifying the problem when they said that materialism had so overwhelmed society that the country had lost its sense of purpose. A vacuum existed, said intellectuals, because the United States had failed throughout the postwar years to generate new ideas. Intellectuals traced this problem to Senator Joseph R. McCarthy's anticommunist smears in the early fifties. "Intercourse is poisoned," publicly observed the legal scholar Zechariah Chafee, Jr., "if one never knows whether his fellow guest at dinner is going to report statements to the secret police." At one level, the problem was psychological. The need was not, as the old New Dealers of the thirties believed, to find policy prescriptions for social ills, nor was it to synthesize national goals. The problem was more subtle. For half a century liberals had generated most of the new ideas in American society; now they seemed uncertain. The left-liberal journalist Carey McWilliams came closer to the truth when he saw "moral discontents" amid a stagnant liberalism. "It lacks a radical dynamic," he lamented, "it cannot arouse enthusiasm." The destruction of the Left had cast liberalism adrift.[6]

The American problem was lodged deep in the nation's consciousness. In part, the Great Barbecue pressed hard upon that portion of the American psyche that, from the Pilgrim founding on, looked with suspicion upon worldly success as evidence of sin and spiritual failure. The more Americans enjoyed the economic boom, the more discomfort they felt: Life was not supposed to be this much fun. "I met many a soul," noted one observer in a letter, "wandering in the shining abyss of materialism between emptiness and nothing." "The whole country," complained the conservative writer Taylor Caldwell to a friend, "has become soft, whiney, whimpering, demanding, cowering, lip-licking, feeble – and stupid." The United States, thought the novelist John Steinbeck, suffered from "a creeping, all pervading nerve-gas of immorality." Underneath the unease about materialism lurked darker fears. The horrors of nuclear war and the fact that the United States had initiated the nuclear age had, by 1960, produced guilt and fear, along with denial. "No one has dared to speak of GUILT," noted the Catholic *Boston Pilot*. "The atom bomb," the old-line Democrat James Farley had observed at a prayer breakfast, "has more or less brought people back to realize there is a God." The fifties brought an upsurge in religion, as the Cold War entangled the United States in the world in new, exasperating ways, and at any moment threatened thermonuclear death. "Sweetness and light," said Carey McWilliams, "are no longer the only notes to be sounded in our land."[7]

More than he ever let on publicly, President Eisenhower understood the country's mood in the fifties. A master of deception, the old general concocted meaningless, ungrammatical answers at press conferences and took innocent drives in the country, prescribed by his physician, to make secret visits to his closest adviser, his brother Milton. Behind the famous wide smile, Ike was ruthless. A credible military commander, he had ended the Korean War by threatening nuclear war. Other results of his activity could be seen elsewhere. The Shah of Iran reappeared, Guatemala's Left-leaning government disappeared, and Ngo Dinh Diem appeared as the pro-American ruler in South Vietnam. Quietly and unobtrusively, Ike moved all over the world. As 1960 dawned, he remained popular, and had he been eligible for a third term, he would have won in a landslide. The Constitution, however, required Ike to step down, and he looked upon potential successors with deep doubt. Lyndon Johnson had no support outside the South, John Kennedy was too young and inexperienced, and Vice President Richard Nixon, the designated Republican heir, did not inspire confidence. At a press conference, Ike was asked to name one contribution Nixon had made to the administration. "If you give me a week, I might think of one. I don't remember," opined the old general. Later, he apologized to Nixon and called his remark flippant. His flippancy is doubtful.[8]

Following two terms in the House of Representatives, Nixon had moved to the Senate in 1950, after defeating Helen Gahagan Douglas, whom he accused of being "pink right down to her underwear." Two years later Nixon became Ike's vice president. In 1960, he was the first sitting vice president nominated by a major party for the presidency since Martin Van Buren in 1836. Despite strong support from party loyalists, Nixon was not an ideal candidate. Although no one doubted his intelligence or hard work, he was widely hated. Speaker of the House Sam Rayburn, a conservative Texas Democrat, neither shook Nixon's hand nor looked at him nor spoke with him whenever the vice president came to the House for Ike's State of the Union speeches. In the early sixties, former President Harry Truman privately called Nixon "a shifty-eyed, god-damn liar." In a letter the British journalist John Calmann described Nixon as "a real middle-class uneducated swindler with all the virtues of a seller of fountain-pens in Naples." Years later, the conservative Republican Barry Goldwater recalled Nixon as "the most dishonest individual I ever met in my life." A brilliant tactician but a poor strategist, the vice president, like many other Americans adrift during the fifties, lacked any moral compass. "I feel sorry for Nixon," John Kennedy observed privately, "because he does not know who he is, and at each stop he has to decide which Nixon he is at the moment, which must be very exhausting."[9]

John F. Kennedy formally declared for the presidency on January 2, 1960. Although he challenged others to join the contest, no one did so at that time. Professional politicians felt it too early to begin an open campaign, which would expose the frontrunner to sniping attacks from all directions. Kennedy understood that problem, but his own inexperience, as well as the hostility of party elders, forced his decision. To have any chance of being nominated, he had to run openly, to campaign actively, and to use television to create an attractive public image. He would try to excite the masses, to confront the vague anxieties that Americans felt by tapping the country's hopeful yearnings about itself, and to present himself as the person best equipped to lead Americans into a promising future. He projected an infectious optimism. Few took Kennedy seriously.

The press, inclined to see 1960 as a Republican year due to Ike's success, greeted the announcement with skepticism. Reporters, like Democratic professionals, considered Kennedy's declaration as the beginning of a campaign for the vice presidency. Throughout the spring, Kennedy insisted that under no circumstances would he leave the Senate for second place. At a dinner party Jackie Kennedy declared, "I will slash my wrists and write an oath in blood that Jack will never run for vice president!"[10]

Wise men doubted Kennedy's chances largely because of his youth. If he won at age 43, he would be the youngest person ever elected. "That kid needs a little gray in his hair," said Senator Lyndon Johnson of Texas. The Soviet leader Nikita Khrushchev fretted, "He's younger than my own son." To win the nomination, Kennedy turned the argument upside down. He insisted that his youth was an advantage, because the nation required a leader with energy and new ideas. "It is time," said Kennedy in speeches throughout 1960, "to get this country moving again." In a triumph of style over substance, he was short on specifics. A promising time did not necessarily require a candidate to make promises. The contrast with Eisenhower, however, was clear. Ike, about to turn 70, would leave office the oldest president in history. (Ronald Reagan later broke that record.) Politicians' complaints about Kennedy's youth were primarily worries about his inexperience. He had never been a governor nor held any executive post. In neither the House of Representatives nor the Senate had he been impressive. "He's smart enough," said Johnson, "but he doesn't like the grunt work."[11]

Kennedy's family proved useful. Jack's father, Joseph P. Kennedy, Sr., was reputed to be worth at least $200 million, one of the country's largest fortunes. The money mattered. Before World War II he had been ambassador to Great Britain, until isolationism forced his resignation. Jack's mother Rose, the daughter of Boston Mayor John "Honey Fitz" Fitzgerald, was a brilliant campaigner. A devout Catholic who attended daily mass, Rose was also a tightwad who made the household staff pay for cups of coffee that they drank. Jack's brothers and sisters helped, too. Sister Patricia, wife of the actor Peter Lawford, introduced Jack to Hollywood donors and superstars Frank Sinatra and Marilyn Monroe. Brother Robert ran Jack's 1960 campaign. Bobby, as he was generally known, was brilliant, ruthless, and feared. "He has all the patience of a vulture," said one observer, "without any of the dripping sentimentality." The journalist Igor Cassini thought Bobby was tough enough to have been in the Gestapo. "He hates the same way I do," said Joe Kennedy. Lyndon Johnson offered a different insight about Bobby. "He skipped the grades," said Johnson, "where you learn the rules of life." Friends praised Bobby's "heart" and loyalty, but numerous enemies cited his temper and arrogance.[12]

Jack Kennedy was a complicated man, more so than his relatives. At Harvard he was one of the first Catholics to be admitted to an exclusive club (Spee). This was less a comment about declining prejudice than proof of his charm. His gift, Senator Clinton Anderson recalled, was lifting people's spirits. In 1960, Kennedy's optimism matched the public mood. As a child, Jack suffered frail health, became a bookworm, and, aided by perfect recall, developed a taste for history. This intellectual side, while by no means dominant, asserted itself at Harvard. He spent school vacations in England with his father, then the ambassador, traveled around the continent, and returned to Harvard to write a stimulating senior thesis on why England failed to prepare for World War II. It was a timely and important topic, and Kennedy's warning that the United States ought to be better prepared put the youth in opposition to his isolationist father. The ambassador arranged for publication through a friend, the *New York Times* columnist Arthur Krock. *Why England Slept* became a bestseller. With his profits, Jack bought a flashy red Buick. In 1955, while convalescing from a back operation, Jack produced, with considerable help from his assistant Theodore Sorensen, *Profiles in Courage*. This book not only was a bestseller, but also, with Krock's aid, won the Pulitzer Prize.[13]

World War II showed another side of Jack Kennedy. After failing an Army physical, Kennedy talked his way into the Navy. Assigned to intelligence, he became involved with Inga Arvad, a woman wrongly suspected of being a German spy. J. Edgar Hoover personally followed the case; the 700-page file later guaranteed the FBI director his job during Kennedy's presidency. (Asked why he was keeping Hoover, President Kennedy replied, "You don't fire God.") To end the romance, Jack was reassigned to captain a PT boat in the South Pacific. Small PT boats tried, with little success, to torpedo much larger, faster Japanese ships in an area the enemy controlled. On a foggy night a Japanese destroyer sliced Kennedy's PT109 in two. The PT109 sank, but Kennedy and ten of twelve crew members swam to a nearby island. With a strap held in his teeth, Kennedy towed one badly burned man. His strength and endurance, developed on the Harvard swimming team, paid off, as did his confidence, instilled by the ambassador as a family trait. Kennedys never quit. Virtually abandoned by the U.S. Navy, which erroneously concluded that there were no survivors, Kennedy rescued his men by sending out a message carved on a coconut. As president, he displayed the coconut in the Oval Office.[14]

In 1946, when Kennedy won a seat in Congress from a working-class district in Boston, being a war hero helped. So did his liberalism, his unpretentious charm, and the fact that his grandfather had been the mayor of Boston. Six years later, after defeating the incumbent Senator Henry Cabot Lodge, Kennedy cultivated new constituencies by hiring Theodore Sorensen, a half-Danish and half-Jewish Unitarian from Nebraska. Ted was a brilliant speechwriter. That same year Robert Kennedy went to work for Wisconsin's anticommunist Senator Joseph R. McCarthy. A fellow Irish Catholic, McCarthy was a Republican who had dated Jack's sisters Patricia and Jean. The ambassador had given McCarthy a contribution, and in 1952 he stayed out of Massachusetts, where he might have ruined Kennedy's Senate bid. By 1954, with McCarthy's reputation sinking, Bobby quit the staff, but Jack still defended McCarthy. When a speaker at a Harvard club dinner equated McCarthy and Alger Hiss, a former high-ranking State Department official accused of being a Soviet agent, Kennedy flared, "How dare you couple the name of a great American patriot with that of a traitor!" Then the Senate censured McCarthy, and Jack Kennedy, hospitalized with a bad back, neither voted nor announced his position. Every other Senate Democrat supported censure. Kennedy's behavior appalled party liberals like Eleanor Roosevelt.[15]

Despite a strained relationship with some liberals, Kennedy had wide appeal. By 1959, a year when Kennedy received more than 10,000 invitations to speak, some polls showed him as the Democrats' strongest candidate. Only one strategy was open to Kennedy. Because of youth and inexperience, he could not expect to win in a brokered convention. To be nominated, he had to demonstrate popularity by main force. He also had to put to rest once and for all the idea that a Catholic could not be elected. Both problems could be solved by winning primaries. By appealing directly to voters, Kennedy proposed to remake American politics. Before 1960, winning primaries had rarely led to nominations. The ambassador saw the issue as one of marketing. "We're going to sell Jack like soap flakes," he declared. The key to this new kind of politics was image-making based on polls, travel, speeches, media, and personal contacts. Although Kennedy was not the first candidate to hire a pollster, he used Louis Harris to do unusually subtle, in-depth analyses that were rare at that time. Extensive travel gave Kennedy wide exposure and enabled him to meet Democrats likely to be convention delegates in 1960. In the past, candidates had bargained wholesale with state bosses; Kennedy cultivated delegates at retail. Admiring the new techniques, the journalist Stewart Alsop concluded, "Kennedy is his own secret weapon." Others sensed manipulation and disapproved. The independent leftist I. F. Stone lamented "the phoney smell of advertising copy." Noting that wealth was crucial to the Kennedys' image-making, the author Gore Vidal wrote, "They create illusions and call them facts...."[16]

As Kennedy laid out strategy for 1960, he dodged two problems. One was chronic poor health. Although he had unusual stamina and energy, he had allergies, a thyroid condition, one shortened leg, an unstable spine, and a bad back. An early operation to fuse disks had failed and left him with a fist-sized hole in his back; an operation in 1955 finally stabilized his back. He often wore a back brace and slept on a bed board or, when traveling, on the hotel floor. After the war, Kennedy suffered periodic high fevers, which were probably malarial. Many men who had served in the South Pacific did contract tropical fevers. Then Kennedy fell ill in London in 1947 and was diagnosed with Addison's disease. Caused by an insufficient production of adrenalin by the adrenal glands, the classic Addison's killed its victims in a few years after producing blotchy skin, a brown tongue, swollen glands, and generally deteriorated health. Although Kennedy lacked these symptoms, he did have some unusual form of Addison's disease. When news about this illness leaked in 1960, both Kennedy and his doctor, Janet Travell, flatly denied that he had Addison's. Years later Travell corrected her statement. Fortunately for Kennedy, cortisone, a fairly recent invention, had been discovered to stimulate the adrenal glands and restore adrenalin to the body. By the early fifties, scientists learned that only one specific portion of the cortisone compound accounted for the adrenalin improvement, and for the rest of his life Kennedy took cortisone-derivative pills to control adrenalin insufficiency. He also received occasional shots.[17]

Persons close to Kennedy wondered if poor health did not explain much of his sexual behavior, which was the other unmentionable topic during his 1960 campaign. Handsome, charming, wealthy, and intelligent, Kennedy was popular with women. After he had served several years in Congress, he remained a bachelor unready and unwilling to settle down. Political success, however, required a public image of respectability, and the ambassador insisted that Jack marry a woman who could please Irish Catholics while confirming that the Kennedys belonged to the upper class. In 1953 Jack married Jacqueline Bouvier at a society wedding at Newport, Rhode Island, before a crowd of 3,000. An upper-class Catholic who brought prestige to the nouveau riche Kennedys, Jackie was a graceful, well-mannered beauty with brains and style. Jack and Jackie's marriage was troubled. "I don't think," said Jackie, "there are any men who are faithful to their wives." In the late fifties there was talk of the Kennedys divorcing, and Joe Kennedy may have given Jackie a large sum to stay married to Jack. Stories about affairs abound. According to one report, Jack was caught with the flight attendant aboard the family-owned airplane, and the woman had to be paid off with oil leases. In 1960, Kennedy apparently began a two-year affair with Judith Campbell that ended only after J. Edgar Hoover informed the president that Judy was being shared with the mobster Sam Giancana. In 1960, before politicians had become celebrities, the media paid no attention to officeholders' private lives.[18]

In April 1960, Kennedy faced Minnesota's liberal Senator Hubert H. Humphrey in the Wisconsin primary. While Humphrey rattled across the state shivering in a decrepit rented bus with a broken heater, Kennedy and his press followers flew smoothly and were served hot meals by a flight attendant aboard Kennedy's 40-passenger jet, the *Caroline*, which the family had bought in 1959. All the Kennedys campaigned, and Humphrey said, "I feel like an independent merchant competing against a chain store." Kennedy won a modest 56 percent of the vote and did well only in Catholic areas. The two candidates then moved on to West Virginia, which was 90 percent Protestant. If Kennedy could win there, he would put the Catholic issue to rest. To carry many counties, it was necessary to deliver suitcases of cash to the local party boss. Both campaigns did so, but Kennedy had more funds, including mob money. (In one county the Kennedys bid up the price from the usual $2 to $10 per vote. Officials refunded Humphrey's money.) One irate citizen complained in a letter that "this type of one-sided campaigning could even put Khrushchev in the White House." Kennedy also used television shrewdly. In a debate with Humphrey, the telegenic Kennedy cleverly brought into the studio a pitifully small amount of food which he said represented the amount of surplus federal assistance that a family on relief might receive in one month. His effort to show that he cared about poverty impressed mountaineers. On Election Day Kennedy won 61 percent, and Humphrey quit.[19]

The frontrunner was now on a roll. For the first time in American politics, Kennedy had demonstrated that primaries could lead to the nomination, at least for a candidate who had money, who could organize, who led in the polls, and who looked good on television in the new media age. In July, the Democratic convention opened in Los Angeles. Famous for its freeways, its sprawling suburbs, and nearby Disneyland, the city combined an image of futuristic progress with the glitter of Hollywood. Los Angeles seemed remote from either eastern city bosses or the smoke-filled rooms associated with political conventions. Instead, this convention was the first media extravaganza staged for the nationwide television audience. The schedule was arranged to favor television over newspapers, and this convention was the first one to use videotape, teleprompters at the podium, split screens, graphic inserts, and remote feeds. The convention, in fact, was about image-making, and so, too, was Los Angeles. Democrats held numerous private parties that mixed delegates, politicians, and stars. At the largest fundraising dinner, 3,000 guests watched Frank Sinatra mingle with the other candidates, Lyndon Johnson, Adlai Stevenson, and Stuart Symington, while Jack Kennedy sat with Judy Garland. Subtly, the notion of the politician as celebrity was being created. Kennedy was on his way to becoming the first televised political star.[20]

Kennedy was nominated on the first ballot, a result that astonished the party's old-timers, including Truman's secretary of state, Dean Acheson, who conceded, correctly, in a letter to a friend that he had been "put out to pasture." Kennedy had supplanted top-down, boss-led politics with a national grassroots campaign based upon popular appeal and youthful volunteers. This convention marked the last time when both delegates and reporters seriously speculated about a candidate being unable to win on the first ballot. In the coming money-based, primary-oriented, television-driven politics, nominations were decided well before the convention, which merely ratified what had already been decided by image and mass appeal to the voters. Kennedy won because he had refused to play the game the old way, which he could not win, and instead invented a new game that gave him victory. Kennedy's success was generational. It represented the coming to power of the junior officers of World War II. The war had both enabled and forced that generation to break down stereotypes and class barriers, and its officers had devised ways to promote collective achievement. Exceptionally meritocratic, they measured each other mainly in terms of competence, and yet they (unlike the baby boomers) also respected hierarchy as necessary to provide leadership for large, powerful organizations. They felt uncomfortable discussing morals or principles, kept ideology at a distance, emphasized the practical, learned to ignore rules, and frequently improvised. Their style was aggressive. Attacking the political structure directly, they seized command from below.[21]

After winning the nomination, Kennedy personally invited Lyndon Johnson to be his running mate. Kennedy's staff was divided on this matter; the party's liberals were opposed. In part, Kennedy made this offer because he believed Johnson to be the person other than himself best qualified to be president, but Kennedy also wanted to unify the party and heal the convention's wounds. Electoral calculation suggested that Johnson would enable Kennedy to carry Texas and win the election. Otherwise, defeat loomed. Near the end of the convention Kennedy held an off-the-record meeting with African-American delegates to reassure them that he was personally committed to civil rights. The Democrats had adopted a liberal platform that strongly supported civil rights. The convention ended with Kennedy accepting the nomination before 80,000 people at the Los Angeles Coliseum. With 35 million watching on television, he declared, "We stand on the edge of a New Frontier...." As he gave the speech, Kennedy probably did not notice a picket carrying a sign that read "Stevenson for Secretary of State." Not everyone liked Kennedy's speech. Alarmed by its liberal tone, Ronald Reagan wrote Richard Nixon, "Under the tousled boyish hair cut it is still old Karl Marx – first launched a century ago. There is nothing new in the idea of a government being Big Brother to us all."[22]

The Republicans nominated Richard Nixon and Henry Cabot Lodge. Ike's personal choice for vice president, Lodge was picked to emphasize foreign affairs in the campaign, but the former ambassador to the United Nations proved to be a desultory, undisciplined campaigner. While Lodge was stumbling, Johnson whistle-stopped by train from Virginia through the Deep South toward Texas. Speaking from the back of what reporters called the "Cornpone Special," Johnson used his thickest southern accent to recall his Confederate ancestry. By the time he reached Texas, most of the South was safe for the ticket. Kennedy began his campaign by again facing the religious issue, which he had once believed had been put to rest in West Virginia. In early September, he spoke powerfully before a fairly hostile gathering of Protestant ministers in Houston. Speaking on statewide television, Kennedy denied any Catholic church influence upon him in his political capacity and promised a rigid separation of church and state in his administration. The event was filmed, and the campaign rebroadcast it frequently on local television in parts of the country where the religious issue remained alive. This speech marked yet another example of Kennedy's mastery of television.[23]

All year pollsters had predicted a close election. No single event was decisive, but one key moment was the country's first televised presidential debate. Of the four presidential debates in 1960, only the first truly mattered. While radio listeners rated Nixon the victor, television viewers believed that Kennedy had won. The camera contrasted a handsome, well-groomed, articulate Kennedy with a poorly dressed and badly made-up Nixon. The debates created excitement, made Kennedy a celebrity, and stimulated turnout. Kennedy may have gained two million votes drawn mostly from new voters. The election ended with the highest percentage of adults of voting age casting ballots in American history. Despite an overall theme of getting the country moving again, Kennedy's campaign was stronger on style than on specifics. Expressing few new ideas, which might divide and alienate potential voters, the candidate instead emphasized vitality and vigor. Beyond the glitter, Kennedy proved ready to seize opportunity. When the civil rights leader Martin Luther King, Jr., was arrested in Atlanta, Kennedy called Mrs. King to comfort her. Ike and Nixon did nothing. Kennedy's call did not offend southern whites, but it did reshape black thinking. King's father, fearing the election of a Catholic, had endorsed Nixon, and he now publicly reversed himself. All over the country, African Americans shifted to Kennedy. On election day Kennedy got 68 percent of the African-American vote; in 1956, Stevenson had 61 percent.[24]

In one of the closest elections in American history, Kennedy squeaked through with a few votes more than Nixon but with less than a majority of the popular vote. The contest broke along religious lines. Of the 15 most heavily Catholic states, mostly in the Northeast, Kennedy won 11, losing only rural upper New England and Nixon's home state of California. Of 16 predominantly Protestant southern or border states, including Texas, Kennedy took ten, six of which were overwhelmingly Democratic ex-Confederate states largely brought to the ticket by Johnson. Of 19 predominantly Protestant states in the rest of the country, Kennedy carried only Minnesota and Nevada. In Minnesota, Humphrey had told suspicious Protestant Scandinavians that Kennedy's fair skin and reddish hair meant, "Why, he is one of us!" Vikings had once conquered Ireland. The argument worked. In most parts of the nation Kennedy had run well behind Democratic candidates for other offices. Although Kennedy's religion had helped him in some places, especially among suburban Catholics in the Northeast, in most areas it had hurt. Estimates ran as high as a net loss of 4.5 million votes. While Kennedy's election proved that a Catholic could be elected president, it did not demonstrate that a political party was wise to nominate a Catholic. Since 1960 neither party has named a Catholic.[25]

On January 20, 1961, barely more than a year after announcing for the presidency, John F. Kennedy was sworn into office. With an eye toward a huge television audience, he launched his presidency with a sparkling inaugural address. For years he and Ted Sorensen had collected ideas and phrases for this speech. Kennedy worried if it was good enough. The night before, reading it over, he had commented that it still was not so good as Jefferson's first address. As he spoke, his audience, both the few on Capitol Hill and the millions watching television across the nation, noticed that this always balanced and often poetic address ignored domestic affairs.

Announcing that the torch of leadership had passed to the globally oriented and experienced World War II generation, Kennedy asked Americans to pay heed to the rest of the world. Rejecting a sugar-coated view, he presented the Cold War as a worldwide struggle for freedom in which, by sacrifice, Americans might decide the outcome. "Ask not what your country can do for you," said the new president in a widely quoted phrase, "ask what you can do for your country." When examined carefully years later, Kennedy's address seemed to exude Cold War excess, but at the time it drew praise from persons as diverse as Adlai Stevenson and Barry Goldwater and excited both supporters and those who had not voted for him in November.[26]

Bursting with energy and optimism, the administration began work the next morning. The most prominent members of the cabinet were Secretary of State Dean Rusk, a weak compromise choice acceptable to both Dean Acheson and Adlai Stevenson; Secretary of Defense Robert McNamara, who had headed the Ford Motor Company; Attorney General Robert Kennedy; and United Nations Ambassador Adlai Stevenson, who still smarted over not being secretary of state. The White House staff included Ted Sorensen in charge of speech writing and domestic policy, Richard Goodwin to assist with speeches, Arthur Schlesinger, Jr., for special assignments, Harris Wofford for civil rights, Larry O'Brien for congressional relations, Kenny O'Donnell for appointments, Pierre Salinger as press secretary, and McGeorge Bundy as head of a small staff advising the National Security Council on foreign policy. The most urgent issues concerned Southeast Asia, especially Laos, and Walt Rostow was assigned to help Bundy in that area. Schlesinger, Bundy, and Rostow were university intellectuals. In a break with Eisenhower, Kennedy gave each aide the same job title and salary. He also refused to appoint a chief of staff on the grounds that such a person would insulate him from his staff and become a kind of internal

White House dictator. The result was creative tension and chaos, which Kennedy enjoyed.[27]

Kennedy abolished the committee system that Eisenhower had used to run the White House and the national security apparatus. Unlike Ike, Kennedy had little use for large, formal meetings. He preferred to deal with officials one-on-one or in small, specialized task forces. The Cabinet and National Security Council met infrequently and rarely dealt with important issues. Often, Kennedy would call lower-level government officials both to learn what was happening and to encourage action. While these calls prodded staff, they also generated conflict and demoralized superiors. Kennedy called this a spoke-and-wheel system in which he was the "hub" and the entire government consisted of "spokes" radiating outward from himself. France's Louis XIV had had a similar conception of centralized administration. While providing more flexibility and overturning lethargic bureaucracy, the system also produced trouble because no single "spoke" knew what the other "spokes" were doing, no one could coordinate activities, and the system was only as wise as the "hub," who was often necessarily only partly informed about highly complex, technical matters. The disadvantages of this "system" became evident later, when the administration's lack of coordination and sustained drive produced chronic domestic and foreign policy failure.[28]

Kennedy fared better with public relations. While the administration used media-driven image-making to promote the president's commitment to a promising future, darker private thoughts were largely obscured from public view. From the beginning, Americans loved Kennedy's live, witty televised press conferences, which were a daring innovation, and reporters gave the administration rave notices. Furthermore, this administration, more than most, liked to cooperate with, even cultivate, the media, and the president himself provided tips. "The American ship of state," privately noted Stewart Alsop, "is the only ship that leaks at the top!" Whenever

Kennedy learned that a leak that he had denounced had, in fact, been made by himself, he had the good sense to laugh along with his staff. Liberal euphoria was everywhere. With so many brains in such high places offering so much sound advice, how, one might ask, could anything go wrong? When Lyndon Johnson told Sam Rayburn how smart the appointees were, the sagacious speaker observed, "Well, Lyndon, you might be right and they may be every bit as intelligent as you say, but I'd feel a whole lot better about them if just one of them had run for sheriff once." Rayburn worried that Kennedy's intelligentsia lacked both common sense and the common touch. In this promising time, no one paid much attention to Rayburn's remark, and for three months liberals were in paradise. This was a giddy fantasy. The Bay of Pigs would provide a rude awakening.[29]

U.S. Air Force rocket launches a space satellite, Cape Canaveral, Florida, 1961.

(National Archives. NWDNS-326-PV-(4)185(1).)

CHAPTER TWO

The Cold War

In the early sixties, Americans publicly expressed confidence in a promising future; privately, they were frightened by, consumed with, and enveloped within the Cold War, which hung like a storm cloud over the nation. Only a handful openly questioned the Cold War. Talk about a bright future may have helped Americans assuage their fears. At no time in the 40-year history of the postwar rivalry between the United States and the Soviet Union did matters seem so dark as in those years. The Cold War was like a long, bad marriage. Starting in the mid-1940s, it had, by 1960, lasted half a generation. It had become predictable, stale, and enervating. Few, in 1960, were in love with the Cold War, but that fact did not mean that it could be ignored. It could not be wished away, although some Americans did at times try to do so, and it often seemed unwinnable. How much longer, or even whether, it could be endured before it turned nuclear was uncertain. Perhaps, some thought optimistically, the Cold War might be tamed or, at least, managed. In any case, it had long existed, it continued, and it gave every prospect of perpetuity. It was the one ongoing feature of American life, a certainty that could be counted upon like almost nothing else, except perhaps death and taxes. To many it promised death, and to all it

23

brought very high taxes. By 1959, defense spending was more than half the federal budget and 9.6 percent of gross national product. As a result, the Cold War put the country on a permanent war footing, gave the military-industrial complex unprecedented influence, and shaped almost everything else in American society.[1]

The Cold War operated on three levels. First, at the level of principle, it was a battle between good and evil, or between freedom and oppression, or between democracy and totalitarianism, or between Christianity and godless communism. In this formulation the United States stood for all that was virtuous and the Soviet Union for all that was not. Much Cold War rhetoric was high-minded, but few saw the issue entirely in terms of values. Second, at the level of power politics, the Cold War was a contest between the United States and the Soviet Union for domination of the postwar world. From 1917 on communists had preached the inevitability of global revolution through the violent overthrow of all capitalist nations. This messianic idea frightened established governments, including that of the United States. To meet this challenge, the United States proposed the doctrine of containment, first articulated during Harry Truman's presidency in the 1940s by Secretary of State Dean Acheson and the diplomat George Kennan. Advocates of containment recognized communism's dangers, but they also held optimistically that communism's own evils and internal contradictions would lead to its eventual failure. In the meantime, vigilance was required to make certain that this dangerous political virus did not spread. Containment was designed to stop the Soviets from bringing communism to the entire world by election, subversion, revolution, or military conquest.[2]

At a third level, the Cold War was about purging American communists and their sympathizers from positions of influence inside the United States. To cold warriors, destroying the domestic Communist party was a top priority in the late forties. American communists were conceived of as Soviet apologists, lackeys, dupes, or even as foreign agents; they were to be identified, harassed, uprooted like noxious weeds, and politically destroyed. The communist policy of using secret party cells and names, clandestine operations, and orders given through authoritarian hierarchy, even when not actually in support of espionage, affronted both democratic values and the openness of American popular culture. In the 1940s the domestic anticommunist crusade was arguably the most important part of the Cold War, because a vibrant communist movement inside the United States potentially would threaten the policy of containment. Domestic communists were crushed rather easily, in part because postwar prosperity made the Left unfashionable, in part because of internal party bickering, and in part because of tough federal government action. Party membership fell from perhaps 50,000 in 1949 to as little as 5,000 by 1960, when one-quarter of party leaders were agents of the Federal Bureau of Investigation.[3]

The government and anticommunist groups used loyalty oaths, blacklists, and pressure to purge communists or their sympathizers from all walks of life. Some ex-communists, like the *Time* magazine editor Whittaker Chambers, became zealous anticommunist crusaders who were now as eager to root out former comrades as they had once been in favor of revolution. In 1948 the onetime party member and Soviet spy Chambers told the House Un-American Activities Committee that Alger Hiss, a former top State Department official, had been a fellow red agent. Hiss denied the charge, but after two sensational trials he was convicted of perjury in 1950 for testifying that he had never known Chambers. The Hiss case remained in public consciousness throughout the fifties, when rooting out communists became an obsession. Government agencies got help from chambers of commerce, private security firms, grassroots anticommunist organizations, and veterans groups. The FBI's American Legion Contact Program used 110,000 veterans to assist in maintaining files on 25 million Americans. In 1956 the FBI started COINTELPRO, a counterintelligence operation to harass and destroy the Communist party. FBI files on the party eventually ran to 26.5 million pages. Although the best known anticommunist, Senator Joseph R. McCarthy, had died in 1957, the hunt for communists continued.[4]

Throughout these years prominent people who had never been communists were also hounded. The independent leftist journalist I. F. Stone was kept off national radio and television for twenty years, and the Atomic Energy Commission investigated the nuclear physicist Hans Bethe for talking with Cornell University students about a possible ban on nuclear bomb tests. Owen Lattimore, a China scholar and sometime government adviser, was blamed for the communist takeover of China in 1949. (His FBI file was 38,900 pages.) Charged with perjury for denying communist affiliations, he won in court but remained under a cloud all during the fifties. Despite tenure, he found his academic post at Johns Hopkins University threatened by Milton Eisenhower, Ike's brother and the school's president. When Lattimore was asked to speak before a small town book club in 1961, the invitation had to be withdrawn because one member had learned that Lattimore had been called a communist years earlier. "Perhaps McCarthyism has gone," a friend told the professor, "but the moral laziness in civil liberties remains."[5]

The U.S. Supreme Court showed little sympathy for civil liberties. In 1961 the justices, in two cases involving witnesses who had refused to cooperate with HUAC, ruled 5–4 against Carl Braden, a civil rights activist, and Frank Wilkinson, organizer of a group seeking to abolish HUAC. (Neither was a proven communist, although there was testimony against both; Wilkinson's FBI file ran to 132,000 pages.) As the sixties began, a number of losers in earlier communist cases remained in prison. Among those behind bars was Gil Green, one of the original top Communist party leaders who had been convicted under the Smith Act in 1949. In 1961, he was released. That same year Braden and Wilkinson went to prison. Despite a quiet lobbying campaign, the Kennedy administration declined to free Braden. "They want to please the Birchers," privately observed the old New Deal liberal Aubrey Williams. Residues from the haunted fifties continued well into the sixties. "I . . . shudder to realize once again," noted one observer in a letter in 1963, "how the remnants of McCarthyism and the whole frightened 'Fifties linger on. It was, I've decided, like a strep throat that can leave in its wake a rheumatic heart for life. We rarely recover completely from the serious diseases of the body politic."[6]

Although the repression eased at the end of the fifties, and a small but noisy peace movement began to be heard, intimidation did not end. Accordingly, public expression of private thoughts was often guarded. When the World Council of Churches tried to publish an antinuclear pamphlet in 1961, two publishers declined, calling the material "subversive." The group then approached the Committee for a Sane Nuclear Policy (commonly called SANE), which was founded in 1957. SANE, however, was not entirely respectable, as evidenced by the fact that the mainstream *Saturday Evening Post* refused to permit the organization to reprint a short extract of an article. The magazine did not wish its name to be printed on any peace literature. Joining SANE might bring official scrutiny. "Ben and I were served subpoenas recently by HUAC," complained one woman in a letter in 1963, "because of our having signed the open letter to Kennedy on Vietnam. . . ." The couple, who had been active in Boston SANE since 1959, had earlier leftist associations that they hoped to keep private.[7]

By the early sixties, however, change was in the air. A more promising time loomed. The most famous case of ritualized humiliation during the McCarthy years involved Robert Oppenheimer, the nuclear physicist partly responsible for the wartime atomic bomb. In 1953, the government acted to revoke his security clearance on the grounds that he was a security risk because he had known numerous communists in Berkeley in the 1930s. Friends suspected that the real reason for revoking his clearance was to punish him for opposing development of the postwar H-bomb and the resultant arms race. Without clearance, he could hold only private thoughts; he was muzzled in any public expression about ongoing nuclear issues. In 1962, President Kennedy began Oppenheimer's public rehabilitation by inviting him to the White House dinner for Nobel and Pulitzer prize winners. Not everyone approved. "I hope," Senator Karl Mundt told the press, "but not confidently, that Alger Hiss won't be the next one invited." Another controversial guest at the same event, the chemist turned peace activist Linus Pauling, picketed the White House before going in to dine. A year later Kennedy honored Oppenheimer with the Fermi prize. Adolf Berle, a former Truman administration official, congratulated Oppie. "In Victor Hugo's tale," he noted, "they first decorated the hero and then shot him. Happily, in your case, the order is reversed."[8]

Despite the administration's softer approach to security, the Cold War remained a hard fact of life, and the government was jarred in April 1961, when the American-backed invasion at the Bay of Pigs in Cuba failed. The U.S. Central Intelligence Agency had trained and armed 1,500 Cuban exiles, who went ashore without proper air cover and were overwhelmed by Fidel Castro's forces. The worst single American foreign policy failure of the Cold War, the bungled invasion set up Castro for long-term survival. (Although the Vietnam War was more disastrous, it was not rooted in a single bad decision.) Reaction to this painful fiasco was both swift and brutal. National attention was focused on Cuba, partly because the invasion was a dramatic spectacle and partly because that island was only ninety miles offshore, as Right-wing bumper stickers began to remind Americans. Personal correspondence was overwhelmingly critical with a frankness that would have been hard to express in public. The debacle, noted the historian Samuel Flagg Bemis, resembled the pre-World War II Munich agreement in that a great power's credibility had been destroyed. The United States had shown itself incapable of planning and executing to a successful conclusion a minor military operation. "The Cuban affair," thought another observer, "tended to make us look like a third rate power." Yet another added that "the CIA is referred to in Washington as the 'Cuban Invasion Agency.' Sad, isn't it?" In the Midwest the reporter and sometime Kennedy aide John Bartlow Martin found "disillusionment and disappointment." About the amateurish, botched invasion, a political science professor declared, "I keep telling my students it didn't happen because men don't act that way."[9]

Private comments inside the administration were also harsh. Kennedy told the reporter Bill Lawrence the operation had been "an unrelieved disaster." To Lyndon Johnson and Arthur Schlesinger, Jr., the president spoke more bluntly, "We got a big kick in the ass. . . ." Despite a public declaration taking full responsibility, Kennedy blamed subordinates, particularly the CIA and the military Joint Chiefs of Staff. "My God," he told Jackie, "the bunch of advisers we inherited. . . ." CIA Director Allen Dulles, who bore primary responsibility for the operation, informed Richard Nixon, "This is the worst day of my life!" Dulles blamed softliners inside the administration for weakening the operation to the point of failure. Particularly inexplicable was Kennedy's decision to withdraw air cover over the beach. Although Dulles had promised that the invasion would occur without American forces, he had assumed that the U.S. Air Force would be used if necessary to save the invasion brigade from direct attack by Castro's planes. For a variety of reasons, including a possible Soviet move against West Berlin, Kennedy took Dulles's promise of no American involvement literally. No one explained to the president that the refusal to use the American military would ruin the country's prestige. Briefed about events afterward, Eisenhower was incredulous that national prestige could be squandered in humiliating failure without any effort to use force to gain success. When the invasion brigade's American beach commander, who had voted for Kennedy, learned that the plan had been wrecked by the president, he concluded, "Superman is a fairy."[10]

The administration's judgment was questioned, especially by those on its periphery. The respected former Secretary of Defense Robert Lovett privately found the plan "lunatic." The force was too small, the landing site inappropriate, and the lack of air cover ludicrous. This preposterous scheme was "a shocking example of what not to do, as well as how not to do it." It was so unworkable that it would have been laughable had it not proved so disastrous. He also noted that plausible deniability of American involvement could not be sustained in something so large and visible as an amphibious landing. "Why we ever engaged in this asinine Cuban adventure I cannot imagine...," Dean Acheson wrote Harry Truman, "The direction of this government seems surprisingly weak." He concluded, "Washington is a depressed town." Republicans held similar views. "Kennedy had clearly lost his nerve," thought Barry Goldwater. Richard Nixon considered the episode "near-criminal." A conservative privately compared the president to "...the man who runs over your child unintentionally, then leaves the scene of the accident." "What shocks me," declared a foreign policy analyst in a letter, "is to think that all of Kennedy's civilian and military advisors were in favor of invasion. While the final responsibility is still Kennedy's and his alone, it is nonetheless disquieting to become aware that he is not better surrounded." About these advisers, the former nuclear administrator David Lilienthal recorded in his diary, "They behave like children...."[11]

Further afield, the reaction was just as negative. A friend of the journalist Arthur Krock privately wrote, "What a lot of mixed up, amateurists." The columnist Stewart Alsop later publicly called it "a minor national disaster." On the eve of the invasion Carey McWilliams, editor of the Left-liberal *Nation*, observed in his diary, "It strikes me as being a tired, hair-brained operation." His magazine had been the first to publish information about the assembling of the exile force in Guatemala. After the failure, McWilliams concluded, "Cuba debacle is an embarrassment. Incredible." Kennedy had pressured the *New York Times* not to publicize the plan. Afterward, he reconsidered. "If you had printed more about the operation," the president told the paper, "you would have saved us from a colossal mistake." What did the president mean? Was the invasion a bad idea, or was it bad because it had failed? Or did he mean that government mistakes could only be stopped by media exposure? Or did he want the *New York Times* to run foreign policy? Kennedy's remark betrays a mental evasion of the responsibility that he publicly embraced. Deep down, he was most embarrassed by failure. Privately, he blamed others.[12]

For Kennedy, the problem was Fidel Castro, who had seized power by a triumphal march into Havana on New Year's Day, 1959. Carefully keeping his communism hidden from public view at that time, Castro displayed a beard, military fatigues, and rough ways that signaled a new-style revolutionary hero. His persona exuded confidence in a promising future. After meeting Castro in New York in 1959, the liberal columnist James Wechsler privately said, "Jesus Christ must have been like this when he walked on water." Although the charismatic Cuban dictator had at first appealed to many Americans, his popularity had faded rapidly. By the time of Kennedy's election, Americans gave Castro a 2 percent approval rating. A handful of leftists remained enthusiastic. Nelson Algren publicly declared, "It's a hell of a good thing Castro's doing." Backing from Algren was less surprising than Castro's support among America's normally apolitical Beat writers. The poets Allen Ginsberg and Lawrence Ferlinghetti were supportive, and the latter, after meeting Castro in Cuba, claimed in a letter that the event had been "a great experience." Not all Beats, however, were charmed. The novelist Jack Kerouac, already breaking with what was to become sixties radicalism, sent Ferlinghetti "fuck-yous about Fidel." While the poet Gary Snyder believed that Cuba needed a revolution, he wrote Allen Ginsberg that Castro's "excessive retribution-violence" made "bad karma."[13]

By mid-1960, before Kennedy became president, the CIA had decided to kill Castro. The assassination became part of the Bay of Pigs invasion plan. The Cuban leader was to be dead before the beachhead was secured. Castro's survival may explain Kennedy's refusal to use American air power to protect the exile brigade, since the larger scheme had already failed. Kennedy's hatred of Castro remained. If anything, humiliation at the Bay of Pigs increased the president's determination to eliminate the Cuban dictator. Many shared the desire. "Castro is a 'demon,'" warned a Cuban refugee in a letter, "very intelligent, put there by the Russians, with great ability, and if this country does not look out, you will have him here very soon." One terrified American fantasized that Castro would invade the United States with an army of 500,000 troops. "I can now evaluate," he added, "how the Japs must have felt when Okinawa and Iwo Jima were swarming with hundreds of B-29s and our crack army and marine corps troops!" Projections of World War II onto the present are an important, curious facet of the sixties. These memories of a distant war distorted the meaning of current events in all sorts of often strange ways.[14]

"It took a long time," noted Kennedy's friend Dave Powers, "to get over the Bay of Pigs." In some ways, the wound was too gaping to enable a complete recovery. The president and his advisers had lost their self-confidence. Three decades later Clark Clifford recalled, "My God, you never saw such a whipped bunch." The damage extended abroad. America's European allies, in the words of Dean Acheson, were "shattered." Khrushchev could feel that he had Kennedy on the run. The Soviet dictator admired both Castro's courage in defying the United States and his Cuban revolution as a model for emerging nations in the Third World. At home, the failed invasion cut both ways. Castro's survival increased the Right's hysteria about losing the Cold War. On the other hand, the attempted intervention disillusioned members of the growing peace movement, many of whom were liberals who had backed Kennedy's election out of a hope for a different kind of foreign policy. SANE's Sanford Gottlieb met privately with the Kennedy adviser McGeorge Bundy. "We must lead social revolution," said Gottlieb, "not follow it. This means supporting the forces representing peasants and workers, countries with mixed economies and even heavy doses of socialism. . . . Cuba is a prime example of a revolution we could have influenced." Bundy replied that Cuba was a communist country that had cut its ties with the United States. Gottlieb responded, "We must recognize that the uncommitted hold the world balance of power." Although the two disagreed about Cuba, Bundy agreed with the importance of the Third World.[15]

On the heels of the Cuban debacle, Kennedy decided to make a deal about Laos. The American–Soviet compromise to neutralize Laos provoked less public discussion than did the Bay of Pigs, probably because compromise was difficult to attack and because Laos was little known and far away. Yet the administration's seeming change of position concerning Laotian neutrality did not go unnoticed. Before the Bay of Pigs invasion, Kennedy had told a reporter privately that he would go to war in Laos if necessary, even if it made him a one-term president, but the Cuban fiasco had caused the president to settle on a nonmilitary solution. For the present, he felt that he could not use troops because he lacked confidence in his military advisers. "Over a month ago," one cold warrior wrote in a letter, "we had brave talk about defending Laos. And now look at it. Haven't we learned yet that to compromise – half communist and half free – is only another name for surrender and eventual take over? At least, if we are going to give Moscow all it wants, why do we go on bragging about the big things we are going to do? Whom do we think we are fooling? Certainly *not* Moscow." A journalist for the socialist but anticommunist *New Leader* privately called both Cuba and Laos "heartbreaking failures." Humiliated at the Bay of Pigs and forced to compromise over Laos, the administration began to ponder showing its toughness by taking a strong stand in Vietnam.[16]

A third disappointment awaited Kennedy that spring, when he went to Vienna to talk with Nikita Khrushchev. Although Kennedy had been warned that a summit was unwise for an inexperienced administration that had nothing to announce at the meeting, the American president decided to meet the Soviet premier in order to establish a basis for doing business. Kennedy arrived ill-prepared; he may also have been tired, jet-lagged, and affected by the drugs he had to take for his various maladies. The presidential party included Dr. Max Jacobson ("Dr. Feelgood"), dispenser of shots laced with amphetamine ("speed"). In any event, Kennedy allowed himself to be drawn away from a discussion of specific problems into a fruitless ideological debate with Khrushchev, who certainly knew Marxism–Leninism better. The Soviet leader later told top communists in a secret meeting that his opponent was "too much of a light-weight." The president ended the summit by telling his rival, "I see it's going to be a very cold winter." Astonished by the Russian's tirades, Kennedy asked his adviser Llewellyn Thompson, "Tommy, is it always like this?" Thompson said yes. Kennedy became petulant. "What was I supposed to do to show how tough I was," asked the president, "take my shoe off and pound it on the table?" Khrushchev had done just that in 1960 during a speech at the United Nations in New York. Later, a depressed Kennedy complained, "So he just beat the hell out of me." Although Americans had to live with the consequences of this failure in the early sixties, Kennedy's poor performance remained partly hidden from view for decades. Transcripts of the sessions were released only in 1990.[17]

The main reason that Khrushchev had wanted the summit was to force a change in the status of West Berlin, that military outpost of the United States, Britain, and France that lay inside communist East Germany. "It's a bone in my throat," Khrushchev had said. West Berlin was a sore point because more than 100,000 East Germans a year continued to pour through the city's open borders with communist East Berlin. Most were ambitious, educated younger workers who could earn far higher wages in West Germany's booming economy. Khrushchev was prepared to turn West Berlin into a neutral free city, an idea that he personally invented, or, under certain conditions, to reunite the two Germanies into an unarmed, neutral country. Americans could accept neither proposal because each forced the United States to back down from its role as military guarantor of western Europe under the North Atlantic Treaty Organization. Because of the geography of western Europe, NATO could not survive the neutralization and disarmament of Germany, and turning West Berlin into a neutral city might well have led to the end of American influence inside West Germany. In addition, 82 percent of Americans believed that United States forces should remain in Berlin. Yet Americans in 1961 could find no easy way to defend West Berlin short of nuclear war. "After listening to Dean Acheson at lunch yesterday for an hour and a half," observed the columnist Stewart Alsop to a friend, "I said, 'What you're saying is that we have no carrot we can honorably offer him [i.e., Khrushchev], and no stick to beat him with but a nuclear stick.' The phrase is mine, but it sums up Acheson's conclusions, and the conclusions of everybody else I've talked to."[18]

The summit did not solve Khrushchev's Berlin problem, and in August 1961 he built a wall to stop the flow of people from East to West Berlin. Some observers believed that the wall was prelude to military action to force the United States out. One visitor to Berlin privately felt that "the Wall leaves little doubt that we are engaged in war." Other personal letters were scarcely less discouraging. "All talk in Washington these days," noted Stewart Alsop, "is on the same subject, as in the old Alger Hiss or Joe McCarthy days, but now it's Berlin, Berlin, Berlin, Berlin." Washington's Eurocentrism showed. The United States might be faring poorly in Latin America or Asia, but most Americans, including the administration, gave a higher priority to western Europe. "I do not have to tell you about the gravity of the situation ...," warned Marcus Raskin. "Berlin," reported the columnist Stewart Alsop to his editor at the *Saturday Evening Post*, "has apparently become something of an obsession...." Others saw the wall as a first step to isolate and strangle Berlin. "I see no way out of our dilemma," declared the foreign policy analyst Hans Morgenthau, who added, "If we go to war we will destroy ourselves as well as the objective for which we would wage the war. If we don't go to war we are likely to surrender our positions piecemeal. As long as we conduct foreign policy under prenuclear conditions, this dilemma is inescapable."[19]

"We shall end up with no war," British Labour Member of Parliament (and later Foreign Secretary) George Brown wrote Joe Alsop, "but we will have to take the loss of Berlin." The American ambassador to Yugoslavia, George Kennan, was more positive. "I can see no compelling reason," he informed Robert Oppenheimer, "why it [the world] should feel obliged to tear itself to pieces over the problem of Berlin. Other problems, no less complicated, have been lived with in the past and endured, in one way or another, by devices less than suicidal." Over time, people realized that the Soviets intended the wall to be the final solution. "Each passing day," privately wrote the American ambassador to France, "makes it more clear that the Soviets are happy with Berlin...." The wall also became a powerful symbol of, as Stewart Alsop told his editor, "the abysmal failure of Communism." It even became a tourist site, and adventuresome American youths found crossing it fascinating. About East Berlin, the columnist Joseph Alsop's nephew observed, "It is the easiest place to get into and the hardest to get out of. Last time it was five minutes in and two hours out." In 1963 young Alsop attended John Kennedy's outdoor speech in West Berlin, where, addressing up to a million people, the president said, "Ich bin ein Berliner." Beleagured Berliners gave a deafening roar.[20]

During the Kennedy years the United States seemed to be in retreat throughout the world. In 1960, 47 percent of Americans believed that the Soviet Union was ahead of the United States in rockets and missiles. Kennedy had campaigned against the (nonexistent) missile gap. In the 1960 contest, Kennedy himself had warned that the sixties were likely to be difficult, even grim for the United States. On the eve of the new president's inauguration, Khrushchev had declared Soviet support for guerrilla wars of liberation all over the world, and Kennedy's inaugural address responded with strident rhetoric that, ignoring domestic issues, called the Cold War "a hard and bitter peace" and urged sacrifice in a "long twilight struggle." At the end of 1961 the administration had few foreign policy accomplishments, and the United States faced bleak prospects. "However the sums are done," one newsman warned privately, "there is a shift which we can hardly grasp in the balance of world power prospects, and all we can do, in an ordinary weekly exercise, is to point to the big gaps in our too complacent certainties about the outlook." How might Americans respond to reports of deteriorating support from most parts of the world? Advice could be shrill. "Save China, Europe, and North America," suggested one letter-writer, "and you can sink the rest of the world."[21]

Khrushchev was confident that the Soviet Union would prevail. "The socialist camp," publicly boasted a Vietnamese communist, "is mightier than the imperialist camp." As a good Marxist, Castro must have felt that he had chosen the side of historical inevitability. Among those favoring the American side in the Cold War, the sense of gloom was palpable. The poet Elizabeth Bishop, living in Brazil, told Robert Lowell that all of Latin America would eventually turn red. For the first time, the rightist Victor Lasky felt that the United States might well lose the Cold War. "I must confess," privately commented Arthur Schlesinger, Jr., "that I feel more gloomy about international developments than I have felt since the summer of 1939." The United States and its allies seemed to be on the defensive amid rising violence all over the world. "The news of Cuba, Laos, Korea, Formosa, Pakistan, Berlin is chilling beyond the memory of man," wrote the diarist Helen Bevington. "The planet explodes daily," she continued. "Even if we survive the decade, let alone the century, we'll have to admit it seemed unlikely. Sometime, somewhere the holocaust will start." Fear gripped many. According to one poll, 53 percent believed that there would be a world war within five years. "Our chances of getting through the next ten years without war are slim," concluded the nuclear physicist Leo Szilard in a speech. "I look forward to seeing you in 1962," wrote a European correspondent to an American friend, "if the world can refrain from blowing itself up in the interval."[22]

What made the Cold War different from other, earlier great power rivalries such as those between Britain and France during the eighteenth century or between Britain and Germany in the early twentieth century was that both the United States and the Soviet Union were, by 1960, armed with large numbers of nuclear weapons of unprecedented destructive capacity that could be delivered cheaply and quickly by bombers and, increasingly, missiles. In the early sixties, the Pentagon did a study of the consequences of an American first strike against both the Soviet Union and China. It concluded that although a few million Americans might die in the subsequent Soviet response, the United States would win the war with about 360 million dead Russians and Chinese. The Pentagon did not address how Americans or anyone else remaining in the world might feel about megadeath. "The Atom has forced us, as individuals and as peoples," wrote David Lilienthal in his journal, "to look into our hearts and souls, to inquire into what life means, in that solitude given us only by vast and unmistakable *change*, change in the foundations of our beliefs and in the structure of our world." The cloistered Trappist monk Thomas Merton privately declared nuclear war "murder and sin." In a letter, the poet

Gregory Corso asked, "Who's to say the second coming shan't be of megaton stuff?"[23]

In 1960 the fear of nuclear war, while large, produced only muted public comment out of concern of being labeled a coward, a traitor, or a communist. "I would rather be DEAD than RED," J. Edgar Hoover declared in a speech. According to a Gallup poll, 81 percent of Americans agreed. Nuclear Armegeddon was preferable to enslavement to communism. Hoover's declaration was ironic because the slogan had originally been rendered in Britain as "better red than dead," to indicate that life, even under the tyranny of communism, was preferable to annihilation. While public remarks might lean toward the "dead" side of the argument, private thoughts revealed the psychological terror of nuclear war that gripped most of the world during the height of the Cold War. The novelist Taylor Caldwell praised the title that her friend Alexander King planned to use for his book, *May This House Be Safe from Tigers* (1960). Nuclear war, Caldwell wrote King, was "the tiger looking into every window." Nuclear fear was not eased by new technology. Each time a guided missile was tested at a base near Pomona, California, all of that town's automatic garage doors flew open. Residents wondered if a garage door opener might not accidentally launch a missile.[24]

The most perceptive observers realized that something fundamental had changed in human affairs, but these thoughts were usually expressed only in private or among intimates. On receiving the news about Hiroshima in 1945, Dean Acheson had called it "frightening." Unless nations learned to cooperate, he observed in his journal, "we shall be gone geese...." The logic of the terror forced new thoughts. As tension grew in the early sixties, tension itself could prove cathartic. In a letter to his father, Allen Ginsberg mused, "I suppose the Cold War is really over.... No way out other than that or blowing up the world." During 1962 Ginsberg, for the first time, had dreams about the bomb. Nuclear fear pushed people to reject the status quo, to examine alternatives, and to seek a new path to peace. Optimism was almost a necessity to handle the bold transition. If the future were not seen as promising, then it was surely bleak. The Jesuit priest Daniel Berrigan confided to a friend that "the overhanging omnipresent threat" pushed him toward an engaged pacifism. He saw a need for acts of courage, including peace marches, as a "new world" was aborning. The monk Thomas Merton guessed that it might be only five years before nuclear war destroyed everything. "This one does not go around saying," Merton admitted to Berrigan, "it seems so foolish."[25]

Children's lives were most affected. Schools not only held regular nuclear air raid drills, sometimes with visits to dark and dank basement fallout shelters stocked with large circular cardboard containers of food and water, but children also overheard anxious parents discuss a series of never-ending crises. The young absorbed new lessons. "What a world this is," reported a family letter about the *Time* publisher Henry Luce's grandson. "Yesterday Kit built a beautiful bridge with some little red blocks that he's been playing with. Today...he is building a bomb shelter (which he just now finished bombing)." Children pushed women into antiwar politics. "My nine year old wakes with bad dreams," noted one mother in a public statement, "and how can I assure her that it is not a nightmare world? Our six year old asks if its only the Russians who drop bombs?" Only her four year old was innocent. When Carl Braden was in prison, his ten-year-old son wrote him, "Berlin pretty hot place...might be war...be carefull...Watch Out...." Braden's cell was far from any nuclear target.[26]

Most were prepared to agree with the writer Clare Boothe Luce, who privately wrote of a nuclear war, "Anyone who is not an idiot knows that a war in which 100-megaton bombs would be used would blot out our civilization." By 1961 Kennedy had realized that nuclear superiority was meaningless; Secretary of Defense Robert McNamara did not reach this conclusion until 1963. The balance of terror in which both sides had the capacity for over-whelming destruction marked the new reality; a delicate hair trig-ger maintained peace. Experts would soon describe this system for avoiding war as an application of the theory of Mutually Assured Destruction. It really was a MAD world. The question, of course, re-mained what to do about the threat. The bomb could turn out to be strangely liberating. "It may put an end to large-scale wars between nations," noted one letter-writer. "It may also push nations into giving up old-fashioned ideas of national sovereignty." Such radical ideas were more often found among the public than among leaders whose careers depended upon successful management of nuclear weapons.[27]

A number of leaders, including Nelson Rockefeller, proposed mass construction of fallout shelters throughout the United States, but the public never accepted the idea. According to a Gallup poll, only 5 percent of Americans believed that they had a "very good" chance of surviving a nuclear war. "One would be fried and crushed," privately wrote a shelter critic, "even though not ion-ized." Shelters also seemed undemocratic. While the masses evapo-rated, Gary Snyder observed to Allen Ginsberg, the wealthy "figure to come out ahead if not dead." John Alsop, brother of the jour-nalists Stewart and Joseph, built a roomy family shelter in Con-necticut. Then he ran for governor on a platform calling for state subsidies to construct shelters and was badly trounced. When the Weavers, a folk singing group led by Pete Seeger that had been blacklisted for its leftist politics during the McCarthy era, played Carnegie Hall in 1963, they sang a short song about a young cou-ple whose love remained intact even as the man was locked out of the woman's shelter. The audience's nervous laughter revealed apprehension. Shelters, many suspected, might provide an excuse to start nuclear war. The public did not know that the government had already built a huge complex under a West Virginia mountain to house members of Congress and their families.[28]

Anxiety over nuclear war, as much as the perception that the Cold War was being lost around the world, goes far toward explaining why a new, militant anticommunist Right gained strength in the early sixties. Eisenhower's leaving office also played a role. It had been difficult to charge the hero of the D-Day invasion with military incompetence or negligence. Even if J. Edgar Hoover did believe that Ike's administration suffered from the "Karl Marx virus," conservatives who did not totally approve of the old general mostly kept quiet during his watch. Furthermore, when the Massachusetts candymaker Robert Welch, who had founded the secretive, ultraright John Birch Society in 1958, suggested that Ike was a communist, he eventually found himself and his fellow anticommunist Birchers under attack from conservative Republicans, including Clare Boothe Luce and William F. Buckley, Jr. Buckley, however, acted cautiously, since he wanted to discredit Welch while cultivating the society's members. Despite Welch's excesses, two California Birchers, John Rousselot and Edgar Hiestand, were elected to Congress as Republicans in 1960, and Gen. Edwin Walker tried to indoctrinate troops under his command with Birchite ideas, until he was fired in 1961. Although only 8 percent of Americans viewed the society favorably in 1962, it grew to 40,000 members by 1963.[29]

Signs of conservative upsurge went well beyond the Birch Society. At the movement's center was the suave, wealthy, Yale-educated William F. Buckley, Jr., whose *National Review* tripled its circulation from 1960 to 1964. A clever, witty writer, public speaker, and television debater, Buckley commanded large audiences. A devout Catholic, he used his magazine to meld conservative Catholics, Protestants, and Jews into a potential political majority. Buckley understood that conservatives, whose politics often reflected deep religious convictions, found it harder to cross denominational barriers than did liberals, who were secular by nature. Although deeply religious, Buckley used a secular tone in his magazine in order to avoid unnecessary divisions among supporters. The key to uniting the otherwise diverse and fragmented Right, Buckley knew, was anticommunism. Furthermore, conservatives saw liberals as fatally tied to the Left. Taylor Caldwell, for one, equated reds and liberals. "I'm perfectly willing to forgive the bastards," she declared in a letter to Buckley, "after I've planted a good firecracker in their careers or rectums." Buckley sought to remake American politics. "Nothing more annoys a Liberal," he wrote a friend, "than to be told that the real radicals are conservatives these days."[30]

For a time Americans seemed obsessed with anticommunism, which was heavily promoted by the *Reader's Digest*, a conservative monthly magazine with the nation's highest circulation. Millions more read J. Edgar Hoover's communist exposé, *Masters of Deceit* (1958), and listened to the Right-wing radio shows of Clarence Manion, Fulton Lewis, Jr., and Dan Smoot. Texas billionaire H. L. Hunt paid for many of Smoot's broadcasts. Thousands flocked to Rev. Billy Hargis's Christian Anti-Communist Crusade and Dr. Fred Schwarz's Anti-Communist Schools. In 1961, when Schwarz filled the Hollywood Bowl in Los Angeles with 15,000 people, four million watched on television. Nixon sent greetings, the actor (later Senator) George Murphy hosted, and John Wayne appeared as a guest. While Schwarz's schools quickly faded, anticommunists began to organize politically. Across the country they emerged from the grassroots to take over many local Republican party organizations. Some conservatives argued that adding fluoride to public water supply systems was a communist plot to cause "lethargy," and many local elections were won on that issue. This ultraconservative idea was brilliantly satirized in Stanley Kubrick's film, *Dr. Strangelove* (1964). The Right frequently found plots in the strangest places. Myers Lowman of the Circuit Riders, a Cincinnati-based group founded by conservative Methodists, insisted that the Revised Standard Version of the Bible was a communist hoax.[31]

Conservatives trumpeted *Operation Abolition*, a HUAC-sponsored film that portrayed a college student protest against the committee in San Francisco in 1960 as a communist-inspired riot. Although sophisticates, including students, found the film unconvincing, it excited many viewers. Conservative groups used the movie to raise funds, and, as the liberal Senator Gale McGee lamented, Democrats had no equivalent, which made them look soft on communism. *Operation Abolition* was just one way in which government itself assisted the Right. Nor was it safe to object. When a student in Miami heckled the film, he was called up by his draft board. After Gore Vidal wrote a rave review of Frank Donner's *The Un-Americans* (1961), a scathing condemnation of HUAC that included excellent coverage of the San Francisco protest, the committee's chair, Francis Walter, attacked Vidal in the *Congressional Record*. As Aubrey Williams privately observed, Americans had been "terrorized into silence" by the Right and its allies at HUAC and the FBI. The people, he predicted, would "vomit them all up." However, he conceded, "I think right now it is indisputable that they are pretty much in control."[32]

Kennedy, moreover, was ripe fruit for conservative picking. Not only had the candidate raised public anxiety during the 1960 campaign by suggesting (incorrectly) that the United States lagged behind the Soviet Union in nuclear missiles, but after the election the youthful, inexperienced president's failure at the Bay of Pigs confirmed, to the Right, that Kennedy was a softy who could not help pandering to leftist, pacifist forces inside his party. Conservatives speculated about who in the administration – Adlai Stevenson was one suspect – had been behind the decision to deny air cover to the exile brigade, and whether that denial showed liberal incompetence, lack of courage, or treason. Rightists, even after they had concluded that McCarthy's tactics were embarrassing, continued to believe that the United States was losing the Cold War due, mainly, to lack of will and moral fiber. "It is amazing," privately noted one observer, "to find out how many people, frustrated by events abroad, lay the blame at home, by believing that the government is cowardly or that it is infiltrated by the communists." To the Right, the Kennedy-led liberal Democrats were hopeless. Finding metooism inside a Republican party dominated by the chameleonic Richard Nixon and the liberal Nelson Rockefeller, conservatives looked for an alternative.[33]

Out of Arizona came the highly quotable Senator Barry Goldwater. His book, *Conscience of a Conservative* (1960), which had been ghosted by Brent Bozell, William F. Buckley's brother-in-law, eventually sold 3.5 million copies. At the 1960 Republican convention, when conservatives expressed dismay over Nixon's nomination, Goldwater told his supporters, "Let's grow up, conservatives. Let's, if we want to, take this party back and I think we can someday. Let's get to work." This comment proved inspirational, and, after Nixon's defeat that fall, conservatives did take control and began to work for Goldwater's nomination in 1964. When Kennedy visited Philadelphia in 1963, he was greeted with picket signs: "We will Barry you!" "It is my opinion that Far Leftists from now on," wrote one conservative in a letter, "will move Heaven and Earth to block Goldwater's nomination, for the obvious reason that he can lick Kennedy." Others were less approving. The moderate Republican Stewart Alsop told his editor that Goldwater was "the kind of 'conservative' who wants to substitute loud noises for money and effort in opposing Communism." Still, Alsop understood the appeal, finding the Arizonan to be "the most saleable political commodity in the country, after Jackie and JFK."[34]

In 1960 M. Stanton Evans published *Revolt on the Campus*, about the upsurge of conservatism among students. That same year William F. Buckley, Jr., helped found Young Americans for Freedom, which grew to 175 chapters with 20,000 members in less than two years. In March 1962, 18,000 young conservatives attended a YAF rally at New York's Madison Square Garden. Outside, a few American Nazis picketed, claiming that YAF was a communist front. About 500 radicals carried signs that read, "YAF–Young

American Fascists" and "Down with HUAC." A thousand liberal protesters, Young Democrats, milled around with their own anti-YAF signs but refused to mingle with those to their Left, and, after proving to everyone that they outnumbered the radicals, they departed for their own rally to hear Hubert Humphrey. Inside the YAF rally, the well-dressed, good-natured, and orderly crowd listened to Brent Bozell call for the invasion of Cuba and the tearing down of the Berlin Wall. George Murphy vowed, "John Wayne will not forget the Alamo." The reference is ironic, but Wayne had directed and starred in *The Alamo* (1960), a film that reeked of so much sentimental patriotism that Wayne nearly jumped off the screen to corral the audience to seize Cuba. Baby boomers had first encountered the Texas martyrs in the popular Disney film *Davy Crockett* (1955). Amid a few paper airplanes sent sailing from the balcony, young conservatives endlessly chanted for Goldwater, who finally appeared to attack the welfare state. Goldwater insisted that Gen. Edwin Walker not be on the platform.[35]

In the early sixties older conservatives were, despite a sense of increased numbers and enthusiasm among the young, restless and uneasy. "From my own standpoint," privately wrote the Seattle surgeon Don Hall, who had married the conservative Senator Robert Taft's niece, "the only encouraging signs I see are those pertaining to the increasing popularity of the Goldwater philosophy – especially in the colleges." Despite these trends, Americans, in the eyes of conservatives, were all too eager to embrace the welfare state. The columnist Constance Brown told a friend, "Socialism is coming upon us with such rapidity from so many directions that there are not enough fingers to hold in the dyke." Or as a steel company president wrote in a letter, "I am increasingly alarmed by the drift in both government and education toward socialism...." Dr. Hall echoed this gloom. "I feel strongly that this drive toward a welfare, socialist state," he told a relative, "is a far greater danger to us than the threat of communism abroad." Hall wondered if he should instill conservative values in his children, "for it will sure make it harder for them to assimilate & conform in the years to come."[36]

The upsurge of youths espousing conservatism was but one aspect of growing political restlessness among young Americans. Demographic change played a role in this development. As baby boomers entered their teens in record numbers in the early sixties, the cohort's large size enabled young people to call attention to themselves. Moreover, youthful boomers who were uncomfortable with the status quo but uncertain about where to go could be found on *all* sides of the political spectrum. In a note to a comrade, the leftist Carleton Smith reported "the youth willing and anxious to forge ahead!" An idealistic Stanford student, according to a friend in a letter, wanted "to join a revolution for the experience." Sensitive to this restless sentiment for change, Kennedy tried to tap the hope for a promising future by directing youngsters into public service. In many ways, the newly established Peace Corps would become Kennedy's finest accomplishment; it showed the president's unique capacity among his peers for understanding the younger generation. "You would be amazed," confided a student, "at the interest that has developed recently in teaching somewhere in the developing countries." Young idealists were everywhere. "I have become extremely interested in contributing my services," wrote Averell Harriman's great niece, a high school student who sought a position at the United Nations. Uncle Ave tried, but failed, in this particular assignment.[37]

At no time did the Cold War seem more frightening than during the Cuban Missile Crisis in October 1962. When Kennedy discovered that, contrary to private assurances, Khrushchev was in the process of putting medium-range nuclear missiles capable of destroying most American cities into Cuba, he was furious. After observing that whether missiles were in Cuba or on submarines was militarily unimportant, Secretary of Defense Robert McNamara candidly told the president, "This is a domestic political problem." Kennedy's humiliation at the Bay of Pigs and in Vienna had been accompanied by a clouded negotiated settlement in Laos and by his acceptance of the Berlin Wall. Pounded in the media daily by Republicans for these failures, he had not a single foreign policy victory to trumpet in reply in the midterm elections, which were about to take place. At the same time, Americans opposed United States forces invading Cuba, and 51 percent believed that such an invasion would lead to war with the Soviet Union. If before, or even after, the elections, Americans suddenly learned that the Soviets had placed missiles in Cuba, that Kennedy had known, and that he had done nothing, the Right would attack the president mercilessly.[38]

The Missile Crisis was the most dangerous event during the Cold War because both sides lacked accurate information. Miscalculation might have led to nuclear war; Kennedy privately estimated the odds at one in five. He offered to evacuate Jackie and the children from the White House, but Mrs. Kennedy declined to go. Since the end of the Cold War, we have learned how close to disaster the world came. The United States nearly invaded Cuba, which almost certainly would have occurred after American bombing of the missile sites, since only ground troops could guarantee their total destruction. The invaders would have faced about 43,000 Soviet soldiers under a commander who had as many as 160 mostly tactical nuclear weapons. The United States had estimated the number of Russian troops at 4,000 and did not know that they had any nuclear arms that were ready to be fired. Worried primarily about submarine-launched weapons, Kennedy had already warned that any nuclear bombs used in the western hemisphere would bring a full-scale retaliatory response upon the Soviet Union. One of the main reasons that Khrushchev backed down by removing the medium-range missiles and all nuclear weapons from Cuba was that he feared losing control of events. Soviet communications technology was poor, and Khrushchev could not be certain that he could stop the local Soviet commander from using tactical nuclear weapons and thereby starting a global holocaust. He also found his overall nuclear arsenal, one-quarter the size of the American one, mismatched.[39]

As the crisis unfolded, terror rose. The British philosopher and peace activist Bertrand Russell publicly declared, "We'll all be dead in a week." As few as eight well-placed bombs could annihilate tiny Great Britain. Columbia University students, privately noted a professor, "were literally scared for their lives." The diarist Helen Bevington, who lived in Durham, North Carolina, was drinking coffee with friends when an air raid siren went off. She said, "This is it!" But it was only a test. During World War II, she and her husband had had a similar panic in New York. Not everyone sat idly. In the middle of the crisis, 15,000 people demonstrated for peace in New York, Los Angeles, Berkeley, and Chicago. In Austin, Texas, thirteen students picketed at the Capitol with signs reading "Invasion means Retaliation means Annihilation" and "Let's use our brains, not our bombs." When the National Student Christian Federation solicited student views on Kennedy's policy, all responses came back negative, and the group, to present both sides, had to seek out pro-Kennedy statements. In Detroit there was hysteria. In a letter an eyewitness reported "practice civil defense drills breaking up in panics, terrific stockpiling of goods, Negro disaffection that they would be the ones to get it while white folks sat fatly in shelters, etc."[40]

Because Khrushchev did agree to withdraw the missiles, Americans generally credited Kennedy with a Cold War "victory" in the Missile Crisis. The president's polls rose, and Democrats, contrary to expectation, gained in the off-year elections, but the episode had badly scared Americans. "Are you as deeply disturbed about the Cuban situation as I am?" inquired Owen Lattimore in a letter shortly before the crisis ended. Detecting a pattern similar to one seen during the Bay of Pigs, he thought that the Democrats felt pressured to match militant Republican anticommunism. The result was an administration that practiced vacillation, decision, more vacillation, and then indecision. It "gives me the gooseflesh," he concluded. Although he expected that the United States would either invade or bomb the missile sites, he also believed nuclear war unlikely. Lattimore saw that Kennedy would gain politically in the short term but worried that American prestige throughout Latin America would suffer over the long term. "I haven't been so depressed for a long, long time," he concluded.[41]

Proclaiming victory in his duel with Khrushchev over the Soviet missiles, Kennedy boasted to friends, "I cut his balls off." Of the president, Lyndon Johnson concluded, "He plays a damn good hand of poker." Others saw the matter differently. Air Force General Curtis LeMay, disappointed that Castro remained in power, told the president, "We lost," while Acheson held that a reckless Kennedy had won only by "plain dumb luck." Neither Castro nor Khrushchev felt like winners. An enraged Castro kicked in a wall and shattered a mirror while shouting that Khrushchev had "no cojones." The Soviet premier, having rejected Castro's suggestion of a suicidal nuclear first strike against the more potent United States, privately said, "Because of Fidel I cannot sleep." In a quiet moment, however, Kennedy offered a more sober assessment. "It is insane," he observed, "that two men on opposite sides of the world, should be able to decide to bring an end to civilization." Khrushchev may well have shared that sentiment. Months later, Dean Rusk noted how new information and arguments presented throughout the crisis had caused top officials to shift positions continually during their deliberations. The overall effect of these twists and turns had been both sobering and psychologically transformative. He told Kennedy, "We have to remember that no one who went through the missile crisis came out the same as they went in."[42]

Had Kennedy really "won?" Private thoughts expressed doubt. "Is it enough that the Soviet missiles and other 'offensive weapons' have been removed from Cuba?" asked Stewart Alsop in a letter,

"Or must Fidel Castro himself be removed, and with him the military base which the Soviets have built in the Western hemisphere?" The costly failure at the Bay of Pigs had encouraged Castro to turn Cuba into a Soviet satellite. After all, one leftist concluded, "I think we can be merry. The USSR has saved Cuba...." Or as a sour voice put it, "I think Comrade Khrushchev is about ready to write a book at this point – 'Profiles in American guts'." So long as Castro remained in power, many Americans would be dissatisfied. "I tried to tell the people in Hancock & Peterboro & Rindge," reported a New Hampshire conservative to a friend, "that Kennedy was a traitor but the women so love Irish Kennedy that they have mostly cut me for daring to suggest their 'loveable' President was a traitor." By 1963, one heard less of this bitter talk. "All the portents," noted Clare Boothe Luce in a letter, "are that the Cuban Issue is dying down as a deep concern of the American people." In the fall of 1963, Mrs. Luce was secretly admitted to a hospital in Boston. Blaming the Kennedys both for her illness and for the nation's political troubles, she named her two ulcers "Jack" and "Bobby."[43]

While Soviet missiles were removed from Cuba (in exchange for American missiles in Turkey, in a secret part of the deal long suspected but disclosed only in 1987), Castro remained in power, and the United States continued to honor Kennedy's public pledge not to invade Cuba. Thus, the missile trade aside, the main consequence of the crisis appeared to be the guarantee of Castro's regime. Appearances can deceive. "Castro walks in fear," said the sphinx-like Rusk off the record. Quietly, the president stepped up Operation Mongoose, a program that used Cuban exiles to harass Castro's regime and sabotage the Cuban economy. (One of the more bizarre projects was a failed attempt to divert a hurricane over Cuba.) At its most secret heart, Operation Mongoose also tried to kill Castro. The CIA planned to do so by continuing to use mobsters who had lost their gambling interests in Havana. But Kennedy's Cuban policy had more than one dimension. On the day that the president was assassinated in Dallas, the CIA-mob plot to kill Castro was going forward in Paris with the attempted passing of a poison pen. At the moment of Kennedy's death Castro was talking with a European journalist who had been authorized by Kennedy to open private negotiations with Castro for rapprochement. The dual policy is no surprise given Kennedy's enigmatic nature.[44]

Meantime, a peace movement had begun to flourish. Kennedy's Cold War failures, the nightmarish quality of the Missile Crisis, and even the rise of the anticommunist Right helped nurture this movement, whose participants, drawn mostly from the educated middle class and disproportionately women and college students, argued that the best way for Americans to avoid nuclear annihilation, to challenge communism, and to win support in the neutral Third World was to work for peace. In part, the movement was spurred by nuclear weapons tests and by growing evidence in the late fifties and early sixties that such tests by both Russians and Americans posed a serious hazard to the environment and to health. Of what use was an arms race that destroyed the human race? But the peace movement also challenged compulsory support for official policy. In the fifties, participation in city air raid drills was mandatory. On one day each spring at a preannounced moment sirens sounded, traffic stopped, radio and television broadcasts were interrupted, and everyone on the street was required to take shelter underground until the all-clear was given. From 1955 to 1959 a handful of New Yorkers openly defied the drills each year; they were arrested. In 1960 the number refusing to participate at City Hall Park grew to 500, only 26 of whom were cited. The next year, when 2,000 defied the local ordinance, no one was arrested. Air raid drills ended.[45]

Ever since 1945, nuclear scientists had been among those most concerned about the destructive new weaponry. On both sides of the Iron Curtain, scientists gradually developed back channels, largely through the numerous Pugwash conferences, in order to discuss both the dangers of nuclear tests and the issue of proliferation. The first of these meetings of American, British, and Russian scientists was held in 1957 at the instigation of Albert Einstein and Bertrand Russell at Pugwash, Nova Scotia, the Canadian birthplace of the industrialist Cyrus Eaton. In Robert Oppenheimer's private view, these conferences were "one of the rather hopeful lights in a picture which generally still seems to be very dark." By 1960 neither the United States nor the Soviet Union could benefit much militarily from further tests. Both countries found it convenient to call for a test ban primarily to prevent other nations, especially China, from gaining nuclear weapons. However, the level of trust between the United States and the Soviet Union was very low, and talks for a test ban treaty stalled.[46]

The most prominent peace organization in the late fifties was SANE, which had been founded in 1957. Like most other McCarthy era political groups, it barred communists. However, the effort to keep SANE free of reds did not prevent Senator Thomas Dodd from attacking the group when a suspected former communist was found in a high position. True to its commitment, SANE dismissed the official. The national board also resisted chartering student groups suspected of containing communists. SANE members, however, resented not only their leaders' obsession with communists but also the organization's authoritarian structure. These irritations suggest the beginnings of a sixties sensibility in which top-down organizations gave way to bottom-up participatory groups. SANE's greatest successes came in two newspaper advertisements. One linked nuclear fallout to unsafe milk, due to a radioactive isotope that cows picked up from contaminated grass, and the other featured Dr. Benjamin Spock, a revered public figure, warning against nuclear danger to children's health. The Spock ad, reprinted in more than 90 newspapers, not only presented a powerful message against the arms race but also propelled the famous pediatrician into politics.[47]

SANE was already in decline when Dagmar Wilson, a children's book illustrator and the wife of an employee in the British embassy in Washington, founded Women Strike for Peace in November 1961. Unlike SANE, WSP did not bar communists. These women took the position that anyone was welcome so long as the person supported WSP's general purpose. WSP was a true grassroots organization. National leaders helped circulate ideas and coordinate among various chapters, but they did not control any local activities. Instead, each particular women's group made plans for its own community. WSP's emphasis upon activity generated from the bottom up became a model for later sixties political movements. Indeed, WSP became a training ground for activists, including those in the ripening feminist movement. Dagmar Wilson personified the do-it-yourself spirit. The well-heeled Mrs. Wilson at times flew to Europe to meet fellow peace activists who were unable, sometimes for political reasons, to enter the United States. She met European women, including Soviets, in Vienna, Stockholm, Helsinki, and Moscow.[48]

WSP grew rapidly, with 90 local affiliates created in the United States within a month, and support groups in foreign countries quickly followed. In January 1962, WSP sent 2,000 pickets to the White House in the rain. Confidence in a promising future spurred women to public expression that overcame reluctance to state private thoughts. The demonstration did not go unnoticed. President Kennedy was said to have watched the protest from inside behind a curtained window. At the end of the year, HUAC subpoenaed Dagmar Wilson. She testified that she was not a communist, that WSP welcomed all, even communists, and that WSP was willing to talk to communists about peace at any time or place. HUAC was routed. "To stand up and tell that bone-picking committee," one supporter wrote Wilson, "that there are some things more important than suspicion and hate and provincial fears was to do a great service for the whole world." WSP sent 51 lobbyists to the Geneva disarmament conference and persuaded both American and Russian delegates to meet jointly with the women. This session marked the first time delegates had ever met informally. To reduce Cold War tensions, WSP proposed cultural and personal exchanges between the United States and the Soviet Union. Although male-run governments resisted, the women continued to lobby. Eventually, the two countries agreed to cultural exchanges, which proved important in increasing Soviet contact with the outside world. In prodding both governments, one woman argued, "The men's way is not working; it has never worked; it has always led to war."[49]

Although we tend to think of the peace movement in terms of large organizations, planned protests, or publications, much important activity involved low-key acts by individuals or very small groups that are much more difficult to document. These modest personal gestures would have been impossible or ineffective during the earlier McCarthyite repression; the optimism of the early sixties stimulated women to act, sometimes boldly. In 1961 Agnes Meyer, the widow of the publisher of the *Washington Post*, was one of a dozen American women who met with Soviet counterparts at Bryn Mawr College. "It is our purpose," she told Robert Oppenheimer, "to study what Russian and American women can do to ease the tensions between our two countries." A year later Mrs. Meyer threw a dinner party to honor Anatoly Dobrynin, the new Soviet ambassador to the United States. She noted that he saw almost no one outside diplomatic circles. In addition to the Russian and his wife, Mrs. Meyer's guests included the McNamaras, the Harrimans, the Oppenheimers, and Adlai Stevenson. As Agnes hoped, Adlai acted as host and put everyone at ease by asking Madame Dobrynin to play the piano and sing. So went one small promising moment amid the large dark shadow of the Cold War.[50]

In 1962, activists decided to challenge the Cold War consensus directly by running candidates for Congress on peace platforms. These candidates campaigned for the end of nuclear tests, for negotiations with the Soviet Union, and for reducing the American military budget. Of the seven Democrats and one Republican who won congressional nominations, three California Democrats (George Brown, Edward Roybal, and Lionel Van Deerlin) were elected. A few independents also ran, and these fared poorly in November, drawing under 3 percent of the vote. The most prominent independent candidate was H. Stuart Hughes, a Harvard history professor who ran for the Senate in Massachusetts against Ted Kennedy. Hughes, the grandson of Chief Justice Charles Evans Hughes, raised money with an auction of works by Gregory Corso, Thomas Merton, Archibald MacLeish, and Lawrence Ferlinghetti. He drew enthusiastic support only on campuses and mostly from students ineligible to vote. In 1962, the voting age was still 21. Nevertheless, he brought young people into politics, and early polls suggested that he might draw 7 percent of the vote. However, the Missile Crisis on the eve of the election hurt all the peace candidates, and Hughes finished with 2 percent.[51]

College students, as potential cannon fodder, had a special interest in peace. The Student Peace Union, founded in 1959, had 1,500 members by 1961. As SANE shrank due to its unpopular top-down leadership, SPU grew. It staged a number of vigorous marches that especially appealed to energetic young people. SPU also shrewdly borrowed Britain's "peace symbol" from that country's large antinuclear movement. The semaphore markers for N and D (for Nuclear Disarmament) were superimposed upon each other inside a circle. Although still a novel symbol in the early sixties, this memorable and easily recognizable device was to become a standard in the antiwar movement during the late sixties. In February 1962, SPU, Students for a Democratic Society, and other groups operating as the consortium Turn toward Peace cosponsored pickets at the White House and other events in Washington that drew a surprisingly large 4,000 people on a cold, wet weekend. "It has to be said for Kennedy," noted Hannah Arendt in a letter, "that he sent coffee out to the students who were demonstrating. . . ." It is hard to imagine another administration that would have undertaken that gesture. With the signing of the nuclear test ban treaty in 1963, SPU declined, and student antiwar activity shifted into SDS.[52]

Peace activism fed into a larger movement that became known as the New Left. The sociologist C. Wright Mills had promoted the concept in a key article in 1960; the scholarly journal *Studies on the Left*, founded in 1959, helped develop the idea. While civil rights played a bigger role both in terms of inspiration and in terms of ideas about organization and tactics, the Cold War also stimulated the creation of a New Left. Simple war weariness pushed young people to look for new paths to peace. For many members of the Student Peace Union, it was a short step from that monocausal organization to Students for a Democratic Society, which had a larger agenda for social change. In some respects the New Left began with the charismatic Fidel Castro, who had stimulated radical enthusiasm among young Americans in the late fifties. When the Cuban leader visited the United States in 1959, he drew large, enthusiastic crowds at both Princeton and Harvard, where then-Dean McGeorge Bundy introduced Castro to a football stadium full of students. Growing repression inside Cuba, however, caused American support to fall quickly. Like others who embraced radicalism, Allen Ginsberg did not mind Castro's expropriation of American-owned property; he did, however, object to the Cuban government's hostility to marijuana and homosexuality. By 1962, Students for a Democatic Society condemned Castro as an unacceptable dictator.[53]

SDS, which became the most important New Left organization during the sixties, was tiny during the Kennedy years. In the fall of 1960 it had only 250 members; a year later, 575. At that time the conservative Young Americans for Freedom already had thousands of members. Despite SDS's small size, it was in the early sixties that the organization adopted the measures that led to its upsurge later in the decade. A number of colleges already showed rising activism during the late fifties, after McCarthyite repression declined. Peace activists at the University of Wisconsin staged an annual Anti-Military Ball, while those at Harvard University created Tocsin, an organization that became involved in the Stuart Hughes election campaign. In 1957, radicals at the University of California at Berkeley created SLATE (a meaningless acronym) to contest fraternity-dominated student body elections. In 1960, many of these same students demonstrated against capital punishment and against HUAC's hearings in San Francisco. In the early sixties ad hoc committees were formed to protest racism in the Bay Area. Both Berkeley and Madison developed unique radical cultures that operated largely through ad hoc committees. In contrast, SDS grew into prominence at Harvard and at the University of Michigan, where it brought together young people concerned about peace, racism, poverty, and capitalist exploitation.[54]

Although SDS banned communists, it did not enforce the ban rigorously. After Khrushchev's revelations of Stalin's crimes, the Old Left was dead, and the purpose of the New Left was to unite all leftists within a democratic framework. Steve Max, from a communist family, played a leadership role, but SDS in the early sixties was not Marxist. It was, however, hostile to the Cold War and emotionally anti-anticommunist. In 1962, SDS proclaimed its principles in "The Port Huron Statement." Largely written by Tom Hayden, former editor of the *University of Michigan Daily*, the statement began, "We are the people of this generation, bred in at least modest comfort, housed now in universities, looking uncomfortably to the world we inherit." Elsewhere, SDS explained that it sought "to create a sustained community ... bringing together liberals and radicals, activists and scholars. ..." Seeking to empower ordinary people to enact "a radical, democratic program," SDS touted participatory democracy, defined as collective decisions reached by a full, honest thrashing out of issues in long open meetings. "We combine," Hayden observed in a letter, "a weirdly paradoxical sense of impatience *and* experimentalism." SDS was congruent with a rising public expression during a promising time. Like WSP, SDS was to be bottom up, not top down. "Think nationally, act locally" was the motto. "Members," privately stated one leader, "are encouraged to act in whatever way and on whatever issues they feel most reasonable." This attitude influenced SDS's approach to the Cold War throughout the sixties.[55]

Youthful idealists, as well as other peace activists, clashed with the administration over nuclear tests. In 1961, Khrushchev broke a self-imposed ban to announce the resumption of tests, and Kennedy, despite pressure from peace groups, resolved to do likewise. Public opinion was split. Kennedy recognized that the tests had little military value, but he felt that he could not afford to look complacent. Peace activists criticized both nations. Over Thanksgiving, 30 students from Swarthmore, Amherst, and Mount Holyoke picketed the White House. Although the SANE leader Homer Jack concluded that the situation was "practically back to where we were in 1957," the reality was different. After tests were completed in 1962, prospects for an American–Soviet limited test ban treaty increased, since both countries had little to gain from further tests. In the aftermath of the Missile Crisis, Kennedy began in 1963 to move toward a more peace-oriented foreign policy. In a key speech at American University in June, he said, "In the final analysis, our most basic common link is that we all inhabit this small planet." Shortly afterward, Averell Harriman went to Moscow to negotiate the first test ban treaty with the Soviet Union. One poll found 63 percent approval. When Harriman returned home, he was greeted by a crowd in a candlelight vigil at his home in Georgetown. They sang, "For He's a Jolly Good Fellow."[56]

Despite the test ban treaty, the administration continued to worry about global trouble spots. During Kennedy's presidency, no Cold War problem, even Cuba, proved more vexing than Southeast Asia. Although the administration had negotiated a compromise over Laos in 1961, a similar outcome appeared impossible in South Vietnam, which many observers felt likely to fall to communist guerrillas. The United States had been involved in South Vietnam since that country's creation in 1954, when the prowestern Ngo Dinh Diem's regime had been installed. His inept government had hung on, but the war against the communist North Vietnam-organized Viet Cong insurgency inside South Vietnam faltered in 1961. While some Kennedy aides wanted to use American combat troops, others were leery. After the Korean War, the United States had shied away from any Asian land war. In 1961 Undersecretary of State George Ball warned, "Within five years we'll have 300,000 men in the paddies and jungles and never find them again." Wishing to preserve options at low cost, Kennedy decided to limit involvement, at least for the time being, by sending military "advisors" in lieu of combat troops. (In late 1963 there were 16,000 advisors.) As the situation appeared to stabilize during 1961, the administration concluded that patience, democratization, and economic aid would eventually produce a robust, anticommunist South Vietnam. Patience, however, was required. In 1962 Averell Harriman privately concluded, "...we are likely to be in Viet-Nam for a long period of time."[57]

In 1961 much of the administration's optimism about South Vietnam came from its enthusiasm for counterguerrilla warfare. The way to beat the insurgents, it was argued, was to use specially trained personnel. This idea was bolstered by British success against communist rebels in Malaysia. Over the opposition of regular officers, Kennedy had established the Green Berets and ordered that all military training emphasize guerrilla activities. The president kept a green beret on his desk, and the Special Forces were invited to demonstrate skills at Bobby Kennedy's home. Vietnam, however, proved a poor place to test counterinsurgency. The regular military's reluctance to train such personnel made it impossible to acquire enough to overpower the Viet Cong. In contrast with traditional warfare, this type of action required a high, 10 to 1 ratio of trained forces to the enemy, and the communists were simply too numerous. The insurgents' continued success then led to a new strategy. In order to cut off rural support, the administration decided to move many Vietnamese peasants to "strategic hamlets." This disastrous policy produced economic and social crises and turned the peasants against the South Vietnamese government. Because low-level American officials knew that Kennedy was personally committed to both counterinsurgency and strategic hamlets, they were reluctant to criticize either policy in reports. They avoided the truth: The communists were gradually gaining control of the country.[58]

By mid-1963 Diem's unpopular regime was near collapse. A Catholic mystic in a country where Catholics were a tiny, educated elite, Diem increasingly turned inward to his family. One brother, Ngo Dinh Thuc, was archbishop and another, Ngo Dinh Nhu, ran the secret police. The government repressed Buddhists, who were the most numerous religious group. Several of that sect's monks protested by setting themselves ablaze, which Diem's sharp-tongued sister-in-law, Madame Nhu, scornfully dismissed as fondness for "barbecue." In August 1963, Kennedy sent Henry Cabot Lodge as ambassador to make one last effort to reform the South Vietnamese regime or, if that failed, to seek a new government. Kennedy had named a prominent Republican to ensure bipartisan support for his policy. The president, who dealt directly with Lodge in secret cables that often used Rusk's name, caused a critical wire to be sent urging either reform or a coup. Although neither Kennedy nor Rusk had signed the message, both had approved it. Lodge reported that the chances for reform were "nil." A few days later, Lodge declared in a secret cable, "We are launched on a course from which there is no respectable turning back: the overthrow of the Diem government." No coup took place at that time, but the stage was set.[59]

In September 1963, Kennedy laid down conditions for further American military efforts in South Vietnam in a television interview. "In the final analysis," he declared, "it is their war. They are the ones who have to win it or lose it. We can help them. We can give them equipment. We can send our men there as advisors but they have to win it – the people of Viet-Nam against the Communists." The president's words papered over the administration's internal divisions. A few days later, Rusk privately warned, "If we do go in with U.S. combat troops, the Vietnamese will turn against us." He sounded tougher when he informed Lodge that "a secure and independent South Viet-Nam" was "the condition for our leaving." Two days later, the secretary of state told the ambassador, "I can assure you that from the President on down everybody is determined to support you and the country team in winning the war against the Viet Cong. There . . . are not quitters here." Maybe not, but after an upbeat Marine Corps general and a gloomy State Department official presented strikingly divergent reports about South Vietnam to Kennedy at the same meeting, an exasperated president asked, "Were you two gentlemen in the same country?" To almost everyone, Vietnam presented a puzzle.[60]

On November 1, 1963, the South Vietnamese generals overthrew Diem in a coup sanctioned in Washington. "If we miscalculated," Kennedy warned, "we could lose our entire position in Southeast Asia overnight." The generals planned the operation, but the CIA Saigon station chief was in coup headquarters during the event constantly on the telephone with Lodge. When Diem realized that his own military, including special troops that guarded the palace, had turned against him, he asked Lodge to be flown out of the country. The ambassador declared that no airplane was available. His response may have been influenced by a warning that Nhu planned to have Lodge killed. The coup plotters did not feel safe leaving Diem and Nhu alive to plan a countercoup or assassinations. Lodge could not have been surprised when a few hours later the brothers were murdered. Kennedy had wanted a bloodless change, and he was visibly upset by Diem's death. "We had a hand in killing him," said Lyndon Johnson privately. Seeing the coup as unproductive and destabilizing, former Ambassador Frederick Nolting later publicly called it "shameful and disastrous." The American role in overthrowing Diem, like the Bay of Pigs fiasco, involved American prestige, which made any quiet withdrawal by the United States difficult. The coup had all the markings of Kennedy's penchant for secret, deadly plots. Although the Pentagon Papers revealed part of the American role in 1971, many details were kept hidden for thirty years. As of 1996, missing data included American cash payments, the payees, and specifics about manipulations of South Vietnam's economy.[61]

Many reacted gloomily to the deteriorating situation in Vietnam. "We are in an awful mess in South Vietnam," privately wrote Joe Alsop, who believed that he had uncovered evidence that Diem's opium-smoking brother Nhu had conspired with North Vietnam to undermine the South Vietnamese government. One scenario had Nhu heading a neutralist government and inviting the United States to leave. In the fall of 1963 the national security expert Hans Morgenthau seemed to support a coup against Diem. "My position," he declared in a letter, "with regard to Vietnam is very simple: get rid of the family one way or the other, put in a general or civilian as the head of a caretaker government and try to establish at least a modicum of democratic freedom." However, after watching the weak, almost comical government that replaced Diem, Morgenthau turned negative. "I am inclined," he wrote privately, "to think that the situation in South Vietnam is beyond redemption." After receiving a report from a well-placed source, Senator Thomas Dodd told Clare Boothe Luce that the situation in South Vietnam was "shocking." Luce herself had a gloomy forecast. "My impression now," she told a friend, "is that after a brief period of military push against the Viet Cong Communists, we will help to bring about a negotiated peace in Vietnam, according to the pattern we have followed in Laos. In time all these countries will, of course, fall under the domination of Red China or Soviet Russia."[62]

Because Kennedy outlived Diem by just three weeks, he did not have time to adopt an effective post-Diem policy. In later years, most of his advisers argued either that he would have sought a neutral Vietnam on the Laotian model or that the United States would have withdrawn from Vietnam after the 1964 election. Although some evidence supports these views, it should be noted that many of these same advisers led Lyndon Johnson into a massive commitment of American ground troops in 1965, and most of the claims for Kennedy's seeking neutrality or withdrawal appear in interviews given in the late sixties, after the Vietnam War was discredited. Furthermore, it is difficult to explain why Kennedy stimulated the coup against Diem if the United States planned to leave Vietnam within a couple of years. Diem's demise created a vacuum that made American withdrawal more difficult. In November 1963, Kennedy probably had made no decision about America's future role in Vietnam. He tended to postpone crucial decisions, particularly about weighty matters, in order to keep options open. As a senator, he had stood silent on McCarthy, the most important vote in his time in the Senate; at the Bay of Pigs, Kennedy had been incapable of action. He often seemed to pursue contradictory policies simultaneously, as with plans in 1963 both to cultivate and to assassinate Castro. His politics could be strangely enigmatic.[63]

It was Kennedy's misfortune to be president during the bleakest years of the Cold War. American power and prestige, clearly supreme at the end of World War II, appeared to be ebbing in the early sixties. Europe mattered less, and the emerging nations were undecided between capitalism and communism. The United States and the Soviet Union competed in a rivalry that threatened war. The Russians were gaining both military strength and new influence in the Third World. At the same time, American self-confidence sagged, in part because of rising Soviet power and Third World restlessness, in part because of racial problems at home, and in part because the waning of McCarthyism allowed doubts to be stated more frankly. Private thoughts increasingly gave way to public expressions. Mostly, however, the gloom that hung over Americans in the Kennedy years was about nuclear war and the growing belief that such a war could not be won and might well be inevitable. Nuclear fear threatened the sense of a promising time. All of these frustrations in the early sixties helped give birth to both the Right and the New Left. In the Missile Crisis, Kennedy went to the brink, but he and Khrushchev acted cautiously, and the result had a purgative effect. Having stared into the abyss, everyone realized that no one wanted to go there. Although the Cold War continued for another generation, it never again seemed so ominous. Kennedy, intentionally or not, moved the world in a less confrontational direction.

Martin Luther King, Jr., confers with civil rights leaders at the March on Washington, August 28, 1963.

(National Archives. NWDNS-306-SSM-4C(51)13.)

CHAPTER THREE

Civil Rights

In 1960 race relations sizzled. Although Hispanics, Asian Americans, and American Indians were few in numbers and quiescent, African Americans, who were 10 percent of the population, were restless. Finding the sixties to be a promising time for the redress of grievances, they gave increasing public expression to previously private thoughts. The mostly white North had long condemned formal systems of white supremacy, including government-imposed racial segregation, but that region's commitment to the ideal of legal equality often clashed with social realities. Although blacks and other racial minorities in the North routinely voted, they were often housed and schooled apart in urban ghettoes. Some blacks worked beside whites, especially in factories, but blacks found few jobs in unionized crafts, sales, or the professions. Mixed marriages remained rare and even illegal in several northern states. Barriers, however, were partially permeable and had been generally eroding during most of the century. In the South, where more than half of African Americans lived in 1960, the situation was quite different. In that region blacks who held low-paying, menial jobs under white supervision often met whites on a daily basis, but the two races seldom lived in the same neighborhoods. In 1960 only

28 percent of southern blacks were registered to vote, and fewer than one in a thousand attended integrated schools.[1]

Although African Americans faced many kinds of discrimination, employment was a key issue. To get higher pay, blacks long had migrated from the rural South to the industrial North. By 1960 31 percent of African Americans lived in just twelve cities. For decades urban blacks had been factory workers. From the thirties to the fifties industrial unions, especially in autos, rubber, steel, and meat packing, had benefited black workers, but by 1960 factories were using automation to cut payrolls or were relocating to low-paying southern states. Although poor schooling and business inexperience hurt blacks, discrimination was more important in limiting opportunities. Nationally, African Americans were less than 1 percent of apprentices in the building trades. When two black plumbers were hired on a Cleveland city project, white plumbers struck. In Washington, D.C., six of thirteen secretarial schools trained only whites; most graduates got federal jobs. In Chicago 98 percent of jobs advertised with private employment agencies barred nonwhites. Retail sales, office work, and local government positions were usually restricted. Spiraling black unemployment produced despair in the North and tension in the South, which could no longer export its surplus rural population. Racial change came to the South with the end of the northern factory safety valve.[2]

Although the white South defended segregation with the doctrine of "separate but equal" first articulated by the U.S. Supreme Court in *Plessy v. Ferguson* in 1896, the reality was that southern segregation was anything but equal. Rather, the entire legal and cultural edifice, constructed solely by powerful whites, promoted white supremacy. When the Supreme Court outlawed the region's segregated schools in *Brown v. Board of Education* in 1954, it did so with the knowledge that segregation as practiced had been inherently unequal. One court ruling, however, had limited impact, and outlawing state-mandated segregation could not, in any case, overturn the many areas of private life in which white southerners demanded separation and traditional black subordination. While African Americans interpreted the Brown decision as a call for moral action, many whites became defiant. In 1957 Governor Orval Faubus of Arkansas tried to block court-ordered school integration in Little Rock, and President Dwight D. Eisenhower had to use Army troops to enforce the law. Little Rock demonstrated the practical limits to using the courts to dismantle segregation. As late as 1962, Mississippi's reactionary Senator James Eastland could boast, "The South has not been breached."[3]

In the 1950s, Martin Luther King, Jr., found a new way to challenge segregation with the doctrine of nonviolence. At the simplest level, his most powerful insight was to recognize that the key to southern white supremacy had been violence. African Americans who protested segregation in any form or, indeed, even those who merely signaled disbelief, were subject to personal harassment, economic pressure, removal from the South, or murder by lynching. White control of the economy, politics, the media, and the law gave blacks no effective way to object. Occasionally, sporadic black violence had occurred, and it had been met with swift, brutal repression. Every act of black protest and its inevitable crushing had confirmed, for whites, the necessity for white supremacy to prevent chaos and disorder. Then came King's idea of nonviolence. "We have the bigoted white man baffled," noted King, "because he does not know how to cope with nonviolence." At a deeper level, sometimes almost subconsciously, King offered both blacks and whites a radical reconstruction of their lives. "Through nonviolence," he said, "courage displaces fear; love transforms hate; hope ends despair." King both depended upon and embraced the widespread optimism of the times. The solution, for this black Baptist preacher, was a system of nonviolent protest that united blacks, that eliminated white fear of black violence, and that offered both races a transformative experience in which violence might be forsaken and society rebuilt on a harmonious basis.[4]

In the protest against segregated buses in Montgomery, Alabama, in 1955–1956, which the 26-year-old King led, he devised a strategy to avoid the violence and repression that had marked prior attempts to challenge segregation. Borrowing from the Christian gospel, from the ideals of twentieth-century pacifists, and from Gandhi's doctrine of nonviolent resistance, King united blacks, aided by a small number of white allies, into a phalanx for moral reform guided by the philosophy and practice of nonviolence. "One of the glories of living in a democracy," said King, "is that citizens have the right to protest for what they believe to be right." News about Rosa Parks's refusal to give up her seat on the bus, her arrest, and the resultant bus boycott largely kept going by Montgomery's awakened church women permeated the South through the new medium of television. Among those who saw the reports was 12-year-old Cleveland Sellers in Denmark, South Carolina; he became a prominent activist in the early sixties. King's ultimate triumph in Montgomery gave him national prominence and led many others to embrace his ideas and his methods. The black magazine *Jet* found that 73 percent of its readers believed nonviolence was the best way to win rights in the South. "No man has ever waged the battle for equality under our law in a more lawful and *Christian* way than you have," an approving Clare Boothe Luce wrote King. Soon after, Luce's husband put King's portrait on the cover of *Time* magazine. In 1957 King and other black ministers founded an organization that quickly became the Southern Christian Leadership Conference (SCLC, sometimes called "Slick") to promote the non-violent struggle for civil rights.[5]

The civil rights movement was part of a global pattern. Clarence Mitchell, then Washington lobbyist for the National Association for the Advancement of Colored People (NAACP), later recalled, "A kind of tide of freedom was sweeping the world." In the last part of 1960 alone, ten African nations gained their independence. On visiting the new nation of Tanganyika, King's associate Bayard Rustin privately wrote, "It makes one feel good to be black." African independence, global communication and trade, and the Cold War forced Americans to rethink race. Catholic college students, the Jesuit priest Daniel Berrigan found, had "a deep anxiety to know others...." "The Big Integration of us less-colored Westerners in a largely colored world," Harris Wofford advised President Kennedy, "is the question that interests me the most." After a global trip, Robert Kennedy concluded, "There wasn't an area of the world that I visited, ... that I wasn't asked about the question of civil rights." Americans living abroad found locals keenly interested in racial problems in the United States. "Our struggles in this country," an American activist told a Liberian, "are very similar to those in your own." America's racism was a source of shame. "We, as a country, talk of equality to other nations," noted one letter-writer, "when we do not have it in our own country entirely."[6]

When new African nations, beginning with Ghana in 1957, sent ambassadors to Washington, D.C., they found widespread discrimination. Nigeria was unable to buy an embassy site that it wanted because the owner refused to sell to an African government. Rental housing was a serious problem. Maryland restaurants often turned away black diplomats who drove from Washington to New York to attend meetings at the United Nations. One incident made headlines in Lagos, Nigeria. President Kennedy, deaf to the insult, suggested that diplomats fly instead. Ambassadors who traveled further afield in the United States found similar difficulties. In 1961, Lyndon Johnson intervened to get the Houston Hilton Hotel to accept the ambassador from Ghana. Nonwhite allies sent military personnel to American bases in the South for training. After the head of the Ethiopian Air Force was arrested and beaten, a cop asked, "Hell, how do you expect me to tell an Ethiopian from a Nigger?" Discrimination existed in all parts of the country. "I am in the process of trying to decide," privately wrote a white civil rights sympathizer in Los Angeles, "whether blatant prejudice á la Alabama or polite prejudice á la Los Angeles is worse." The journalist Stewart Alsop, after finding rampant racism in a northern poll, told a friend, "God,

what a lot of intolerant slobs the great rancid American people are."
The problem, however, was worst in the South.[7]

In February 1960, four freshmen at the all-black North Carolina
Agricultural and Technical College in Greensboro sat at the all-
white lunch counter at Woolworth's and demanded service. "I felt,"
one of the four later said, "as though I had gained my manhood."
The store, like others across the South, sold goods to black customers but did not allow blacks and whites to eat together. Unlike
other forms of sales, eating, according to southern mores, was a
sociable activity that suggested equality among those who broke
bread together. For blacks and whites to eat in common was to
challenge the heart of southern racial doctrine. As a private facility, Woolworth's was not required to provide dual lunch counters.
Under southern law and custom – the exact legal situation varied by
state and city – a store could bar persons on the basis of race from
certain areas, or, indeed, from the entire premises. No federal law
required serving all customers, and, unlike the use of schools, parks,
buses, or other public facilities, the federal courts had no basis to
overturn private business discrimination. In the case of Greensboro,
the four freshmen who sat in at Woolworth's were challenging
custom rather than *law*. The attack against segregation had moved
into a new phase.[8]

Although sit-ins to protest lack of service in restaurants or at
lunch counters had taken place as early as 1942, prior demonstrations had generated little publicity. Because the civil rights movement was large and growing in the promising year 1960, and because
the media had a keen interest, the ongoing sit-ins in Greensboro
attracted notice. Southern black college students, ripe for protest
psychologically and prepared for conducting sit-ins by King's doctrine of nonviolence, quickly carried the movement to other cities.
Within three months there were similar sit-ins in more than 78 cities
with 2,000 arrests. By the end of the following year 70,000 had sat
in. The mood was euphoric. From a prison in South Carolina, Tom

Gaither informed a friend, "Our chins are up high[.] We know we are right. Democracy and equality are our goals. . . . For we realize that it is not only our Freedom that is at stake but the ultimate survival of our Nation. Integration or disintegration." King said, "What is new is that American students have come of age. You now take your honored places in the world-wide struggle for freedom." Furthermore, civil rights groups in northern cities picketed national chains' northern stores if those chains did not change their policies in the South.[9]

Results of the campaign varied. In a few cities, including Winston-Salem, North Carolina, negotiations led to rapid desegregation. In other places, city ordinances or state laws required segregation in eating facilities, even though local business leaders favored change. Stores had powerful incentives to avoid costly boycotts and add customers. Calculating possible new profits, the owner of a Memphis department store privately predicted, "The Southern businessman will become the most dedicated integrationist." In Greensboro, the protests brought the racist Ku Klux Klan into town, and the Klan's menacing presence made it more difficult for the local business and political elite to reach an agreement with the black students. In Nashville, Tennessee, Diane Nash, a black student leader, confronted the mayor with the basic immorality of a store accepting a patron's money in one part of the store but not in another. The mayor understood her point immediately, reversed his position, and quickly brokered desegregation. Although such changes of heart were rare, the fact that they did occur suggests something about the moral force that the sit-ins represented. Student determination and persistence were also important. "The most hopeful thing that has happened in the South in my lifetime," the white activist James Dombrowski wrote Eleanor Roosevelt, "is the student protest movement."[10]

Two months after the first protest in Greensboro, 120 or more southern black college students met in Raleigh, North Carolina.

They arrived filled with excitement about the promising future that they envisioned and determined to give public expression to their deep moral convictions. A number of student organizations sent observers, and a dozen southern white students attended, too. Inspired by King, but influenced even more by Ella Baker, who had worked for King and other civil rights organizations, the students decided to form their own group, the Student Non-Violent Coordinating Committee (SNCC, pronounced "Snick"). Although King and some of his aides had hoped the students would become the Southern Christian Leadership Conference's youth division, Baker discouraged this idea. She had worked closely with King and the other black Baptist ministers who had dominated the SCLC, and she knew that these men, none of whom had small egos, would expect the students to take orders. Baker, who felt keenly that she had been ignored because she was neither male nor a minister, advised the students to create their own group to avoid conflict with King. The students agreed, and Baker became SNCC's first administrator.[11]

The SCLC ministers were surprised that the students did not join their organization. These clergymen belonged to an older generation that believed in authority and hierarchy and that engaged in activities inside large, disciplined structures. The SNCC students conceived of themselves quite differently. They had no desire to be an appendage to a group of oldsters, and as much as they admired King, whose reception at Raleigh had been tumultuous, they took from King's message of nonviolent protest a somewhat different meaning than did the clergy. To the students, the significance of nonviolence was the possibility for righteous expression by persons committed to truth, honor, and virtue. Although almost all had been raised inside southern black churches, and many had come to civil rights through church-sponsored colleges, their philosophy did not necessarily mesh with that of the preachers. Even when the students held strong religious views, they stressed personal intensity and mixed principle with emotion. "Many of the Negro students," a close observer told the press, "are Christian revolutionaries." They had little use for the church as an institution because it lacked feelings found among individuals. The movement gave them purpose and intensity. "You find out," the activist Charles Sherrod said publicly, "the difference between being dead and alive." Devoted to each other, the students spoke of themselves as the "beloved community."[12]

The commitment of this particular generation of southern black college students to civil rights was striking. They were prepared to sacrifice their own comfort or even long-term career prospects. "Some of us," said Sherrod, "have to be willing to die." Civil rights, at the minimum, consumed time that threatened academic success, but at southern state colleges in particular the mere suspicion that a student might be engaged in such activity often brought instant expulsion. Induction into the military under the then-existing draft might follow. After seven activists were expelled from Southern University in Baton Rouge, black high school and college students held a vigil in New Orleans. An admiring Phil Berrigan, a white Catholic priest who taught some of them, confided to his brother, "They're a new breed – they see the issues as clearly as the best of us – There's no bullshitting them – no confusing them with semantics." Poorer blacks were especially proud. "We were all excited about these young people," recalled Unita Blackwell, "because they was educated and they treated us so nice." King commented to the press, "They are seeking to save the soul of America." Traditional leaders were less enchanted. "They don't take orders from anybody," publicly complained the NAACP's Roy Wilkins. "They don't consult anybody. They operate in a kind of vacuum: parade, protest, sit-in."[13]

Activist students were most likely to come from elite, private black colleges that drew from higher status families. Those who sat in lived in more sophisticated urban settings where African

Americans had a greater awareness of white society and had more contact with white students or faculty. During the 1950s, African Americans had made gains in education and were catching up with whites. While more blacks held white-collar jobs, racial barriers hindered advancement. The Brown decision raised hopes and expectations, especially for the younger generation, and by 1960 these upward aspirations, stimulated further by the atmosphere of a promising time, clashed with limitations imposed by segregation and white supremacy. The black middle class, observed the writer James Baldwin in print, was an "unlucky bourgeoisie" trapped "between black humiliation and white power." These youths did not believe in white supremacy and therefore rejected bargaining with the white power structure. African American students were self-confident and optimistic about both black and white support for civil rights. Whereas earlier generations of poor students had been burdened with helping needy relatives, a fact that tended to make such students more willing to accept modest, secure jobs, such as teaching school, this new generation came from families that were doing better. Rising prosperity in the postwar South enabled students to take more risks.[14]

African Americans were also more sophisticated. As late as 1950, when James Meredith had attended high school in Mississippi, his school had no working toilet and not a single teacher had a college degree. Only 2 percent of the African American population in Mississippi had high school diplomas. During the 1950s, both before and after the Brown decision, southern states upgraded black education in an ultimately futile attempt to stop desegregation. Some progress was made. In 1960, 4 percent of Mississippi blacks had completed high school; 24 percent of whites had. Better education did not necessarily translate into jobs. "We are training the Negro," privately noted one Jackson businessman, "and then, refusing him the employment he is trained for." Educated blacks in Mississippi were forced to leave the state due to job discrimination. By 1960, the southern black population as a whole was better educated and more sophisticated than had been the case in earlier years. "The young colored people today," said one white Mississippian off the record, "aren't like they once were. These have had more schooling and they know more about things. They probably know more about a lot of things than I do." Nevertheless, as late as 1962 nine counties in Mississippi provided no high schools for African Americans, and the state had only seven accredited black high schools.[15]

The changes had started with World War II. As one corporal from Alabama put it, "I went into the army a nigger; I'm comin' out a *man*." A combat veteran jailed for civil rights activity in the sixties privately wrote, "Yes, the Government that I went to war for, jailed me like a murder[er], rob[b]er, rapist[,] etc. Just because I want to be free." For more than one million black veterans, the war had brought eye-opening experiences. Blacks from the segregated South found themselves thrust into integrated settings in the North or overseas. The journalist Carl Rowan, for example, broke the color barrier during the war as one of the Navy's first black officers; he had been trained in an integrated unit at Oberlin College. Sgt. Whitney Young, who eventually headed the Urban League, had acted as a racial mediator between white officers and black troops. The NAACP's Medgar Evers had been welcomed by the French as a conquering hero and had fallen in love with a French woman. Hitler's racist Holocaust also challenged southern tradition. After the war, veterans transferred organizational skills that they had learned in the military to civil rights. In the sixties, many black college students were Cold War-era veterans.[16]

The great migration to the North had significance even for those who remained in the South, as friends and relatives moved back and forth to work or visit. Lifelong Mississippians Medgar Evers and his wife Myrlie had lived, worked, and courted in Chicago, and native Georgian Charlayne Hunter, one of the first two blacks admitted to the University of Georgia in 1961, had first attended an integrated school in Alaska, when her father was in the Air Force. While her

application to the University of Georgia was in the courts, she studied at Wayne State University in Detroit. Northern black publications like the *Chicago Defender*, the *Pittsburgh Courier*, *Ebony*, and
Jet circulated in the South. All contained stories that were bolder
than those found in southern black periodicals and gave public
expression to what had long been black private thought. Finally,
television had swept across the South in the 1950s. "The Negro
sharecropper and Old Massa," Medgar Evers told the press, "have
the same TV antenna." Although some southern stations refused
to carry shows that included black performers, television made an
enormous impact. One participant in the Greensboro sit-in said that
he had been impressed with a television documentary on Gandhi's
passive resistance. "They learn," Evers noted, "there is a different
world outside Mississippi."[17]

SNCC was the first of the sixties-style activist organizations.
To outsiders who did not understand the premises behind SNCC,
it seemed hopelessly chaotic and disorganized. To the students who
founded it, and to Ella Baker, the principal purpose of the group
was to serve as a clearing house. The organization enabled information to be shared and made fund-raising possible. SNCC students, however, would not accept a policy-setting board. In part,
this conclusion came from experience. The dynamics of civil rights
protests at the local level had to govern how "indigenous people,"
to use Ella Baker's phrase, ought to proceed. At a more philosophical level, SNCC members resisted top-down authority. They did not
want to dismantle white supremacy only to replace it with rule by a
black elite. African Americans, especially those from poorer back-
grounds, noticed the movement's commitment to local talent and
democracy immediately. "For the first time," recalled the plantation
worker Fannie Lou Hamer, "I ever been treated like a human being,
whether the kids was white or black." The movement's psychological commitment to egalitarianism should not be underestimated as
a force that helped shape SNCC's specific structure.[18]

Because SNCC was not an organization in any traditional sense, it could not truly control who participated at the local level. This opened SNCC to the charge of communism, which was widely made by Right-wing opponents throughout the organization's existence. A few communists may have been involved in SNCC, but the Communist party had all but collapsed inside the United States by 1960, so the charge meant little outside conservative circles. "Would to God," said the white civil rights lawyer Charles Morgan, "there *were* communists in Snick.... They would be a moderating influence." The white activist Clarice Campbell called the movement "essentially Christian." At a SNCC Executive Committee meeting, Charles Sherrod indicated how his thinking had changed. "When I was in college," he noted, "they said CORE was communistic – and I started running away." Protests had made him more broadminded. "I don't care who the heck it is," he added, "if he is willing to come down on the front lines and bring his body along with me to die." Commitment to the cause was all that mattered at a promising time when participants believed that they could shape the future. SNCC's founders, however, failed to recognize that the lack of any mechanism to control membership made SNCC an ideal target to be taken over. SNCC's later downfall came not from the Old Left but from advocates of Black Power.[19]

As a consortium, SNCC's real strength was at the local level. In each community, SNCC members had to make decisions constantly about what to protest, what to ignore, when to negotiate, when to demonstrate, and how far and how hard to push issues. Each situation was different, and results depended upon both the local business community and white officials. Some were intransigent, others were flexible. Success also depended upon whether there was intense opposition to black demands and whether that opposition came from the legalistic Citizens' Council or the violent Ku Klux Klan. Because protest required active participation by large numbers of persons, SNCC held lengthy meetings to thrash out alternatives and to try, as much as possible, to build consensus among supporters. A certain amount of unity was necessary to enable those participating in protest to act together. This process, later adopted by the white New Left under the title of "participatory democracy," used full, frank discussion and consensus building rather than decisions governed by majority votes.[20]

The most important consequence of the sit-ins in 1960, along with the subsequent organization of SNCC, was to show that blacks were demanding not only the dismantling of legal segregation but also a change in custom. The movement's slogan, "Freedom Now," expressed both impatience and the basic idea. Subsumed in the concept of freedom was a notion of equality that sought to obliterate the existing racial hierarchy. While the movement was steeped in popular American values, this particular mode of expression also resonated with the optimism of a promising time. Freedom required the practice of equality, and real equality could only come about through the triumph of freedom. By transforming the issue from a legal battle that had to be fought and won in the courts, as the NAACP had long done, into a moral issue that demanded immediate redress, the black movement moved civil rights to center stage. Furthermore, the shift from law to human rights made the North subject to protest as well. In the early sixties, however, grievances were worse in the South, and because northern white support was necessary to put pressure on intransigent elements in the South, civil rights leaders largely ignored the North.[21]

During the last half of 1960, sit-ins subsided. For one thing, a number of southern cities with moderate white leadership had already desegregated. Some white leaders may have hoped that this decline indicated that the protests were largely over, but the retreat was mainly strategic. Although the students could not always be contained, considerable pressure was put upon them to stay quiet until after the presidential election. Both John Kennedy and Richard Nixon had good civil rights records, but most black leaders gravitated to Kennedy. Not only did the Democrats have a liberal wing

eager to push civil rights, but Kennedy was likely to have more influence than Nixon over recalcitrant southern Democrats. Attitudes
toward sit-ins also played a role in this calculation. In the 1930s
labor unions had used sit-ins, and many unions remained favorable
to the idea, whereas Republican businessmen, like 57 percent of
Americans, opposed sit-ins, which could be viewed as assaults on
property rights.[22]

In 1961 another civil rights organization, the Congress of Racial
Equality (CORE), decided to resume protest in a different form. In
1946 the Supreme Court had ruled that black interstate bus pas-
sengers could not be required to sit at the back of the bus. In 1947
CORE and the Fellowship of Reconciliation, both northern biracial pacifist groups, had tested that decision by sending 16 interracial riders into the South. They did not get far. After being arrested in Virginia and mobbed in North Carolina, the first Freedom
Ride was abandoned. CORE's decision to hold a new Freedom
Ride in 1961 was rooted in the partial success of the sit-in movement, in the growing national interest in civil rights, and in John
Kennedy's arrival in office. The enthusiasm and energy that surrounded Kennedy's inauguration suggested that it was a promising time to challenge the old order. In some ways, CORE proposed to test both southern mores and the new administration's
will to enforce court rulings. "We follow Gandhi, and Thoreau
in their emphasis upon non-cooperation," privately wrote James
Farmer, the black head of CORE, "...as well as their emphasis
upon nonviolence as a philosophy and as a tactic." Farmer, John
Lewis, a black SNCC leader, and James Peck, a radical white minister who had been on the 1947 trip, were among the first
13 volunteers.[23]

The Freedom Riders passed though Virginia, the Carolinas, and
Georgia with little trouble, but in Atlanta, Martin Luther King, Jr.,
warned the group, "You will never make it through Alabama."
They didn't. One bus entered Ku Klux Klan territory in northern
Alabama and had its tires slashed in the Anniston bus terminal.

The driver quickly left the station, but the tires failed, and the bus had to stop several miles outside town. There, followed by a mob of 200 in 50 cars and lacking any police escort, it was fire-bombed. The Freedom Riders barely escaped from the bus, and many were badly beaten by the angry mob that was driven off mainly by one armed undercover state patrolman who had been aboard. Riders on a second bus were mauled by thugs who boarded in Anniston. Nursing an aching head after being hit, Hank Thomas, a Howard University student, publicly said, "I see what Martin Luther King means when he says suffering is redemption." When that bus reached Birmingham, the mob there beat the Freedom Riders savagely with iron bars. Peck, attacked in both Anniston and Birmingham, required 53 stitches. No local police appeared. It was Mother's Day, and they were all visiting their mothers, explained Birmingham Police Commissioner Bull Connor. An FBI informant privately reported that Connor had agreed to give the Klan 15 minutes alone with the Freedom Riders. The Klan had close ties to Connor's department.[24]

Alabama Governor John Patterson promised to provide security, but when a bus arrived in Montgomery, no police were present. Riders exited the bus into the middle of an angry, howling mob of 500 to 1,000. The crowd first attacked crews from NBC News and *Life* and then turned on the Freedom Riders. Most were badly beaten. When Kennedy's personal emissary, John Seigenthaler, tried to help two female Freedom Riders escape, he was attacked, knocked out, and left unconscious on the pavement. FBI agents were present but did nothing. They stood calmly and took notes, which FBI officials ordered burned. "It galls me," Seigenthaler later said, "to think that the FBI stood there and watched me get clubbed." Virginia Durr, Supreme Court Justice Hugo Black's sister-in-law, watched the riot from her husband's law office. "I felt absolute stark terror," she recalled, as the mob chanted over and over, "Go get the niggers!" Feeling betrayed by Patterson, the Kennedys ordered 400 federal marshals to Montgomery. This marked the first time that marshals were used, and while not entirely satisfactory, marshals proved superior to Army troops, who reminded southerners of Reconstruction. The public knew no real marshals, but they enjoyed an excellent reputation due to the fine performance of Marshal Matt Dillon of Dodge City on the long-running hit television series *Gunsmoke*. Whereas only 24 percent of Americans sanctioned the Freedom Rides, 70 percent approved of Kennedy sending marshals to Montgomery.[25]

Urged to call off the remainder of their trip to New Orleans by the Kennedy administration, the Freedom Riders defiantly announced that they would travel by bus from Montgomery to Jackson, Mississippi. Diane Nash told James Farmer, "We can't stop it now, right after we've been clobbered." To the press, King said, "Unearned suffering is redemptive." Many, including some volunteers, thought this a suicide mission, because Mississippi had a reputation for being uniquely bloody. "Freedom Riders," declared King, "must develop the quiet courage of dying for a cause." One said, "I feel like I'm going to war." As another activist's bus approached the Mississippi state line, he said, "I feel like Daniel about to meet the lions." Enroute they sang "We Shall Overcome." Robert Kennedy was desperate to avoid a repetition of the violence in Alabama, and he finally struck a deal with Mississippi's powerful Senator James Eastland, after former Governor J. P. Coleman warned Kennedy not to trust Governor Ross Barnett. Mississippi authorities were to provide protection from the Alabama state line to Jackson. When the Freedom Riders left the bus, they were to be arrested when they attempted to desegregate the bus station. The Freedom Ride would end in Jackson. Eastland kept his word, and there was no violence in Mississippi. State officials had told racist elements that arrests stopped Freedom Rides better than did burning buses.[26]

The arrestees in Jackson sang "We Shall Overcome" in the paddy wagon. While they were being booked, cops kept saying,

"Niggers don't do things like this." The police could only explain the strangely aggressive behavior of the Freedom Riders as being due to either payoffs or communism. Eastland announced that the Freedom Riders were "part of the Communist movement." Local whites showed no understanding how a promising time stimulated African Americans to make a public expression of their long-held private thoughts about equality. The protesters adopted a "Jail, No Bail" policy. Jailers could not understand the white Freedom Riders, but one told James Farmer, "If I was colored, I'd be doin' the same thing...." In a *Jet* readers' poll, 96 percent thought the Freedom Rides should continue. Still, Americans were uneasy. "Even more than the sit-ins," claimed one new leftist, "the Freedom Rides were disruptive of the conventional liberal mentality." Movement activists felt strength. "The 'Ride' gave convictions to some," said one in a letter, "and deepened the convictions of others." "I note," Carl Braden wrote his wife, "that most of our friends are in jail in Montgomery or Jackson, so the world moves forward through jails."[27]

In Jackson, 2,000 excited blacks packed the Masonic Temple. "The Negro population is definitely on the march," privately declared James Dombrowski, "and will never be the same again because of these freedom rides." Freedom songs were heard everywhere, especially inside jails. In a letter from the Hinds County Jail, James Farmer asked, "Who says jail is a place of seclusion? It is bedlam. At least under present circumstances." Several prisoners were beaten for refusing to say "Sir." At the notorious Parchman State Penitentiary, where many Freedom Riders served harsh sentences, songs offered a way to bond, even when guards took away mattresses as punishment for singing. One activist called out, "Take my mattress. I'll keep my soul." Through singing, Cordell Reagon concluded, "... we were much more powerful than them." Bernice Reagon explained, "If you cannot sing a congregational song at full power, you cannot fight in any struggle.... This transformation in yourself that you create is exactly what happens when you join a movement." For activists, prison invited reflection. "There was this very strong feeling," recalled John Lewis, "we could change the hard-core segregationist attitudes and feelings. There was just a great many young people who believed in that hope – what we later came to call the beloved community." While in Parchman or while attending later court hearings in Mississippi, many Freedom Riders decided to stay in the state as civil rights activists.[28]

The Freedom Riders so impressed rural blacks in the Deep South that afterward civil rights workers were called Freedom Riders, or, sometimes, Freedom Fighters, a name that lingered from the failed Hungarian Revolution of 1956. Children said, "I'm going to be a Freedom Rider when I grow up." By summer's end 328 Freedom Riders had come to Jackson, where they were routinely arrested. Amid declining publicity, the rides eventually fizzled with Mississippi making no concessions. Jackson's bus terminal remained defiantly segregated. Bail drained the NAACP, and Roy Wilkins complained, "Man, Mississippi is a *bitch!*" Civil rights groups spent more than $100,000 on bail; Mississippi ten times that on prosecution. In 1965 the Supreme Court overturned the Jackson convictions. Meanwhile, segregation elsewhere slowly crumbled. The Montgomery Greyhound station quietly desegregated in late May 1961. By June only a third of southern terminals had racial signs. A year later, after the Interstate Commerce Commission had banned segregation, the Justice Department's Burke Marshall privately declared the problem "virtually eliminated." Despite the trend, white Mississippians were convinced that they could stop desegregation by a combination of unity, toughness, and legal vigilance.[29]

In 1960 Mississippi occupied a unique position. The poorest state in the union, its per-capita income was only about half that of the typical northern industrial state. More than half its residents used privies. Mississippi was also the nation's blackest state at 42 percent, and black incomes were one-third that of whites. From its earliest days until the 1930s it had had a black majority. During World War II, large numbers of African Americans migrated via the Illinois Central Railroad to industrial jobs in Chicago. After the war, when cotton planters increasingly replaced tenants with picking machines, that migration continued. More than 300,000 blacks left during the fifties. Mississippi was overwhelmingly rural. A small number of extremely wealthy cotton planters dominated the state. They owned vast acreages of lush land near the Mississippi River in a region called the Delta. Senator Eastland, for example, owned 5,800 acres. The Delta counties all had black majorities, but few African Americans owned land or houses, schools were limited, voting was rare, and virtually no black practiced a profession or engaged in a business. Uneducated and unsophisticated, Delta blacks were increasingly unemployable anywhere. They were, privately thought the civil rights leader Bob Moses, "surplus people." Planters refused to see problems. One publicly said, "They're happy. We're happy. Everybody's happy here." Planters or their overseers controlled access to the plantations and did not hesitate to evict any tenant before nightfall if a tenant was seen talking to a stranger disapproved of by the owner.[30]

Throughout Mississippi racism, poverty, and ignorance were entangled. In contrast with other southern states, white attitudes about race were frozen at the level of 1890, when a strong belief in biological determinism had been at the core of white supremacy. The state's poverty had hindered public education. In 1961 only 58 percent of white children and 31 percent of black children attended nine-month schools. A poor economy drove a third of the state's white college graduates out of the state. More black college graduates stayed, but they were mostly teachers; in 1959 African Americans could count among themselves only 60 doctors, five lawyers, and one dentist. The level of sophistication was low. When Rust College served jello in its cafeteria in 1961, several poor black students said that they had never seen it before. About 70 percent of adult blacks were functionally illiterate. Four-fifths of black women were domestics or farm workers; three-quarters of black men were laborers, farm workers, or factory operatives. Mississippi provided little incentive for black self-improvement. An African American who had been a plumber in the Army could not work in Hattiesburg, which licensed no black plumbers or electricians. He got a job at the city water works and actually did plumbing but was paid as an assistant. The white plumber on the payroll did no work.[31]

Politics was backward-looking. In a policy that dated to the end of Reconstruction, virtually no African Americans were allowed to vote. Of more than half a million registered voters in 1963, no more than 26,000 were black. Even in relatively moderate Jackson 42 percent of whites but only 13 percent of blacks were registered. The lack of votes encouraged police harassment. For example, Mississippi remained legally dry. African Americans were routinely arrested for illicit drinking at black clubs. The clubs, however, were never closed. Instead, white deputies entered and singled out four or five blacks for arbitrary arrest. Snooping was common. Mail was opened: "Plain envelopes," observed Bob Moses in a note, "have a lower mortality rate." Telephone operators monitored and reported long distance calls to authorities. Blacks sometimes protested with boycotts, but these were done without publicity so that no one could be charged with organizing a boycott. It was dangerous to give public expression to private thoughts. White Mississippians clung to the past with a vengeance. In 1954 the University of Mississippi ("Ole Miss") celebrated Dixie Week with a Rebel Flag Raising, a reenactment of Lincoln's assassination, and a slave auction.[32]

Senator James Eastland was a Delta bigwig. His estate was close to Parchman State Penitentiary, a state-owned plantation. Comparing the two, Carl Braden said in a letter, "Not much difference, I'd say." From a prominent family, Eastland maintained a patriarchal image. The family had a certain notoriety. At the turn of the century his father had helped burn a black man alive in a lynching. This deed caused the senator no embarrassment. A longtime practitioner of racial politics, he had helped organize the Citizens' Council, and in 1956 he spoke to the Council's largest ever rally before 15,000 in Montgomery. As chair of the Senate Judiciary Committee, Eastland made certain that every federal judge in Mississippi was a diehard segregationist. He demanded the appointment of the egregiously racist Harold Cox to the district court in Mississippi as the price for putting the black Thurgood Marshall on the Court of Appeals in New York. "Tell your brother that if he will give me Harold Cox," he is reputed to have said to Robert Kennedy, "I will give him the nigger." The Kennedy administration honored Eastland's request. Cox, who once called blacks "chimpanzees" in his court, had been a close friend of Eastland's in law school. On the bench Cox was reversed on appeal in about three-fourths of civil rights cases, which was more than any other judge. Times change. In 1995 Eastland's portrait hung in Jackson's Old Capitol, but a vandal had removed the nameplate, and a swastika had been drawn in its place.[33]

In July 1954, within two months of the Brown decision, Mississippians quietly began to organize the Citizens' Council to defend segregation. Every community in the state was to have a local Council coordinated through a statewide office in Jackson. William J. Simmons, son of a wealthy banker, ran the organization. His politics was not subtle. "The only real solution," he said publicly, "is a return of Negroes to Africa." Although Simmons was important, some people believed that Eastland secretly called the shots; the first Council was organized in the senator's Sunflower County. Eventually, the Council spread into other Deep South states. Within two years it claimed 300,000 members, of whom 80,000 were in Mississippi, the only state where the organization gained total control. The main goal was to enforce ideological conformity for segregation. Within three years the Council had taken charge of school materials and had issued more than two million items of propaganda. "Do black birds," asked one piece, "intermingle with blue birds?" This line came from a minister. Conservative clergy were among the strongest supporters. In contrast, liberal ministers who warned that segregation was doomed were driven from their pulpits and the state. The Council blacklisted the NAACP, the Methodist Church, Young Women's Christian Association, Elks, and liberal unions. Many top Council leaders, including Simmons, belonged to the ultraright John Birch Society. Leaders used secretive Birch ties to control the organization.[34]

The Council quickly became a great force in politics. Toleration disappeared. By 1960 only two members of the legislature routinely opposed Council-backed bills. Colleagues called Joe Wroten a "nigger lover," and Karl Wiesenberg had a cross burned on his lawn. In 1962 Frank Smith, the only member of Congress not identified with the Council, was defeated by a pro-Council candidate in the primary. Jamie Whitten won with this song:

> Skunks in the stump holes, monkeys in the trees,
> Frank's crawled in bed with the Kennedys.
> Frank has Kennedys and their money, too,
> But Jamie's good for me and for you.
> Jamie's got the ball and he's on the team,
> Let's run up the score on the Kennedy machine.[35]

The Citizens' Council made special efforts to enlist the media. The powerful Hederman brothers, owners of two Jackson newspapers, were enthusiastic. The editorial cartoonist for one paper also drew cartoons for Council literature. Both papers avoided national columnists in favor of racially pungent local ones. The *Jackson Daily News* once described two of its political enemies as "sleazy, rodent-brained, prize-happy, fractional-minded frauds unworthy of brotherhooding with skunks." The *Clarion-Ledger*, nicknamed the *Klan-Ledger*, headlined the March on Washington as "Washington Is Clean Again with Negro Trash Removed." The papers contained so many falsehoods that one reader privately complained, "Really, they make Joe Goebels look like an amateur." The Hedermans also owned one of Jackson's two television stations. Both stations took Council positions editorially and broadcast Council propaganda shows, many of which were prepared in Washington

through subsidized government studios courtesy of Senator Eastland and Representative John Bell Williams. The stations also censored national network news about race. "Sorry, Cable Trouble"
was a common message. In 1962 both stations resisted selling air
time to a black congressional candidate. Seven years later racism
cost WLBT-TV its license.[36]

In the mid-fifties Charles Evers became Mississippi's first black
radio disc jockey. He played blues and gospel music, but after he
used his show to register 200 new black voters, the Council drove
him to Chicago. Only a few newspaper publishers showed independence. "They were a bunch of sniveling cowards," declared Karl
Wiesenberg. Hodding Carter II, whose assets outside Mississippi
made him less vulnerable, successfully resisted the Council, even
though his Greenville *Delta Democrat-Times* supported segregation. Carter privately considered the Brown decision "morally right"
but "impossible to be carried out." After he wrote an article on
the secretive Council for *Look* magazine in 1955, the Mississippi
House of Representatives censured him for "selling out the state for
Yankee gold." Hazel Brannon Smith's *Lexington Advertiser* sur-
vived off of donations, after the Council ordered a boycott. Ira
Harkey, publisher of the *Pascagoula Chronicle*, won the Pulitzer
Prize, but lost advertisers and left the state. The acerbic and nearly
subscriberless P. D. East sent *The Petal Paper* to Bill Minor, the top
out-of-state reporter based in Jackson, with an address label that
read "foreign correspondent."[37]

Mississippi was suspicious of outsiders. The Presbyterian student adviser at Ole Miss, a Georgian, confidentially said he "felt
like an alien." "All you have to do to be called an agitator in
Mississippi," privately said the moderate Claude Ramsey, president
of the state AFL–CIO, "is to cross the state line." In 1961 John R.
Salter, Jr., later prominent in the Jackson Movement, first entered
Mississippi to take a job at black Tougaloo College. Half white and
half American Indian, he had grown up in Arizona, where he had
been an organizer for the leftist Mine Mill union. He came out of

the Wobbly (Industrial Workers of the World) tradition rather than the communist tradition. When Salter and his wife drove over a rickety toll bridge into Mississippi, they were questioned intensely by heavily armed toll takers. "I had the feeling," he later recalled, "that we were crossing into another world, into another country, and that certainly proved to be the case." Mississippi was a "police state" where *Time* magazine and the *Wall Street Journal* were considered "subversive." Even William F. Buckley, Jr., was suspected of being a fellow traveler. "I wasn't prepared for the existence of state orthodoxy," Salter conceded. Within a few weeks, the Salters were evicted from their apartment for having a black student to dinner.[38]

The Citizens' Council was determined to keep out anyone who might stir up the state's blacks. Private thoughts were not dangerous to the old order so long as there was no public expression. According to the Council, black ignorance produced bliss for both races. The Council blamed racial turmoil in neighboring Alabama at the time of King's Montgomery bus boycott, as well as the ability of blacks to organize themselves effectively, on insufficient vigilance against outsiders, including the Atlantan King, combined with bombings that destroyed white unity. As of 1960, Virginia's legalistic defense of segregation had proven more successful, but the Council also believed that a strictly legal defense might collapse in court. The trick, thought the Council, was to combine a vigorous legal defense, intense economic pressure, and robust political activity. Violence was to be discouraged but not totally ruled out. Thus, a black might win an occasional court case, but such an isolated victory would not truly end segregation if all the forces in white society stood in solidarity to defend the system.[39]

To maintain white solidarity, the Council needed total control. Keeping blacks from voting was paramount, and economic pressure was often used. "If you can afford to vote," one Council member said, "you don't need a loan." More important was the continuing displacement of black cotton pickers, who were encouraged to leave the state. Industrialists who located factories in Mississippi did so with the understanding that most jobs were reserved for whites. The Council hoped to move out 500,000 blacks in a decade. Seeking information on growing black restlessness, the Council turned to the State Sovereignty Commission, which, under Governor Ross Barnett, began to give the Council $5,000 per month in 1960. In addition to helping the Council send more than 1,000 speakers around the country to defend segregation, the Commission subsidized Council radio and television shows and operated statewide espionage, including paid informants and wiretaps. The full scope of this system was revealed only in 1989.[40]

The middle-class Council had a strained relationship with violent racists, many of whom operated through the rural, populist Klan. So long as the "respectable" Council appeared to be successful, the Klan attracted few followers, but Council leaders knew that the depth of feeling on the part of white Mississippians was so great that as soon as the Council was perceived to be ineffective, then Klan membership and violence would rise. One businessman who belonged to the Council said, "Now I wouldn't think about joining the Klan myself . . . , but you know there are times when you need organizations like the Klan." Presumably, he did not mind violence so long as he did not soil his own hands. Many Council members had a sympathy for the Klan that constituted a kind of tacit approval for its bloody actions. Both the Council and the Klan had ties to local members of the secretive John Birch Society, even though that group's national leaders condemned racism. "If I were a Catholic in Mississippi," announced the journalist P. D. East in 1962, "I'd be worried. If I were a Jew, I'd be scared stiff. If I were a Negro, I would already be gone." When the Klan erupted in Mississippi in the mid-sixties, it was more hostile to whites whom it considered to be race traitors, especially Jews, than it was to blacks.[41]

The most important black leader in the state was Medgar Evers, the head of the state NAACP. A World War II combat veteran, Evers had returned to Mississippi after the war. Shaped by the experience, he said, "I knew if I didn't fight for what we are entitled to, I'd be less than a man." In 1946 he and five other black veterans, against overwhelming odds, registered to vote. However, when the group went to the polls on election day, they were greeted by armed whites, and they retreated without casting ballots. So much for the public expression of private thoughts; it was not yet a promising time. Evers graduated from Alcorn College and became an agent for a black-owned life insurance company. While traveling around the state, he was appalled by the poverty in the Delta. Shortly before the Brown decision, Evers applied to the Ole Miss law school. He was rejected, even though Mississippi, unlike many other southern states, provided no law school for blacks. Evers impressed national NAACP leaders as intelligent, hard working, and courageous, and in December 1954 they offered him the post of state chair.[42]

In the late fifties Evers's main task was to research, document, and report to the national office incidents of discrimination or violence in Mississippi. This proved to be a fulltime job. Evers recorded the murders of Rev. George Lee, who was killed for trying to vote in 1955; of Edward Duckworth, shot in 1956; and of Mack Charles Parker, lynched in 1959. Emmett Till's murder in 1955 was especially vicious. The 14-year-old black Chicagoan had spent the summer with older relatives in the Delta. Oblivious to Mississippi's racial etiquette, he had talked to, whistled at, or touched a white woman storekeeper. Till was then kidnapped, mutilated, killed, and dumped into the Tallahatchie River. The story got prominent coverage, including a gruesome picture in *Jet*, and as many as 10,000 mourners viewed the body in a Chicago funeral home. After the murderers were speedily tried and acquitted, they sold their confession to *Look* magazine. This murder horrified Sam Block, Anne Moody, and other southern black youths, who often cited it as stimulating later interest in civil rights. The black songwriters Berry Gordy and Janie Bradford wrote "Money (That's What I Want)." In 1960 it was a Motown hit for Barrett Strong; three years later the Beatles recorded it. The song's themes of money and sex were entwined in classic rock double-entendre. Till had been killed in Money, Mississippi.[43]

The Kennedy administration took more seriously the issue of black voting rights than had the Eisenhower administration. In the close presidential election of 1960 African Americans had cast only 6 percent of the votes in the South. "I am more and more convinced," privately wrote one observer, "that voting is the key. . . ." Vice President Lyndon Johnson, based on his experiences in Texas, felt that greater black participation would force the political system to respond to concerns about police violence, jobs, education, and housing. Kennedy and Johnson expected liberals to gain from a large southern black vote. "Their whole idea of civil rights," privately complained one conservative, "is purely negro votes!" Attorney General Robert Kennedy and his top aides at the Justice Department also believed that there was little opposition, even in the South, for black votes. Mississippi had a uniquely bad record on this issue, and Justice began to build cases against the state's county registrars. The cases, however, proved slow to prosecute, in part because of flawed federal law, and in part, especially in Mississippi, due to recalcitrant federal judges.[44]

After the sit-ins and Freedom Rides, the administration urged civil rights activists to register voters. This idealistic plan was in keeping with the notion of the early sixties as a promising time. A vote could be a dignified way for a person to give public expression to a private conviction for change. Robert Kennedy persuaded the liberal Taconic, Field, and Stern foundations to finance the Voter Education Project (VEP). He arranged for donors' tax exemptions and for activists' draft deferments. The VEP, in turn, supported SNCC, CORE, the NAACP, and other groups that began to sign up voters. Many restless activists at first rejected this approach, because they argued that the government was manipulating the movement, altering its goals, and changing the issue from one of radical social change that included jobs, housing, and education, into the 'minor' issue of voting. Although the manipulation was true, the rights groups nevertheless took $870,000 in VEP money, because it enabled them to operate much larger programs than would otherwise have been the case. Furthermore, both the administration and the activists had miscalculated. Neither realized that diehard segregationists considered black voting to be a frontal assault. Thus, what had seemed like a way to defuse the situation actually turned out to inflame matters. In the end this result did not displease the activists.[45]

The Freedom Riders and the Voter Education Project broke open the possibility of radical change in Mississippi. Public expression might, in a promising time, upset the old order. One key person in this new movement turned out to be Bob Moses, an African American, a former Harvard graduate student, and a New Yorker of southern ancestry. Moses became involved after he saw a picture of the Greensboro sit-in in the *New York Times*. "They were kids my own age," he recalled, "and I knew this had something to do with my own life." In 1961 he went to Mississippi to register voters. This mild, modest man had a remarkable effect upon those with whom he worked. Julian Bond later said, "We thought he was a Communist because he was from New York and wore glasses and was smarter than we were." Black southerners found him exotic: He read Albert Camus in French, had participated in Quaker workshops in France, had studied the Chinese philosopher Lao-tze, and had explored Zen Buddhism in Japan. He admired the writer J. R. R. Tolkien. Often silent in meetings, Moses had a softspoken charisma. "One of the greatest human beings on earth," declared Fannie Lou Hamer. Working for SNCC, but cooperative with CORE, and occasionally even with the cautious NAACP, he quickly became the state's most important activist. He became the head of the Council of Federated Organizations (COFO), which was designed to coordinate among the various groups.[46]

After a false start in McComb, Moses moved the registration project to the Delta, where the population was blacker, and where there were fewer of the poor whites who had caused so much of the violence around McComb. Moses placed volunteers in a number of Delta counties and worked hard to develop indigenous talent. Sam Block went to Greenwood, in Leflore County, where the Citizens' Council had once been headquartered. Police advised Block to say "Sir" or "I would end up on the concrete, getting up without any teeth." After he took four blacks to the registration office, a Citizens' Council official warned, "If you take anybody else up to register you'll never leave Greenwood alive." A few days later 18 white men invaded the SNCC office, and the staff had to make a quick exit through the bathroom window. Throughout 1962 few actual registrations took place in the Delta. Mississippi's bizarre voter registration test was difficult to pass even when it was administered fairly, which it seldom was in the Delta. Workshops were held about registration procedures, and mass meetings, mostly held in black churches, built collective confidence through singing, but blacks remained afraid to go to the courthouse to take the test out of fear of being fired, evicted, or killed.[47]

While the Freedom Rides had failed in Jackson, and while voter registration remained stymied, a new player appeared. In January 1961, James Meredith, a Mississippi native and an Air Force veteran, applied to transfer from Jackson State to the University of Mississippi ("Ole Miss"). Having gained a new understanding of race while stationed in Japan, he was also influenced by the Democrats' strong civil rights plank and by Kennedy's election. His choice of Ole Miss as a target was a calculated psychological attack. This university was where Delta planters sent their children, and its graduates, despite their parochialism, formed the state's business, professional, and political elite. He sought to breach this citadel precisely because it was the highest. "I am a soldier at heart," he later wrote, "and I suppose I always will be." Desegregating Ole Miss first, before the state's other schools, would shock and enrage. Furthermore, the name "Ole Miss" had a double meaning. On a plantation, the planter's wife was called Ole Miss. Thus, the school was its students' mother. "Meredith will be the first Negro with a white Alma Mammy," publicly wrote Langston Hughes. "So many white folks down there have had black mammies in their childhood. It is time for a black boy to have a white mammy now." Integration mixed incest with miscegenation. In a significant role reversal, Meredith was about to deflower Ole Miss.[48]

Although older and more mature, the somewhat haughty Meredith was not the ideal person to attack segregation. "Nobody," privately said an exasperated Medgar Evers, "controls him." Disciplined, hard-working, and able to handle pressure, Meredith was also independent, shrewd, and calculating, qualities that helped him win a cat and mouse game in the federal courts. After many delays and much subterfuge, including masterly inactivity by a federal district judge, the Fifth Circuit Court of Appeals and the U.S. Supreme Court ordered Meredith's admission in September 1962. Meredith would become the first known black to attend any white school in Mississippi. His victory over Governor Ross Barnett required help from Medgar Evers, the NAACP, and its articulate lawyer, Constance Baker Motley. Nor would he have succeeded without the Justice Department and the U.S. Army. The obstacles to be overcome were not merely legal. A source close to the Sovereignty Commission privately reported, "Ross [Barnett] had ordered them to kill Meredith." The fact that the story was taken seriously is itself chilling evidence of the official hostility that Meredith's action generated.[49]

For two weeks Governor Barnett and Robert Kennedy held 22 telephone conversations trying to arrange for Meredith's registration and arrival at Ole Miss. The governor proved hard to pin down.

> Kennedy: "Governor, you are a part of the United States."
> Barnett: "We have been a part of the United States but I don't know whether we are or not."
> Kennedy: "Are you getting out of the Union?"

Kennedy, desperate to avoid federal troops, wanted Barnett to agree to use state forces to guarantee Meredith's safety. Barnett, a self-made millionaire trial lawyer best known for having installed gold-plated bathroom fixtures in the governor's mansion, consistently exuded charm, but on the crucial issue his behavior was so vacillating and bizarre that Kennedy concluded that he was "loony." The Kennedys did not know that the Citizens' Council's William J. Simmons was with the governor during these conversations and controlled Barnett's responses. Barnett had been a creature of the Council since his election in 1959. The governor's erraticism would have been easier to comprehend if one had known that Simmons had once been diagnosed with a serious psychiatric disorder. Ole Miss Professor James Silver was not far from the truth when he privately called the state's top leaders "psychopaths."[50]

At one point the governor asked the attorney general to stage a sham battle, a plan that Senator Eastland called "silly." While Robert Kennedy frantically tried to negotiate, the Court of Appeals lost patience with Barnett's stalling, held him in contempt, and threatened to fine him $10,000 per day until he complied. To the materialistic governor the prospect of financial ruin was probably worse than that of a heroic death defending segregation. Under this cloud, as well as Kennedy's threat to have the president expose the sham battle plan on television, the governor suddenly grew more pliable. On Sunday, September 30, 1962, Barnett and Robert Kennedy agreed to move Meredith to Ole Miss that very afternoon. The slippery governor never entirely acceded to the Kennedys' request for a pledge to maintain order, although he left the attorney general with the impression that the highway patrol would be in Oxford when Meredith arrived. About dark, Meredith was quietly flown from Memphis to Oxford and taken directly to his dorm, where he was surrounded by two dozen marshals. That night no one learned his whereabouts, and Meredith slept through the nighttime disturbances across campus at the Lyceum.[51]

Nick Katzenbach, one of Robert Kennedy's chief deputies, had been sent to Oxford to oversee the arrival of the federal marshals and Meredith. Late in the afternoon Katzenbach installed himself in a command post inside the Lyceum, Ole Miss's oldest building and administrative headquarters. Much about this operation proved to be slipshod. Federal officials had no campus maps, and important supplies, including loudspeakers for crowd control and most of the tear gas, had been left at the airport. The marshals lacked medics, and the Lyceum did not even have a first-aid kit. Still, they improvised. In the kind of action that made World War II veterans famous, Katzenbach located a payphone in the Lyceum, called the White House collect, and kept the Kennedys informed about events as they unfolded. This communications link proved crucial. The president was surprised (and annoyed) to find that Katzenbach's live reports ran about 40 minutes ahead of the Army's official communications.[52]

Almost 200 marshals, nearly half of those in the Oxford area, stationed themselves in a close order line in front of the building facing onto a lightly treed, grassy area called the grove. According to a number of witnesses, the marshals looked slightly ridiculous, which did not help crowd control. To avoid appearing militaristic, they wore business suits rather than uniforms, but to identify each other they also displayed orange vests and wide yellow arm bands inscribed "U.S. Marshal." As a precaution against rocks, they wore steel helmets or white helmet liners. Their concealed side arms, gas mask pouches, tear gas guns, and three-foot riot batons dangled around their bodies. When they later donned their gas masks, they looked like aliens from a cheap science fiction movie. About 150 students gathered in the area and jeered the marshals. The highway patrol stood in front of the marshals and discouraged violence. Some protesters chanted, "Two, four, one, three, we hate Kennedy!" and "We want Meredith. Get a rope." Some taunts made reference to the Cuban Missile Crisis, which was unfolding at the same time. "Go to Cuba, nigger lovers," shouted one student.[53]

Until dusk, the crowd had been sullen and angry but not violent. After dark, however, its size grew considerably to 2,500 to 4,000, and its character changed. Students were joined by brawny working-class youth and sunburned older men who came in battered cars and pickups with out-of-state license plates from across the South. General Edwin Walker, recently dismissed from the U.S. Army for insubordination after trying to indoctrinate troops with John Birch Society propaganda, had given a radio address from Dallas urging all Right-thinking patriots to make their way to Oxford with their "skillets." This remark could be interpreted as a call to arms. "It is time to move," declared the general. "We have talked, listened and been pushed around too much by the anti-Christ Supreme Court." He called for "10,000 strong from every state." Walker declined to rule out guns: "We will move with the punches." Walker had been cultivating Mississippi for some time. In a speech to a large audience in Jackson in 1961, he had attacked Lyndon Johnson, the United Nations, the Peace Corps, the national media, and Harvard Marxists. Praising Mississippi's sovereignty, he announced, "I came here to meet the Communists on their battlefield right here in Mississippi."[54]

At first the mob jeered and chanted, tossed lighted cigarettes, and threw gravel and eggs, but it then switched to rocks and bottles, slashed tires, and set fire to the canvas top of an Army truck used by the marshals. Shortly before 8 p.m. a marshal was felled by a lead pipe, and Katzenbach ordered tear gas. President Kennedy learned about the gas just moments before he went on television to tell the nation that Ole Miss had been peacefully integrated. The mob, hearing the president on car radios, was antagonized, gave a rebel yell, and hurled debris. The gas temporarily surprised the mob and drove it back across the grove, but it also enraged them. Because the wind blew much of the gas back toward the marshals, it did not quell the crowd. While gas masks protected the marshals, dozens of Mississippi highway patrolmen who had stood passively between

the crowd and the marshals suddenly melted away. One patrolman had been injured seriously by a gas canister. Many lacked gas
masks, and all were angry that they had not been told that gas was
going to be used. The crowd surged toward the marshals aggressively. With the patrol gone, attackers charged the marshals again
and again with Confederate flags and cursed "the Yankees." (Most
marshals were southerners.) As the melee continued, dozens of marshals, felled by rocks and debris, were taken inside the Lyceum,
which looked like a field hospital.[55]

Around 9 p.m. General Walker appeared amid the rioters to
give a rousing speech under the Confederate monument. Growing
surly, the mob hurled bricks from a construction site, acid stolen
from the nearby Chemistry building, and Molotov cocktails made
from empty Coke bottles. The marshals were pushed back closer
to the Lyceum. They faced spray from a firetruck hose, a bulldozer,
and a driverless car sent hurtling into their ranks. As snipers began
to fire shots sporadically, most students prudently left for campus
residence halls or fraternities. Five cars parked around the grove
were set ablaze. Much of the fury came from a rumor that the
marshals had killed a coed. Although this statement was untrue, it
was repeated on Mississippi radio stations even after the riot was
over. Throughout the riot members of the press had been singled
out for abuse. Six press photographers had cameras smashed or
taken, a Memphis radio station's mobile broadcasting unit was
burned, a reporter who admitted to being from Atlanta was attacked, and a French reporter was shot in the back of the neck at
close range, execution-style. These attacks were so systematic that
one suspects a calculated plan to drive away the out-of-state and
foreign media so that local propaganda blaming the violence on the
marshals might prevail.[56]

As the riot continued, the marshals ran low on tear gas, and volunteers had to drive through the mob to obtain a new supply from
the airport. President Kennedy recognized that the 400 marshals

were too few in number, too ill equipped, and too poorly trained to deal with the situation. At 10 p.m. he ordered 23,000 troops, about half federalized Mississippi National Guard and about half regular Army who had been standing by in Memphis, to proceed to Oxford. On the telephone to the Lyceum, Robert Kennedy asked his aide Ed Guthman how matters stood on campus. Guthman replied, "It's getting like the Alamo." Kennedy said, "Well, you know what happened to those guys, don't you?" Kennedy's wit did not reassure Guthman. Within an hour, a few dozen local national guardsmen, under command of William Faulkner's nephew, arrived. The commander's arm was broken by a brick, and the Guard showed no sympathy for the raging mob. It took the bulk of the Army four hours to get to campus. When they arrived, they found the roadway in front of the Lyceum about six inches deep in bricks, rocks, pipes, bottles, gas shells, and concrete rubble. They cleared the area with bayonets fixed. By then, the marshals had almost exhausted their tear gas. At dawn the Army was in control, and the mob, after making sporadic attacks upon the adjacent town of Oxford, had faded away.[57]

Governor Barnett ordered flags flown at half staff due to the "invasion" and "bloodshed." In addition to the French reporter, a local resident watching the riot was killed by stray gunfire. On President Kennedy's orders, no federals fired, except to disable the firehose. The injured included 166 marshals, 29 of whom required treatment for gunshot wounds. There were 160 arrests, of whom only 25 were Ole Miss students, but charges were not pressed. In a legally dubious move that raised the ire of conservatives, federal officials took General Walker to a federal prison hospital and put him under observation as a possible psychiatric case. On Monday morning, Katzenbach escorted Meredith from his dorm to the Lyceum to be registered. Afterwards, he attended his first class. Meredith was an outcast on campus. An effigy dangling from a dorm window was labelled "Go back to Africa where YOU BELONG." The first time that Meredith ate in the campus cafeteria students outside jeered, "Kennedy is a coon keeper." A fraternity put up a sign, "Ole Miss may surrender but the Dekes NEVER." A draftee on duty at Oxford observed, "The most disturbing thing about Mississippi is its superficial resemblance to the United States." Few students or faculty dared speak to Meredith. Those who did were ostracized. In the summer of 1963, Meredith graduated from Ole Miss.[58]

The Ole Miss riot of 1962, which took place 100 years after Lincoln's preliminary Emancipation Proclamation, was the last major all-white male riot in defense of white supremacy. Committed to the past, the rioters had shown no faith in the present as a promising time. A public expression of private thoughts, the "insurrection" failed. One Deep South congressman privately said, "There aren't many of us who're willing to dust off our muskets and leave the Union to preserve a dying order." The Army, including local Guard units, quelled the disturbance, and Mississippi's elite became frightened by the riffraff rioters' disrespect for private property as evidenced by burning cars at the grove. WLBT-TV, the notoriously racist Jackson station, called for General Walker's arrest. Two days after the riot 127 state leaders met in Jackson and signed a statement condemning violence. However, another 30 walked out of the meeting. Then, too, the riot had attracted only a tiny portion of the millions of southern whites who opposed desegregation. The diehards' weakness suggested to the moderate Hodding Carter that "perhaps the tide has turned." Had it? It cost $5 million to put and keep Meredith at Ole Miss, and enrollment fell by half in the ensuing year. "Ole Miss has not been integrated!" declared the Citizens' Council, "It has been invaded and occupied by the United States Army, but Meredith is a prisoner on the campus...."[59]

As the Kennedys feared, the use of soldiers antagonized the Right. "The display at Oxford awakened millions of Americans to the dangers of Kennedyism," said Lieutenant Governor Paul Johnson, who was elected governor in 1963. One conservative letter-writer asked, "...are the Russians really as rotten as our own government?" Another advised Lyndon Johnson, "Why don't you tell your boss to tend to Castro and leave Ole Miss alone." A French nobleman privately said, "It is very strange that a nation which whimpers before Castro and cowers at the Berlin Wall can so bravely bayonet and threaten and beat young white American students in Mississippi." Unlike Khrushchev, Governor Barnett lacked nuclear weapons. The "agreeable rogue," to use Robert Kennedy's description, was, however, capable of considerable mischief. With remarkable psychological insight, a Citizens' Council official privately wrote, "Ole Miss was not integrated, for she never submitted. It can only be said that she has been subjected to integration by overwhelming and unlawful force. Thus, Ole Miss's honor is still intact." The Kennedys, in other words, had abetted Meredith's metaphorical act of rape.[60]

At the beginning of 1963, Martin Luther King, Jr., struggled to regain control of the movement. While the sit-ins, Freedom Rides, and Meredith's admission had increased King's prominence and brought him publicity, the SCLC had lost ground to CORE and SNCC. King's problems began when attempts to desegregate Albany, Georgia, through mass marches in 1961 and 1962 failed. Almost everything had gone wrong. Local black leaders were divided, SNCC volunteers derisively called King "De Lawd," and Albany's large black underclass never accepted King's doctrine of nonviolence. Once when demonstrators hurled rocks, Police Chief Laurie Pritchett asked, "Did you see them nonviolent rocks?" The media provided little coverage to a town far from reporters' bases and, in those presatellite days, beyond the television networks' capacity for a feed. Finally, Chief Pritchett practiced nonviolence. Although arrests were numerous, the disciplined, well-trained police avoided incidents that the Albany Movement could exploit to gain wider support. One time when King was in jail, the mayor's law partner secretly paid the fine and forced King's release in order to end publicity about his incarceration.[61]

Albany offered many lessons. For King, the underlying issue remained the nation's endemic racism as well as the poverty that accompanied it. Philosophically, he led a moral movement to change the society's views about both race and poverty. Asked on the witness stand whether his pray-in in the street did not violate the Bible's admonition to pray privately, King answered that religion should not be "outward, but inward and spiritual." Christ urged "individual diagnosis, not universal surgery." To change consciousness, King needed to alter the views of whites as well as blacks, of northerners as well as southerners. The starting point had to be the South's egregious, institutionalized racism. White allies, and especially nationally powerful northerners, were crucial. Congress would have to pass an effective civil rights law. He was prepared to use the political system. The law, he once said, might not change hearts, which was his larger goal, but it could coerce good behavior. Albany had also taught the importance of publicity, community organization, indigenous leadership, and of having southern officials whose outrageous conduct, unlike that of Laurie Pritchett, could add support among blacks, generate northern sympathy, and bring pressure upon the federal government to intervene. The confrontation over Meredith at Ole Miss suggested that the Kennedys, however reluctantly, would find it difficult to resist being drawn into a new dispute on the side of civil rights.[62]

King chose Birmingham as the site for his battle. He chose well. No southern city presented a more inviting target. Race relations in that steel capital, which was 40 percent black, had never been harmonious. Throughout the century, employers had played black and white workers against each other. Many local white unions, still powerful in 1963, were vehemently racist; some had ties to the Ku Klux Klan. Race relations were made more tense by the fact that the steel industry had been in decline since the 1930s. Whites were determined to hold on to the few opportunities for advancement inside this fading industry in a city that had generally poor prospects. The city had lost 10 percent of its jobs in five years; no new factories had opened, and one was scared off by the Freedom Rider violence. During that same period there were 17 race-related bombings, and more than 50 crosses had been burned. Despite its crudeness, "Bombingham," as the city was sometimes called, was convenient for visiting reporters. Local media were cooperative, and television networks could air footage via a one-hour flight to Atlanta. As a former Montgomery minister, King had known many Alabama clergy for years, his wife Coretta was from North Alabama, and King's brother, another Baptist minister, lived in Birmingham. King was also encouraged by A. G. Gaston, a local black millionaire, and by Rev. Fred Shuttlesworth, who had already organized a significant local movement.[63]

The most important reason for selecting Birmingham as a target may have been Bull Connor. The elected police commissioner had long boasted, and few disputed it, that his city was the most segregated in the United States. In other southern jurisdictions, limited interracial contact took place, but this was all but impossible in Birmingham due to Connor's spies and vigorous enforcement of a law that virtually prohibited mixed meetings. Police tapped telephones, racial activists got numerous obscene phone calls, and anyone who had talked to an out-of-town reporter might well be subpoenaed and interrogated. Originally a steel industry union buster, Connor opposed activities that crossed the color line almost as much to prevent interracial unions as to maintain white supremacy. By 1963 Connor had learned to accept white unions. He also tolerated prostitution and other underworld activities. Connor's police force was, not surprisingly, entwined with the Klan, which also had connections to the white unions and the underworld. Police ties to the Klan dictated that Connor do the Klan's bidding. The person who actually called the shots in Birmingham was Bobby Shelton, head of the 5,000–7,000 member North Alabama Klan. Connor was only his agent.[64]

In April 1963, the day after Connor lost a bid to become mayor, King launched the campaign to desegregate Birmingham. He demanded not only the end to discriminatory lunch counters downtown but also the hiring of blacks by businesses and the police department, and desegregation of parks, libraries, swimming pools, and schools. The white political establishment and business community refused even to discuss these demands. Because African Americans were only 10 percent of the city's voters, they had little political influence, but a black boycott of downtown businesses hurt. Every day hundreds of blacks marched and were arrested. Reporters and camera crews came. The demonstrations always ended by noon so that the film could be processed in time to appear on the national nightly news. King understood the importance of public expression in pressing for change. More blacks marched. On Good Friday, April 12, King personally led a march and was jailed. He was put in solitary confinement, which produced hysteria among movement leaders, who did not know his whereabouts. Finally, a phone call from President Kennedy located King, who was allowed to reassure his distressed, pregnant wife that he was okay. Kennedy privately told King, "Bull Connor has done as much for civil rights as Abraham Lincoln."[65]

While locked up, King wrote his remarkable "Letter from Birmingham Jail." This message, partly written on toilet paper, was smuggled out of jail by a black trusty. In it, King denounced segregation as a moral evil and expressed his own willingness to remain behind bars to defeat that evil. He distinguished between proper obedience to a just law and the moral necessity to disobey an unjust law. Nonviolence, then, was not just a negative pledge to avoid the destructive and self-destructive evil that violence unleashed. Rather, King proposed that moral righteousness required positive action to oppose wrongs such as segregation. Being jailed might be the price, but self-abnegating action was necessary to show the oppressor the true nature of bad law. The oppressor's blindness would dissolve, and morality would triumph. In a promising time, a public expression of private thought through moral witness could change a nation. King's words jarred the country's conscience. He had found a way both to attack segregation and to force Americans to rethink and remake their society. Among those profoundly moved was Daniel Berrigan. "His thoughtful and prophetic statement," the Jesuit priest wrote a friend, "cast a great deal of light on the subject for me...."[66]

Over time, black support for the marches dwindled, press coverage dropped, and organizers despaired. King then allowed thousands of black children to join the marches. "Real men," the radical Malcolm X complained to the press, "don't put their children on the firing line." However, the movement had excited very young blacks, who enthusiastically marched, clapped, and sang "We Shall Overcome." Lacking detention facilities, Connor tried to control the protesters with dogs and fire hoses. Television showed the result. "What is happening in Birmingham, Alabama," wrote one angry viewer in a private letter, "is shocking the *whole world*!" Large, snarling police dogs jumped on small children, scratched them, and bit them, while high-pressure fire hoses washed angry youths down the sidewalks bumping and bruising them against walls and walks. After Rev. Shuttlesworth was hosed and hospitalized, Connor said, "I wish they'd carried him away in a hearse." Connor's forces, rather than King's disciplined followers, appeared to be the source of disorder and violence. National revulsion brought, as King had planned, federal intervention. Burke Marshall, Robert Kennedy's top civil rights lawyer, flew to Birmingham to mediate. The business community, suffering severely from the black boycott, wanted to settle. So did King. Connor resisted, until the Kennedy administration exerted pressure by calling top executives of companies that did business in Birmingham. Connor had greater loyalty to business than to the Klan. A desegregation plan was adopted. Bombs exploded all over Birmingham, but the deal held.[67]

King's victory proved bittersweet. Although he had gained prestige, was heralded by some as the black "Messiah," and could take credit for moving civil rights to the top of the national agenda, these changes did not take place without cost. Relations between King and Rev. Shuttlesworth became strained and ended in bitterness. Implementation of the Birmingham agreement proved difficult. The demonstrations and their repression had killed good will on both sides. Minor disputes over the deal were interpreted darkly as attempts to destroy it. Marshall found himself entangled in protracted negotiations. Connor's departure from office left a power vacuum, and no new powerful figure took his place. In September 1963, the Sixteenth Street Baptist Church, where many of the marches had been organized, was bombed. "The terrible dynamiting shocked me into a better metabolic state...," privately wrote the ailing white southern integrationist Lillian Smith. "I felt I couldn't die – yet." Four black girls died in the blast. "If this outrageous action is not met by firm, relentless pursuit and punishment of culprits," the black union leader A. Philip Randolph warned President Kennedy, then blacks would turn to "violent direct action...." Birmingham's angry blacks attacked whites, and whites responded in kind. By then, King's doctrine of nonviolence seemed on the wane.[68]

The Birmingham protests made civil rights the top domestic issue. King's aide Wyatt Tee Walker had declared, "We've got a movement!" African Americans, said Bayard Rustin publicly, "cannot be contained." Michigan's former Governor G. Mennen Williams privately warned, "The grass roots of the Negro population is clearly aroused." "Birmingham," predicted the journalist Ralph Gleason in a letter to a friend, "has started a chain reaction. There will be demonstrations and riots in all the cities. Over 20,000 marched in San Francisco last Sunday for human rights. Pretty wild." By the end of the summer there were 600 protests in 169 cities in 32 states. A pleased Aubrey Williams told Jim Dombrowski, "It seems to be breaking all over – at long last the tide has begun to flow in." A worried white woman wrote Lyndon Johnson, "I'm scared!!" In a speech Harlem's Rep. Adam Clayton Powell said, "We have America by the throat." What did rising black restlessness mean? The NAACP's Roy Wilkins told the press, "99 percent of the Negroes want in," but the Urban League's Whitney Young noted, "In previous generations the Negro believed what is white is right.... This has changed. The Negro is ... rejecting many of the white man's values and codes of behavior." Robert Kennedy privately told a group of Alabama editors, "If King loses, worse leaders are going to take his place. Look at the black Muslims." King enjoyed the attention and liked being seen as a moderate alternative to Malcolm X. "We are on the threshold of a significant breakthrough," he said privately, "and the greatest weapon is mass demonstration."[69]

By early June the Kennedys, and Robert in particular, understood the urgency of federal involvement. The issue was no longer, as it had been in the Meredith case, about federal court orders, nor was it about registering black voters in the South and dismantling that region's segregation laws. Demands in Birmingham for jobs and for the right to eat in restaurants and to shop in stores pushed for changes in the private sector that applied to the North as well as the South and which, if pursued aggressively, meant that race relations in the United States would be placed upon an entirely different basis. "We are," Ralph Gleason wrote privately, "in the midst of a revolution...." This was precisely Martin Luther King, Jr.'s intent. A public expression of private thoughts favoring equality in a promising time pointed to momentous change. The federal government would, as a practical matter, have to be involved, and a new civil rights law was imperative. Earlier in the year President Kennedy had proposed a tepid bill on the grounds that a more robust law could not pass the Senate, but Birmingham and the resulting restlessness had revealed the need for federal action and changed calculations about the Senate.[70]

That same month the University of Alabama was desegregated. Unlike Ross Barnett, Governor George Wallace knew how to play the political game. He demanded that the Klan, which had supported his election, stay away from the university, and he promised "to stand in the schoolhouse door." Wallace planned to do so both metaphorically and literally. Mostly, he intended to stage an act of powerful symbolic value. He sent signals that the two black students could be registered after he left. In front of 150 patrolmen and 400 reporters on live daytime television in 95 degree heat, the governor confronted Nick Katzenbach, not the students. Wallace wanted the public, especially southerners, to see that he opposed desegregation with courage but without violence. Robert Kennedy felt that the governor's defiant pose looked ridiculous. It certainly did not stop integration, but ever since the Civil War, southerners had not required political leaders to be victorious. By making himself the focal point of opposition, the governor knew that he would become a folk hero for segregationists. He calculated, correctly, to launch a national political career.[71]

President Kennedy responded to Wallace's antics with a televised speech of his own that same night. He could not allow the governor to go unchallenged. Against the advice of his staff, but at the insistence of his brother, the president decided to speak about civil rights and morality. For a long time, King had pleaded with Kennedy to do just that. In one of his finest speeches, which was still incomplete as he went on the air, and with the best parts at the end ad-libbed, Kennedy argued, "We are confronted primarily with a moral issue." Always keen to play the Cold War card, the president noted that the United States was a mostly white country in a mostly nonwhite world, and that treatment of nonwhites in the United States affected American prestige abroad. But he also said, "The Negro baby born in America today...has about one-half as much chance of completing a high school as a white baby born in the same place on the same day, one-third as much chance of completing college, ... twice as much chance of becoming unemployed, ... a life expectancy which is seven years shorter, and the prospects of earning only half as much." He suggested that this unequal outcome was due to segregation and discrimination. "He was really great," King said in a private conversation recorded by the FBI that reached Kennedy almost immediately. The president was finally committed to a strong civil rights bill and a policy of federal enforcement.[72]

While the media had focused on Birmingham and Wallace's televised stand in the schoolhouse door, the most astonishing challenges to the old order had been taking place in Mississippi. In the heavily black Delta town of Greenwood, African Americans in early 1963 had begun to try to register to vote. In the seven years before SNCC's Sam Block arrived only 40 blacks had tried to register. In nine months 30 more tried, and then in March 1963, 336 attempted to register. Ten may have passed. This result came about largely because of the hard work over many months of Block, Willie Peacock, and Lawrence Guyot. Harassment had been constant. "In the state of Mississippi," Block said publicly, "every animal has a season but the Negro; you can shoot him anytime." He was arrested seven times. He had a certain gutsy style. A local officer accosted Block:

> "Nigger, where you from?"
> "I'm a native of Mississippi."
> "I know all the niggers here."
> "Do you know any colored people?" The sheriff spat.
> "I give you till tomorrow to get out of here."
> "If you don't want to see me here, you better pack up and leave, because I'll be here."

The next day Block led 50 blacks to the courthouse to try to register.[73]

Shortly after the first registration attempts in 1962, Leflore County had cut off welfare payments and surplus food to punish African Americans, but after the black comedian Dick Gregory had chartered an airplane to bring in seven tons of food, county aid had been restored to prevent private assistance from being used to encourage blacks to register. After Jimmy Travis was shot and SNCC's office was burned, Wiley Branton, head of the Voter Education Project, put 35 paid workers into the county. He then visited and disclosed that Greenwood Leflore, the county's founder and a major planter, was his great-grandfather. (Branton was so light that he was often mistaken for white.) During one protest march a police dog bit Rev. D. L. Tucker. The preacher said, "God is still my helper." A cop replied, "Shut up, Kennedy is the only God you know." A white mob gathered and said "kill him" and "throw him in the river," where Emmett Till's body had been found. "The predominant mood of the masses of Negroes in Mississippi," SCLC's Andrew Young told the press, "is religious." Faith made them fearless. "They sing all the time," he added. Block recalled, "Music served as a drawing card and the organizational glue...." Gregory sponsored an interracial musical fundraiser on a black farm that featured Albany's Freedom Singers and the white folksingers Pete Seeger and Bob Dylan. The still obscure Dylan performed his first hit, "Blowin' in the Wind," which had been inspired by events in Mississippi.[74]

Meanwhile, protests began in Jackson, and after the mayor denounced agitators on television, Medgar Evers demanded and got time to reply. In a prime time telecast, he said, "Tonight the Negro plantation worker in the Delta knows from his radio and television what happened today all over the world....a Congo native can be a locomotive engineer, but in Jackson he cannot even drive a garbage truck." On May 28, 1963, an interracial group of eight that included the student Anne Moody sat in at Woolworth's. Angry white toughs smeared ketchup, mustard, sugar, and blood on the protesters and left Moody in tears. Three days later 600 black high school students marched in the streets, were attacked by police, and, upon being arrested, were hauled off in city garbage trucks to a makeshift prison at the state fairgrounds. The mayor boasted that he could house 10,000 demonstrators. Males were kept in the cattle stockade; females in the hogpens. Police threw the prisoners slices of bread in the dirt. One night the captives were sprayed with insecticide. The usually placid NAACP chief, Roy Wilkins, flew in from New York and gave a rousing talk. "There remains," he said, "the establishment of the ovens to complete the picture of Nazi terror." The next day Wilkins and Evers picketed Woolworth's and were immediately arrested. The national NAACP leader's arrest made national television news and showed that events were forcing the organization to take a new, more militant position. King said, "We've finally baptized brother Wilkins."[75]

On the night of Kennedy's civil rights speech Evers returned home late from a meeting and was shot by a sniper in the driveway of his home. As he lay dying he was surrounded by sweatshirts that he had been carrying that read "Jim Crow Must Go." Like the later Birmingham church bombing, Evers's murder enraged the local black community. On the *Today* show, Wilkins said, "Evers went overseas to fight for his country and what did he get for it – a bullet in the back." During the funeral march, leaders had a difficult time maintaining order. When the 4,000 to 6,000 marchers passed black homes, residents shouted, "Freedom! Freedom!" Black youths screamed at police, "Shoot us! Shoot us!" After the Justice Department's John Doar calmed the crowd, a black youth muttered, "The only way to stop evil here is to have a revolution. Somebody have to die." One mourner said, "Let's stop this non-violence and get at it. I did it in '43 and I'll do it again." King attended the service in Jackson but dared not speak. "This is an NAACP affair," Wilkins told King. "We have not invited you here to come and take over." Relations between the NAACP and SCLC had been tense, and they grew worse when the SCLC and other groups tried to raise funds off of Evers's death.[76]

The sensational shooting led to a thorough search of the area near Evers's home and the recovery of the murder weapon. It contained fingerprints, which the FBI traced to Byron De La Beckwith, a Greenwood fertilizer salesman and longtime activist in racist groups. A wounded combat veteran of World War II and a heavy drinker, he was a charter member of the Citizens' Council. In 1964 Beckwith was tried for the murder. While he waited in jail, General Walker visited, a fact that led Burke Marshall to ask Robert Kennedy, "Isn't this enough to turn your stomach?" During the trial Ex-Governor Ross Barnett, who had called the slaying "a dastardly act," entered the courtroom and made a point of shaking hands with the defendant in the presence of the jury. The trial ended with a hung jury. So did a retrial. In 1989 evidence turned up showing that in the second trial the Sovereignty Commission had tampered with jury selection in the hopes of gaining an acquittal. In a third trial in 1994 Beckwith was convicted.[77]

Evers's murder was the first political assassination of the sixties. It was not, alas, the last; much of the optimism that made the early sixties a promising time turned to despair with leaders' deaths. Part of the shock about Evers came from what was then the novelty of that idea. At least 145 memorial services were held in 33 states. His death and Beckwith's two shameful trials curdled race relations in Mississippi. "I regard Evers death as cruel, senseless, heartless and unforgiveable," wrote one white activist to a friend. Intelligent, perceptive, disciplined, organized, and courageous, Evers also had an unusual ability to get along with other civil rights leaders. The only one in the state who could play that role, he had constantly stroked the egos of both the vain Aaron Henry and the idealistic Bob Moses. Within days of the murder, the movement in Mississippi was in a shambles. Evers's half-brother Charles got the NAACP job but commanded little respect. Sovereignty Commission spies did everything in their power to sow mistrust. Eventually, when blacks gained the vote and a certain amount of power, the absence of credible leadership, compared to other southern states, mattered. Evers's murder was a cynical act designed to make the exercise of black power impossible. The deed painfully echoed across an entire generation.[78]

The administration tried to find a formula for a civil rights bill strong enough to meet King's demands while still mild enough to get through the Senate, where votes had to be found to cut off a southern filibuster. A consensus existed for a bill that improved access to voting and promised speedier court cases about schools, parks, or other public facilities, but covering service in restaurants was still a problem because of the need to get Republican votes to end the filibuster. Many Republican senators had powerful business constituents who opposed rights to public accommodations. Lyndon Johnson urged the president to seek support from the key Republican, Senator Everett Dirksen, and to stress the moral issue. The vice president privately said, "What Negroes are really seeking is moral force...." By this point, King had concluded that the administration's commitment to civil rights was based strictly on being pushed. The administration saw matters differently. As a Democrat, Kennedy depended upon the party in Congress to carry all of his legislation. If he alienated southern Democrats, he risked losing his entire program. Already tax reform had been held hostage in an attempt to derail civil rights. To Kennedy, avoiding a split in the party was more important than any particular piece of legislation. In 1963 Congress passed only 27 percent of Kennedy's proposals, the lowest percentage in modern times.[79]

After Birmingham, as King's prestige grew, the administration became keenly interested in King's plans. So was J. Edgar Hoover. When an FBI memo in 1961 stated that King was not under investigation, the director asked, "Why not?" Close scrutiny led top FBI officials to clear King. Presented with this conclusion in 1963, the director angrily replied, "This memo reminds me vividly of those I received when Castro took over Cuba. You contended then that Castro and his cohorts were not Communists and not influenced by Communists. Time alone proved you wrong." Hoover's staff

quickly reversed course and intensely examined King. For years
the FBI had claimed that King had two key communist advisers,
Stan Levison and Jack O'Dell. Levison, a New York businessman
who became a strong supporter of King and civil rights after the
Montgomery bus boycott, helped raise funds for the SCLC, gave
King shrewd political advice, and wrote some of King's speeches and
books. According to the FBI, Levison had also been a secret courier
who brought Moscow gold to the United States. In the party's secret
organizational chart, according to FBI sources, he ranked second
in the country. Levison may, without King's knowledge, have sup-
plied secret Soviet funds to King, and his advice to King could have
been calculated both to stir racial trouble and to build an intellectual bridge between King and the party. The FBI was sufficiently
concerned that it began to tap Levison's telephones in 1962.[80]

Those taps showed that Levison did influence King, and after
the Kennedys saw the role that Levison played, they decided to
warn King of the danger of this connection. If King could be publicly tied to communists, various administration officials privately
pointed out to King's friends, the civil rights movement would be
discredited, and so would the administration. At first King did not
take the charge seriously. He found nothing in Levison's conduct
that suggested communism. Rather, the New Yorker seemed only
eager to help civil rights. Finally, John Kennedy confronted King
about both Levison and O'Dell in the White House Rose Garden.
"They're Communists," he said, "You've got to get rid of them. If
they shoot *you* down, they'll shoot us down too – so we're asking
you to be careful." To end rumors circulating in Congress, Robert
Kennedy announced that King and other civil rights leaders were
free from communist influence. King broke off direct contact with
Levison, but the phone taps, which he apparently never suspected,
showed that the two continued to communicate through interme-
diaries. King's defiance undermined the administration's confidence
in him and enraged J. Edgar Hoover.[81]

Although Jack O'Dell had played only a minor role in King's life, his communist background was less secretive. According to the FBI, O'Dell had been elected to a high post in the party in 1959. After the administration's warnings about O'Dell went unheeded, the FBI leaked stories to conservative newspapers. A master of public relations, King announced that O'Dell had tendered his resignation. FBI taps, however, showed that he actually continued to work for SCLC, at times under the name Rev. Tom Kilgore. King found it hard to fire O'Dell because he was excellent at doing mailings to raise funds. After the FBI noted that O'Dell continued to work for King almost a year after the 'resignation,' Hoover concluded that King was a "vicious liar." Offended, Hoover obtained permission from Robert Kennedy to tap King's phones. The administration found all of these taps useful. Thus, King's approval of Kennedy's June 1963 civil rights speech, picked up on the Levison tap, reached the Kennedys within a couple of days. Private thoughts about public matters, it turned out, were not entirely private during this promising time.[82]

In June 1963, King began to plan a mass civil rights protest march in the nation's capital. "The threat itself," he said privately, "may so frighten the President that he would have to do something." King was eager to get a civil rights bill passed. "If there is a filibuster in Congress," he warned publicly, "we will have a nonviolent peaceful demonstration in Washington." Birmingham had shown the segregationists' weakness, it had excited the black masses, and it had created the possibility for federal support. A large protest in the nation's capital could serve multiple purposes. It would celebrate present-day success, affirm vast support for civil rights, bring new supporters into the movement, and put pressure on Congress to pass a strong bill. King was following a tactic originated by A. Philip Randolph. The head of the Brotherhood of Sleeping Car Porters had first advocated a March on Washington in 1941; the idea had sufficiently alarmed President Franklin

Roosevelt that he banned discrimination in industry during World War II. However, black industrial job gains made during and after the war were threatened in the early sixties. Chrysler had employed 200,000 workers in 1957, but only 50,000 in 1962, and in 1960 International Harvester had lost half of its jobs in three years. In 1962 black unemployment was 11 percent, more than double the rate for white males. Black income, as a percentage of white, had fallen from 69 percent in 1952 to 57 percent in 1960. As black job troubles rose "with the inexorable advance of automation," Randolph had talked about a march for jobs as early as 1962.[83]

The two leaders agreed to combine their issues into the March for Jobs and Freedom. Already assured of support from CORE's James Farmer and SNCC's John Lewis, King and Randolph lobbied Roy Wilkins of the NAACP and Whitney Young of the National Urban League to participate. Those more conservative leaders resisted so long as the March envisioned sit-ins at the Capitol with "Senator Eastland stepping over supine bodies to get to his office." The Urban League feared losing its tax exemption, which would have dried up contributions, and the NAACP, experienced at political lobbying, knew that Congress would be enraged by a sit-in on the hill. Young and Wilkins wanted the March to be peaceful and interracial. Their groups had many white members and enjoyed substantial white financial support. They defined racial progress as gradual gains won in lawsuits, legislation, and quiet lobbying. Randolph wanted the March to focus on the North, where jobs for unskilled workers were disappearing rapidly. Many unions, and especially the United Auto Workers, participated in the March largely because it concerned jobs. The AFL–CIO's powerful George Meany, however, kept his distance, much to the irritation of Randolph and the UAW's Walter Reuther. King hoped that the March would give the administration the backbone to push Congress to enact a strong civil rights bill. He brought support not only from black churches but also from northern white churches. Next to unions, churches were the most important organizations in the March.[84]

King, in an FBI tap quickly conveyed to the Kennedys, said that he wanted at least 100,000 people to march. The sheer size would put pressure on both the administration and the Congress. King also believed that a majority of the participants should be black. Psychologically, African Americans needed pride of authorship to show both to themselves and to whites that they could mount such a protest. Still, King understood the importance of white participants, whom he hoped would come in large numbers. He wanted "a symphony of love and brotherhood." King believed, "God wants freedom for all people. This is what we are striving for." Black supremacy, suggested by the Muslims, was "evil and godless." The National Council of Churches promised to bring 40,000 mostly white Protestants; Catholic groups pledged 10,000. White marchers would generate greater media interest and bring powerful allies who could lobby effectively on Capitol Hill. In addition, a biracial March – little thought was given to Hispanics, Asian Americans, or American Indians – would be less threatening to whites. The Japanese American Citizens League participated in the March but was given no place either on the program or on the platform. Union and northern religious support brought many whites to the March, which exceeded organizers' hopes by reaching up to 250,000 and was more than one quarter white.[85]

In July the administration decided to coopt the March. In return for support, the organizers, led by Bayard Rustin, agreed to certain conditions. The event was set for a Wednesday to avoid weekend rowdiness, and special buses and trains were scheduled so that everyone would arrive in the morning and depart before nightfall. Expensive overnight lodging was avoided. The marchers would not congregate on Capitol Hill, even though Congress was a main target. Instead, small numbers of participants would meet informally with members of Congress and staffs. As it turned out, 75 members, mostly liberals, attended the event. When the legislators appeared, the crowd chanted, "Pass the bill." No cabinet officers and few from the administration came. The focus of the March would be speeches in front of the Lincoln Memorial, a reminder of Emancipation. Although black leaders of the six main civil rights groups would be featured, the rest of the program would be biracial. No women, however, were to speak. After the event, if it were peaceful, the leaders would meet with President Kennedy at the White House.[86]

Wednesday, August 28, was a typical hot, steamy Washington summer day. Organizers had required that all signs be approved. Some read "We March for Integrated Schools NOW," "Kill Jim Crow – Detroit NAACP," and "We March for Jobs for All NOW." The actual March along the Mall was vast and confusing, and some program leaders had trouble reaching the Lincoln Memorial. "Americans don't know how to march," said a reporter, who added, "Thank God." A marcher said, "We don't need no leaders. We know the way to go." As the crowd moved forward, they chanted "Freedom Now" and sang "We Shall Overcome." The speeches went well, except for a flap over John Lewis's intention to use inflammatory language. Washington's Catholic Archbishop, who had smoothed details behind the scenes, refused to be on the platform with the SNCC leader unless the speech was toned down. The Archbishop objected after Burke Marshall and Robert Kennedy had read and conveyed their disapproval of Lewis's speech. Finally, Phil Randolph persuaded Lewis to make changes, but the angry version had already been given to the press. Entertainers included Mahalia Jackson, Odetta, Bob Dylan, and Joan Baez. Celebrities present included the black entertainers Dick Gregory, Lena Horne, Harry Belafonte, and Josephine Baker, who had flown in from Paris, as well as the white film stars Paul Newman and Marlon Brando. The program ended with "We Shall Overcome," which became the March's anthem. At the conclusion, Randolph cried.[87]

The highlight, as anticipated, was Martin Luther King, Jr.'s "I Have a Dream" speech, as moving a piece of rhetoric as there was in the twentieth century. Millions saw the event on television, which was broadcast worldwide on the new Telstar satellite. The organizers may have postponed the event until August to make certain that it could be watched globally. The poignancy of King's call for an end to racism worked its way into the nation's conscience. Kennedy, watching at the White House, said, "He's damn good." The ending to King's address, partly ad-libbed, brought stunned silence, then ecstacy from the crowd. Coretta Scott King called it "a great spiritual communion." Catching the optimistic mood of a promising time, King's public expression challenged the nation to transform itself. For millions of others, the reaction to King's message was subtle rather than sudden, but time would prove that some sort of watershed had been crossed. The fact of the March combined with the power of King's speech meant that race relations would have to be managed and reorganized on a new basis. Among the few critics was King's bitter rival for black leadership, Malcolm X. Condemning "the Farce on Washington," he said, "Who ever heard of angry revolutionists all harmonizing in 'We Shall Overcome' ... while tripping and swaying along, arm-in-arm, with the very people they were supposed to be angrily revolting against?"[88]

In reflecting upon the March, participants stressed the event's hope and joy. "It was the living end," one wrote privately. On the train home a number of Chicagoans told the press that the March had been "beautiful," "swinging," "an hour of triumph," and "the most wonderful experience of my life." A Unitarian minister from Massachusetts said, "The soul of America has finally been stirred." Hubert Humphrey recalled, "There was a spirit of love and kindness everywhere." "It's going to be a great big Sunday school picnic," Dick Gregory had predicted. Organizers had been subtly pushed into holding a positive event by the administration's decision to embrace the March. Had the administration not done so, noted

Burke Marshall, the activists would have turned on the government. Marchers came away with renewed faith in the righteousness of their cause but also with a strong feeling that they were sufficiently numerous that, in a pluralistic democracy, they would ultimately triumph. Chances for a strong civil rights bill also improved. The combined participation of both unions and northern churches brought pressure on members of Congress from different constituencies. For southern blacks, the March indicated vast support for local struggles from outside. A Mississippi farmer said, "I never realized all of these people were on my side." From a jail cell in Louisiana, James Farmer wept at seeing the huge crowd on television.[89]

No one knew what would happen next. The March did not in and of itself break the filibuster in the Senate against the civil rights bill, but the majesty of the event and the eloquence of King did make a new law more likely. "My concept of equality," said King publicly, "means the untrammeled opportunity for every person to fulfill his total individual capacity...." The administration finally seemed prepared to commit energy and prestige to King's goal. Although such a bill could bring access to the ballot and better chances to win lawsuits, it was not clear how a law could create jobs. Changes taking place in the economy were difficult for any government to manage. King's larger point, of course, was a moral one, and at that level government officials were almost helpless. Consciousness might be in the process of being changed, but racism remained, as news from Mississippi provided frequent reminders. "I do not object," said James Baldwin publicly, "to the fact that Senator Eastland is alive, but I do object to his power....I certainly reject with vehemence, any notion that I, as a Negro, should ever become 'equal' to such a man." Furthermore, if racism was purged from America's heart, as King recommended, how would Americans of all races work with and relate to each other? King's speech suggested compassion, charity, and Christian love; it did not present a method for implementation.[90]

Americans found that King expressed both a conviction of hope about the future and an idea that resonated with the creed of equality and liberty first articulated by the Founding Fathers. He exuded the optimism of a promising time, but King's idealism also clashed with nasty racist realities. A black Baptist preacher was perhaps entitled to noble principles that transcended present-day truths. King's ability to project traditional ideals mocked the present in a way that jarred. If whites found it disconcerting to be reminded of the republic's failings, it was even more so to be told this by a black preacher. "We are," A. Philip Randolph told the press, "the advance guard of a massive moral revolution." Frightening though this was, as King shrewdly knew, the country had little choice but to cling to its ideals. But only a tiny minority felt confident that those values were about to be realized for all Americans. To the majority, the dissonance between idealism and reality produced much doubt and a shattering of the complacency and smugness that had long gripped American culture and which had predominated in the postwar world. Who were the American people? What did they stand for? Where were they going? King raised those questions. He did not provide answers.[91]

The importance of the civil rights movement in the early sixties was not that it dismantled legal segregation in the South. The NAACP had begun that task long before, and the courts had gradually moved to end segregation even without the civil rights movement. Of course, the movement did accelerate the process, but its larger accomplishment was to challenge the role of race in American life and the definition of what being an American meant. When middle-class black students challenged segregation, they also challenged the myth of white supremacy and the power of the white elite. As a consequence, they caused a crisis in identity for whites. "The liberation of Americans from the racial anguish which has crippled us for so long," James Baldwin observed publicly, "can only mean, truly, the creation of a new people in this still-new world."

"The enormous, frightening massive inner sufferings of good people," Daniel Berrigan wrote privately, "are helping a new world get born. We are in the strange twilight zone where the child is herself unsure of what she will be...." In linking the attack against racism to traditional ideals of equality and liberty, King challenged the nation to redefine itself.[92]

This impetus for redefinition formed the core of the civil rights movement, and it explains why participants in that movement described the experience as transformative. "The social revolution now in full swing," wrote one activist in a letter, "has painfully awakened our consciences...." Another privately observed, "It seems to me that we are having a conservative revolution. For certainly the goals are conservative. Our supporters and participants want in to American society. They want television sets and cars and the right to vote and everything that anyone else has. But there is a new conception of their own role in that society and of their own ability to change that society." The personal changes that resulted from participation were accompanied by visions for a transformed society. "One era," recalled the white activist Mary King, "was drawing to a close and another was beginning." By giving public expression, through participation in the movement, to private thoughts upholding American ideals during a promising time for social change, each activist, as a matter of individual conscience, had shown that the personal was the political. The implications would be worked out in other social movements and in changed conceptions about society and politics that took place during the remainder of the decade and, indeed, throughout the rest of the century. No other movement in the early sixties had such profound long-term consequences for the United States.[93]

Yo-yo champion Glen Beckner wins passes for his family to the Seattle World's Fair, October 2, 1962.

(*Seattle Post-Intelligencer Collection.* Museum of History and Industry, Seattle. 86.5.2862.)

CHAPTER FOUR

Families

The comedian Vaughn Meader had a brief career. Possessed of an uncanny ability to project a remarkably exact rendition of the strange New England twang of John Kennedy, Meader burst upon the public stage in 1962. A minor nightclub performer, he became a star by recording *The First Family*, an album that reputedly sold four million copies. Even the Kennedys loved it, and why not? Meader's innocent, slapstick jokes, some of which were about the idea of family, seemed to partake of the family's high spirits in an uncritical way. If he poked fun at the Kennedys' wealth and style, he did so with good humor. To avoid criticism that he was ridiculing the presidency, the album presented John Kennedy in a reserved fashion and made other family members bear the brunt of the cracks. Most importantly, the album conveyed the essential clannishness of the Kennedys, their loyalty among themselves, and a devotion to family that met a yearning public need in the early sixties. Although the American love affair with the Kennedys that began in those years was shaped by the family's power, wealth, and glamor, it was also influenced by that sense of family. Meader's success in large part came from his ability to tap a part of the rising public concern about the meaning of family at a time when the postwar family was in increasing crisis.[1]

The Kennedys quickly became ersatz American royalty. They were well dressed, articulate, energetic, and engaging on television. They presented elements of tragedy, which would unfortunately grow in later years. The premature deaths of Jack's brother Joe, the young war hero, and of sister Kathleen made the otherwise fairy-tale family seem more human. Sister Rosemary's mental retardation, hidden during the campaign, was now used to raise funds for charity, sometimes to the resentment of those who felt pressured to contribute. Much was made of sister Pat's husband, the film and television star Peter Lawford, and Lawford's "rat pack" friends, Frank Sinatra, Dean Martin, Sammy Davis, Jr., and Joey Bishop. Public service kept family members in constant view. Brother-in-law Sargent Shriver set up the Peace Corps, while brother Robert became Attorney General, and brother Ted soon occupied Jack's old Senate seat. Robert Kennedy's Virginia home was filled with children and visitors. France's Minister of Culture André Malraux visited and said, "This house is 'hellzapopping.'" Top members of the administration gathered there to found the Hickory Hill Seminars, where eminent persons led political and philosophical discussions. It was also there that Arthur Schlesinger, Jr., among others, was pushed fully clothed into the swimming pool. The strait-laced former Harvard professor was not amused, and catty Republicans declared the Kennedys vulgar. To the Kennedys, such high jinks broke the tension that prevailed in Cold War Washington and helped bond outsiders to the family.[2]

No one dared push John Kennedy into any swimming pool. The president was a naturally dignified, reserved man who sought to preserve the aura of both his person and his office. If rumors of clandestine affairs abounded, Kennedy offset them with public relations that emphasized a happy, wholesome family life. Photographs of the president with his daughter Caroline ("Buttons") or, somewhat later, with John, Jr. ("John-John"), were not only handed out throughout Kennedy's time in office, but the press often found the children inside the Oval Office. At age two, John, Jr., liked hiding under the president's desk. Caroline and her friends played in the adjacent Rose Garden, and the president took breaks from his work to visit. Sometimes he gave them candy. During one official reception that was televised, Clare Boothe Luce noted in a letter to a friend, "Three-year-old John Kennedy was permitted to do a long solo marching sequence on the balcony overhead." Once, at the family compound at Palm Beach, Florida, Kennedy was upstaged at a press conference when Caroline showed up thumping along in Jackie's high heels. Such scenes of domesticity helped endear Kennedy to both the media and the public. "Family," the journalist Stewart Alsop wrote privately, "is a subject on which JFK is as passionately sensitive as Harry Truman."[3]

Kennedy's secret weapon, as shrewd old Joe had long recognized, was Jackie. The mysterious and alluring first lady had special appeal to both men and women. Jackie's natural good looks were enhanced by genteel manners, by a carefully trained voice, and by the extreme care with which she dressed. When she hired Oleg Cassini as her private designer, she gave him instructions to dress her as if she were the wife of the president of France. Within six weeks of the inauguration, the "Jackie look" had swept the country. Department store advertising featured drawings of women who looked remarkably like Jackie. The style that she set prevailed for the remainder of Kennedy's presidency. She changed fashion in a daring way by wearing a formal gown that showed bare shoulders. In 1961 Jackie spent $105,446 on personal expenses. The glamor that she conveyed reinforced the sense that it was a promising time. She carried her sense of style into the project of redecorating the White House. After this monumental task was completed, Jackie showed off the results in a televised tour watched by 56 million Americans. Vaughn Meader joked about the tour, but Jack was jealous of his wife's popularity. Crowds doubled when she accompanied the president on trips. After the couple visited Los Angeles, an eyewitness recalled, "They looked more like movie stars than most movie stars." Their tumultuous state visit to France in 1961 led Kennedy to say, "I am the man who accompanied Jacqueline Kennedy to Paris."[4]

Americans have always been fascinated by the rich, and Jackie, unlike the upstart Kennedys, had been born into the upper class. She found the Kennedys "terribly *bourgeois*." Although her father had squandered the family fortune, her mother had remarried real money, and Jackie's upbringing had been consistent with that wealth: Her mother kept 25 servants at the family summer hone at Newport, Rhode Island. Jackie learned to ride at an early age, won championships at horse shows, and spent a year in Paris as a young woman. Thirty-one-year-old Jackie played the role of first lady with taste, imagination, and self-assurance. She gave neither speeches nor interviews, but her spare comments showed incisive intelligence and psychological insight. Unlike Mamie Eisenhower, Mrs. Kennedy served hard liquor at the White House, put ashtrays in the public rooms, and encouraged guests to talk with reporters who covered social events. Flattering the press encouraged favorable stories that gave public expression to the view that it was a promising time. Emphasizing high culture, she had the musical composer Igor Stravinsky, the cellist Pablo Casals, and the dance choreographer George Ballanchine perform after formal dinners. Her sphynx-like public silence created an aura of mystery that excited the public, and particularly women, who avidly read articles about her. Any magazine with Jackie's name on the cover sold an extra 500,000 copies. Cover stories became common.[5]

Jackie's appeal, and the desire many women had to be like Jackie, came in part from a crisis that was brewing in the middle-class family. During World War II, unprecedented numbers of

American women had worked outside the home. At the end of the war, many women lost these jobs. While some were forced to make way for returning male veterans, many married women workers in 1945 did not object to leaving the workforce to return to a "normal" life as childbearers, childrearers, and homemakers. Before the war very few married women had worked outside the home. (Among those ousted was the labor journalist Betty Friedan. She was bumped by Jim Peck, who reclaimed a job lost while imprisoned as a conscientious objector.) Cultural expectations strongly supported married women staying home. Older female relatives and husbands did not believe that married women ought to work outside the home permanently. Practical considerations played a role, too. In the days before fast food and frozen food, and at a time when eating out was expensive and rare, cooking was a major home occupation. So was doing laundry in those days before automatic washers and no-iron fabrics. (Women routinely spent two days per week at home washing and ironing.) Furthermore, daytime child care or after school care was rare after the war. The baby boom that began in 1946 marked the return of "normal" family life, with the birth of many children who had been postponed either from the depressed thirties or from the war years.[6]

America prospered, veterans went to college on the GI Bill and thereby qualified for good jobs, and government-backed mortgages stimulated a housing boom. Between 1947 and 1960, real wages rose almost 50 percent. Even the unskilled did well, especially in unionized industries. In 1960 nearly one-third of American workers belonged to unions. For men, higher earnings meant that they could provide better for their families. High wages help explain why Americans considered the early sixties a promising time. For women, the situation was more complicated. As the oldest boomers grew up, and as household chores declined with time-saving inventions, housewives increasingly entered the workforce, although many did so only part time. During the fifties the percentage of women who worked outside the home passed World War II levels, although women were poorly paid. The typical female college graduate earned less than a male high school dropout. Women often worked for a specific purpose, such as to buy a house or to put a son through college. By 1960 37 percent of women worked, and 30 percent of married women worked. Few, however, thought of themselves as having careers. Although male attitudes about working wives also changed, the ideal type was still a family with one male breadwinner. In 1960 few women, even among the large working minority, questioned this stereotype. Infatuation with upper-class Jackie provided a way to express dissatisfaction with middle-class life without challenging basic premises. After all, wasn't Jackie a housewife, too? But nobody really believed that. Jackie lacked dishpan hands.[7]

Another profound change evident by 1960 was the breakdown among whites of older ethnic and religious class barriers. For three generations after the Civil War the country had been dominated politically, economically, and culturally by a tiny upper-class white Anglo–Saxon Protestant elite heavily concentrated along the eastern seaboard. In many ways, Rockefellers, Mellons, Lodges, and Roosevelts had run the country primarily for the benefit of themselves, but they had always taken seriously notions of public service and top-down responsibility for others. The columnist Joseph Alsop, who was born into that upper-class world of British ancestry, Episcopal boarding schools, exclusive private clubs, and debutante balls observed late in life that before World War II the Protestant Ascendancy had made all the society's crucial decisions. (Joe Kennedy thought the inner circle numbered only 50.) Most were related by marriage, business, and school ties. Alsop's mother, for example, was Eleanor Roosevelt's first cousin, and Alsop got his first job as a reporter because the publisher of the *New York Herald Tribune* was a family friend. Although the depression of the thirties had destroyed the elite's cockiness, WASPs remained in firm control of the country at the beginning of World War II.[8]

The war, however, proved fatal to the establishment's power. Military expenditures in the South and West had produced new elites, war industries created meritocratic tycoons, such as the shipbuilder Henry J. Kaiser, and younger Catholics and Jews had gained confidence, experience, and acceptance as officers on the battlefront. After the war, veterans who had little use for ethno-class divisions battled older leaders over this issue in the business world. Over time, meritocracy triumphed. Part of what made the early sixties a promising time was the sense of Americans having greater opportunities that came from the decline of ethnic prejudice. Barriers, however, crumbled unevenly. In the late forties white ethnic politics waned, and many white Americans married across ethnic lines for the first time, but Protestants, Catholics, and Jews well into the fifties tended to marry inside each of those three major groups. College fraternities often discriminated on religious grounds, but by the early sixties hostile public opinion sometimes forced fraternities to deny the existence of the discrimination that they actually practiced. Race was a different matter. Interracial activities, especially marriage, remained generally taboo.[9]

The generation that had come of age before the war found it hard to accept the new, more open reality. The fifties boom tended to obscure the tensions under the surface in that supposedly placid decade. Private doubts seldom produced public expression, but the name Levittown suggested who was moving to the suburbs in large numbers for the first time. Controversies over "exclusive" country clubs occurred throughout the fifties and usually ended with Jews and Catholics founding their own clubs, ostensibly open to all moneyed persons but commonly failing to attract any WASPs. As late as 1963, 72 percent of country clubs barred Jews. During the fifties the elite retained control of key institutions. For example, Yale University continued to discriminate against Jews in admissions, and every top administrator at the University of California was a WASP. Control, however, clearly was slipping. The WASP-owned and establishment-oriented *New York Herald Tribune* lost ground to the more broad-minded *New York Times*, whose owners were Jewish, and the rising entertainment industry was predominantly Jewish. Labor leaders, too, were Catholics and Jews. Despite these trends, the old guard resisted change. As late as 1962, the historian Carl Bridenbaugh, descended from the Virginia gentry, questioned, in his presidential address to the American Historical Association, whether Americans whose ancestors had arrived after the Revolution were qualified to write colonial history.[10]

Richard Goodwin, who became a speechwriter for Kennedy, was one member of a talented younger generation of upwardly mobile Jews. In the fifties he had triumphed at Harvard Law School, clerked for Justice Felix Frankfurter, and went to work on Capitol Hill. As a committee staffer, he helped uncover the television quiz show scandal in 1959. According to one account, he used his Jewish identity as a bond with an embittered and unappealing Jewish contestant to draw out the truth about the payoffs and manipulations. The show's Jewish managers had preferred, based on audience research, to have the top prize won by a handsome young WASP, Charles Van Doren, the son of a prominent Columbia University professor. Using his Ivy League identity as a bond with Van Doren, Goodwin extracted a confession from the bewildered phony winner. Goodwin was incredulous. Van Doren, scion of privilege, had thrown his reputation away for a cheap payoff – largely so he could have his own apartment in trendy Greenwich Village. The epiphany came to Goodwin when he realized that smart, savvy, upwardly mobile men like himself would, if they too could avoid succumbing to cheap temptation, triumph in the years ahead over hothouse WASPs who, perhaps in power uncontested for too long, had known no struggle and had lost their moral bearing. By 1960 young Catholics and Jews, rallying around Kennedy, were eager to push aside what remained of the Protestant Ascendancy. Their enthusiasm and sense of arrival also made the early sixties a promising time.[11]

This was not a contest for power. Rather, it marked the point where the WASP elite lost its energy, or indeed even its reason to exist. One of President William Howard Taft's great-granddaughters, shortly before marrying an Italian American, perceptively observed that energetic people seemed to come from newer immigrant stock. (Her fiancé had an MBA from Stanford.) She hoped, but was not certain, that this point would offset likely family criticism for a religiously inappropriate marriage. The new forces, and they included Mormons in Utah and Baptists in the South as well as Catholics and Jews in the older cities, were excited by opportunities. Although business would be the main focus, government was also important to these younger Americans. Generationally tempered by World War II, they embraced government with enthusiasm. "I am *strongly* allergic to conversation," wrote John Kenneth Galbraith, "as a substitute for action." (Galbraith was an outsider as a rural Canadian-born Baptist of Scottish ancestry.) They were confident that problems could be solved, and they blamed society's existing problems largely on the old elite's lack of will to tackle difficult issues. There was some truth in this argument. But the WASP establishment's preference for the status quo, although no doubt convenient to those who were comfortable, also came from a kind of wisdom derived from experience. The fading elite knew, better than did the newcomers, that it was difficult for government to accomplish goals and that overpromising and overreaching could prove disastrous.[12]

The Kennedy administration attempted ethnic balance in its major appointments. Until it was learned that Robert McNamara was Episcopalian and not Catholic, as his name might suggest, no cabinet post could be offered. Kennedy was determined that his brother would be the only Catholic in the cabinet, lest the administration be termed a Catholic one. The WASP facade at the top obscured from view the predominant Catholic–Jewish character of the lower appointments and especially of the White House staff. Goodwin, Myer Feldman, and Walt Rostow were Jewish, while Arthur Schlesinger, Jr., Ted Sorensen, and Pierre Salinger had partly Jewish ancestry. Ralph Dungan, Harris Wofford, Kenneth O'Donnell, and Lawrence O'Brien were Catholic. Despite jokes about the administration's ties to Harvard, what was more striking inside the White House was the absence of the WASP elite. The only member of that group to rank high in the administration was McGeorge Bundy. Ethnicity on the staff was not an issue inside the administration, which was concerned only with merit and loyalty to Kennedy, but ethnic consciousness did affect the way the administration approached certain situations, especially where elite WASPs were perceived as obstacles. Hence, Bundy and Sorensen declined to join any club to avoid awkwardness over discrimination against others, Kennedy eventually cancelled 22 White House subscriptions to the *New York Herald Tribune*, and the administration showed disdain for the WASP-dominated State Department.[13]

Much of the talk inside the government about youth and vigor were code words disparaging stuffy old WASPs. Ever since the days of Joe McCarthy, the State Department had been suspected of harboring, if not communists, at least an effete elite. In a country where knowing a language other than English was often embarrassing admission that one was an unassimilated immigrant, the middle class rarely mastered foreign languages. In 1960, 56 percent of American high schools taught no foreign languages. Members of the upper class were among the few who did learn languages in prep schools and elite colleges. The State Department had long harbored the offspring of the upper class dripping with Ivy League degrees and elite surnames as first names. (One official had the curious name of Outerbridge Horsey; he went by the nickname Inner.) State Department pay was low, but since one was presumed to have family money, poor compensation mattered less than one might expect. To the Kennedys, and to their hatchet man, Chester Bowles, a thorough cleaning of State was in order. The administration, however, found that it could not drastically change the pattern of employment. However, Kennedy did appoint younger ambassadors, which favored those who had entered the Foreign Service after the war, when ethno-class barriers had begun to decline.[14]

In addition to crumbling ethnicity, another part of the upheaval in family life had to do with changing sexual attitudes and practices. As late as 1920, if a teenage girl from a prominent WASP family got pregnant, she might well be sent away permanently and never mentioned again. Sometimes the family would move to a new locale to avoid gossip. European immigrants were scarcely less conservative, and those who sought upward mobility had to conform to elite norms. Women at Wellesley College were told never to allow a man to kiss them unless they planned to marry. The students knew so little about sex that most believed that kissing produced babies. Before World War II sex was rarely discussed, publishing information about sex was illegal, and movies were censored. During the war millions of men went overseas and met women who had freer attitudes; some brought back brides. At home, women became more assertive. Wartime upheaval caused traditions to be challenged, including prudish ideas about sex. The postwar rise of Freudianism and the decline of the Protestant upper class accelerated the change. By 1960 the country was ripe for a sexual revolution. "This administration," joked the Kennedy aide Theodore Sorensen, "is going to do for sex what the last one did for golf." In Washington society, conquest was more highly valued than chastity. "Power and marriage," privately wrote the Kennedy adviser and journalist John Bartlow Martin, "are not compatible."[15]

Popular culture changed, too. In this promising time, public expression of private thoughts about sex challenged older mores. After the Korean War ended in 1953, Hugh Hefner launched *Playboy*

with Marilyn Monroe on the cover of the first issue. Ten years later
Hefner explained his sex-focused, hedonistic ideas in a series of es-
says called "The Playboy Philosophy." In 1956 Grace Metalious's
Peyton Place was published. A year later, this story of multiple
extramarital affairs in a small New England town came out in paperback and sold six million copies. Its female characters rejected
traditional values. In 1962 Helen Gurley Brown articulated a female pleasure-seeking view in *Sex and the Single Girl*. Movie directors found ways of challenging the censorship code indirectly.
The Cold War spoof *One, Two, Three* (1961) opened with a West
Berlin billboard showing a bosomy blonde drinking Coca-Cola as
the voiceover hailed "all the blessings of democracy." Facing falling
ratings, the comedian Groucho Marx revamped his television quiz
program by adding "a spritely young semivirgin with oversized
knockers...." Standards, however, did still exist in the early sixties. For example, the words "rape" and "abortion" could not be
spoken on NBC News. A stodgy editor at the *Saturday Evening Post*
declared that readers had no interest in sex scandals, but in 1963
the writer Stewart Alsop advised that financially troubled magazine,
"We need more tits...."[16]

Censorship about sex declined. In 1956 Lawrence Ferlinghetti,
owner of San Francisco's City Lights Books, had published Allen
Ginsberg's *Howl*. A year later a landmark local court ruling cleared
both the author and publisher of obscenity. Despite that case, censorship remained a serious issue in the early sixties. In 1961 Grove
Press published Henry Miller's *Tropic of Cancer*. In addition to
foul language, the book presented an "anarchic" worldview. After
the *New York Times* accepted an advertisement, Greenwich Village bookstores were willing to stock or even display the volume.
Ferlinghetti had no problem selling it in San Francisco. Nevertheless, Miller's book drew 61 court challenges for obscenity, until it
was cleared as a serious literary work by the U.S. Supreme Court in

1964. Success with Miller led Grove Press to sell the Beat novelist
William Burroughs's more daring *Naked Lunch*. Originally published in Paris in 1959, that novel was imported in 1962. Grove did
not dare print it in the United States until after the Miller decision.
Court approval of Burroughs's book in 1966 ended attempts to
censor serious literature. In the early sixties publishers encountered
other forms of resistance. Ferlinghetti's printer refused to set the
word "fuck" in the first issue of *City Lights Journal*, and Ferlinghetti
could not replace the printer because of money owed which could
only be paid through sales of the publication. By 1963 censorship
faced frontal assaults from Ed Sanders's *Fuck You* magazine and
from the sexually explicit performance art of the comedian Lenny
Bruce, whose frequent arrests drove him out of every city except
liberal San Francisco.[17]

In the early sixties freer attitudes were found especially among
young Americans. Youth culture had emerged after World War II.
By the mid-fifties teenagers, sensing upheaval, no longer took cues
from parents. Instead, they clumped together in peer groups that
were influenced by popular culture and mass media. Although
movies and television played a role, white teens were especially
drawn to black music. Affluence enabled middle-class youths for
the first time to own personal radios or record players. They listened to Little Richard and Chuck Berry as well as Elvis Presley.
"Rock and roll," as it was called, appalled parents, but teens found
that the new music expressed their own feelings with an honesty
that was lacking in the adult middle-class world. Young people understood and appreciated the lyrics as a subversive counterattack
upon mainstream propriety. Rock and roll gave public expression
to private thoughts, undermined the old order, and helped create the
mood of a promising time. Alarmed adults became hysterical about
juvenile delinquency, which became a major theme in movies such
as *Rebel without a Cause* (1955) and *Blackboard Jungle* (1955).

Ironically, actual teen crime was low. Young people received mixed messages about sex. While 72 percent of adults believed that birth control information should be available to anyone, only 13 percent approved of high school students going steady, a practice that was blamed for premarital sex. In contrast, 59 percent of high school students approved of going steady.[18]

College students were puzzled by changing sexual standards. When the Catholic activist Dorothy Day lectured at secular colleges, she got many questions on overpopulation, birth control, and abortion. Despite freer talk, old practices largely remained: 75 percent of single female college graduates were virgins in 1965. Perhaps this fact is not surprising, since half the men said that they wanted to marry virgins. Middle-class men did not expect to have premarital sex with middle-class women. Prostitutes and working-class women sustained the middle-class double standard. As changes in popular culture spread throughout the society, children were also affected. Kate Corwin had a conversation with her eight-year-old son.

> Tony said, "I don't like Paul."
> Kate asked, "Why?"
> Tony explained, "He says things like 'Aw, fuck.' "
> She said, "That's a very offensive word."
> He asked, "What does it mean?"
> She stalled, "What does what mean?"
> He said, "Offensive."[19]

For most of the twentieth century, Margaret Sanger and other feminists argued that the crucial difference separating men and women was childbearing. Women, according to Sanger, had been deprived of opportunities because of pregnancy. Sanger devoted her life to the invention and perfection of a reliable female birth control pill, so that women themselves could control childbearing. After trials during the 1950s, the pill was marketed in 1960. As is often the case with innovations that have profound long-term consequences, its use at first caught on slowly rather than rapidly. By

1965, 20 percent of women of childbearing age used the pill or other contraceptives. Only in the late sixties did birthrates drop dramatically. While the pill's popularity grew during the rising hedonism of the decade's later years, cause and effect are difficult to prove. Because this medical innovation gave women the freedom to plan pregnancies, they could choose to have careers. In the early sixties, however, female careers were still rare, the age of marriage remained low, and birth rates remained high. In 1960 the average American woman married at 20; her husband was 22. In 1940 the comparable numbers were 22 and 24. In two decades the average family had grown from two to three children. Jackie Kennedy even got pregnant in the White House, although the baby, Patrick, died almost immediately after birth.[20]

In contrast with shifting class, ethnic, and religious lines, and with freer talk about sex, marriage seemed stable as an institution in 1960. Few considered living together out of wedlock; landlords routinely evicted unmarried couples. The double standard prevailed, and premarital sex for women was condemned as sluttishness if not prostitution. Young, single women were terrified of pregnancy, which could only be terminated through abortions, which were usually dangerous, expensive, and illegal. According to rough estimates, from 750,000 to two million of these operations each year killed 5,000 to 10,000 pregnant women. Many believed these deaths just punishment for illicit sex. The topic, however, had long been "taboo" for public discussion. When the journalist John Bartlow Martin reported on abortion in the *Saturday Evening Post* in 1961, the magazine's mail overwhelmingly condemned both the procedure and any mention of it. Unprecedented coverage in a mainstream publication showed how a promising time promoted public expression about private matters. Abortion was illegal in all 50 states, and few legislators in the early sixties wanted any change. In those years young, single, pregnant women often were euphemistically said to be "visiting an aunt in the country." They entered secretive homes for unwed mothers, with babies placed for adoption. The word "pregnant" was considered sufficiently off-color that conservatives avoided it. Instead, women were "in the family way." Single parenthood as a concept did not exist. Widows or divorcees might be single parents, but no one could imagine that a young woman would seek to have a child out of wedlock and raise it on her own.[21]

The concept of same-sex marriage also did not exist, and homosexuality could only be discussed in whispers and almost never in print or on camera. In the fifties conservatives considered homosexuality a crime; liberals, influenced by Freud, urged treatment with psychoanalysis. Oddly enough, it was during the conformist, homophobic fifties that gays and lesbians began to organize among themselves. To the public, the word "gay" still meant "light-hearted" and had nothing to do with sex, although gay did have a coded meaning among male homosexuals. The decline of censorship led to mainstream books that incorporated homosexuality, such as Allen Drury's *Advise and Consent* (1959), James Baldwin's *Another Country* (1962), and Mary McCarthy's *The Group* (1963). In 1961 Illinois became the first state to allow homosexuality among consenting adults. In another example of rising public expression about private matters, the press by 1962 began to report on gay communities. Because most homosexuals remained closeted, however, few demanded rights. Public understanding was limited. When Jackie Kennedy's stepbrother, Gore Vidal, ran for Congress in 1960 in a rural district, he was advised to counter rumors about his sexuality by bringing a woman to his campaign appearances. Marriage was the norm, and virtually all Americans either were married, had been married, or expected to be married. Despite obvious tension and hypocrisy, such a system had the advantage of defining roles clearly.[22]

The pressure for marriage can be seen in the life of Allard K. Lowenstein. By 1960, the still single 31-year-old lawyer and budding politician seemed increasingly at loose ends. "You will be far happier," one friend advised, "...when you are married." His mother had already introduced him to suitable Jewish women, none of whom impressed him. Instead, Al fell madly in love with Barbara Boggs, the vivacious daughter of Rep. Hale Boggs, a liberal congressman from New Orleans and Democratic party whip. Part of the attraction was her father's connections, but 21-year-old Barbara also moved in a circle that included other lively young people, notably her brother Tommy, her sister Cokie, and Cokie's good friend, Steve Roberts. Barbara, who, like her sister, had been educated in Catholic schools, was swept away by Al. They shared a belief in social change, a contempt for leftover, useless tradition, and a desire to improve race relations. Both felt that they lived in a promising time. In 1960 civil rights workers stayed in the basement of the Boggs's home in Washington before heading South, a fact that would have angered most of the congressman's white constituents if they had known about it.[23]

The love match of Al and Barbara appalled both sets of parents. The Lowensteins could not understand why their son wanted to marry a southern Catholic. As a secularized Jew, Al's father – who counted ham among the specialities in his restaurants – had no particular concern about religion, but both Lowensteins worried that Barbara would raise devoutly Catholic grandchildren. The Boggs family's objections were religious and personal. Barbara's mother had doubts about crossing the religious barrier; Hale questioned Al's lack of a stable career. As a practicing Catholic, Barbara took marriage seriously. For months, she agonized. Barbara, who went to work in the Kennedy White House, resolved to go through with the marriage, but the wedding date was postponed several times. In the end, religion mattered. Al was willing to marry in a Catholic service, but when Barbara insisted that their children be raised Catholic, he balked. Unable to imagine her children being brought up without her religion, she broke the engagement.[24]

If Al and Barbara had met five years earlier, in the mid-fifties, their friendship would probably never have blossomed into love. In that more conservative age, each would have found crossing the religious divide too difficult. But because barriers had been crumbling during the postwar years, and because the civil rights movement, which was important to both Al and Barbara, had shown that barriers inhibited contact and stifled humanity, both were open to make the effort in the more promising time of the early sixties. "The ecumenical search," privately wrote one Protestant minister, "is interconnected with all the other longings to bridge other disunities in our lives." In the end, however, both Al and Barbara were sufficiently traditional that they could not imagine defying convention and simply going their own way – in a civil marriage, for example. Had Al and Barbara met five years later, they might well in that more secular, self-centered era have lived together. Marriage might or might not have followed, but there would have been no concerns about parental approval, society weddings, or signing promises to priests. In that curious in-between period of the early sixties, they could accept neither total conformity to convention nor bold radicalism. Avant-garde enough to attempt to challenge tradition, they lacked the zeal, the confidence, or the later supportive social environment, to execute their hopes.[25]

Barbara Boggs later married a Catholic political science professor at Princeton University. She served as mayor and died young of cancer. Her sister Cokie married Steve Roberts, who was Jewish, and both became prominent journalists. The Catholic ceremony was performed by Hale Boggs's brother, a priest. Al Lowenstein married a WASP, a Boston Brahmin who complained that he was virtually never home. When he did occasionally show up, Al usually was surrounded by an entourage of young political enthusiasts. His wife rarely had private moments with him. They divorced. In 1964 he helped organize summer volunteers to go to Mississippi and work for civil rights, and in 1968 he engineered, largely through contacts with thousands of friends, Eugene McCarthy's presidential challenge and Lyndon Johnson's defeat. Lowenstein's many diverse friendships had helped persuade him that the Vietnam War lacked any public support. In 1980 he was assassinated by a deranged former admirer whose emotional problems had first become evident during the Mississippi project.[26]

So went the public record. The broken engagement, however, was more complicated than it appeared on the surface. Lowenstein visited many colleges to discuss politics, and he often used student drivers. A number of male students have testified about a peculiar Lowenstein routine. He would travel all day with a driver, fall behind schedule, announce that he was near collapse, and suggest that the two of them check into a cheap motel. Lowenstein would leave the car to book a room and return to tell the student that the only room left had just one double bed, which, unfortunately, they would have to share. After Lowenstein and the student had undressed and gotten into bed, the student would usually turn away. Al would then grab the student from behind in an oddly clinging manner. If no objection was raised, Al might silently hold the young man in this fashion for hours. One friend asked Al bluntly if he was homosexual. He denied it but said that he had a need for this strange form of intimacy. The students that Lowenstein approached in this way were blond, athletic WASPs. One of them was his murderer. It is impossible to sort out the full meaning either of Lowenstein's embraces or of his broken engagement, but that fact itself offers a comment about the period's rigid certainties, conformity, and hypocrisy.[27]

Although attitudes about marriage remained largely conventional in 1960, there was a growing acceptance of divorce, which occurred more frequently amid changing cultural patterns. In 1960 one in four marriages ended in divorce. Before World War II, the rate had been one in six. Opponents, although on the defensive in 1960, wanted divorce to be expensive and even humiliating. It often

was. An assistant professor at Wesleyan University was forced to
withdraw his divorce case from the local court in order to get tenure.
His wife and children then left town, which was socially acceptable.
Presumably, she filed for divorce elsewhere. By early 1963 Peter and
Pat Lawford had decided to divorce, but they agreed to wait until
after the 1964 election so as not to hurt the Kennedy family. They
divorced in 1966. In 1960 no state had no-fault divorce, although
a few, notably Nevada, came close in practice, but in almost every
jurisdiction a well-paid lawyer was needed. In New York, where
adultery was the only practical basis for a suit, witnesses often had
to commit perjury by swearing to imagined unseemly details in
court. When that travesty seemed too great a burden, one spouse
could take an eight-week vacation to Nevada, gain residency, and
thereby a far easier divorce, as shown in Marilyn Monroe's film,
The Misfits (1961).[28]

Monroe's personal life, unfortunately, bore great resemblance
to her role as a loser in the film. Born in 1926 into poverty as Norma
Jean Mortensen, she had after World War II dyed her hair blonde,
painted her lips red, adopted a certain walk, and became Marilyn
Monroe. Although she was the most memorable film star of the
fifties (her cameo in *All About Eve* (1950) remains one of the great
performances of all time), her genius was to create a larger than
film life persona that fitted the decade perfectly. Persons as diverse as
Andy Warhol and Madonna later paid iconographic tribute. In that
last decade of the WASP Ascendancy only a Nordic blonde could
truly be the national paragon of beauty. The only other contender
was the actress Grace Kelly, but she retired to be a princess. The
fact that Monroe's hair was dyed made her more appealing, since
it suggested that Aryanism was as close as a bottle of Miss Clairol.
During the fifties, 30 percent of American women dyed or bleached
their hair blonde. It was the color that went best with popular pastel
pinks, baby blues, and light greens. In that whitest of decades, oak
and mahogany furniture was blond; even margarine was white.

Skin lightener was a major product advertised in *Ebony* magazine. Dark-haired Betty Friedan could not be blonde, so she settled for red-dyed hair, which, unfortunately, turned green in the sun at the beach.[29]

In 1955 Monroe told friends that she had had 13 abortions. She had already been married and divorced twice. The next year she married the playwright Arthur Miller; they divorced in 1961. She was deep into psychoanalysis. By then she was enamored of John Kennedy, who saw much of her whenever he visited Peter and Pat Lawford in Santa Monica. Kennedy and Monroe may or may not have had an affair; Marilyn's testimony to friends often involved fantasy. She certainly sounded willing, even eager, to have a relationship when she sang "Happy Birthday" to Kennedy at a fundraiser in Madison Square Garden in 1962. Dispensing with underwear, Marilyn wore a see-through gauze dress studded with rhinestones. She had to be sewn into the gown, which was so tight that she could not sit. The president thanked her for her "wholesome" song. Jackie was not present. At a private party afterward, Arthur Schlesinger, Jr., watched from a distance as Adlai Stevenson stared at Marilyn's nondress, while a frenetic Bobby Kennedy, according to Stevenson, acted "like a moth around the flame." Marilyn saw the president privately. She had believed, friends reported later, that Jack would get a divorce, marry her, and make her first lady. Marilyn learned that this would not happen. Eleven weeks later she died from an overdose of sleeping pills. Newsstands sold out all their papers. Dark Jackie, not blonde Marilyn, would be the icon of the sixties. WASP was over, and black was beautiful.[30]

The decision to seek a divorce was difficult. When a husband deserted a wife who had never worked outside the home, she felt abandoned and without an identity. A friend of Clare Boothe Luce's disclosed her crumbling marriage. She reported no appetite, insomnia, and fear of a breakdown. She had no plans, no future. This was not a promising time. She worried about the children, who were adopted. If wives could be chosen and "*un*chosen," could adopted children? "It's a sort of murder. . .," she concluded. The wife of an alcoholic considered divorce several times, but she felt too dependent upon her husband, perhaps both psychologically and financially, to do so, despite the fact that she earned a small income in sales. Sometimes a spouse felt there was no choice. Despite counseling and children, Marthe Rexroth finally left her husband, the critic Kenneth. She told him, "I wonder what it would be like not to expect to be socked or slapped or stepped on or spit on." Her husband's lover advised Kenneth, "Divorce is always so miserable, it lightens the emotions to get away from scene of crime." Rexroth quickly fled to Europe. Attitudes about divorce could be quite rigid. At a celebration of a wedding anniversary, one woman was asked if she had ever contemplated divorce. She replied, "No, divorce never – murder often." To some, divorce and murder were equally immoral. Her husband mused, "I do not think it was too far from the truth."[31]

One of the major reasons for a growing acceptance of divorce was the spread of Freudian or neo-Freudian views throughout the culture. Earlier generations had subsumed questions about the conduct of sex inside the permanent institution of marriage as a matter for adjustment and accommodation, but younger Americans held a more sex-centered view of the world that linked sex and happiness in quite specific ways. In this new view, marriage was the by-product rather than the core value. If a particular marriage did not bring sexual fulfillment, the resulting unhappiness was sufficient grounds for divorce. Furthermore, the new psychological way of looking at matters recognized that people changed over time. A once satisfactory relationship could turn bitter or boring, and these states of unhappiness could form the basis for divorce. In a promising time, was not unhappiness by itself reason enough to part? Furthermore,

the widely read Kinsey reports (1948 and 1953) promoted divorce
by suggesting that a married couple's sexual incompatibility, which
might develop over time, was a problem that, in the absence of successful marital therapy, might require a change in partners. In 1960
few Americans yet subscribed to marriage or divorce as matters
of personal freedom, as would be the case a decade later, but the
trend toward that outcome could be seen in the self-indulgence suggested by the proposition that relationships were mostly a matter
of self-defined personal happiness.[32]

The growing acceptance of divorce in the early sixties, as well
as its changing nature, can be seen in the life of Supreme Court
Justice William O. Douglas. The justice scandalized much of official Washington by marrying four times, with a hasty divorce pre-
ceding each of his last three marriages. Furthermore, each bride
was younger than the one before. He was more than double the
age of the last two. A brilliant intellect, a prolific writer of popular
books, and a global traveler who loved the wilderness, the justice
was a rugged individualist who cared little for public opinion. A
talented professor at Yale University, Douglas had been brought to
Washington in 1934 by Joe Kennedy to work for the Securities and
Exchange Commission. Three years later Douglas, with Kennedy's
support, chaired the agency. The two remained close friends, and for
years Kennedy sent Douglas a case of expensive scotch each Christmas. (In his second divorce, an irate Douglas accused his wife of
stealing four cases of the scotch from the house.) In 1939 Franklin
Roosevelt was sufficiently impressed with the 40-year-old Douglas
that he named him to a seat on the Supreme Court, where he served
an unprecedented 36 years.[33]

In 1953 Douglas shocked Washington by divorcing his first
wife, Mildred. They had been married nearly 30 years. Divorce was
not acceptable at that time, and the justice received letters suggesting
that he should resign, because it was improper for a divorced man to

serve on the court. Adlai Stevenson, who was also divorced, became the first divorcee to run for president in 1952, and his marital status was an issue in the campaign. Douglas did not take the controversy about himself seriously. He saw no reason to mix public and private matters. The justice was more concerned about the high cost of the settlement with Mildred, which he had felt pressured into accepting. Not only did she get the townhouse that was located near the court on Capitol Hill, but Douglas was forced to pay her such a large monthly alimony, including an escalator clause that captured part of the justice's increased outside income, that he had to step up his speaking and writing schedule to earn enough money to live on.[34]

In 1954 Douglas married Mercedes Davidson, a divorcee. Nine years later the 64-year-old Douglas divorced her and almost immediately married a 23-year-old college student, Joan Martin. Given the justice's previous divorce and contempt for public opinion, Washingtonians were not surprised by this turn of events. They were, however, pained by the age difference between the bride and groom. "Think of that," marveled President Kennedy. Many believed that the powerful, wealthy, and charming Douglas was shamefully exploiting a naive younger woman. However, attitudes toward divorce had changed so much in just a decade that few advised the justice to resign. "People," one conservative confided to a friend, "don't have the same standards they did." Nelson Rockefeller, also recently divorced, counted on this change in attitude when he decided to run for president in 1964. His divorce did not matter, apparently, but his poll ratings dropped nearly in half after he remarried. Second wife Happy gave up custody of four young children to her ex-husband. When Happy got pregnant, his polls dropped further. Many believed that the timing of the birth in 1964 cost the New Yorker the key California primary and the presidential nomination. Times change. In 1981 Ronald Reagan became America's first divorced president. His divorce was never an issue.[35]

In 1963 Douglas was terrified that Mercedes would cost him as much money as Mildred had. "I don't see how you can finance another divorce," the justice's sister warned. She urged him to stay single temporarily. The justice was pleasantly surprised to learn that divorce had become so acceptable in the intervening decade that in Washington state, which had jurisdiction, a court had recently declared that alimony was not a right. Unlike the first divorce, Bill found both the court and the attorneys speedy, accommodating, and unquestioning. Bill and Joan soon separated, but Bill could hardly afford a third divorce, either financially or psychologically. Joan, however, proved to be a modern woman; she sought little compensation. They divorced in 1966. By then Bill had met an even younger woman, 22-year-old Cathy Heffernan, who not only enjoyed the outdoors but had a rigorous mind. Bill married Cathy, put her through law school, and coached her as a lawyer. The pair lived apparently happily until his death.[36]

Divorce was not the solution to all marital problems. In 1940 Phil Graham wed Kay Meyer, the daughter of Eugene and Agnes Meyer. Eugene, of German-Jewish ancestry, had made a fortune in finance before World War I. He had married the Lutheran Agnes Ernst over her family's objections. In the 1920s the Meyers became part of Washington society. He headed the Federal Reserve, and she collected art. In 1933 Eugene bought the bankrupt *Washington Post* for $825,000 and turned it into a liberal voice backing Franklin Roosevelt. The paper lost $1 million per year, which Meyer subsidized with Allied Chemical profits. Phil Graham grew up Methodist in Miami, graduated from Harvard Law School, and clerked at the Supreme Court for both Justices Stanley Reed and Felix Frankfurter. After military service in World War II, he joined the *Washington Post*. Meyer retired and in 1948 gave the paper to Phil and Kay. Meyer died in 1959. As publisher, Phil hired brilliant editorial writers, bought radio and television stations, made the newspaper profitable by merging it with the *Washington Times-Herald* in 1954, and obtained *Newsweek* in 1961. In the promising early sixties he showed keen interest in satellite technology and began to plan a global media empire. A liberal Democrat, Phil was close to both Jack Kennedy and Lyndon Johnson. He claimed credit for creating the winning ticket in 1960.[37]

A manic depressive whose moods swung from penetrating, upbeat brilliance to dark despair, Phil had a serious breakdown in the late fifties. He was hospitalized and psychoanalyzed. This was the most common treatment for mental illness at a time before drug therapy existed. The fact that Kay's brother was a psychiatrist reinforced this mode of treatment. Phil was also a chainsmoker, an alcoholic, and a womanizer; he and Jack Kennedy whored together, which was a Kennedy family technique for male bonding. In this case, the results may not have been what Kennedy desired. Phil reputedly complained, "I'm better-looking than Jack Kennedy, I'm more successful with girls, I'm a lot smarter. Why is he president?" In 1962 Phil fell in love with Robin Webb, an Australian. He eventually installed her in a house in Washington and introduced her to friends as the new Mrs. Graham. In "a war of nerves," he called Kay "a Jewish cow" and forced mutual friends to choose sides by hosting a series of parties with Robin. Kay considered Phil mentally ill and refused to file for divorce. Agnes, drowning in martinis, was furious that Phil was trying to steal ownership of the *Washington Post*.[38]

In January 1963, at a publishers' meeting in Phoenix, a drunken Phil grabbed the microphone and began to talk about Kennedy's ongoing affair with Mary Meyer (unrelated to Eugene and Agnes). The niece of the conservationist Gifford Pinchot and the ex-wife of the CIA's Cord Meyer, Mary was a WASP, an artist, and a prominent Washington socialite. Her sister Tony was married to the journalist Ben Bradlee; the Bradlees frequently socialized with the Kennedys. According to some accounts, Mary and the president smoked pot in the White House. She was also friends with Harvard Professor Timothy Leary and may have given Kennedy LSD. During Graham's tirade in Phoenix, someone called Kennedy at the White House, and the president, with Kay's approval, sent a military jet to Arizona to fetch Phil. Robin was told to go away. Phil was put in a straight-jacket and shipped to Washington. Kay helped sign Phil into a hospital, but he quickly checked himself out to rejoin Robin in New York.[39]

In Spring 1963, Phil and Robin flew to London, where he tried and failed to introduce her to society friends. Phil did dine with Lady Pamela Berry, a prime source on the emerging Profumo sex scandal. Still a newshound, Phil had sniffed that something important was happening in Britain. John Profumo, the British Secretary of Defense, had been sleeping with Christine Keeler, a high-priced call girl who had also slept with a spy from the Soviet embassy. British law made it hard for newspapers there to print the story, which circulated as gossip for months. Rumors from London trickled to the United States. After Phil's visit, the scholar Isaiah Berlin pointedly wrote to Kennedy's adviser Arthur Schlesinger, Jr., "I am still more concerned about Phil than Profumo." Top Kennedy aides became interested in the Profumo scandal because two of Keeler's stablemates had plied their trade in New York. There was fear that the trail could lead into the White House.[40]

In June Phil returned to Washington, renounced Robin, and checked himself back into the hospital. While he was being treated, a movie was filmed at the hospital starring the actress Jean Seberg. Seberg and her boyfriend, Romain Gary, were invited to dine informally with the Kennedys at the White House. Told that Jean planned to marry Romain, Jackie advised, "Don't. They lose all interest in you once you do." Sebring did marry Gary, but they later divorced. In early August, Phil Graham checked himself out of the hospital, lunched with Kay at their Virginia retreat, and shot himself. Kay became the publisher of the *Washington Post*. Phil, a mixture of brilliance and illness, is somewhat difficult to assess. To William F. Buckley, Jr., Phil was "profoundly and primarily in love with himself." For Phil, an unstable optimist, the euphoric early sixties had proved to be anything but a promising time. The fall guy for the Profumo affair, Stephen Ward, committed suicide the same day that Phil did. Meanwhile, Bobby Baker's Capitol Hill sex ring had been uncovered. One call girl, Ellen Rometsch, had visited with the president. Suspected of being a communist agent, this East German was hustled out of the country on Bobby Kennedy's orders. Even Lady Pamela Berry would have had trouble sorting out all of these sordid events.[41]

By the early sixties intrigue, family disarray, and personal disintegration were beginning to run in all directions. In part, the problem was the era's excessive optimism, which led people to push themselves beyond personal limits. Then, too, Cold War fear increased stress. At the same time, the civil rights movement, which had already gathered massive support inside the black community, was beginning to conduct itself in ways that would force whites to reexamine ideas and practices about race and, more subtly, about other forms of hierarchical power. The collapse of the WASP establishment's power along with the rise of a new Catholic and Jewish middle class created a destabilization that raised questions about the shape of the society. Amid all these changes, the institution of marriage remained outwardly unchallenged, but as we have seen in the case of Al Lowenstein and Barbara Boggs, changes in ethnic relations were beginning to clash with traditional ideas about marriage. Justice Douglas's multiple divorces show the way in which traditional ideas about marriage were beginning to unravel in favor of a more personalist and hedonistic way of approaching sexual relations. Phil Graham was simply out of control. If one looked closely at the institution of marriage as it actually existed for millions of Americans around this time, one found deep anxieties, at least among many educated, middle-class women.[42]

In 1963 Betty Friedan published *The Feminine Mystique* and thereby launched the women's movement. Friedan, who had

written widely as a freelancer for women's magazines throughout the fifties, had noticed for years, in casual conversation, in
interviews, and in surveys done with her former college classmates
(Smith '42), that many educated middle-class women expressed dissatisfaction with their lives as nonworking spouses, mothers, and
homemakers. "I feel so empty somehow," one housewife said, "useless, as if I don't exist." Friedan's attempts to get this story into print
in women's magazines had been resisted, often by male editors, who
declared women contented with their lot. The magazines were filled
with articles telling women how to cook, clean, keep house, and
make children and husbands happy. Advertisers took a similar line
and suggested that women could remove any unhappiness that they
might feel by redecorating, buying furniture, choosing clothes, or
getting a facelift so as to retain or regain sexual attraction from husbands who no longer seemed to pay much attention to them. One
widely recommended cure for boredom was to have another child.
As Friedan noted, postwar women had gotten married at unprece-
dentedly young ages and had a record number of children. Half of
American women were married by age 20. Of those who attended
college, 60 percent dropped out to get married.[43]

Friedan personally recalled an earlier era when at least some
women who graduated from college had planned careers. In most
cases, including her own, they had instead chosen marriage and
children. She recognized her own guilt about her decision to forego
graduate study in psychology, despite a prestigious fellowship, and
she suspected that this feeling was widespread, but, as she had observed, in her youth the only women who actually seemed to have
careers were either old maids or childless women. In her generation,
those role models had been unappealing, but what appalled Friedan
about the conformist fifties was the cultural pressure for women to
marry, have children, and never work outside the home. "Career
woman," she told the press, "is a dirty word now." Because Friedan
had developed a career as a writer, she perhaps could not identify

very well with women who found being homemakers satisfying. To Friedan, one bizarre aspect of the current situation was the way in which professional women writers wrote in the women's magazines as if they themselves were primarily homemakers who happened to write occasionally as amateurs. In other words, the idea of a woman having a profession was so unacceptable that even those who did have such careers tried to hide the fact. Editors, often men, played a role in this deception, but the writers themselves, Friedan knew, were also succumbing to a cultural expectation that women were not supposed to be professionals.[44]

Friedan's discovery of the discrepancy between women's actual lives and the projected happiness inculcated by popular culture and cheered on by the media proved momentous. In her book, which attacked the difference between public expression and private thoughts, she called this split "the problem that has no name," because although she came to recognize a pattern, women lacked language to describe their frustrations. Millions of women, and especially well-educated suburban housewives, had vaguely recognized their own unhappiness. To cope, some had had additional children, and others, including Friedan, had tried the psychological therapy so widely recommended in the fifties. Still others had turned to prescription tranquilizers. In most cases, women found that these attempted cures for their vague, uneasy anxiety had failed. As Friedan stated, the most important aspect of the nameless problem was not the inability to describe it accurately in the conservative language of the fifties, but the fact that women, through the process of inculcation of family and home as the sole reason for women's existence, had lost any sense of identity. "Who am I?" Friedan asked. Women who had been taught by mothers, by husbands, by peers, and by women's magazines to define themselves around family and housework could not imagine themselves existing in any other framework. At the same time, clean floors and clean shirts provided neither intellectual nor spiritual satisfaction.[45]

Suburbanization had no doubt made the problem worse. Women who lived in cities often retained ties to older relatives, to neighborhoods, and to institutions, often ethnic or religious, that enabled people to play more complex roles interacting across generations. The postwar move to the suburbs had largely been about the youthful, upwardly mobile new Catholic and Jewish middle class leaving behind its now embarrassing ethnic neighborhoods and non-English speaking older relatives. The inculcation of a cult of domesticity fitted a suburban reality where male breadwinners commuted, often by train, to jobs in city centers, while women ran households filled with young children. From nine to five the "burbs" belonged to women. As the children grew, much time was spent transporting them in neighborhoods too sprawling to support services within walking distance. By 1960 millions of suburban women were deeply unhappy, but no one talked about the fact publicly, and so each woman privately rationalized that her problem was a personal one. "She was so ashamed to admit her dissatisfaction," wrote Friedan, "that she never knew how many other women shared it." For every woman who took tranquilizers or tried psychoanalysis, there must have been several who either cried quietly or busied themselves in meaningless frantic activity, such as constant redecorating.[46]

When Friedan published a preliminary, short version of her discovery in *McCall's* in March 1963, the magazine was overwhelmed with letters. Sending the mail to Friedan, the editors noted that the response was unprecedented. The letters are fascinating to read, because they are so strikingly similar. Well-written and articulate, the letters are usually written in ink (not typed) and occasionally contain food stains, because the writer has been interrupted by a child while writing at the kitchen table. Frequently, the authors state that they have never written a letter to any magazine before. Often, they disclose that they dropped out of college to get married, a decision that frequently left them feeling ambivalent. In many cases, their children are now half-grown and need little attention. Sometimes, they would like more children, to escape from the boredom, but they state that they cannot have more children for biological, health, or financial reasons. Many writers thank Friedan for putting into words vague feelings of discontent that they have long felt but have been unable to articulate due to inadequate language. A number of writers express relief at learning that they are not the only unhappy women, and some excitedly report that the article has led them to discussions with other women who share similar feelings.[47]

In her book, Friedan did not advocate a feminist revolution, although during a promotion tour she did say that she was leading "a delayed revolution." The women's movement would come later, after millions of women had digested the "problem with no name." (Friedan was the founding president of the National Organization for Women in 1966.) Although Friedan had considered herself a feminist for two decades, she was shrewd enough in 1963 not to get ahead of her audience. At the time the word "feminist" was an epithet. The first feminist movement at the turn of the century had stalled, once women's suffrage had been adopted in 1920, partly because its leaders had gotten too far ahead of ordinary women. The fact that so many women, and especially younger women, were well-educated in 1960 gave Friedan a better chance for success. Of baby-boomer women, 20 percent were college graduates; only 8 percent of boomers' mothers were. As many people had recognized, there was something odd about the postwar habit of middle-class women going to college and then either dropping out to marry or marrying after graduation with no prospect for a career. Women's educations were serving little purpose, a point that frustrated many middle-class women, for whom the early sixties was not necessarily a promising time. Partly drawing upon psychology, Friedan believed that women needed careers to attain identities. A career was not about a job but about "being somebody yourself."[48]

Although Friedan was criticized both then and later, especially by militant feminists in the 1970s, for ignoring both race and class, her own background suggests that her middle-class approach was based upon calculation. After World War II, Friedan had worked as a labor journalist for the United Electrical Workers, one of the Left unions kicked out of the Congress of Industrial Organizations for refusing to rid itself of communists. In that job she had become painfully aware of the problems faced by working-class women, including women of color. In the early fifties, Friedan and her husband had lived in an unusual multiracial apartment project. In *The Feminine Mystique* she portrayed herself as a suburban housewife. At the time she wrote the book, she did live in the suburbs, although her home was an 11-room Victorian rather than a tract house, but her career as a freelance writer meant that she was not a typical housewife. Downplaying her former union work to avoid being smeared as red, she had become sufficiently disillusioned with the working class's rejection of the Left, embracement of consumerism, and endorsement of the stay-at-home mom that she did not look for support from that quarter. Friedan realized that the educated suburban housewife was a more reachable target whose sympathy could be gotten by claiming that the author was also such a person. This was shrewd politics.[49]

While the Cold War was a given, and while the civil rights movement profoundly affected the African-American minority, Friedan's discovery of a contradiction between popular, media-driven happy perceptions and unhappy realities in the lives of many women had far more important implications for American society. The social crisis that Friedan uncovered was broad, deep, and profound. It contradicted the notion that the era was a promising time. Although the crisis had not yet expressed itself in protest and indeed existed only at the level of vague misery, its existence and its large size meant that when it did finally manifest itself during the course of the decade, the entire society would, to some extent, be reconstructed. Women's roles, gender relations, marriage, and sexual practices would change. Few of these profound alterations could have been predicted from the publication of Friedan's book, even after it generated wide publicity, sold more than three million copies, and made its author famous. In 1963 Friedan had disclosed an unpleasant truth: that the supposedly happiest person in the nation, the well-educated, middle-class, suburban housewife with a sparkling new home and impressive time-saving appliances, who was happily married to her hardworking, professionally successful sweetheart and surrounded by cheerful children, was in fact miserable. If such a person was not happy, then what was truly wrong with America?[50]

Friedan's book appeared just as the Kennedy administration tried to grapple with the emergence of women's issues. For 40 years Alice Paul and the tiny Woman's party had advocated the addition of the Equal Rights Amendment to the U.S. Constitution. Since 1940 the Republicans had included support for one version of the ERA at each presidential nominating convention. The Democrats, however, were divided over the ERA. Prominent party leaders, most notably Eleanor Roosevelt, opposed the ERA, because it threatened to undo laws to protect women workers that had been passed during the first part of the century. The Supreme Court had made it clear that it would approve no laws that restricted male workers, but the court, taking a sexist line, had long been sympathetic to laws that protected women workers, because, like children, women were considered incapable of taking care of themselves. Progressives and many union leaders had long held that laws that protected only women by requiring rest breaks or limiting hours of work were better than leaving women in the same unprotected position as men. In the closely fought campaign of 1960, however, some Democrats perceived that the election might be won or lost due to lack of support for the ERA. John Kennedy, taking a cue from union leaders, opposed the ERA, but a zealous supporter issued a letter over Kennedy's fake signature endorsing the measure. After the election, the discrepancy became an embarrassment to the administration.[51]

The deception over the ERA angered women on both sides of that issue, and women's groups also noticed Kennedy's failure to name a woman to his cabinet. Esther Peterson, assistant secretary of labor and the highest ranking woman in the administration, bluntly told Kennedy that he had a problem. The president decided to appoint the President's Commission on the Status of Women. Because Kennedy's relationship with Eleanor Roosevelt had been strained ever since she expressed reservations about his candidacy in 1960, the president named Roosevelt to chair the commission. The world's most famous woman, however, played only a minor role and died before work was completed. Peterson, who came out of the labor movement, stage-managed the commission. In keeping with union opposition, she made certain that the ERA issue was buried. However, she could not prevent commission members from discussing the issue, and support for the ERA inside the commission gave backers the courage to continue the fight elsewhere. Among those stimulated was the black lawyer Pauli Murray, who found striking similarities between the problems of women and those of African Americans. To sidestep the ERA controversy, Murray urged litigation over gender discrimination under the Fourteenth Amendment as well as making certain that the next civil rights bill covered both gender and race. The commission played an indirect role in having gender covered by the later Civil Rights Act (1964).[52]

Although Peterson had buried the ERA issue, which could only have divided the Democratic party at that time, she also recognized that the commission would be regarded as a flop unless it led to some concrete result. Again drawing upon her experience in the labor movement, Peterson steered the commission into recommending a federal law requiring equal pay for equal work by women and men. Members of the commission could agree on this proposal, and it was easy to find congressional sponsors to introduce a bill. The Equal Pay Act (1963), the first "sex discrimination" law, was passed with broad support, although the business community worried about increased federal interference. In practice, the new law accomplished little, since employers who discriminated often simply gave male and female employees different job titles, even when they did the same work, in order to justify pay differences. *Time* employed male writers and editors and female researchers. No researcher could ever become a writer, much less an editor. In 1960 labor markets were rigidly segregated by gender with women trapped in low-paid work: The average woman earned 60 percent of a male wage. Even after passage of the law, newspapers, including the liberal *Washington Post*, routinely advertised jobs by gender. The Equal Pay Act did not ban such categorization as discrimination. Such advertising was prohibited only in 1968.[53]

Tiny changes, often having little real effect, marked much social change in the early sixties. Attacks against bulwarks had to be calculated strategically to have any chance for success. Public expression of private thoughts did occur during this promising time. In a decade that witnessed many pathbreaking books, including Rachel Carson's *Silent Spring* (1962), Joseph Heller's *Catch-22* (1961), and Ken Kesey's *One Flew over the Cukoo's Nest* (1962), Betty Friedan's *The Feminine Mystique* was the most brilliant and the most consequential. A powerful call for middle-class women to reconceptualize their roles, it ultimately was a spur to the greatest upheaval in American society in the twentieth century: Women reconceived and remade themselves. None of that was clear in 1963. Friedan's shrewdness ultimately came less from her leftist background, although her youthful radical values did help her analyze the situation at the end of the fifties, than from her capacity to merge multiple concerns about women, work, and family amid the gradual crumbling of the WASP elite's hold upon the society and its institutions. Without the more fluid culture that was emerging in the postwar years, without the blurring and ultimate collapse of white ethnic lines, without more flexible attitudes about ethnicity, race, marriage, and divorce, it is difficult to imagine Friedan's plea gaining the massive reception that it did. All of that took time, and yet in 1963 the stakes were already visible. The adventure called the sixties was about to begin.[54]

The folksingers Joan Baez and Bob Dylan perform at the March on Washington, August 28, 1963.

(National Archives. NWDNS-306-SSM-4C(53)24.)

CHAPTER FIVE

Cosmologies

In this promising time of political and social change, there was also cultural upheaval. Private thought was less important than the way in which literature, music, and art gave public expression to new ideas. Amid the avant-garde challenge, however, most Americans remained committed to traditional values. In 1960 Americans believed in God and country. According to the Gallup poll, 97 percent believed in God, and three-quarters worshipped at least once a month. Church membership rose from 48 percent of the population in 1940 to 69 percent by 1960. Amid the Cold War, nationalism was so universal that it scarcely needed measuring. Perhaps there were good reasons for all this religion and patriotism. The fears and hopes of the thirties had played out in internal ideological warfare, and then World War II had overwhelmed everyone. In less than four years Americans had been shocked by the attack on Pearl Harbor, by the Holocaust, and by the nuclear bombing at Hiroshima. Each of these slaughters revealed new horrors about the human capacity for destruction. The cumulative effect of these momentous bloody events, not yet fully absorbed in consciousness in the early postwar years due to their recency, their magnitude, and their strangeness, tended toward numbness. When the terror-laden

Cold War was added in, the result was spiritual crisis. The turn to religion in the fifties was, like other aspects of that decade, an attempt to use traditional structures to cope with new, harsh realities. Results proved problematic.[1]

In a mostly Protestant country, the main beneficiaries of a conformist religious upsurge were mainline denominations. In 1960 Methodists outnumbered Southern Baptists, and Episcopalians and Presbyterians, although small in numbers, enjoyed unusual influence in colleges, in the media, and in public life. When an unchurched Dwight Eisenhower became president, Secretary of State John Foster Dulles persuaded him to attend the capital's leading Presbyterian church. Among Protestants, the Rev. Billy Graham urged Americans to turn to God, while the Rev. Norman Vincent Peale offered self-help through the power of positive thinking. A bland product for mass consumption, mainline Protestantism meant mainstream, which was the safest place to swim even after the Senate censured Senator Joseph McCarthy. In 1954 Congress added "under God" to the Pledge of Allegiance. Two years later, in what could be construed as sanctification of postwar consumerism, "In God We Trust" was put on paper money. During most of the fifties the Catholic church remained traditional; its prelates spent much energy denouncing communism. Reform Judaism prospered by pursuing traditional social uplift. Although these approaches were quite different, they shared a common practice of meeting a religious need by giving public expression to traditional practice.[2]

Outward conformity took place in a society badly shaken by World War II. Throughout the fifties, Americans made reference to the war; life was divided into times "before" or "after." Recalling his own prewar innocence, Jack Kerouac in 1953 privately wrote, "No idea in 1939 that the world would turn mad." Because of the trauma of the depressed thirties, few expressed nostalgia for that decade, but older people noted that the country had been changed in a single generation. The writer Janet Flanner observed in a letter that Americans in the twenties had been "naive, silly, hopeful"; now they were "completely different ... less and less tenderhearted or unselfish." Money-grubbing seemed especially pronounced. By the early sixties, the prewar years had become remote and no more relevant as a guide for living than practices in colonial Virginia. Upheaval and loss of confidence in traditional values were powerful stimuli toward conformity. The reorganization of American life that had come about during and after the war had been so drastic that its full meaning had yet to be absorbed. Much of what was called conservatism in the fifties was a sort of contented befuddlement, an inability to comprehend or explain profound change amid a need, partially produced by exhaustion brought about by rapid change, to absorb matters slowly. To accept religious platitudes or to indulge in consumerism were ways to make a comfortable zone for habitation while avoiding hard questions about where the country was or ought to be heading.[3]

Despite the conservatizing influences that weighed heavily upon the fifties and despite the fact that opportunities to push for change were relatively limited, the decade did witness important changes, including unprecedented American involvement with the world, increasing calls for minority rights, rising racial tolerance, and the decline of religious bigotry. In 1958 the new Pope John XXIII began to modernize the Catholic church, and the following year a Zen Buddhist monastery opened in San Francisco. What has made the decade appear to be conservative is the fact that, amid massive conservative rhetoric praising stability, this tendency toward change came largely from the grassroots, was piecemeal, and operated usually without a frankly stated philosophical framework. In the fifties, the artist Andy Warhol later observed, rebellion meant joining a motorcycle gang but ultimately staying in one's place; in the sixties people broke old conventions and did whatever they wanted. The folksinger Phil Ochs caught the ironic duality of the fifties when he said in an interview that the decade had "great perception leading to inaction." In the fifties reformers offered no coherent worldview because they lacked the ability to reconcile the war's horrors with any concept of a good society. Such a concept could no longer be derived from the prewar period, either in a New Deal or anti-New Deal mode, because events had so shattered the assumptions of the thirties that prewar ideals no longer mattered, while the postwar period was still too new, unformed, and undigested to have generated a broadly shared, coherent worldview.[4]

In the fifties conservatism predominated not because of better ideas or the public mood, although many Americans welcomed inaction and tranquility, but because the New Deal's liberalism seemed outdated and thirties' radicalism either ludicrous or traitorous. Conservatism, in other words, temporarily filled a vacuum, in large part because it was fairly benign and made few demands upon anyone, except for those who objected to the command to consume, but the cataclysmic wartime and postwar changes that had weakened liberalism and destroyed radicalism had also shaken conservatism, which traditionally had isolationist and xenophobic tendencies. Fifties conservatism, like the religion of Graham and Peale, was popular but airy. Without a tougher philosophical stance, as William F. Buckley, Jr., argued in the *National Review*, this popularity would, like any light gas, quickly dissipate. Although few except Buckley and the emerging New Left recognized the point in the late fifties, American society was at a crossroads. The lumbering giant of a nation was grazing contentedly, like Elsie the Borden cow, in rich fields, but the overfed beast meandered in cockeyed fashion, seemed at times blind to perils ahead, and appeared ready to tumble off a cliff if not jump a fence. For more than a decade Americans, bewildered by events and scarred by the high cost of thirties ideology, had declined to chart any course. Wandering, however, also had a price.[5]

During the fifties most Americans complacently accepted prosperity with little concern for strong values or principles. For those who appeared to be troubled, Freudian psychology, then at its zenith, blamed the maladjusted individual rather than society and offered redress through personality transformation. During a not yet promising time, when public expression of unorthodox ideas could be dangerous, private thoughts had to be kept to oneself. Analysts were swamped. Social ills no longer needed society's attention or governmental action because they were personal problems best handled on a psychiatrist's couch. Any defiance of social norms, such as homosexuality, also brought calls for treatment. Nonconformists were committed involuntarily to huge state-run mental hospitals or given electric shock treatment. Despite the advice of the pediatrician Benjamin Spock, father's belts and schoolhouse paddles coerced the young. Conform to norms voluntarily or be changed forcibly was the rule. Americans were expected to adhere to a narrow range of acceptable behaviors in an increasingly homogenized society in which overt ideology was rarely stated. The culture of conformity served both as a conservatizing influence and as an implicit, ersatz value system. Because this intellectual structure denied the validity of alternative ideologies, it all but foreclosed direct ideological challenges, and even led the sociologist Daniel Bell to declare *The End of Ideology* (1960). However, the structure's anemic nature also invited sidewinder attacks.[6]

One of the earliest attacks on the postwar social order came from the self-proclaimed Beat Generation, which really meant Allen Ginsberg, Jack Kerouac, and their friends. In 1944, 18-year-old Ginsberg, a Columbia University student, had met 22-year-old Kerouac, a Columbia dropout. Sharing a commitment to writing, they soon became acquainted with 30-year-old William Burroughs, a deeply alienated Harvard graduate. All three were profoundly affected by the war. Kerouac and Burroughs had been thrown out of the military for an inability to adjust, while Ginsberg had avoided the Army by sailing as a merchant seaman. They shared other burdens. Ginsberg was homosexual, while Burroughs was conflicted by his desire for boys, and Kerouac denied his bisexuality. Burroughs, from a prominent Protestant family in St. Louis, was tormented by the class privilege to which he had been born; he received a monthly retainer – largely, it appears, to stay away. Kerouac's parents were French Canadian immigrants to Lowell, Massachusetts. The father had been a printer, the mother a devout Catholic. The son, devoted to his mother, had entered Columbia to play football but quit to write novels. Ginsberg was Jewish. His father was a socialist high school English teacher in Paterson, New Jersey; his mother had been a communist and had such serious psychiatric problems that she had been committed to a mental hospital.[7]

In the early postwar years the trio read widely, talked freely, and wrote prodigiously without publishing. Although not yet committed to giving public expression to their private thoughts, their willingness to share thoughts that challenged prevailing values was unusual. They believed that they were on a holy quest for what they called a New Vision. Disillusioned by the war, the Holocaust, the Cold War, the collapse of the Left, consumer culture, and conformity, they desperately wanted to remake society but recognized that they lacked tools to do so. In their lives and through their writings, they rejected America and its values. "I don't believe at all in this society," wrote Kerouac in a letter. "It is evil. It will fall. Men have to do what they want." They believed that the first step in their quest was to oppose the status quo. Burroughs told Allen Ginsberg, "Repressive bureaucracy is a vast conspiracy against life." Only when all the psychological and ideological poisons generated by society had been purged from their own bodies would they be free to propose a new order. So long as they felt downtrodden, they could not generate their New Vision. Uncertain how they would fulfill that spiritual desire, they knew that writing would be key. By 1948 Kerouac had declared the group "beat," a word that suggested general despair about the world and themselves. To be beat was to be beaten down and out. Beat also stood for jazz and to beat the system. Later, Kerouac defined beat as beatific, but this added meaning, while clever, appears to have been an afterthought.[8]

To gain inspiration, the Beats drew upon Walt Whitman and the alienated nineteenth-century French intellectuals Charles Baudelaire and Arthur Rimbaud. They listened to jazz, and especially to the new "hot" bebop of Charlie Parker and Dizzy Gillespie. "You ain't known nothing about the new hipness in America," Kerouac wrote privately, "till you've dug the younger Negroes who call New York the Apple." Jazz influenced both Kerouac and Ginsberg to write with an open, expressive, long-line rhythm. As time passed, they became aware of vision-seekers in other cultures and noticed the importance of nonwestern religion and drugs to visionary experiences. Eventually, they sought mystical religious experiences outside western faiths. For a time Kerouac tried Buddhism and then returned to Catholicism. Ginsberg studied Hindu ideas and later turned Buddhist. They took drugs. Although Kerouac used amphetamines ("speed"), he never seemed comfortable with drugs and, like so many other American writers, was alcoholic. For almost 15 years Burroughs was a heroin addict. Ginsberg, who was both more sociable and less alienated, tried many drugs in search of vision. He drank little and generally avoided heroin. The Beat nihilist philosophy inspired few followers, and the original Beats remained a tiny group well into the fifties. They could even be viewed as whiny crackpots amid America's Great Barbecue.[9]

In the mid-fifties the Beats suddenly burst into prominence through their writings. They were the first cultural figures in those years to give public expression to private thoughts that challenged traditional values. In 1955 Allen Ginsberg, a performance artist who believed that poetry's power came from recitation before an audience, read his stunning poem, "Howl," before 150 people at the Six Gallery in San Francisco. After each line, Kerouac shouted "Go!" Both poet and audience ended the performance in tears. Sweeping aside McCarthy era repression, Ginsberg expressed honest feelings about both the self and society with a startling and rare public candor. The poem spoke openly about poverty and drugs, alluded to homosexuality, expressed Ginsberg's pain and alienation, and condemned a society that ignored misery, punished nonconformity, and worshiped materialism. According to the poet Michael McClure, who was present, the event unleashed a cascade of emotion because Ginsberg had stated certain truths, had confronted society's hypocrisy, especially about homosexuality, and had claimed the right to criticize the era's conformist culture. "We were ready for it . . . ," recalled McClure, "None of us wanted to go back to the grey, chill militaristic silence . . . we wanted vision." It was not insignificant that Ginsberg had been committed to a mental hospital in 1949 after involvement in a criminal escapade and had been psychologically coerced into an uncomfortable heterosexuality. In the years since, he had tried therapy without success until a San Francisco psychiatrist gave him permission to live an openly homosexual life. Relief at this affirmation of self had inspired "Howl." Not only did Lawrence Ferlinghetti immediately offer to publish the poem, but the respectable *New York Times* covered the Beat poetry movement. *Howl* sold 400,000 copies in 12 years and made Ginsberg a celebrity. The poet had inadvertently opened what would become a countercultural goldmine.[10]

Not long after Ginsberg's triumph Jack Kerouac published *On the Road*. Wishing to give public expression to his deepest private thought, he wrote this novel in a new way. Depending upon total recall, he sat at a typewriter for three weeks in 1951 and, drinking pots of coffee, generated a single 120-foot teletype paper roll of autobiographical utterances. Kerouac later called the method "spontaneous prose." The novelist Truman Capote later declared,

"It is not writing. It is only typing." Although there was more control in Kerouac's technique than he admitted, especially considering his phenomenal memory, he had also reached an important conclusion about fiction writing. Retaining the narrative form, he was determined to purge niceness, politeness, social convention, artful construction, and convoluted subterfuge from his work. "There is nothing to do but write the truth," he confided in a letter. Kerouac tried to capture the zaniness of American life, to present its low-life qualities, to strip away middle-class hypocrisies and pretensions, and to show how people really acted, felt, thought, and talked. When *On the Road* appeared in 1957, some six years after it had been written, it drew a rave review in the *New York Times*, largely because the conservative regular book reviewer was on vacation, and, while other reviews were hostile, the book did well, especially among young people. Half a million paperback copies were sold by 1959.[11]

The book's popularity had little to do with Kerouac's method of writing and a great deal to do with the subject matter and especially the personal philosophy espoused. The author and his friends, the original Beats, were shown enjoying kicks and thrills. The book's hero was the zany, impulsive Neal Cassady. Contemptuous of consumer culture, unafraid of hard labor when necessary to earn subsistence, but unwilling to be tied down to family, career, or place, Cassady embraced a seemingly richly rewarding life of vicarious experience uninhibited by all the rules laid down by postwar conformist culture. It is surprising how many young people read *On the Road* and decided to move either to New York's Greenwich Village or San Francisco's North Beach, where bohemian communities flourished. Ken Kesey left Oregon to take a writing fellowship at Stanford University. He spent much of his time in North Beach, and influenced by the local counterculture, including psychedelic drugs, wrote *One Flew over the Cuckoo's Nest* (1962). After reading *On the Road*, Tom Hayden hitchhiked from Michigan to California.

There he met young western radicals and forged a continental link. The future actor Nick Nolte suddenly bolted Nebraska. Janis Joplin said, "Wow!" and fled Port Arthur, Texas. "It changed my life," recalled Bob Dylan, who moved from Minnesota to Greenwich Village. "Kerouac," said Burroughs, "opened a million coffee bars and sold a million Levis."[12]

The popularity of Ginsberg and Kerouac in the late fifties, especially with younger readers, challenged that decade's conformity and marked the point where massive cultural change began. The sense that norms were crumbling encouraged many to believe that the country was entering into a promising time. Diane di Prima, who became a major Beat poet, had felt the insecurity of being both an outsider and an outcast in New York until the day she accidentally came across *Howl*. Unable to put the book down, di Prima suddenly realized that she shared Ginsberg's sensibility and hostility to the status quo, and she shrewdly reasoned that if there was enough of an audience to warrant publication, then there must be many more such people than she had believed. Instead of seeing herself as one of a hundred oddballs, di Prima now felt that she shared a bond with thousands of people. In New York and San Francisco the mass was large enough to be a self-defined community. Media attention generated more interest in the Beats and in young followers, truly of a different postwar generation, who were soon termed Beatniks. Herb Caen, the San Francisco newspaper columnist who publicized the label, may have devised the -nik ending from the Yiddish suffix -nik, signifying a person, but the -nik spelling also suggested a reference to the Soviet satellite Sputnik, which was put into orbit in 1957. Beatniks, in other words, were of the present moment and possibly, like the space vehicle, dangerously subversive to American tranquility.[13]

The media quickly exploited the Beatnik movement, commercialized it, and satirized it. In an ironic twist that could be read as the beginning of the postmodernist self-referential mocking mode, business shamelessly exploited a counterculture that had denounced the commercial exploitation of culture. Plans to film *On the Road* were abandoned, in part because Kerouac proved difficult, but sensational movies were made, including *The Beat Generation* (1959) and *The Subterraneans* (1960). The latter, based on a Kerouac novel, had to be altered drastically both to obscure the then-explosive interracial love affair that formed the heart of the story and to avoid lawsuits from living persons that Kerouac had described in ways that were too easily recognizable. Television sometimes handled the Beats sensitively, as when 30 million people watched Kerouac read poety to background jazz on *The Steve Allen Show*, but that medium found Beatniks tempting to mock. While the comedy character Kookie, a parking lot attendant on *77 Sunset Strip* (1958–1964), was harmless and lovable, the quintessential media Beatnik was Maynard G. Krebs on *Dobie Gillis* (1959–1963). Straight-arrow Gillis's Beat friend not only had a name suggesting crab lice associated with casual sex among the unwashed, but Krebs went to elaborate and often hilarious lengths to avoid any kind of work, which he seemed to regard as possibly fatal. To most Americans, Beatniks were scorned as unclean, sexually promiscuous freeloaders who sponged off society.[14]

By 1960 media interest in the Beatnik craze had subsided, but the number of young people who chose a bohemian lifestyle was increasing. Coffee houses sprang up in medium and smaller cities all over America. To the annoyance of residents, tourists filled Greenwich Village and North Beach on weekends. Many came dressed as Beatniks. Real Beatnik women wore their hair long, dressed in black slacks or tights, wore dark blouses, and occasionally displayed pieces of odd, handcrafted jewelry. They avoided lipstick or makeup. The men had fairly short hair but often had beards, which were so rare in the United States at that time that they often brought stares, dressed in Levi's blue jeans or hand-me-downs, put on rough work shirts, and donned brown or black French berets.

Originally a sign of leftist solidarity with the working class, berets had become identified with Paris's countercultural Left Bank. Both men and women wore sandals, sometimes made in Mexico from old automobile tires. Unlike later colorful hippie clothes, Beatnik garb was simple, practical, drab, and cheap. It often came from second-hand stores. To a country tiring of fifties conformity, Beatniks offered a highly visible alternative. Furthermore, unlike an organized political movement, they were difficult to repress. Indeed, many Beatniks were conservatives of a sort – libertarians or anarchists, in fact.[15]

By 1961 Ginsberg's poetry sold sufficiently well that he used royalties to make a major trip abroad. Although he had already traveled to Latin America, Europe, and Morocco, this new trip would be his first to the Middle East and Asia. In 1948 Ginsberg, without drugs, had had strange, powerful visions that left him feeling close to or even part of God. For a time, he worried that he was crazy; he feared following his mother into a mental asylum. But wide reading had persuaded the poet that such experiences, similar to visions had by the poet William Blake, were occasionally found among holy men in nonwestern cultures. To attempt to re-realize the transcendant visions that he had once experienced, Ginsberg tried many psychedelic drugs: peyote (New Jersey, 1952), LSD (California, 1959), yage (Peru, 1960), and psilocybin (New York, 1960). Describing one of his Peruvian drug trips as more powerful than LSD, he claimed that "the whole fucking cosmos broke loose around me." Although he had powerful drug episodes, he had no spiritual visions. Ginsberg, however, came to understand that psychedelic drugs could alter the psyche so that personal and social experience had new meaning. This marked the beginning of Ginsberg's personal crusade to change the world by using chemicals to alter inhabitants' mindsets.[16]

In 1961 Ginsberg stopped in Tangier, where Burroughs was living in heroin-hazed exile. After drug experiments there, Ginsberg went to India, where he studied with a Hindu holy man, learned to chant "om" and "Hare Krishna," and took various drugs, including opium. Finding that he could live in India on $2 a month, he stayed 15 months. In 1963 Ginsberg reached Japan, where he and the poet Gary Snyder entered a Zen Buddhist monastery to meditate. By then Ginsberg had to admit that he had been unable to replicate his 1948 visions. While on a train in Japan, however, he had an epiphany and suddenly realized that the quest for spiritual purity had to begin within the self. Any drug-induced vision would not outlast the chemicals, whereas spiritual inspiration could transform the soul and forever change the self. That point, he now realized, was the secret of the world's holy men. His conclusion was breathtaking. "Hurrah," he wrote, "all we gotta do is really love each other." Psychedelic drugs might give assistance in seeking spirituality, but they had to be understood to be of lesser importance. This insight would eventually lead Ginsberg to Buddhism. He then returned to the United States. Arriving in San Francisco three months before Kennedy's assassination, the poet sported a long beard, wore flowing robes, chanted "om," and played tambourines, a new habit that may have inspired his friend Bob Dylan to write "Mr. Tambourine Man."[17]

By the early sixties the Beat writers could not be ignored. Their public expression of private thoughts mattered; their demand for personal change promoted the idea of a promising time. Both Ginsberg and Kerouac had not only sold many books, but both authors, along with a number of other Beat writers, found that major critics began to take their work seriously. The Beat analysis of the ills of American society was, at one level, devastating. Because they were outsiders who denied any allegiance to existing society, their criticism was systemic and total. Freed from loyalty to conservatism, radicalism, or liberalism, their views were not political in any traditional sense. Yet they were not so much apolitical as offering an entirely different kind of politics rooted in new understandings about consciousness and the self. "A revolt in the WAY of thinking," said the poet Gregory Corso in a letter. In that sense, the Beats could be seen as libertarian anarchists. Lawrence Ferlinghetti, who called himself an anarcho-pacifist, declared the poet "the natural born enemy of the state." Their hostility to the Cold War and consumer culture challenged two main anchors of postwar American society, but by expressing this challenge as a personal quest for a New Vision they showed a tendency toward the spiritual rather than the political. Their respect for nonwestern religions opened new avenues for exploration. They were globalists at a time when Americans were having unprecedented interactions with other peoples.[18]

The Beats called upon Americans, particularly young people, to remake themselves in order to remake society and the world. Kerouac's *The Dharma Bums* (1958) envisioned a future in which thousands of young Americans, many Zen-trained, donned rucksacks and hiked in the wilderness both in search of a spiritual communion with nature and to find deeper meaning within the self. The locus of change was to be the self. The methods were to be meditation, drugs, and spiritual seeking. Those with raised consciousness would renounce materialism, racism, imperialism, and war, which was seen as a mass sickness that had infected all societies in the twentieth century. Weariness with the Cold War and fear of nuclear war played major roles in stimulating the Beats to address a general yearning to end war. Rather than seek a political, military, or social solution, they envisioned war as a deeply psychological and spiritual problem, and they urged the global reconstitution of personas so as to make war, the institutions of war, and the political structures that sustained war obsolete. In this sense, the Beats offered a counterculture to existing society. The Beats, however, also advocated tolerance and compassion, free and easy sex, and a generally hedonistic and easygoing attitude toward life. Because they had rejected consumer culture, they cared little about working for money.[19]

In 1960 few Americans subscribed to the Beat philosophy, which remained well outside the mainstream. Even those young persons tempted to try a Beat life were pressured by relatives, friends, lovers, and, in the case of men, draft boards, to go to college, to get married, and to work at a regular job, which meant the five-day, 40-hour week and living and dressing in traditional ways. Nevertheless, the Beats had tapped a nerve, and a good many people found themselves pulled in contradictory directions. Beat ideas, courtesy of the media, had entered mainstream culture and had begun to change it. That explains why curiosity seekers and part-time Beatniks descended upon Greenwich Village, North Beach, or similar neighborhoods in other cities on weekends or on evenings during the summer vacation season. One could go to a Village coffeehouse to hear a Beat poetry reading, which might be accompanied by jazz, Kerouac's favorite music; take in low-budget off-Broadway plays, a new concept, at the Circle on the Square; or attend Julian Beck and Judith Malina's Living Theater, which was founded in 1951. Beck and Malina challenged audiences with confrontational performances that resembled psychological encounter sessions. In 1963 their last play, *The Brig*, explored dehumanization inside a Marine Corps prison. Although the Holocaust lurked unmentioned beneath the surface of this performance, the larger issue was modern civilization itself with its rigidities, stupidities, cruelties, and inhumanity. Their theater closed when these two anarchists were, with appropriate symbolism, jailed for failing to pay taxes.[20]

In the late fifties and early sixties the avant-garde grew, explored new art forms, combined forms, and attracted new, larger audiences. Performance artists such as Claes Oldenburg broke the barrier between visual and theater arts at "Happenings," which started in 1957. Sometimes artists painted whimsically before audiences while jazz musicians improvised; no two performances were ever alike. Three years later Yoko Ono was staging productions that combined art and action in her Village loft. All of these events celebrated an emerging culture of spontaneity. The sudden movement or unplanned gesture was considered psychologically, physically, and culturally liberating and marked the triumph of self over inhibitions, habits, or rules. Avant-garde films included those by the young directors Stan Brakhage and Jonas Mekas as well as Kerouac's *Pull My Daisy* (1959). The Judson Dance Theater staged strange productions, which, beginning in 1962, were designed to break down middle-class inhibitions about the body and sexuality and to bond performers and audience in a shared experience. Dancers flowed freely among spectators and among themselves in a nonchoreographed way. That troop performed 20 public concerts over three seasons. All of these activities challenged norms, crossed traditional disciplinary boundaries, and jarred audiences by juxtaposing concepts that were in tension. Spontaneity and the body were celebrated. The goals were to show that the culture was stodgy, unrealistic, warped, and false, that ideals and practice diverged hypocritically, and that modern life was exploitative and cruel. To those who came to watch, the cumulative effect was powerful. For many, cultural breakthrough was part of what made the early sixties a promising time. Others sensed collapse. "Total distortion ... may be the only vehicle appropriate to the times," observed Ralph McCabe to a friend in 1961. "Error is everywhere," he continued, "and the civilization in which I thought I lived, may not even exist."[21]

The avant-garde artist Brion Gysin, influenced by randomly created collage paintings, suggested to William Burroughs that novels could be composed by randomly combining words from cut-up pages of newspapers or magazines. When Burroughs tried the method, he was surprised to find the results quite comic. More important, Burroughs saw that this method for constructing literary work – it could scarcely be called writing – enabled the creator to escape from the deep psychological and social meanings imbedded in all language that made authors captives of the past. "Words," said Burroughs, "are the principal agents of control." Culture, ultimately, was about language, its usages, and its historical antecedents. Every time an author used a word, it invoked layers of meaning buried deep within that particular culture. Human beings, then, were imprisoned by language, which was the basis, according to Burroughs, of all the world's evils. After all, did not oppression and repression begin with control of language? All who held power, whether the state, the church, or the wealthy, sought to control language. That was why censorship had been so important throughout history. The cut-up method enabled the novelist Burroughs to advance beyond *Naked Lunch* (1959) and to liberate himself and the reader from control, from logic, and from culture in *The Soft Machine* (1961), *The Ticket That Exploded* (1962), and *Nova Express* (1964).[22]

The main goal of avant-garde participants was to break down barriers. During the first half of the century the avant-garde had questioned principles, values, and traditions within customary aesthetic realms. Expressionists, Dadaists, and Surrealists had attacked traditional art's rules, whereas authors such as James Joyce had challenged norms imposed upon writers. Experimental musicians such as Arnold Schoenberg had tried the 12-tone row in place of the usual European musical scale. Jazz had marked another new mode of expression. At that time any rule-breaking within a particular art form was so daring that few could imagine a time when avant-garde practitioners would eagerly cross traditional disciplinary boundaries to explore new terrain at the borders. Although the avant-garde had lurched forward, World War II and the postwar nuclear threat had taken place before new cultural values could influence social or political questions. The postwar avant-garde tried a different approach. Believing strongly that political disasters, past or pending, were rooted in multiple, complex, and pervasive attitudes and behaviors, cultural innovators, considerably influenced by Freudianism, vowed to smash all existing structures, linkages, and lines of authority. Only a general cultural dissolution could free the human spirit from its unnatural, tormented, and repressed condition. The main emphasis was on liberation through destruction of cultural underpinnings. Results could be shocking.[23]

The avant-garde could also influence traditional forms, such as folk music. The late fifties brought a popular upsurge in folk, which was widely available in both the Village and North Beach. Neither Kerouac nor Ginsberg liked folk music, which had been associated with leftist, and especially communist, political activism in the thirties. The old-time melodies were too pretty for the Beats, who reveled in despair, and smacked of nostalgia, which could not appeal to the avant-garde. The Beats had little use for simple declarations of love or for political songs that contradicted their demand to reject politics, in any of its traditional manifestations, in favor of exploration of self and consciousness. Nevertheless, Beat neighborhoods also became the center of a significant folk music revival in the late fifties and early sixties. One reason, perhaps, was that folk music gave public expression to the upbeat mood of a promising time. Then, too, this music appealed to the era's democratic ethos, since almost anyone could learn to play or sing folk songs. In a society where top-down control prevailed, the act of performance gave adolescents a sense of empowerment. Those drawn to folk included the youthful Joan Baez and Bob Dylan. Professional groups provided inspiration. The Kingston Trio, which had played at the Purple Onion nightclub in North Beach, shot to the top of the pop music charts with a single, "Tom Dooley," in 1958. It sold almost four million copies. For the next two years that folk group dominated popular music with five number one albums. Folk music, clearly, had an audience, especially among college students, who bought most long-playing records.[24]

In some ways, the folk revival seems curious and strange. Ever since Elvis Presley had swiveled his hips to stardom on *The Ed Sullivan Show* in 1956, it had seemed certain that young Americans were smitten by rock and roll, as it was then called. A form of black music that had evolved out of rhythm and blues, rock and roll had crossed the racial barrier largely through radio and records, including white artists' toned-down cover recordings. Elvis had soared to the top with a handsome persona, an excellent voice, and an authentic devotion to the music – a white singer with the black sound. Many white teens also listened to Chuck Berry and Little Richard records, although parents may not have known that both artists were African American. White performers like Jerry Lee Lewis and, especially, Buddy Holly also embraced the new music. Rock and roll's popularity tailed off in the late fifties. Presley was drafted, Holly died, Berry and Lewis, in legal trouble, were more or less banned, and Little Richard temporarily returned to his gospel music roots. In the early sixties rock and roll rebounded with a dance song called "The Twist." At the McDowell Colony, a retreat for working writers and artists, middle-aged residents in 1962 danced as four teen rockers played the new music. "I had the awful feeling," one participant conceded in a letter, "of being present in some wondrous spiritual experience and was rather frightened by this performance." Fear, perhaps, explains why rock penetrated no further at that time.[25]

Nevertheless, it was a long way from Presley's "Hound Dog" or Little Richard's "Tutti-Frutti" to Pete Seeger's "Where Have All the Flowers Gone." There was something distinctly retrogressive about the turn from the rock and roll of the mid-fifties composed and sung by youthful performers to the reappearance of Seeger, who had first gained notice before World War II. Seeger's Almanac

Singers had enjoyed success just before the war, but the way in which he had followed the zig-zags of the Communist party line had turned off many from his topical songs. After the war, Seeger, who supported the communist-backed Henry Wallace for president in 1948, learned to use songs in more metaphorical, less overtly political, and therefore palatable ways. In 1950 his new folk group, the Weavers, sold two million copies in six months of "Goodnight Irene," which became the group's signature song. Written by the great black folk artist, Leadbelly, the song embodied the new emphasis on the personal over the political, but for a white group in 1950 to make a hit out of a black composition also made a statement. The Left's longtime commitment to civil rights was one ingredient in the rise of folk music in the early sixties. So, too, was the civil rights movement and its songs.[26]

Also important to the folk revival was the end of the McCarthy era blacklist. Although the Weavers had been crippled commercially in the early fifties after their communist ties were publicized, Seeger and the other Weavers had been able to make a living without either regular radio play or a major recording contract through occasional concerts at Carnegie Hall and a few other venues that refused to honor the blacklist, by occasional guest appearances on radio, and by playing at private schools and summer camps. As a result, a new generation had learned folk songs from old Weavers records as well as school or camp. Because Seeger had always insisted upon audience participation in performances, and because he had written many children's songs, these children had emerged familiar with and sympathetic toward folk songs. In 1955 Seeger was called to testify before Congress about his communist connections, refused to do so, and was charged with contempt. Although his case was ultimately overturned on a technicality, it kept Seeger off of ABC's *Hootenanny* (1963). Other major performers refused to appear so long as Seeger was banned. Ironically, Seeger had popularized the word hootenanny to describe audience singalongs.[27]

The blacklist had no effect on the next generation of folksingers, who were too young to have been part of the Left. The Kingston Trio had, however, shied away from political songs. In keeping with their collegiate image, they had sung mostly about romance, often with considerable humor, or drinking. Drawing on traditional ballads as well as songs from all over the world, they had no coherent style and seldom composed songs. While the Trio's breadth enabled them to gain a broad audience, it also limited their development. As the folk revival gained steam, shrewd observers noted that a more coherent approach might produce greater long-term success. Albert Grossman, an older man who frequented Greenwich Village coffeehouses and bars, spent two years trying to create a new trio. Recognizing the advantage of a female lead singer, he eventually brought together Peter Yarrow, Paul Stookey, and Mary Travers. In 1963 Peter, Paul and Mary had a number-two pop hit with "Blowin' in the Wind," a pro-civil rights composition by the youthful Bob Dylan. Their album containing that song, *In the Wind*, reached number one. Peter, Paul and Mary, unlike the Kingston Trio, did no drinking songs and showed their belief that the era was a promising time by expressing a commitment to the two major political issues of the day – peace and civil rights.[28]

The resurgence in the early sixties of the topical political song, freed from any ties to communism but still distinctly leftist, shows the particular way in which politics flavored this period. ("There are no Republican folksingers," Mary Travers once said.) It was primarily a time of great hope and uplift. About the Village at that time, Dylan recalled, "It was a movement then, a real movement." Unlike the thirties, a good many young people had no faith in political parties and preferred moral movements to political crusades. Thus, they embraced both civil rights and the peace movement with enthusiasm, but support was at the level of a generalized commitment rather than adoption of specific programs. As a practical matter, movement support could often be turned into participation in particular events, such as the March on Washington. However, this style of politics, while creative, inspirational, and capable of uniting large numbers of people either in favor of noble principles or to make protest about specific grievances, lacked the kind of cohesive organizational structure and institutional means to articulate long-term programmatic views or to pick and choose battles for strategic or tactical reasons. Singing folk songs in coffeehouses or at rallies bonded the like-minded young, suggested the power that could come from solidarity, created a sense of generational specialness, and made it easier to organize young people for numerous causes in the later sixties.[29]

The folk revival might well have sputtered out if new stars had not burst upon the scene. Joan Baez, half-Scottish and half-Mexican, first brought her pure soprano to notice in the coffeehouses of Cambridge, Massachusetts. She gained celebrity as the star of the first Newport Folk Festival in 1959. That Rhode Island town, long a summer vacation spot for America's wealthiest families, including Jackie Kennedy's mother and stepfather, had somewhat improbably become the site for a well-known jazz festival. Due to the rise of folk music, and due to the belief that both jazz and folk authentically expressed the feelings of oppressed groups, it had seemed natural for the festival to add folk to its repertoire. In practice, however, the audiences were different, and the folk festival became separate. There was always a certain tension between the thousands of lovers of folk music who descended upon the posh resort and the local residents. Folkies dressed casually, often wearing attire that was considered Beat, spent little money, which annoyed merchants, and sneered at Newport's ostentacious wealth. Although the audience was young, white, and collegiate, the performers included a number of blacks, which further unsettled a community where African Americans were rare.[30]

After turmoil in 1960, Newport banned the festival, which resumed in 1963. That year the well-known Baez invited a still

obscure and unscheduled Bob Dylan to join her on stage in Dylan's
"With God on Our Side." In 1960 Baez's first album had reached
number three in sales. She had large followings on campuses, could
draw up to 10,000 people for live concerts, and appeared on the
cover of *Time* in 1962. She sang both traditional ballads and topical songs about civil rights and peace. Brought up a Quaker in
California, where both Anglos and Hispanics had rejected her due
to her mixed heritage, she had become a devout pacifist. She often
sang benefit concerts for the peace movement, a fact that made her
more attractive to many in her audience. Baez's career had risen
as she sang Dylan's many excellent new songs, and her admira-
tion for Dylan led to a brief, intense affair. Al Grossman, Dylan's
manager, asked, "Can you imagine the offspring of a union of
those two?" The July 1963 Newport Folk Festival ended with Baez;
Dylan; Seeger; Peter, Paul and Mary; and SNCC's Freedom Singers,
who had come out of the Albany Movement, arm-in-arm on stage
singing Dylan's "Blowin' in the Wind" and "We Shall Overcome,"
the movement anthem. The audience of 15,000 joined in. A month
later all of these performers sang at the March on Washington.[31]

Dylan was now a star. His rise had been meteoric. Born Robert
Zimmerman, he had grown up in Hibbing, Minnesota, a decaying
mining town where his family had operated a furniture and ap-
pliance store. After some months at the University of Minnesota,
where he pledged a Jewish fraternity and then dropped out to live
and play music among the local Beats, the 19-year-old folksinger
moved to New York City in December 1960. He changed his name
to Bob Dylan, either to honor the poet Dylan Thomas or, more
likely, inspired by the western television hero, *Gunsmoke*'s Matt
Dillon. (Before becoming Bob Dylan, he called himself Bob Dillon,
wore boots, and claimed to be a western cowboy.) Dylan played his
first gig at an open amateur night at Gerde's Folk City, Greenwich
Village's principal bar for folkies. An early rave review in the
New York Times mattered. In the beginning, he performed other

composers' songs. Especially devoted to Woody Guthrie and his music, Dylan spent hours with Guthrie, who was already seriously ill with the genetic disease that would kill him. A committed leftist, Guthrie had been a prolific composer and popular performer during the folk surge before World War II. Seeger had performed many of his songs. Dylan openly (and brazenly) wanted to be Guthrie's successor, a mantle which could make it easier to gain fame, but which also promised to entangle Dylan in quarrels about the Left. Although Dylan's career moves were usually shrewd, it is not clear that he fully understood the political dimensions. In any case, Dylan became Guthrie's heir.[32]

Dylan began to write his own songs. His politics at this point paralleled the amorphous moralism of the young folk audience. "Bobby Dylan," observed Joan Baez, "says what a lot of people my age feel but cannot say." In a promising time, he gave public expression to widely held private thoughts. As a composer of fashionable topical songs, he embraced peace ("Masters of War") and civil rights ("Blowin' in the Wind"). He could express compassion for prisoners ("The Walls of Redwing") and outrage at injustice ("The Lonesome Death of Hattie Carroll"). In June 1963 the assassination of Medgar Evers had led Dylan to pen "Only a Pawn in Their Game." In one sense, his songwriting resembled that of Phil Ochs, who was a more overtly leftist folksinger. Both men sang about Evers, and both condemned war. Ochs's "I Ain't Marching Anymore" became the anthem of the antiwar movement during the Vietnam War. But there were differences, too. Ochs, unlike Dylan, enthusiastically endorsed revolution. Dylan's "When the Ship Comes In" could be read as a text favoring revolution, but it could also be interpreted as a warning to Americans to take moderate action lest revolution be the result, or it could be considered as an invocation of Judgment Day. (Baez said it was provoked by a hotel that had denied accommodations to a grubby-looking Dylan.) In contrast, Ochs's "Ringing of Revolution" celebrated not only the toppling of an oligarchy but also the overthrow of a middle class in a bloody revolt. Dylan had a generally pacifist stance, especially while he was close to Baez, and never reveled in vicarious bloodshed.[33]

From the beginning, Dylan reshaped and redefined both folk music and popular culture. In keeping with a promising time, Dylan's "With God on Our Side" challenged Americans to live up to the country's high ideals. Questioning the older generation's devotion to the Cold War, the songwriter redefined the idea of being for peace as an act of patriotism. He showed how Americans could give public expression to private thoughts that had long been difficult or impossible for many to articulate. A similar devotion to principle can be seen in his idealistic civil rights song, "Blowin' in the Wind." Both songs demonstrated Dylan's commitment to use frankness to destroy outmoded pieties. His work, like John Kennedy's call for a fresh politics, or like the avant-garde performance artists' experiments, attacked the old order. Ironically, while Dylan called for a new outlook, and while John Kennedy pursued performance politics on television, Jackie Kennedy promoted the status quo's high culture. Like Allen Ginsberg, Dylan was a performance poet whose words worked best when they were heard rather than read. As a composer-lyricist-performer, he could record his own songs, even when they challenged his limited technical skill as a singer, with more power than when they were rendered by other excellent singers.[34]

As Dylan gained experience, he began to write elliptical messages to be deciphered. Such songs were unlikely to be banned on the radio and created meaning inside the listener's head only insofar as the listener had prepared a mental state. When Dylan penned "A Hard Rain's A-Gonna Fall," his most powerful antiwar song, he drew upon both angst about the Cold War turning nuclear and upon metaphorical songwriting technique. Although Nat Hentoff in the liner notes attributed the song to the Cuban Missile Crisis, this was

not true, since it was performed two weeks before that event. However, the Cold War was tense throughout Kennedy's presidency, and
the Missile Crisis only made concrete a general fear that was the
basis for Dylan's lament. In using rain as a metaphor for war, Dylan
may have been influenced by Guthrie, who wrote "Why Do You
Stand There in the Rain?" in 1940. If so, the borrowing had a twist.
In the spring of 1940 Guthrie had defended leftist students who, following the communist line during the Hitler-Stalin pact, had gone to
the White House to protest American preparation for war. While
the students stood in the rain protesting, the president had criticized them to their faces. Although Guthrie implied a rain/war
metaphor, he mainly suggested that militant action would have been
better than polite protest, which was a very different message from
Dylan's ominous nuclear warning.[35]

In the fifties, as a high school student, Dylan had been caught
up in the rock and roll boom. At night he listened to and drew
inspiration from faraway radio stations that brought black rock
and roll, rhythm and blues, and jazz from Memphis and beyond
up the Mississippi River valley to white Hibbing. He sought out
and learned much from a black radio disc jockey who was one of
the few African Americans in northern Minnesota. Forming a rock
and roll band, Dylan drove teachers to fury by playing loud at a
concert in the high school auditorium. He might very well have
begun to write folk songs using metaphorical language based on
his familiarity with rock and roll. It did not take a genius to recognize that Presley's "Hound Dog" was not about a dog. Nor was
Little Richard's "Tutti-Frutti" about chewing gum. Rock lyrics, like
so many other elements of black culture, were subversive, insinu-
ating, teasing, and powerfully and wonderfully destructive toward
authority. Indeed, it was less the quality of the vicarious thrill or the
overt gesture, although one should not underestimate that aspect
of rock and roll either, than it was the explosive sidewinder attack
to the rear that explained rock's power and appeal to powerless

youth. "I played all the folk songs," Dylan later said, "with a rock and roll attitude."[36]

Dylan's earliest lyrics had a straightforward earnestness that both enraptured folkies and turned off a larger audience. He gradually learned from Guthrie, from Pete Seeger, and from rock and roll that subtle, mysterious lyrics pleased better. Word play, rhyme, and onomatopoeia could all be used; popular culture provided context. The "real" meaning of any song was inside the listener's head. In order to stimulate this effect, Dylan used what might be called associational language, that is, he devised lyrics so that each word or phrase was linked to others that followed, preceded, or were unstated but available through popular culture. Psychiatric free association, popular as a parlor game in the fifties, offered a parallel. This use of language could be provocative, as in "Subterranean Homesick Blues," where people, objects, slogans, and events zip by phrenetically, just as in real life, including the memorable final line about the vandals' theft of the pump handles. Critics declared that the smoke rings of the mind in "Mr. Tambourine Man" were proof of drug use, but Dylan denied this interpretation. There is no denying, however, that the song presents powerful images of a man dancing with tambourines. It would be hard for a listener not to envision the scene. The combination of words, then, through linkages, shared values, or juxtaposed opposites builds composite imagery inside the listener's head. Although this process is ultimately self-generated, it is heavily influenced both by popular culture and by Dylan's cues.[37]

This new style of songwriting indirectly owed a debt to the pervasive Freudianism of the fifties. Earlier generations expected song lyrics to be descriptive, persuasive, argumentative, lyrical, or romantic. Using traditional linear thinking, Tin Pan Alley's hits had always stated the obvious, usually repetitively, and thrown in choruses for emphasis. Even as late as the mid-fifties, if someone had tried to write songs in Dylan's associative fashion, audiences would have fled, and recording companies would have had no use for "gibberish." By the late fifties, however, the Beat spiritual quest, the avant-garde assault on traditional culture, and a Freudian-influenced understanding of the way people used words to manipulate society and politics had created doubts about the purity and objectivity of linguistic building blocks. The beginning of what would later be called the postmodern turn could be seen. A good many Americans, especially young people, were ripe for change. About Dylan, Peter Yarrow observed, "He has his finger on the pulse of America's youth. . . ." The novelist Ken Kesey found Dylan's imagist method "subversive." Dylan was no theoretician, but by adopting the particular practice that he did, he led a revolt that undermined the way people thought and felt about abstractions, events, and themselves. Other songwriters, including the Beatles, quickly adopted his technique. This entanglement of emotion and reason in a matrix of associative language would become a hallmark of the sixties.[38]

Although Dylan exploded on the scene in 1963, his best work and greatest influence would occur in the future; during the next 22 years he sold 35 million albums. His first record, produced in late 1961 and released in March 1962, sold only 8,000 copies in one year. As a new artist, Dylan had little control over album content. He recorded four of his own songs, but Columbia Records, reluctant to allow a new performer to do his own work, put only two on the album. By the time of Dylan's success at Newport in July 1963, he had hired the shrewd Al Grossman as his manager and had recorded *Freewheelin'*, which was released in May 1963. That album included the powerful "Blowin' in the Wind" and "A Hard Rain's A-Gonna Fall." Although three songs that used electrical music were recorded and released on a preview version, they were dropped from the final record. The studio seemed determined to typecast Dylan as a folksinger. In October 1963 Dylan recorded his third album, *The Times They Are A-Changin'*, which was released in January 1964. By then, Dylan was aware of the pathbreaking rock music produced by the Beatles, who catapulted to the top of the charts after arriving from England to appear on *The Ed Sullivan Show* in February. Realizing that the folk revival was dead, Dylan appeared at the Newport Folk Festival in 1965 backed with an electric band. The folkies booed and Pete Seeger threatened to cut the power lines, but Dylan's later electric albums easily outsold his early recordings.[39]

The folk revival had occupied a brief period between the rise of the Kingston Trio in 1958 and the arrival of the Beatles in America in 1964. During that time young people of a particular generation looked perhaps backward as well as forward. Not only were the songs of the folk revival often old, familiar melodies known to parents and grandparents, even when the lyrics were updated, but the mode of group singing was a standby in churches and union halls. The political content, stressing peace and brotherhood, was sufficiently vague that it could unite rather than divide the audience and express a generalized hope rather than pledge listeners to commit to a particular program. In many ways, folk music both gave public expression to private thought and fitted the optimism of a promising time. At some level, the political nature of these songs is important because it shows that young people in the early sixties shared aspirations, in a general way, with the youth of the thirties. If the oldsters had had vast dreams but lived large nightmares in the depression and global war, the youth had more tempered dreams marred by nuclear fears. What had been lost, in addition to ideology, was the capacity for ordinary political organization. The civil rights movement, and all the movements that followed, offered new definitions about politics as well as new modes of organization, but the absence of traditional political forms limited how issues could be handled. In the end, as Dylan realized when he abandoned folk music, the folk revival marked the end of an older era more than it marked the beginning of a new one.[40]

Despite its backward-looking aspects and aesthetic limitations, the folk revival clearly did form a part of the country's cultural transformation in the early sixties. The trend is most evident in Bob Dylan's work. As we have seen, Dylan, like Allen Ginsberg, was primarily a performance poet who used imagery through psychologically significant associative language that both partook of and contributed to popular culture in order to attack the old order. In a sense, the Beat writers, rock musicians, avant-garde performance artists, experimental filmmakers, and folk composers shared a common enterprise during a promising time. As part of a larger movement, all of these practitioners, as well as new Pop Artists like Roy Lichtenstein and Andy Warhol, challenged the society's political, social, and cultural norms. They attacked the country's complacency and stodginess, supported the civil rights movement's demand for freedom and equality, defied censorship to pursue artistic freedom, and argued that high culture, generally considered to be the traditional preserve of the elite, was undemocratic and, therefore, of no value for Americans. At the very moment that cultural innovators were moving in new directions, the Kennedy administration was creating the National Endowment for the Arts and the National Endowment for the Humanities in order to strengthen the nation's high culture in the competition with the Soviet Union in the global propaganda arena. Official policy and cultural practice diverged glaringly. This cultural split, like so many others, would generate heated controversy at the end of the sixties.[41]

One of the best areas for examining the cultural turn of the sixties is in painting. At the decade's beginning the Pop Art of Roy Lichtenstein and Andy Warhol suddenly challenged the Abstract Expressionism that had dominated the postwar United States. To understand the significance of this startling development, we must recognize that Abstract Expressionism was itself a shocking departure from tradition. Before World War II American artists, seeking to develop a national style that separated the United States from Europe, expressed this idea by painting American people and places, including workers and industrial sites. To portray the ordinary as heroic was a main idea of Socialist Realism, which was sanctioned by the Left as an art to inspire the masses. The war had destroyed the isolationism that enabled painters to work apart from the rest of the world and had called uplift into question. The Cold War made any style that was communist-approved suspect and put artists, who often retained leftist sympathies while disapproving of communism, in the position of finding a mode of expression that could be critical of complacent American capitalist culture while at the same time not fall victim to McCarthyite repression.[42]

Unlike literature or music, art traveled poorly. In the thirties American artists could not afford to go abroad. In the prewar years reproductions were expensive, scarce, and generally of poor quality. Few European avant-garde artists' works reached the United States. American collectors did not buy such art, galleries did not show it, and museums did not acquire it. Paris had long been the world's art center, and when the Germans invaded in 1940, the Paris art market effectively closed. The fall of Paris shocked many in America; when the writer Aldous Huxley heard the news, he turned white. Many avant-garde artists, including Max Ernst, Fernand Léger, and Piet Mondrian, fled to New York. They joined earlier emigrés who had arrived after the Nazis took over Germany in 1933. Suddenly, New York galleries were filled with the works of leading European painters. The number of galleries increased from 40 in 1941 to 150 by 1946. Many of these artists were Surrealists or had been influenced by that movement. Their brightly colored, wildly distorted, and highly symbolic paintings used semiabstraction to present psychological explorations of personal topics. American artists, already bored with Socialist Realism, could not help but be influenced. Unfamiliar with the subtleties of European culture, American painters did not become Surrealists, but they were influenced by both the abstract elements in these paintings and by the psychological focus.[43]

The war, the Holocaust, the bomb, and the Cold War led to Abstract Expressionism. Traumatized and even enraged by these events, painters grappled for a way to express fear, anger, and desperation. Angst fed Abstract Expressionism, a style of painting in which the artist, often a war veteran, conveyed deeply personal meaning through abstraction and affirmed the importance of individual vitality through a particular mode of expression. To Robert Motherwell, Mark Rothko, Jackson Pollock, and other practitioners, the key was the painter's devotion to the blank canvas and the paint laid upon it. Pollock, the most brilliant and innovative of these painters, placed his canvases on the ground and splashed and dripped house paint upon them. His pictures exploded like atom bombs. Although a painting's design was abstract, that is, nonrepresentational, that did not indicate that the painting lacked meaning. "You cannot separate me from my paintings," he declared, "they are one and the same." The artist, after all, chose working materials, preparation, and technique. Each precise color had quite different effects on viewers, especially when placed in conversation with other colors, and different styles of workmanship produced varied results. By emphasizing personal expression of their own feelings in these pictures without reference to represented objects, artists affirmed both individuality and their commitment to humanity, and by engaging the viewer emotionally, they hoped to generate a dialogue between the viewer and the work which would invoke a sense of humanity and to prod the viewer through this process toward a personal psychological reconstruction.[44]

Leading abstract expressionists frequented the Cedar bar in Greenwich Village, where they drank heavily, boasted constantly, quarreled frequently, and brawled. Elaine de Kooning described their attitude: "Live fast, die young, and have a good-looking corpse." (Pollock died in a car crash at 44 in 1956.) These painters, like the Beat writers, embraced a bohemian style. By the fifties Abstract Expressionism had support from critics, collectors, and museums, but the public did not like the new art, which portrayed nothing concrete and seemed puzzling. In 1961 Aldous Huxley declared, "I think it's *time we grew out of it.*" As the original Abstract Expressionists came to dominate American painting, younger artists found it difficult to get noticed. In the later fifties Jasper Johns began to paint American flags. Although Johns had seemingly rejected abstraction, his flag portrayals were not representations but calculated commentaries that used some Abstract Expressionist ideas in a nonabstract manner. The flag pictures suggested that artists could convey emotion through the use of icons that were charged with widely shared symbolic meaning. Instead of the blank slate of abstraction, iconographical usage might enrich the associations that both painter and viewer could bring to a work. Johns's flag pictures were akin to the associational language found in Dylan's lyrics. In both cases the artist prodded and even directed the viewer or listener in certain psychological directions due to emotional resonances with borrowings from popular culture.[45]

Robert Rauschenberg used a slightly different approach. Rejecting both abstraction, which offered only limited associational resonances between painter and viewer, and the use of any icon that was so highly charged with symbolism as the American flag, he instead turned to the detritus of consumer culture and created three-dimensional collage paintings out of junk and paint. Rauschenberg's technique not only offered a wicked commentary about the country's glutted commercialism during the postwar boom, but it also enabled the artist to converse with the viewer through the many advertising-based resonances contained in cast-off products. While such associations lacked the power of Johns's flag icon, they were arguably more significant because they cumulated multiple images based on daily interactions generated by common household products into a complex matrix of associations. The paintings, then, struck a resonance with viewers that enabled the artist to communicate readily. To Rauschenberg, communication was the key. When the filmmaker Emile de Antonio defended Rauschenberg and Johns to the Abstract Expressionists, he was attacked as an anarchist. "Maybe I was an anarchist," de Antonio recalled. Although primarily a painter, Rauschenberg was also interested in performance art and for a time staged events, similar to those presented by the Judson Dance Theater, to the accompaniment of music by the avant-garde composer John Cage.[46]

By 1961 Claes Oldenburg was ready to break with the Abstract Expressionists' fundamental ideas. While he remained prepared to drip paint, he did so on small sculptures of pies, cakes, and other objects which he sold at a gallery called The Store. Oldenburg clearly had been influenced by the popularity of the nonabstractions of Johns and Rauschenberg, but rather than depend upon highly charged icons like the flag or deconstructed waste, Oldenburg returned to a more traditional artistic idea of representation. Although his sculptures resembled the everyday objects that they represented, they were deliberately made in such a crude way that they could not be mistaken for the actual objects. They were parodies. Oldenburg offered both a parody and a symbolic celebration of at least some of the items of consumer society that Rauschenberg had ridiculed, but by focusing on recreated whole items, he also satirized their importance. This was especially true in the case of vastly overlarge pieces of cake or pie, which both promoted consumption and warned against gluttony. This self-mocking quality was one of the hallmarks of postmodernism. By the late fifties the avant-garde was beginning to reject the modernist devotion to pure form and abstraction. At the same time, Oldenburg intended his sculptures to perform a function analogous to that of abstract paintings. His expressive works offered his sardonic, postmodern commentary upon contemporary society and its values. In selling them at The Store he self-reflexively both affirmed the importance of the commerical art market and satirized the nature of capitalism. "I am for an art," he said publicly, "that does something other than sit on its ass in a museum."[47]

While Johns and Rauschenberg can be seen as precursors of Pop Art and Oldenburg through his playful duality as an early practitioner, the movement is more clearly identified with Roy Lichtenstein and Andy Warhol, both of whom rocketed to fame in 1962 with paintings that marked a radical departure. In 1960 Lichtenstein, at the request of his daughter, painted his first oversized cartoon. Both fascinated and pleased by the result, the artist launched a series of large canvases based on panels in comic books. Lichtenstein, however, did not merely reproduce an enlarged copy of the original strip. The panels he chose to use often showed violence or emotional intensity. Men frequently were flying combat aircraft, while women were portrayed suffering in traumatized romantic relationships. Some complicating elements in the original panels were dropped, the lines were often thickened, and slight redesigns took place. A color palette of a particular red, blue, and yellow, slightly off the true primary colors and close to those used in the printing industry, was developed, and colors were added in the form of dots, as if the new cartoon was a blowup of a colored comic section from a Sunday newspaper. Word copy in balloons above the pictures was rewritten to enable the panel to stand alone. The overall effect was startling, as unlike Abstract Expressionism as could be imagined. These pictures sold well, and Lichtenstein quickly produced multiple prints and other variant forms of a picture type that was to become his trademark as an artist.[48]

Although visually distinct from Abstract Expressionism, Lichtenstein's work expressed both aesthetic connections and differences. His work was not abstract, but he was using emotionally charged found objects, just like Johns and Rauschenberg. The comic strip avoided the intensity of the flag, but it had more meaning than cast-off junk. While comics could be seen as items of throwaway mass culture, they also had a popular following. The strip artists were highly skilled professional illustrators who had learned during the twentieth century to develop character, to convey complex plots, and to present emotional intensity in restricted space. They used stylized lettering, exclamation marks, exaggerated closeups, and sweat drops on brows to create a new language of mass culture. Their coded cues were widely and easily understood. To viewers familiar with comics, Lichtenstein's pictures resonated with powerful emotional associations. The large scale, however, enabled the painter to transcend representation and to encourage the viewer to ponder the picture's meaning. Use of a single panel eliminated the strip's original plot and forced a certain amount of reinterpretation. The painter, in other words, offered commentary about the society that produced such items of mass culture. These paintings revealed an obsession with war, male heroism, and female romance. Like the best Abstract Expressionism, they cut close to the bone.[49]

While Lichtenstein's comic panel paintings were the first great Pop Art, he never moved beyond that promising beginning. In the long run, Andy Warhol proved more important. Born into the Catholic working class in Pittsburgh, he had moved to New York, where he was a successful commerical artist in the fifties. When he switched to fine art in 1960, he found it difficult to get gallery representation because of his commercial background and his fey homosexuality. As a result, Warhol's first significant one-man show took place in 1962 in Los Angeles, where he displayed 32 paintings of enlarged Campbell's soup cans. Like Lichtenstein, Warhol had used the cans not as junk but as found objects worthy of representation. They could even be considered as iconic representations of modern American consumer culture. These works were rendered, again like Lichtenstein, not as enlarged exact copies but as freely painted commentaries upon the original objects. Like comics, Campbell's soup was both an easily recognized symbol of middle-class life and a part of pop culture. Warhol said, probably facetiously, that he had eaten it every day for lunch for 20 years. Although the use of a commercial product at first glance suggested the anticapitalist sneer of Rauschenberg and Oldenburg, such was not the case. Warhol, as a commercial artist, celebrated the aesthetic appeal of the Campbell's design (which was of higher quality than the soup inside). In doing so, he, like other pop artists, also challenged the high culture definition of "art" by suggesting that common objects were worthy of representation. The Dada artists had done so, too, in the twenties. Both Pop Art and Judson Dance Theater attacked the high art idea that art should be good, true, and beautiful. This attempt to mix commercial enthusiasm with fine art made Warhol anathema among many critics, even though it expressed a basic truth about the American people.[50]

The original soup can pictures proved enormously popular but had been tedious to paint, and Warhol, like other artists throughout history, decided to make profitable multiple copies. He made silk-screen prints, and in the process of screening realized that each print could, depending upon inking, pressure, or alignment, be unique. Because ink could be applied in different color combinations and in different sequencings, which also varied the effect, the result was that a single original design could lead to almost limitless variation. Each print was both an original and a copy at the same time. Warhol was fascinated by the fact that modern industrial technology made endless variation possible. In an interview he said, "I switched to manufactured paintings because they're easier. . . . I wish I were a machine. I don't want to be hurt. I don't want human emotions." Whereas others had seen industrialization necessarily producing dull, repetitive sameness, Warhol envisioned those same processes, through either structured or random variation, yielding an exciting array of individually differentiated results. Each subsequent picture, he recognized, enjoyed the appeal – and commanded the high price – of a preindustrial original, unique work, while at the same time crude mass production itself offered a commentary about the industrial age in which the item was produced. The writer Tom Wolfe described Warhol's attitude toward commercialism: "It's so awful, it's wonderful."[51]

Although Warhol proceeded from soup cans to Brillo boxes, which were also silk-screened, he quickly gave up commercial objects for icons of popular culture. Returning, in a sense, to Johns's flag idea, Warhol's art used images that resonated with an American audience, its emotional concerns, and the associative language that could be related to such images. In a promising time, Warhol sought a public expression of his own private thought as it was encapsulated in popular culture. His insight was remarkably similar to Bob Dylan's. Fascinated by fatal auto crashes and executions, he did a series of black and white photographs overlaid with varied colors that used newspaper pictures of accidents or a somber picture of an empty electric chair. The public ignored these pictures because they lacked appropriate emotional resonances. Then, in 1962 Marilyn Monroe committed suicide. Warhol used an old studio publicity shot of a heavily made-up Monroe to create multiple Marilyns in a variety of colors. Many of these pictures featured oversized ruby lips, dense turquoise eye shadow, and intense yellow hair. These freaky Marilyns captured the suicidal actress's tragedy, her sense of desperation amid stardom, her remoteness and unreality. "The artificial fascinates me," he said, "the bright and shiny." The pictures conveyed the way in which Marilyn had been a glitzy, hyped product for mass consumption, but they also showed compassion and did not descend into satire. Warhol, a devout Catholic, knew better than to ridicule an icon. Even today, Warhol's Marilyns are haunting.[52]

Warhol's best work (e.g., portraits of Marilyn Monroe, Elvis Presley, and Jackie Kennedy) resembled Bob Dylan's best songs (e.g., "Mr. Tambourine Man" and "Subterranean Homesick Blues"). Both artists used new techniques not only to break through formal compositional barriers but also to test cultural limits. The Marilyns presented mass-produced commercial items as hand-produced unique fine art objects in a juxtaposition dripping with irony, forced the viewer to reconsider celebrity, and, ultimately, through the mediation of Warhol's representation, offered a reexamination and reinterpretation of both Monroe and the culture itself. Dylan's "Mr. Tambourine Man" similarly contrasted the songwriter's declarations with the listener's understanding, which depended upon the listener's insight into highly associational language, forced rethinking about the song, and, ultimately, through the mediation of Dylan's lyrics, reinterpreted both that song and the culture that had produced it. Both Warhol's Marilyn paintings and Dylan's song shared the irony, satire, and self-reflexivity commonly found among postmodern works. In late 1963 Warhol moved into the silver-painted Factory. Bored with Pop Art, he became an avant-garde filmmaker and produced such bizarre movies as *Sleep* (1963), which focused a camera on a man asleep for six hours. Warhol tried to recruit Dylan to star in a film. This attempt failed, even though Warhol bribed Dylan by giving him an Elvis portrait. Dylan reciprocated by stealing Warhol's girlfriend.[53]

All of these artistic movements tested limits. The challenge had started with the Beats' hostile, sweeping criticism of American society and culture. According to the Beats, the entirety was rotten and had to be swept away. The self had to be extricated from the monster's grip and remade one person at a time. Only then could people begin anew to build a decent, humane world. Despite the Beats' bitterness, their critique took place from within the culture they despised. In reality, they scarcely knew how to begin their spiritual quest. Although the folk revival, as we have seen, had a more optimistic outlook, gained strength from the civil rights movement, and expressed the widely felt fear of nuclear war, it had the serious limitation of being too closely linked to the outmoded politics of the thirties. That historical connection both inhibited broad support and restricted folk music's capacity for criticism of the culture. Only if music were remade, as Dylan showed, could it break down cultural barriers. In contrast, Pop Art captured the public imagination. Its playful mixture of commerce and culture fitted the American psyche during the early sixties. As a critique of society, Pop Art suggested that mass culture was fragile, that celebrities were hollow, and that consumerism was a cult, if not a religion. Worshipping materialistic idols might well be the devil's work. "Advertising," the monk Thomas Merton wrote in a letter, "is one of the great *loci classici* for the theology of the devil." These ideas aside, it is difficult to identify Pop Art with any spiritual quest.[54]

What common themes can we find among these various cultural movements, including the Beats, the folk revival, and Pop Art? In the early sixties, Americans were in a state of cultural confusion that approached a crisis. Although the sense of a promising time encouraged cultural experimentation, the result both enhanced and threatened the sense of promise. The Beat challenge had already rattled a once complacent society, and while the folk revival asserted an apparently more benign desire to continue reforms from the past, that reform message itself predicted further instability. Pop Art appeared to lack any weighty philosophy, although its self-reflexive irony, parody, and satire signaled the beginning of postmodernism, but its popularity and resonance with mainstream cultural values gave it the greatest influence of these three movements during the remainder of the century. Consumerism thrived, and Warhol had correctly identified celebrity as a key element in American culture. "In the future," he had said, "*everyone* will be famous for 15 minutes." All three movements, however, were incapable of producing spiritual satisfaction or a purposeful cosmology. Ever since World War II, many Americans had felt a need for a new holistic system of values and principles that tradition no longer provided. The Beats were too negative to offer a cosmology, the folkies too rooted in the past to offer a new system, and Pop Art too shallow. If the old order was dying, how might a new one be born? Perhaps, thought Aldous Huxley, the answer should come from science. Ever since Charles Darwin, science had been blamed for loss of faith. Maybe science could now help people regain faith. Psychedelic drugs, Huxley felt, could be the basis for a new cosmology.[55]

Huxley, one of the most brilliant and far-sighted minds of his age, was born in Great Britain in 1894 into a remarkable family. His older brother Julian was a leading scientist, his maternal great-uncle was the poet Matthew Arnold, and his paternal grandfather Thomas Huxley had been a leading scientist and the major promoter of Darwinism. When Huxley was 16, he was blinded by a streptococcus infection. In two weeks he had taught himself to read Braille. Two years later he regained enough sight in one eye to be able to read in bright light. Blocked from a science research career by poor vision, he was also saved from World War I. Two-thirds of his Eton College classmates were killed in the war. Afterward, survivor guilt drew him to pacifism and brooding. He became a writer of philosphical novels. In 1932 he published his most famous work, *Brave New World*, the portrayal of an alarming dystopia in which individuality had given way to regimentation and manipulation in the name of progress. In the fifties it was one of the top ten books used in American schools. Equally hostile to communism and fascism, he watched Europe slide toward war in the later 1930s. In 1937 he moved to Hollywood to write film scripts, which paid better than serious novels. Falling in love with Los Angeles and especially with its bright sunlight, he stayed the rest of his life.[56]

Huxley continued to read science, partly out of fascination and partly to develop material for novels. In 1953 he read a technical report by a Canadian psychiatrist, Humphry Osmond, on the use of a new drug, lysergic acid diethylamide, that is, LSD. The drug had been synthesized in the Sandoz laboratory in Switzerland, and in 1943 its inventor, Albert Hofmann, accidentally contaminated himself and discovered its mind-altering qualities. By the early fifties

LSD research was underway both by psychiatrists, who hoped to use it to treat schizophrenia, and by the Central Intelligence Agency, which saw it as a truth serum. Huxley wrote Osmond, learned that the doctor was about to visit Los Angeles, and arranged a meeting. To acquaint Huxley with psychedelic drugs, Osmond brought mescaline, a drug similar to but much milder than LSD. Decades earlier mescaline had been synthesized from the peyote cactus used by Indians in religious rites in Mexico and the American Southwest. By removing impurities, mescaline reduced the nausea and vomiting that often accompanied use of peyote. Huxley took the mescaline. His first psychedelic trip had far-ranging consequences. Determined both to make sense of his experience and to share it with a larger audience, Huxley wrote *The Doors of Perception* (1954) as the first philosophical study of psychedelic drugs. (In honor of Huxley's contribution, Jim Morrison later named his rock music group The Doors.)[57]

In 1955 Huxley tried LSD and had an even more remarkable experience. Feeling close to the entire world, he concluded that love was "the primary and fundamental cosmic fact." In *Doors* and in a later book, *Heaven and Hell* (1956), Huxley laid out a theory about the nature of the individual mind and how culture enabled it to relate to the larger society. Mescaline and LSD had given Huxley an insight into the oneness of the world and the interconnectivity of everyone and everything. To Huxley, the realization of these truths after one had taken psychedelics (a word that Osmond and Huxley coined) and passed through the doors of perception (a line from the poet William Blake) was so clear that it overturned all previous psychological, social, and political training. Psychedelics promised to transform both mind and soul. "I have known that sense of affectionate solidarity with the people around me and with the universe at large," he later wrote in a letter, "also the sense of the world's fundamental All Rightness. . . ." The author had long wrestled with how to bring the world to reject traditional values, especially war and nationalism, and accept his pacifist vision. Rather than using words to change minds, he discovered that minds could be altered through chemicals. Psychedelics, if properly employed, he thought, promised a revolution in global consciousness as great as any that had ever been produced by mass religious transformation.[58]

Huxley's enthusiasm encouraged psychedelic experiments in Los Angeles. As a sophisticate, he worried that vested interests would become antagonized. The entrenched military-industrial complex profited from the present socio-political system. So did vast bureaucracies. Superstition and fear among the ignorant also mattered. Furthermore, too little was known about the effects of LSD to launch a mass campaign. More research was needed. Huxley's strategy was to promote the expansion of that research with continued emphasis upon a medical model. Governments usually left physicians and their patients alone. Early on, however, Huxley recognized another problem. While psychiatrists might find uses for LSD to treat the mentally ill, Huxley was more interested in expanding consciousness among normal people. A strictly medical experimental model would not allow many people to try the drug. Huxley encouraged doctors to broaden participation and especially to encourage use by the rich and powerful, who could be allies in the event of any attempt to ban LSD, and among creative people, such as actors, writers, and artists. Among those who tripped were the actor Cary Grant, the writer Anaïs Nin, the nuclear strategist Herman Kahn, the *Time* publisher Henry Luce, and his wife Clare Boothe Luce. Huxley personally gave LSD to the Zen Buddhist advocate Alan Watts.[59]

As the circle of experimenters expanded, LSD attracted Allen Ginsberg's attention. In 1956 Burroughs had recommended the drug to Ginsberg as a possible cure for his schizophrenic mother. The poet had already tried peyote and read *Doors* by the time he took his first LSD trip in 1959 in a government-sponsored experiment near Stanford University. Because he had had earlier psychedelic experiences, Ginsberg had limited expectations. The result shocked him. "It was astounding," he wrote. The duration, intensity, and profundity of the experience surpassed his previous drug trips. Perhaps one reason for the more striking effect was LSD's purity. Peyote contained impurities that caused vomiting and other side effects that adversely affected psychedelic results. The poet was left almost speechless. He believed, at least for a time, that he had seen the godhead. Comparing LSD to a trance state, he saw part of his own consciousness as a transcendant part of the universe; he described "beautiful images" with "Hindu-type Gods." In 1960 Ginsberg traveled in South America. In Peru he tasted a brew made from the yage vine that yielded a powerful trip with vivid colors, imagined insects, and "a realization of infinite intimacy." He found this trip even more potent than LSD. By the time he returned to New York, Ginsberg, like Huxley, believed that psychedelics were so potent that, if handled shrewdly, they could change the world by altering everyone's psyches and worldviews.[60]

In late 1960 both Ginsberg and Huxley met Dr. Timothy Leary, a Harvard University psychology professor. Leary had first taken psychedelic mushrooms in Mexico the previous summer. At the time he had not read *Doors*, had not heard of LSD, and had never tried marijuana. Overwhelmed by the mushrooms, the professor returned to Harvard and acquired the mushroom's active ingredient, psilocybin, from Sandoz in Switzerland. Leary soon had a thousand pills for research. He gave one to Huxley, who, under the influence, asked, "So you don't know what to do with this bloody philosopher's stone we have stumbled onto?" Huxley warned of trouble. Leary replied, "But society needs this information." Huxley urged caution. Ginsberg found psilocybin made him "very high" and declared, "*The Revolution Has Begun*." God derived from the self. Ginsberg and Leary agreed that psychedelics could change society drastically, and both intended to see that transformation occur quickly. Ginsberg wrote Cassady, "We're starting a plot to get everyone in Power in America high – Hurrah!" Ginsberg then told Leary about LSD and urged him to use it in research. Leary ordered his first batch from Sandoz. Ginsberg also suggested that Leary restrict his experiments, at least for the time being, to either prominent persons or to writers, artists, and musicians. The former would keep the program respectable, while the latter would provide useful data.[61]

In early 1961 Ginsberg introduced Leary to a number of intellectuals in New York. Many took Leary's psychedelics, but not everyone had a happy experience. Artists often found drugs exciting due to the unusual vividness of their visual minds, and writers, disciplined in word use, sometimes were able to recall specific details after their trips. Jack Kerouac, however, was unimpressed. "Walking on water wasn't built in a day," he said, complaining of bad aftereffects. Jazz musicians proved disappointing. Following Huxley, Ginsberg warned Leary that departure from a medical research model would bring trouble. It was, the poet thought, necessary to try the drug on members of the elite before widespread publicity. As a celebrity, Ginsberg had a better sense of political reality than Leary did. Ginsberg then left on his global tour, and Leary proceeded to conduct LSD experiments in his own way. It was not so much that Leary intended to disobey the advice of Huxley and Ginsberg, but Leary was impetuous and excitable, understood that he had stumbled into the most important research of his career, and was determined to make the most of his opportunity. Besides, deep down Leary did not agree. Huxley was an English aristocrat who distrusted the masses, while Ginsberg, despite an egalitarian ethos, seemed to favor a priesthood of poets and artists. Leary, an Irish democrat, could not resist a more far-ranging program.[62]

Leary's influence spread quickly. In April 1961, Ginsberg reported that William Burroughs and Brion Gysin had gained familiarity with psychedelics. Gysin had invented a "flicker machine" strobe light system that produced the same kinds of optical fields as psychedelic drugs. "It's like being able to have jeweled biblical designs and landscapes without chemicals," marveled Ginsberg, "Amazing. It *works*." A few years later Gysin's invention became the basis for light shows at rock concerts. In summer 1961 Leary and Ginsberg visited Burroughs in Tangier, and Leary invited the novelist to join drug experiments at Harvard. "I think Bill & Leary at Harvard are going to start a beautiful consciousness alteration of the whole world," Ginsberg wrote in a letter. Two months later Burroughs took psilocybin with Leary in London. "Bill was funny, wise, creative, close," the professor reported to Ginsberg, but a few days later, after Leary and Burroughs reached Harvard, they quarreled over Leary's shallow methods. Burroughs, according to Leary, feared the development of "a religion, do-good cult." Unable to contain his excitement, Leary claimed, "Mushroom fever is sweeping Cambridge." He advocated "freedom of your own nervous system." In a dubious experiment, Leary had given psilocybin to hardened inmates in a state prison, and while the drug appeared to improve the prisoners' dispositions and promised to reduce recidivism, the new mellow behavior, along with guards taking the drug, had so alarmed the administration that the experiment was cancelled.[63]

Leary was careless about who got LSD. When the Washington artist Mary Meyer showed up and asked to take a sample back to the capital, Leary obliged. He got the impression that Meyer would introduce the drug to prominent political figures, perhaps including the president. Any prudent person would have been aghast. One did not seek to influence the elite about something so potent as LSD by using a peripheral figure as a conduit. It looked underhanded, and in any case one had no idea what the whimsical and impulsive Meyer would actually do with the LSD. Leary had also discovered that "set and setting" determined whether or not a trip was pleasant. The best trips were taken with friends in a comfortable location. Leary moved his experiments from Harvard to his own living room. Parties at Leary's house grew strange and wild. Since Leary was often stoned himself, he did not pay much attention to guests. Nor to his duties at Harvard. "I see Leary has been thrown out of Harvard," Burroughs wrote Ginsberg in 1963, "for distributing his noxious wares too freely. . . ." If the novelist sounded gleeful, it was because he felt vindicated for having broken with Leary in 1961. After Leary tried but failed to establish an LSD colony in Mexico, he moved to an estate at Millbrook, New York, that was owned by a follower. He and other LSD users lived there until the place was raided in 1966.[64]

Even before Ginsberg had met Leary, Ken Kesey was engaged in LSD experiments at the Veterans Administration Hospital near Stanford University in California. Unlike most subjects, Kesey was sometimes, by sheer force of will, able to write about a trip while on the drug, and he could enlarge and adapt these notes afterward. Government researchers were grateful. The novelist, however, drew a different conclusion. Like Huxley, Ginsberg, and Leary, he believed that psychedelics were destined to change the world by altering individual consciousness. As a libertarian, he found it refreshing that revolution could begin with the self. Unlike Huxley and Ginsberg, Kesey did not wish to keep LSD research in the hands of an elite. He agreed with Leary's notion that such an idea was undemocratic and snobbish. On the other hand, Kesey, like Burroughs, found Leary's ideas about research pretentious. Kesey reasoned that no one could know what LSD would do either to individuals or to societies because no potent psychedelic had ever been widely available before. He felt intuitively that the drug should be disseminated as widely and as rapidly as possible. Mass use would prevent a crackdown. Kesey was not prepared to predict the consequences of a psychedelic revolution, but he believed that both individuals and society would be changed drastically.[65]

In 1963 Kesey used money from *One Flew Over the Cuckoo's Nest* to buy a house on six acres at La Honda in the hills behind Stanford University. Gathering followers, he performed LSD experiments on anyone game enough to try. Using various sound systems, he tried different kinds of music and identified a particular type of rock music as surprisingly pleasurable with LSD. Jerry Garcia, who went on to found the Grateful Dead band, worked with Kesey on the music. In 1964 Kesey and his Merry Pranksters took their experiments public by traveling around the country in a wildly painted bus; the driver was Neal Cassady. Cassady, Kesey, and Kerouac met in New York, but Kerouac showed no interest in LSD. The Pranksters then visited Leary at Millbrook, which they found boring. Always fascinated by the bizarre and the unexpected, Kesey turned on the hard-drinking and violent Hell's Angels motorcycle gang, an unlikely group of psychedelic experimenters. When the Angels threatened to beat up antiwar protesters in 1965, Allen Ginsberg gave them LSD and taught them to chant. The Angels stayed stoned for two days and gave up molesting the protesters, but their worldview did not change.[66]

In the long run, LSD proved no more successful at launching a new cosmology than had the Beat spiritual quest, the folk revival, or Pop Art. All four of these attempts to change worldviews showed an almost desperate effort to escape from the present. LSD perhaps proved the least durable, because its limitations for inspiration quickly became obvious. Ginsberg's insight in Japan into the limitations of drugs proved correct. LSD, however, for a time showed great promise in a culture obsessed with scientific improvement. Aldous Huxley was diagnosed with tongue cancer in 1960. Two years later he published his last book, *Island*, which was a drug-based utopian novel. In that perfect society, taking an LSD-like psychedelic drug was common practice. Huxley's cancer treatment failed, and by late 1963 he knew that he was dying. On the morning of his death, he asked his wife to give him LSD intravenously. A bit later he took a second dose. He remained peaceful all afternoon, quiet, unable to talk, but he indicated with a squeeze of his hand that he could hear and was contented. At 5:20 P.M. he died. It was November 22, 1963. Kennedy had been killed hours earlier, but Huxley never knew it. And so the early sixties, a promising time marked by the increasing public expression of private thoughts, ended in a burst of gunfire amid a pastiche of weird new art, music, literature, and drugs.[67]

The Kennedys arrive in Dallas, November 22, 1963.
(John F. Kennedy Library. ST-C-420-13-63.)

CHAPTER SIX

Dallas

The shock of John Kennedy's death in Dallas brought the promising time of the early sixties to a sudden end. The assassination startled and jarred; mostly it seemed incredible. One moment the president was a youthful, vital presence, a handsome, animated face, and a clever wordsmith whose charm and glamor had captivated most of the country and much of the world. He had given public expression to the private thoughts of millions. The next moment dark horror filled the airwaves, and but a moment later Kennedy, like some Irish leprechaun, was gone. Unlike the leprechaun, however, his presence could be recalled instantly in pictures and sound. Videotape, only recently invented and still too expensive for home use, enabled the television networks to recapture and replay the horror during four days of national mourning. These commercial-free televised repetitions imprinted the stark brutality of Kennedy's death on consciousness like no other event in American history. What might have been the consequence if videotape had been available to show Roosevelt's fatal stroke?; the attack on Pearl Harbor?; Lincoln's assassination?; the firing on Fort Sumter?; or the British burning the White House in the War of 1812? Kennedy's death angered, appalled, and fascinated. He personified the emerging age of celebrity that Andy Warhol had so shrewdly identified as central to the times. Indeed, Kennedy, by the act of becoming a celebrity, had helped create that new era.[1]

When the assassination took place, Adlai Stevenson was in New York. A month earlier, he had been heckled when he gave a speech in Dallas. Afterward, he had crossed a picket line to get to his car. A woman hit him on the head with a sign; a man spat. Wiping his face with a handkerchief, the ambassador asked, "Are these human beings or are these animals?" The coolness impressed Kennedy. Stevenson told Arthur Schlesinger, Jr., that the atmosphere in Dallas was "ugly" and questioned whether Kennedy should go there. Schlesinger did not repeat this comment to the president, and the ambassador at the time was relieved by that act of discretion. Stevenson was lunching with Chilean delegates at the United Nations when an aide interrupted to tell him that Kennedy had been shot. Stunned, the ambassador and the aide rushed back to United States mission headquarters. In the cab, both were silent until Stevenson said, "Maybe I should have *insisted* that he not go to Dallas." He watched events unfold on television. When news came that the president had died, Stevenson, cool under pressure, began to scribble on scraps of paper. He composed an official press release, which the United States mission was expected to issue immediately to other members of the United Nations.[2]

Also in New York that day was Kay Graham. Just three months after Phil's suicide, she had recently become the publisher of the *Washington Post* and had flown to New York in her private jet. She had brought along Arthur Schlesinger, Jr., and the two were joined by John Kenneth Galbraith for a meeting with the editorial staff at *Newsweek*. The trio watched the news on television in the editor's office and then returned to Washington. Hours later, after night fell, they could be found in the White House. Galbraith had tears, Schlesinger cried, and Mrs. Graham sat sobbing on a couch near the Oval Office. Schlesinger asked, "What kind of a country is this?"

Adlai Stevenson wandered in, and Schlesinger perceived "glee" in the ambassador's eyes. Stevenson and Kennedy had had a strained relationship, and the ambassador's remorse might well have been tempered by anticipation of rising influence with now-President Lyndon Johnson. That hope proved false. Also at the White House was the Kennedy aide Theodore Sorensen. Badly wounded in spirit, he was aloof and incommunicative. On a helicopter on the way to Andrews Air Force Base to meet the plane carrying Kennedy's remains, Jackie Kennedy, and Johnson, Sorensen told Johnson's aide George Reedy, "George, I wish to hell that god-dammed State of Texas of yours had never been invented." Reedy recognized that the remark was irrational, but Sorensen was overwrought. Late at night, at the White House, Sorensen complained, "They wouldn't even let him have three years." It was understood that "they" meant Texans.[3]

The tension aboard the flight of Air Force One from Dallas to Washington was palpable. The Kennedy staff, totally in shock, had been unprepared for any action with regard to the transfer of power. For half an hour after the president's death, the fact had gone unannounced. Lyndon Johnson, on the other hand, was a take-charge guy. Almost paranoid about a coup or a world war, he was determined to be sworn in as president immediately in Texas and then flown to the Washington nerve center as quickly as possible. To reassure the public, Johnson insisted that a grieving Jackie Kennedy be photographed with the new president taking the oath. She refused to change out of her blood-stained pink dress and then insisted on sitting with the coffin all the way to Washington. Kenny O'Donnell sat with her and pulled out a bottle of scotch. All the Kennedy staff drank together. It was the first time that Mrs. Kennedy had ever tried scotch. Gesturing toward Johnson, O'Donnell confided to another aide on board, "He's got what he wants now. But we take it back in '68." The former first lady later said of the staff, "They were all lost."[4]

J. Edgar Hoover called Robert Kennedy about the shooting and, later, with news of the president's death. The FBI director's matter-of-fact manner offended the attorney general, who never forgave him. Hoover, an old friend of Johnson's, had little use for the suddenly unimportant attorney general. Kennedy's phone calls on the direct line to Hoover's office were no longer answered, and the FBI director quickly relocated the phone to his secretary's office. Robert Kennedy met the plane at Andrews and asked, "Where's Jackie? I want to be with Jackie." At the attorney general's suggestion, Robert McNamara accompanied the pair to the official autopsy and proposed, with Robert Kennedy's approval, that John Kennedy be buried in Arlington Cemetery. Kennedy's Irish aides had wanted Boston. The president, like so many in Arlington, had been killed in line of duty. Not long before, the president had visited Arlington and had found it beautiful. McNamara selected the spot. Most of the cabinet had been flying to Japan when the assassination had taken place. The plane turned back to Washington and arrived very late, long after Kennedy's body. On the tiresome flight across the Pacific there was silence and sobbing. Finally, to break the tension, Kennedy's press secretary Pierre Salinger suggested that the group play poker. He won a big pot of $800.[5]

Rose Kennedy was resting after lunch at Hyannisport when Robert called to tell her of the shooting and, later, that the president was dead. Joe, who was napping, was not disturbed. Later, Ted and Eunice Kennedy arrived and told their father. The incapacitated ambassador said nothing, but tears rolled down his cheeks. Peter Lawford had been performing late the night before at Harrah's at Lake Tahoe, Nevada. He slept in and was awakened by his valet with news of the shooting. After learning from television that the president was dead, Lawford threw up in the kitchen and then lay on the floor and cried. He headed to Washington for the funeral. So did Jackie's stepbrother Gore Vidal, who was living in Rome.

Jackie's sister Lee and her husband Stas Radziwill also crossed the Atlantic from their home in London. They spent the night in the White House. The Radziwills were given Jack's bedroom, but Stas refused to sleep in the late president's bed, and a cot was brought into the room. Robert Kennedy slept in the Lincoln bedroom. After the president's body was placed in the East Room, the attorney general threw his hands over the casket and talked to his brother. After the funeral, there was an Irish wake with much drinking and joking. Eventually, the party moved upstairs, where John, Jr., celebrated his third birthday with cake and ice cream. Robert Kennedy tried to tell his nephew what had happened, but he was too young to understand.[6]

After returning to Washington from Dallas, Lyndon Johnson and Lady Bird had gone home to The Elms. Looking at a favorite portrait of his longtime friend Sam Rayburn on the wall, the new president raised a glass of orange soda and said, "Oh, Mister Sam, I wish you were here now. I need you." By the next morning President Johnson was ready to begin work. Robert Kennedy had had all of his brother's belongings removed from the Oval Office. Files were already on their way to storage. At 8 A.M. Johnson called Pierre Salinger, who had had only a couple of hours sleep, and asked him to help with the press. Salinger did his duty, but a few months later, after realizing that he was drinking a bottle of scotch a day, he quit. Arthur Schlesinger, Jr., wanted to leave immediately. "It has been a terrible time," he told Adolf Berle, "The worst I have ever known." Kennedy's staff was too shattered to continue. They were unusually close, and their loyalty to Kennedy bordered on love. "The heart has gone out of us all," stated Marian Schlesinger, "though we go through the motions of living each day." It was odd, in a way, because Kennedy never socialized with his staff. Still, he had this emotionally intense connection to people. "Never in my time in public life," recalled Walt Rostow, "have I ever known a man who drew so much affection from those with whom he closely dealt." Years later Lawrence O'Brien said simply, "There was an aura around him."[7]

"How utterly horrible, how evil," David Lilienthal wrote in his diary. His wife listened to television with her hands on her face; he lay on the sofa, face down. Suddenly, he cried, realizing that Kennedy's death showed the uncertainty of life. The monk Thomas Merton thought the death had created a "spiritual crisis." It was "almost an apocalyptic event." It proved that all evil was not behind the Iron Curtain. The *Esquire* editor Rust Hills was on the telephone with Norman Mailer when the news came; Hills told the author, who replied, "It was in the cards." The magazine's editor, Harold Hayes, was struck by the sudden change in Kennedy's image. In life, views about Kennedy had varied widely; now, suddenly, there was a common shared view. Andy Warhol was painting with the radio on when he learned the news; he continued painting. Later, he watched the assassination coverage on television with John Giorno. They sat together on a couch in Warhol's townhouse crying, hugging, and kissing. Giorno recalled, "It was exhilarating...." Afterward, Warhol did "16 Jackies" as a tribute. The violinist Isaac Stern was in Dallas to perform a concert on November 22. He played only one piece, Bach's Chaconne from the Partita No. 2. Stern and the audience left in tears. Three weeks later a memorial service for Aldous Huxley was held in London. The violinist Yehudi Menuhin, an old friend of Huxley, played the same piece.[8]

Because Kennedy was a television celebrity with global appeal, his death touched the entire world. In Copenhagen, where the news came to Ambassador Bill Blair over shortwave radio after dark, thousands of Danes went to the embassy, carried candles, and maintained a nightlong vigil around the compound. The next morning flowers were stacked six feet high at the embassy gate. Thousands more tried to attend a memorial service in Copenhagen's Catholic church, which seated only a few hundred. Kennedy was not Danish, had never visited Denmark, and had rarely, if ever, expressed any opinion that had importance in that country. Virtually no Danes had met Kennedy, and he did not dominate local news. Nevertheless, he had somehow touched a nerve. Danes, like others, sensed that Kennedy was committed to social justice and world peace. His aristocratic demeanor exuded confidence rather than arrogance. In a promising time, he had represented hope and uplift. In Sweden, King Gustav VI Adolf took the astonishing step of visiting the embassy to express condolences. Kennedy had visited Sweden years earlier and had approved its welfare state, a fact that Swedes remembered.[9]

In France, wrote the visiting priest Daniel Berrigan, "the murder brought love to light" in what had been tense Franco-American relations. Suddenly, the French discovered that they loved Kennedy. They had always loved his francophone wife. Berrigan felt that Kennedy's death had so shaken the moral order that the Catholic church would have to find a way to come to terms with Marxism. Grief was expressed behind the Iron Curtain, too. In Moscow, Nikita Khrushchev cried over the death of a man younger than his own son with whom he had quarreled so bitterly that nuclear war was only narrowly averted. Still, Khrushchev, like many others, had grown fond of Kennedy and saw in the president a man with whom he could negotiate. Khrushchev went to the American embassy to offer written condolences in an official book. His visit was shown on American television. In Budapest, a priest preached three times on the president on the Sunday after his death "and the whole congregation was in tears." In Prague, 3,000 Czechs filed through the embassy to sign the register; a mass for diplomats was crowded with wet-eyed ordinary people. The communist regime cooperated by directing the extra traffic. Throughout Europe, even in neutral Switzerland, grief was "*immense.*"[10]

Grief was expressed throughout the world. In a Tokyo hotel, the Democratic party lawyer Harry McPherson, an American visitor, learned of the shooting before dawn. Americans gathered in the hallway and then moved to the lobby in silence. An old colonel sat in a chair, wide-eyed. McPherson went to have tea at a Buddhist shrine, and the hostess said, "Very sorry about your President." McPherson cried. So did the Japanese, which was a most unusual public display. In New Delhi, thousands of Indian peasants placed flowers at the embassy gate and attended an outdoor memorial service at the entrance. An Indian poll shortly before Kennedy's death found him more popular than Prime Minister Jawaharlal Nehru. In their homes, villagers placed Kennedy's picture next to those of Mohandas Gandhi and Nehru. Young leaders of the new African nations liked Kennedy, and local television anchors who reported his death did so through tears. In Guinea, Sékou Touré said, "I have lost my only true friend in the outside world." In the Dominican Republic, 5,000 people signed the embassy consolation book; more than a week later special masses continued to be said throughout the country. In Brazil taxi drivers and shopkeepers offered condolences to Americans even two weeks after Kennedy's death. Months later villagers in the Peruvian Andes still mourned.[11]

The Supreme Court was in conference when the news came by messenger. Earl Warren read the announcement and then wept. When Lyndon Johnson asked the chief justice to head a commission to investigate the assassination, Warren accepted only after the president warned that there might be a nuclear war if he refused. From the beginning, the Warren Commission had an impossible task. Many believed that rightists were behind Kennedy's murder; others blamed communists. A few speculated that the FBI or the CIA were responsible. Among the more bizarre theories was that of a Sino-Soviet plot to kill Kennedy because he had authorized an attack on Chinese nuclear facilities. There was a grain of truth in this idea. Averell Harriman had, at Kennedy's request, asked the Soviets to bomb the Chinese facilities. Khrushchev had declined. After Lee Harvey Oswald was arrested, television had almost immediately identified his leftist ties. The alleged assassin wanted to be represented by John Abt, a longtime Communist party attorney. Abt declined. Oswald then asked for an attorney through the American Civil Liberties Union, and William Kunstler, a New York attorney who had handled many civil rights cases in Mississippi, agreed to take the case. Just as Kunstler was about to fly to Dallas, he learned that Jack Ruby had shot Oswald. Kunstler later aided Ruby's defense.[12]

From the beginning, many suspected a Cuban connection. Within days of the assassination, Elizabeth Churchill Brown, wife of the anticommunist columnist Constance Brown, argued that Castro had authorized Kennedy's death to retaliate for a CIA-led attempt to kill Castro. "Castro learned that he was to be Diem-ed," she wrote a friend. The ever astute Clare Boothe Luce privately agreed. Madame Nhu, Diem's sister-in-law, had pointedly and publicly said, "The chickens have come home to roost." Mrs. Brown, however, gradually backed away from this claim. "The more we learn," she wrote in a letter in 1964, "the more mysterious that [event] becomes." The original hunch may have been correct. "Kennedy was trying to get Castro," Johnson later privately told a number of people, "but Castro got him first." Years later, the Church Committee publicly disclosed details about various CIA plots to kill Castro, including the fact that the CIA had used mob elements with traditional gambling interests in Cuba as go-betweens. The CIA-mob tie-in made it hard to sort matters out, but undertaking the assassination of a president was more dangerous for Castro than for the mob. In addition to the mob, prosecuted vigorously by Robert Kennedy, others had good reasons to want Kennedy dead: Jimmy Hoffa; Cuban exiles, bitter over the Bay of Pigs fiasco; or die-hard segregationists who incorrectly believed that they would fare better with Lyndon Johnson.[13]

The Warren Commission did not seem eager to pursue all leads. Lindy Boggs, widow of Hale Boggs, a commission member, later stated that the family had accepted the report's conclusion that no evidence had been presented for a conspiracy. "I am reasonably sure," cautiously wrote Justice Hugo Black, a friend of Warren's, "that those gentlemen reported what they believed to be true." The assassination produced excitement in odd places. William Baker, a Toronto advertising executive with intelligence ties, told David Ogilvy, an American ad man who had headed British intelligence in the United States during World War II, that rumors were flying all over Toronto. Perhaps this is not surprising when one considers that Canada and Cuba maintained relations during these years. Just minutes after the shooting, CIA Chief John McCone rushed from headquarters to Robert Kennedy's nearby home. They talked privately on the lawn. The reporter Arthur Krock, who had long been close to both the Kennedys and McCone, prepared memoranda about the assassination for his files on November 22 and December 16. On the latter date Krock had met with McCone and Robert Kennedy. Krock did not use these notes in his memoirs, and they were missing from his papers when inventoried at Princeton University in 1977. On Lyndon Johnson's first day as president, J. Edgar Hoover privately told Johnson that the Lee Harvey Oswald who had entered the Soviet embassy in Mexico City was not the same man as the Oswald in Dallas.[14]

Americans shared many different feelings. According to one poll, 92 percent felt sorrow for Jackie and the children, and three-fourths had offered special prayers for them. Jackie Kennedy received more than a million condolence letters; a volunteer staff of 3,000 sent out more than 900,000 acknowledgments. "I can only wonder," one American wrote privately, "how Jackie will be able to live with the memory for the rest of her life." Another common feeling was loss of hope, and the end of what had been seen as a promising time for America. "We thought the world could be changed," recalled the staffer Roger Hilsman, "We thought one man could make a difference." There was also humiliation. "How could this awful thing have happened in our country?" asked the writer Kay

Boyle in a letter. To Dean Acheson, the United States looked like the terrorist-racked Congo. Agnes Meyer privately complained, "We're nothing but a goddamned banana republic." Dwight Macdonald said, "Let's move to Guatemala or some civilized place...." Assassinations were not supposed to occur in contented middle-class nations. Was America peculiarly violent? The writer Janet Flanner, who lived in Paris, thought so. She blamed money-grubbing and thwarted freedom-seeking. "It seems as if a mask has suddenly been torn off of this country," Hannah Arendt wrote Karl Jaspers, "And behind it we see an abyss of potential violence and pure bloodthirstiness." The diarist Helen Bevington recorded that "the violence is in us all."[15]

Television coverage mesmerized and massaged. Over four days, the typical American watched eight or more hours per day about the assassination. Not to watch was almost un-American. "Never has tv been so great," wrote one enthusiast to a friend. This reaction, while common, is curious, because television was rife with repetitive videotape, speculative interviews, and unconfirmed rumors. Questions about Oswald's motivation or whether he had acted alone gained prominence on television and were magnified in importance by their mention. While fresh and exciting, these live broadcasts created a cascade of confused, disjointed facts rather than any coherent, rational interpretation of events. The overall effect, however, was to bind the nation to a common experience – the televised assassination – to create acute emotional intensity and to present a chaotic, inchoate event as holistic and, therefore, capable of being cathartic and therapeutic. If Kennedy's death made the country look berserk, then the public expression of the televised proceedings imposed a form of order, not through rational discourse, but through the Beat, postmodern method of the intensely shared vicarious experience. "It all shows how impermanent are things," Louis Ginsberg wrote his son Allen. "Nothing is constant but change." If one rejected that perspective, one might be forced, like Hannah Arendt, to see in Kennedy's death that "everything could collapse like a house of cards." That could be a dangerous thought.[16]

The funeral, carefully planned by Jackie Kennedy, was stunning, orchestrated pageantry. Television viewers would remember the horse-drawn hearse, General Charles De Gaulle and other world leaders walking through the streets, Jackie Kennedy dressed in impeccable black and, "like Medea," grimly holding her children's hands, and John, Jr., saluting his father's coffin. The reporter Bill Lawrence was proud that, as a professional, he had not cried, but Kennedy's three-year-old son's act proved to be too much. If Dallas had represented chaos with Kennedy's murder, with Oswald's shooting a policeman during his arrest, and with Ruby killing Oswald inside a police station on national television, then the funeral in Washington was designed to reimpose order with the coffin, the hearse, the family, the mass, the dignitaries, and burial at a grave in Arlington marked by an eternal flame. "How much one could learn in these 72 hours," wrote one astute letter-writer, "about the shortcuts to gloire by violent death; about the irrationale in history; about the making of a myth which for a long time will preside over the destinies of this nation. About the fact that sacrificial death – however involuntary and imperfect – derives some of the magic and redemptive power from Christ's death on the Cross; that by such a death the victim quasi participates in the divine...."[17]

And so, one is tempted to say, Kennedy was deified. "So far," wrote one jaded observer, "neither the United States nor Washington have been renamed Kennedy, but almost everything else has." Honors included New York's major airport; Washington's projected arts center; Cape Canaveral, Florida (later restored); the nearby space facility; and numerous schools and roads. Twenty years after his death, Americans rated Kennedy, despite a lack of accomplishments, as one of the two or three best presidents. In 1983 almost a third wished he were president then; nearly two-thirds thought that the country would have been different if Kennedy had lived. The promising time, it was widely believed, would have continued. The principal source of this adulation was the unity created by the funeral; its underlying dynamic was fear. Stanley Levison attended Kennedy's funeral. "It was more solemn than even the nature of the tragedy could explain," he told a friend. The reason, he believed, was "fear." Kennedy's violent death, according to some, came close to being a coup. That was why Lyndon Johnson begged Kennedy's staff to stay on and pledged to push Kennedy's agenda. The Cold War, racial unrest, family crisis, and cultural decomposition were all real. Kennedy had shown an unusual confidence that he could manage the United States through a decade that he had predicted would be difficult. The assassination suggested that a crackup, nuclear, racial, or otherwise, might not be preventable.[18]

Because television made Kennedy's death into a unifying event, his presidency gained a coherence in public memory that had been lacking in his lifetime. The administration's contradictions were overlooked. As the columnist Roscoe Drummond publicly noted, "President Kennedy has been on both sides of so many big questions." The reporter George Herman agreed. For most politicians pretended agreement was a strategy, but Kennedy enjoyed ambiguity. This two-sidedness puzzled Edward R. Murrow. "I have had great difficulty in trying to reach some judgement regarding that young man's relation to his time," he wrote Robert Oppenheimer. "...there remains for me a considerable element of mystery....I always knew where his mind was, but I was not always sure where his heart was." The ambiguity suggested transcendance. "There was an unknown quality about Kennedy," recalled the diplomat Chip Bohlen, "despite all his realism, that gave you infinite hope that somehow or other he was going to change the course of history...." Critics interpreted matters more harshly. The New Dealer Harry McPherson complained that Kennedy "was unable to get anything done." The journalist I. F. Stone thought Kennedy a

"Prince Charming" whose reputation was saved only by death before the problems overwhelmed him. While some believed that, had he lived, change would have "progressed," others dismissed him as a historical footnote. Years later the cartoonist Jules Feiffer declared Kennedy "a wonderful stylist and a bad president."[19]

Kennedy's death especially affected African Americans; they felt that he cared. At the Capitol, many blacks stood in line for hours to have a chance to file past the casket. Although Bayard Rustin dismissed the Kennedy administration as "horribly overrated," other civil rights leaders knew grief. Andrew Young was at a training session in South Carolina when the news came; everyone cried. Years later, John Lewis, whose militance had nearly wrecked the March on Washington, recalled, "It was the saddest day of my life." Given Kennedy's limited accomplishments, his appeal is difficult to explain. Lewis thought that Kennedy had, for a politician, an unusual capacity to listen; he created optimism. Martin Luther King, Jr., watched the assassination with his wife at home on television. He told Coretta that he, too, would be killed. She felt that he was correct. Their daughter Yoki came home from school and said, "Oh, Mommy, we're never going to get our freedom now." Kennedy's death affected Coretta King more deeply than any event in her life to that time. Not everyone was so moved. Elijah Muhammad gave careful instructions to members of the Nation of Islam to be silent on this potentially divisive topic. When Malcolm X disobeyed by stating publicly that Kennedy "never foresaw that the chickens would come home to roost," he was thrown out of the Muslim movement.[20]

Among white southerners, Kennedy had dwindling support in 1963. Many incorrectly blamed him for the rising civil rights movement. To some extent, they felt betrayed by a man who had sought their votes as a fellow Democrat but had, from their viewpoint, proved unreliable in upholding white supremacy. Although Byron De La Beckwith, under arrest for Medgar Evers's murder, publicly called Kennedy's assassination "fearful," he privately expressed a different view. When the late president was honored with new half dollars, Beckwith wanted to flush the coins down the toilet, and he wrote his son, "That fellow sho' done some fancy shooting didn't he HAW HAW HAW. I'll bet Medgar Evers said I thought you'd get down here pretty soon boss. HA HA HA." Although Beckwith's views were extreme, plenty of southerners had reasons, as one astute observer noted, to feel guilty. In parts of the South, white students, still in segregated schools, cheered when Kennedy's assassination was announced. Hugo Black's sister-in-law, Virginia Durr, lived across the street from a high school in Montgomery, Alabama. When the news came, teens honked their car horns and shouted hurrahs. In one town in Mississippi two businessmen announced an Oswald appreciation fund.[21]

Some white southerners aside, Kennedy had held an especial appeal to the nation's young. Parents reported that nearly a quarter of the country's children were "very upset" by the assassination. Kennedy captured youth with excitement and idealism; with a style that emphasized wit, vigor, sexiness, and physical fitness; with a commitment to civil rights and social change; with specific programs, particularly the Peace Corps and the space program. What most drew youth to Kennedy, however, was that more than any other leader of his time, and regardless of chronological age, Kennedy seemed interested in, fascinated by, and committed to the future. His speeches, no matter the topic, always had an eye on tomorrow. He bonded with youth because he himself seemed youthful, and he made others feel that way. "When Kennedy was alive," said 72-year-old Averell Harriman, "was the last time I felt young." That was why Sam Behrman and Sir Isaiah Berlin could agree that "the air was de-oxygenated with JFK gone." Kennedy's unique angle of vision may have been the result of his upper-class origins. If the middle class cared mostly about comfort in the present, perhaps an aristocrat could afford the luxury of looking toward and seeking to do what was best for the future. Kennedy's ambition, the newscaster Walter Cronkite later recalled, had not been personal but "for the country."[22]

While adults could regard the assassination as an unfortunate incident in a lifetime of good mixed with evil, Kennedy's death to the young had a different message. The president's demise crushed their idealism. This result could be seen almost immediately in pop music. The folk revival, rooted in the idea of a promising time, abruptly ended. The Kingston Trio never had another album that charted. More curiously, the insipid rock and roll of the early sixties also ceased. For the month after the assassination, the pop charts were dominated by a strange record called *The Singing Nun* (1963). The Belgian Sister Luc-Gabrielle, who spoke no English, sang religious songs in French. Although few Americans could follow the lyrics, the beautiful melodies were not an inappropriate form of mourning for a Catholic president and his francophone wife. In early 1964 the nun's lamentations faded, and the Beatles arrived in America with a stunning new kind of rock music rooted in black rhythm and blues. If folk had expressed youth's hope for a better tomorrow, the Beatles' clever lyrics and breathtaking beat suggested a frontal assault on traditional culture. The Beatles' name, after all, could be interpreted as paying homage to Jack Kerouac, Allen Ginsberg, and other Beat rebels. No longer would young people strum folk guitars and express vague hopes; now they intended to be in charge of their own destiny. Bob Dylan understood, when he called his first electric album *Bringing It All Back Home* (1965).[23]

Kennedy's death also reshaped the civil rights movement. To many activists, Kennedy seemed reluctant and sometimes lacking in courage, but few doubted his basic commitment to equality. In a Senate eulogy, Mike Mansfield had called the late president "a good, kindly, and decent man." Those qualities meshed well with the movement's demand for fairness and social justice. Lyndon Johnson, in contrast, was a shadowy figure known for wily manipulations. Although he proved more effective at getting civil rights bills through Congress than Kennedy had been, activists found the atmosphere less hopeful. The southern movement was based upon the idea of a redemptive love so powerful that it would end hate and nonviolently dissolve the power of white supremacy. The assassination mocked the movement's idealism and called into question the practicality of its philosophy. In 1963 the movement had not yet reached the northern cities, which were already seething, as indicated by the rising influence of the separatist Malcolm X. If the movement was rooted in hope, and if it depended, ultimately, for its success upon federal power, then the assassination threatened both that hope and the government's self-confidence. In truth, the assassination had jarred the political system, bewildered the public, and created doubt and uncertainty. Hesitation in high places did not benefit the movement. In the late sixties the movement turned violent and collapsed amid increasing political paralysis.[24]

Kennedy had understood that the Cold War was the key to the era. Preventing nuclear war and avoiding lesser wars were important goals. The former would destroy everything, while the latter could become nuclear or could weaken the United States through long, bloody conflict. More than anything else, patience was needed to manage the Cold War. Patience was neither a Kennedy virtue nor an American trait. "The problems were bigger than we thought," conceded Roger Hilsman. At the time of Kennedy's death, Cuba and, increasingly, Vietnam remained sore subjects. No American president during the Cold War could easily concede any country to communism. Because Kennedy had failed in Cuba, he could not afford to lose again in Vietnam. Kennedy's weak foreign-policy team remained in place in the Johnson administration. Although Kennedy had a sense of history and respect for Third World autonomy, he may not have understood the limits of American power. In the nineteenth century great powers moved at will in remote parts of the world; the postwar experience proved different. Kennedy would have been tempted to use American ground troops in Vietnam, as Johnson did. That successor was led into the Vietnam War by Kennedy's team, which almost certainly would have given Kennedy the same advice. He would have found resistance to their arguments very difficult. "This was an interventionist administration," observed Hilsman.[25]

Kennedy's sudden, brutal death ended both the early sixties and the promising time that it had come to represent. The era's problems and the changes that were beginning to occur continued. The Cold War lasted another quarter century, until the Soviet Union collapsed. Race relations gradually improved, as African Americans and other racial minorities made great strides in joining the middle class. Few among the next generation subscribed to white supremacy. Family life continued to evolve, sexual mores grew looser, at least until the AIDS epidemic brought greater caution, and women played new roles in American society. Over time, Americans enjoyed a cultural flowering based on growing diversity. Public expression of private thoughts, even when prudence might suggest otherwise, became the norm. The result was a nation with a franker politics, society, and culture, which often in postmodern fashion projected self-reflexive irony and satire. Those qualities, exemplified by the work of Allen Ginsberg, Bob Dylan, and Andy Warhol, contrasted with the values of John Kennedy in the more earnest early sixties. Setting sights lower prevented disappointment, but the loss of confidence in a promising time, while realistic, also reduced hope. That is why the early sixties have so often been seen as a golden age. Golden it was not; promising it was.

Conclusion

What conclusions can we draw about the early sixties? First, although John Kennedy was the dominant public figure of that promising time and virtually invented television-driven celebrity politics, he did not, with the possible exception of the Missile Crisis, ever control events. Unlike most politicians, Kennedy understood that staggering, even breathtaking changes were taking place throughout the world; globalization was a reality. Although he showed a keen understanding of the big picture, he had a poor grasp of details: He did not envision Asia's future explosive economic growth; he sometimes accepted too readily exaggerated estimates of the Soviet Union's economic and military strength; and he seemed to assume that some sort of welfare state would eventually prevail in most of the world, including the United States. While future-oriented, he tended, like other World War II veterans, to emphasize military power and "toughness," an attitude that could be dangerous in a nuclear world. Secretary of State Dean Rusk cited Neville Chamberlain's agreement with Adolf Hitler at Munich as a kind of weakness to be avoided. Rusk missed the fact that while Nikita Khrushchev was expansion-minded, he was not Hitler. Kennedy and his entourage were, unfortunately, warped in judgment by traumatic historical events that were not germane.

Second, the Cold War was the most important fact in American life for 40 years after the end of World War II. Relations between the United States and the Soviet Union ranged over time from a tense rivalry with undercurrents of improvement to downright hostility. No period was more hostile than the early sixties. After the death of Joseph Stalin in 1953, there had been a slight thaw in American–Soviet relations, but the early sixties reversed that trend. The Soviet crushing of the Hungarian revolution of 1956 confirmed permanent Soviet control of Eastern Europe; Germany remained divided, and West Berlin, though controlled by the United States and its allies, was militarily indefensible. Fidel Castro's triumph in 1959 suggested the possibility for numerous guerrilla revolutions in Third World countries. Africa, Asia, and Latin America were ripe for communist takeover, a point that Khrushchev publicly emphasized in 1961. Kennedy faced especially hostile criticism about the loss of Cuba to communism because of its proximity to the United States. He felt obligated to try to avoid defeat elsewhere, including Vietnam. The failure of the invasion at the Bay of Pigs led Castro to seek and get missiles from the Soviet Union, which provoked the crisis in October 1962, when the world nearly came to nuclear war. Throughout Kennedy's presidency the Cold War was frightening. This fear permeated all aspects of American life and undercut the feeling that the early sixties was a promising time.

Third, the civil rights movement, which began before 1960, reached new heights during the early sixties. Brilliant leadership from Martin Luther King, Jr., and mass participation, especially by young black college students, caused an explosion of activity that rattled the strongholds of white supremacy by 1963. The movement combined traditional political lobbying with the new tactic of the mass sit-in, and as arrests spread throughout the South, segregation was challenged in a way that guaranteed that it could not long survive. Had there been no Cold War, the federal government might well have pursued the traditional post-Reconstruction policy of allowing the white-controlled South, where the race problem was worst, simply to go its own way. The Cold War, however, required the United States to make alliances with nonwhite nations, especially Japan, and to seek to prevent communism from spreading to the nonwhite Third World. As a result, the federal government had to oppose white supremacy at home. A sympathetic federal government, especially during the Kennedy administration, often led civil rights activists to feel encouraged. In the long term, the movement left three legacies from this promising time. Most important was the end of legalized white supremacy, but consciousness among Americans about the evil of racism also grew. Then, too, the movement encouraged other groups to organize using similar tactics. In particular, feminists took notice.

Fourth, as early as World War II, the American family had begun to change in important ways, especially as married women entered the workforce in large numbers for the first time. Although some women left jobs at the end of the war, many continued to work, and by the fifties the number of working wives was reaching unprecedented numbers. At the same time, a distinct youth culture began to emerge. The war had also loosened traditional sexual mores and attitudes about censorship of sexual materials. By the late fifties *Playboy* had millions of readers, and avant-garde books and films were challenging restrictions against publication or dissemination. In the early sixties Betty Friedan publicized the powerful discrepancy between the home-oriented housewife promoted by women's magazines as an ideal and the unhappy reality of many American women. When Friedan published her observations, she received inordinately large numbers of letters from disgruntled women, who began to rethink their role in society. Although feminism, per se, dates from the later sixties, the origins of that movement can be seen in events in the decade's promising early years.

Finally, profound upheavals took place in American culture in the early sixties. The Beat writers, scathing critics of mainstream values, had first gained public notice in the fifties, but only in the early sixties did they achieve sufficient stature to be taken seriously. Their importance was that they dared to criticize a smug, self-contained society that had considered itself to be above criticism. The folk revival marked a curious, almost nostalgic return to the popular music of the late thirties. Because of its connections to the past, it was probably doomed to a short life, but it was partially rescued by Bob Dylan's unique abilities as both a composer and a performer. The poet Dylan remade the way pop songs were written and in the process challenged the culture frontally. Pop Art was not just a fad, although it was popular. Rather, Roy Lichtenstein and Andy Warhol reconceptualized art in a way that both embraced and challenged the emergent consumer culture. The rise of LSD, although it did not move outside elite circles until after 1963, suggested how older values were being threatened. Collectively, these changes in culture suggest that the early sixties both showed mainstream culture to be vulnerable to attack and marked a promising time of unusual experimentation.

The early sixties ended abruptly. What came after was not entirely predictable, because when societies undergo upheaval, and especially drastic cultural change, the old order is a poor guide to the new one. In some ways, the cultural changes proved the most important and the most interesting. Certainly, the verities of fifties culture are long gone, and those aspects which passed for avant-garde then, such as Abstract Expressionism, seem passé now. After 1963, families continued to be transformed, and large numbers of women began to redefine themselves in the women's movement. Race relations were also reconfigured, although the changes did not entirely meet the goals of civil rights activists. The Cold War ended with the collapse of the Soviet Union; the Berlin Wall came down in 1989. Looking back, we can see now that the Cold War in part filled a vacuum for Americans frightened by all the changes unleashed by World War II. As questions of race, gender, and culture unfolded in the postwar years, the Cold War provided an organizing framework that both gave conservatives, at least for a time, the hope of stopping change in its tracks, and gave liberals, pressing for more change, an argument to make changes in order to win the Cold War. The Cold War proved usable by different people for different purposes.

How much about the early sixties John Kennedy understood is unclear, although he certainly both expressed and helped sustain the idea that it was a promising time. Like most politicians, he was often vague. When talking, he preferred to give questions rather than answers, to offer wit rather than conclusions. Or he obfuscated by reciting information. Perhaps the tendency toward witty questioning marks Kennedy as an appropriate symbol for the early sixties, a time caught between the truths of traditional society and those of the postmodern age. Although Americans in those years found life clearly distinct from the quieter, more predictable, and more anemic Eisenhower years, they could not in the early sixties entirely separate themselves from that earlier time or from the mainstream culture that had then prevailed so overwhelmingly. The early sixties, as we have seen, remain linked to the fifties. While trends in the early sixties can be seen leading to the later sixties, there is also a sense in which the decade's two portions are marked by the sharp break of Kennedy's assassination. The Vietnam War, which heated up in 1965, also played a major role in dividing the more peaceful first portion of the sixties from the later period. That unpopular war rattled the government, enraged the young, and led many Americans toward pessimism and despair. African Americans rioted, college students rebelled, and feminists marched for rights. The seeds had been planted in the early sixties, if not before, but, as we have seen, they remained largely underground sprouts in 1963.

Abbreviations

AG-CU	Allen Ginsberg Papers, Columbia University
AG-SU	Allen Ginsberg Papers, Stanford University
CIA	Central Intelligence Agency
COH	Columbia University Oral History
CORE	Congress of Racial Equality
FBI	Federal Bureau of Investigation
HUAC	House Un-American Activities Committee
JFK	John Fitzgerald Kennedy
JFK NSF	John F. Kennedy, National Security Files
JOH	Lyndon B. Johnson Library Oral History
KOH	John F. Kennedy Library Oral History
LAT	*Los Angeles Times*
LBJ	Lyndon Baines Johnson
MLK	Martin Luther King, Jr.
MLK-SL	Martin Luther King, Jr.-Stanley Levison
MOH	Mississippi Department of Archives and History Oral History
NAACP	National Association for the Advancement of Colored People
NYT	*New York Times*

RFK	Robert Francis Kennedy
SANE	Committee for a Sane Nuclear Policy
SCLC	Southern Christian Leadership Conference
SDS	Students for a Democratic Society
SEP	*Saturday Evening Post*
SNCC	Student Non-Violent Coordinating Committee
SPU	Student Peace Union
SRC	Southern Regional Council
SRC VEP	Southern Regional Council, Voter Education Project
UCLA OH	University of California, Los Angeles Oral History
VEP	Voter Education Project
WP	*Washington Post*
WSJ	*Wall Street Journal*
WSP	Women Strike for Peace

Notes

Chapter One

1 Stephen E. Ambrose, *Nixon* (New York, 1987–1989), 1:585; George H. Gallup, *The Gallup Poll* (New York, 1972), 3:1703 and passim.

2 (automation) David F. Noble, *Forces of Production* (New York, 1984); Charles R. Walker, *Toward the Automatic Factory* (New Haven, 1957); (interstates) Mark H. Rose, *Interstate* (rev. ed., Knoxville, 1990); (69 elected) Joseph C. Goulden, *The Best Years, 1945–1950* (New York, 1976), 229; (leaders) Curt Gentry, *J. Edgar Hoover* (New York, 1991); George Q. Flynn, *Lewis B. Hershey, Mr. Selective Service* (Chapel Hill, 1985); Archie Robinson, *George Meany and His Times* (New York, 1981); John Cooney, *The American Pope* (New York, 1984).

3 John Calmann to Fionn O'Neill, Oct. 2, 1959, in JC, *The Letters of John Calmann* (London, 1986), 42 (quote); Ambrose, *Nixon*, 1:513–514, 589; Theodore H. White, *The Making of the President, 1960* (New York, 1961), 219, 222; J. B. West with Mary L. Kotz, *Upstairs at the White House* (New York, 1973), 159.

4 Quotes from Goldman in Jim F. Heath, *Decade of Disillusionment* (Bloomington, IN, 1975), 5; Hannah Arendt to Karl Jaspers, June 20, 1960, Arendt–Jaspers, *Hannah Arendt–Karl Jaspers*, ed. Lotte Kohler and Hans Saner (New York, 1992), 396; Richard N. Goodwin, *Remembering America* (Boston, 1988), 73; Joseph W. Alsop to Sol Sanders, Dec. 22, 1960, Box 17, Alsop Papers; Stevenson in White, *President, 1960*, 119. Authorship is in John B. Martin to Arthur M. Schlesinger, Jr., Jan. 17, 1960, Box 31:1, JBM Papers. See also Dwight Macdonald, *Against*

the *American Grain* (New York, 1962); John Kenneth Galbraith, *The Affluent Society* (Boston, 1958); John Andrew, "The Impending Crises of the 1960s: National Goals and National Purpose," *Viet Nam Generation*, 6:1–2 (1994), 30–41.

5 U.S. Bureau of the Census, *Historical Statistics of the United States, Colonial Times to 1970* (Washington, 1975), 49; U.S. Bureau of the Census, *Census of Population: 1960, V. 1. Characteristics of the Population, Pt. 6, California* (Washington, 1963), 6:471; Gallup, *Gallup Poll*, 3:1685.

6 *I. F. Stone's Weekly*, Nov. 7, 1960, p. 1; Stephen J. Whitfield, *The Culture of the Cold War* (Baltimore, 1991), 179–180. An astute observation on sterility is offered by William Preston's 1989 introduction to Cedric Belfrage, *The American Inquisition, 1945–1960* (2nd ed., New York, 1989), xv–xxi. Quotes from Victor S. Navasky, *Naming Names* (New York, 1980), 44; Carey McWilliams, "The Issues in 1960" (unpub., 1960) and "Horizons for the Independent Voter," (unpub., 1957), 6, both in Box 42, CM Papers.

7 Quotes from J. T. Fraser to William F. Buckley, Jr., Sept. 3, 1961, Box 14:49, WFB Papers; Taylor Caldwell to Alexander King, May 25, 1960, Box 1:13, AK Papers; Steinbeck in Whitfield, *Culture*, 177; *Boston Pilot*, Aug. 13, 1955, copy in Box 13:7, WFB Papers; Farley in Belfrage, *Inquisition*, 194; Carey McWilliams, "The Sixties Will Be Different!" (unpub. lecture, ca. 1960), Box 38, CM Papers.

8 Fred I. Greenstein, *The Hidden-Hand Presidency* (New York, 1982); Gallup, *Gallup Poll*, 3:1596; Arthur Krock, *Memoirs* (New York, 1968), 274–276, 313–315; Arthur Krock Memos #335, Apr. 7, 1960, and #339, July 7, 1960, AK Papers; Eisenhower quoted in Ambrose, *Nixon*, 1:559.

9 Quotes from Nixon in Whitfield, *Culture*, 19; Truman in Merle Miller, ed., *Plain Speaking* (New York, 1974), 188; Calmann, *Letters*, 122; Goldwater in David Halberstam, *The Fifties* (New York, 1993), 314; JFK in Fawn Brodie, *Richard Nixon* (New York, 1981), 414.

10 Theodore Sorensen, *Kennedy* (New York, 1965), 108, 122–123; Calmann, *Letters*, 66; Chalmers M. Roberts KOH, 1; John B. Martin to Arthur M. Schlesinger, Jr., Jan. 17, 1960, Box 31:1, JBM Papers; Jacqueline Kennedy quoted in William Attwood, *The Twilight Struggle* (New York, 1987), 223.

11 Quotes from Robert G. Baker with Larry L. King, *Wheeling and Dealing* (New York, 1978), 45 (1st, 4th quotes); Michael R. Beschloss, *The Crisis Years* (New York, 1991), 34; Sorensen, *Kennedy*, 178.

12 Quotes from David Burner and Thomas R. West, *The Torch Is Passed* (New York, 1984), 201; *National Guardian*, Jan. 30, 1961, p. 7; Beschloss, *Crisis Years*, 296. See also John H. Davis, *The Kennedys* (New York, 1984); Richard J. Whalen, *The Founding Father* (New York, 1964); Charles

Higham, *Rose* (New York, 1995); James Spada, *Peter Lawford* (New York, 1991); Arthur M. Schlesinger, Jr., *Robert Kennedy and His Times* (Boston, 1978).

13 Clinton P. Anderson with Milton Viorst, *Outsider in the Senate* (New York, 1970), 307. Most useful on early life is Nigel Hamilton, *JFK, Reckless Youth* (New York, 1992). The Buick is in Joe McCarthy, *The Remarkable Kennedys* (New York, 1960), 84. On *Profiles* see Sorensen, *Kennedy*, 67–70; Phil [Graham] to Drew Pearson, Dec. 13, 1957, and DP notes, n.d., both in Box G121, 1 of 3, DP Papers.

14 (Arvad) Gentry, *Hoover*, 402, 467–470, 472 (quote); Hamilton, *JFK*, 453–458, 470–478; Athan S. Theoharis and John S. Cox, *The Boss* (Philadelphia, 1988), 371n, 372–376, 381–382, 388; (PT109) Hamilton, *JFK*, 525–633.

15 (elections) David S. Broder, *The Party's Over* (New York, 1971), 18–22; Charles Bartlett KOH, 1–18; Thomas P. O'Neill JOH, 1:18–20; (Sorensen) Lester Tanzer, ed., *The Kennedy Circle* (Washington, 1961), 3–28; Sorensen, *Kennedy*, esp. 60–64; (McCarthy) Burner and West, *Torch*, 55; Arthur M. Schlesinger, Jr., *A Thousand Days* (Boston, 1965), 12; Sorensen, *Kennedy*, 49; Robert Amory KOH, 7 (quote).

16 (invitations) *WP*, Jan. 24, 1960, p. F1; (polls) Gallup, *Gallup Poll*, 3:1622, 1629–1630; *Los Angeles Mirror*, June 4, 1959, and *Parade*, June 21, 1959, both in Box 53, Adlai E. Stevenson Papers; (strategy) Sorensen, *Kennedy*, 28, 96–97, 99, 127–128; White, *President, 1960*, 54–55. Quotes from Whalen, *Founding Father*, 446; Stewart Alsop, "Kennedy's Magic Formula," *SEP*, Aug. 13, 1960, p. 59; *I.F. Stone's Weekly*, Nov. 7, 1960, p. 1; Gore Vidal, "The Holy Family," *Esquire*, Apr. 1967, p. 204.

17 Beschloss, *Crisis Years*, 187, 189; Davis, *Kennedys*, 138–139, 170–171, 182, 211; India Edwards, *Pulling No Punches* (New York, 1977), 228–230; Sorensen, *Kennedy*, 38–39, 41; Janet G. Travell, *Office Hours* (New York, 1968), 323, 327, 330–333. Travell is more candid in Travell KOH, 2–16, 19. See also American Medical Association, *Archives of Surgery*, 71:5 (Nov. 1955), 739–740. Case 3 is JFK.

18 Beschloss, *Crisis Years*, 473–475, 610–617; Davis, *Kennedys*, 197–201, 228–231, 468–471; Seymour M. Hersh, *The Dark Side of Camelot* (Boston, 1997), 110–117; C. David Heymann, *A Woman Named Jackie* (New York, 1994); Richard Reeves, *President Kennedy* (New York, 1993), 289–292; Jacqueline Kennedy quoted in Spada, *Lawford*, 251. (flight attendant) Jack Anderson memo to Drew Pearson, Dec. 20, 1960, Box G121, 1 of 3, DP Papers; (Campbell) Judith Exner with Ovid Demaris, *My Story* (New York, 1977); Hersh, *Dark Side*, 294–323; *New Times*, Jan. 23, 1976, p. 21ff; Campbell in *People*, Feb. 29, 1988, p. 106ff; *Vanity Fair*, Apr. 1990, p. 162ff. For another case, see Florence M. Kater to Gore Vidal, n.d.; to

Jack Paar, Oct. 28, 1961; to Dwight D. Eisenhower, Nov. 2, 1961, all in Box 92:3, GV Papers.

19 Hubert H. Humphrey, *The Education of a Public Man* (New York, 1976), 149–159; Sorensen, *Kennedy*, 133–142 (1st quote at 135); White, *President, 1960*, 92–107; Joseph Rauh JOH, 2:1–10. On West Virginia corruption see Drew Pearson convention notes, Box G121, 1 of 3, DP Papers; DP notes, Box G269, 2 of 3, DP Papers; Lee Hendrik to DP, May 13, 1960 (2nd quote), Box G266, 1 of 2, DP Papers; H. L. Hunt-Walter Jenkins call, May 17, 1960, Box 2, WJ Ser. 2, LBJ Papers. Evidence of mob money is on FBI taps. *People*, Feb. 29, 1988, p. 111. On timid reporting see Hersh, *Dark Side*, 90–100; George Reedy to LBJ, May 16, 1960, Box 430, LBJ Papers-U.S. Senate Papers. David Brinkley personally saw vote-buying. *The Great Campaign of 1960* (2000 film).

20 Mary A. Watson, *The Expanding Vista* (New York, 1990), 8; *NYT*, July 10, 1960, p. 47; *WP*, July 12, 1960, p. A11; July 15, 1960, p. A14 (Childs).

21 The best account of the roll call is in Sorensen, *Kennedy*, 158–162. Broder, *Party's Over*, 18–22; Kenneth S. Davis, *The Politics of Honor* (New York, 1967), 421, 429–432; Tanzer, *Kennedy Circle*, 298; White, *President, 1960*, 154–156; *NYT*, July 15, 1960, p. 22 (Reston); Dean Acheson to A. Whitney Griswold, Aug. 16, 1960, DA, *Among Friends*, ed. David S. McLellan and David C. Acheson (New York, 1980), 192 (quote).

22 (LBJ) Most useful are Phil Graham's memo in Theodore H. White, *The Making of the President, 1964* (New York, 1965), 408–413; Philip Potter, "How LBJ Got the Nomination," *Reporter*, June 18, 1964, p. 16; Katharine Graham, *Personal History* (New York, 1997), 261–267, 364. (civil rights) Simeon Booker KOH, 7–8; (acceptance) White, *President, 1960*, 177–178 (1st quote at 177); Ronald Reagan to Richard Nixon, July 15, 1960, Ambrose, *Nixon*, 1:546 (2nd quote). The sign is in Carey McWilliams Diary, July 15, 1960, CM Papers.

23 (Lodge) Ambrose, *Nixon*, 1:553–554, 580; (LBJ) Leonard Baker, *The Johnson Eclipse* (New York, 1966), 80–86, 89; (JFK) Sorensen, *Kennedy*, 189–194, 217.

24 (polls) Gallup, *Gallup Poll*, 3:1652, 1657, 1660, 1672, 1681–1683, 1687, 1690; (debates) Richard Nixon, *Six Crises* (2nd ed., New York, 1990), 323, 337–346; Sorensen, *Kennedy*, 197–199, 202, 211, 213; White, *President, 1960*, 276, 289–294, 331, 350; (MLK) Morris B. Abram, *The Day Is Short* (New York, 1982), 126–132; Coretta S. King, *My Life with Martin Luther King, Jr.* (New York, 1969), 193–197; Harris Wofford, *Of Kennedys and Kings* (New York, 1980), 11–28; (vote) George C. Roberts, *Paul M. Butler*

(Lanham, MD, 1987), 99; Russell Middleton, "The Civil Rights Issue and Presidential Voting among Southern Negroes and Whites," *Social Forces*, 40:3 (Mar. 1962), 209–215. Compare the Nixon and JFK ads in *Ebony*, Nov. 1960, pp. 8–9, 14–15.

25 My computations use Douglas W. Johnson, et al., *Churches & Church Membership in the United States, 1971* (Washington, 1974), 3–14. Humphrey, *Education*, 171 (quote). The best study is Philip E. Converse, et al., "Stability and Change in 1960," *American Political Science Review*, 55:2 (June 1961), 269–280.

26 "Inaugural Address," *Public Papers of the Presidents: John F. Kennedy, 1961* (Washington, 1962), 3.

27 Pierre Salinger, *With Kennedy* (Garden City, NY, 1966), 63–72, 74, 80; Schlesinger, *Thousand Days*, 124, 165, 167–168, 207–209, 213–214; Sorensen, *Kennedy*, 232, 258–264; Tanzer, *Kennedy Circle*, 29–57; Joseph Kraft, "Kennedy's Working Staff," *Harper's Magazine*, Dec. 1962, pp. 29–36; James M. Burns, "Political Craftsman in the White House," *NYT Magazine*, Jan. 15, 1961, p. 72.

28 Chester Bowles, *Promises to Keep* (New York, 1971), 304n4, 628–630; Helen Fuller, *Year of Trial* (New York, 1962), 43–44, 49–50; Salinger, *Kennedy*, 73–75, 209–210; Sorensen, *Kennedy*, 282–285; Amory KOH, 13–16.

29 (press) David Brinkley, *Memoirs* (New York, 1995), 139–140; Bill Lawrence, *Six Presidents, Too Many Wars* (New York, 1972), 4–5, 243, 247, 250; Salinger, *Kennedy*, 31–33, 46, 54–57, 60–61; Stewart Alsop to Martin Sommers, Jan. 16, 1961 [actually 1962] (1st quote), Box 31, Alsop Papers; (euphoria) Hannah Arendt-Mary McCarthy, *Between Friends*, ed. Carol Brightman (New York, 1995), 132; Goodwin, *Remembering*, 8–9; Heath, *Decade*, 60 (2nd quote).

Chapter Two

1 Statistics in H. W. Brands, *The Devil We Knew* (New York, 1993), 39. See also John L. Gaddis, *The United States and the End of the Cold War* (New York, 1992), and *We Now Know* (New York, 1997); Walter LaFeber, *America, Russia, and the Cold War, 1945–1996* (8th ed., New York, 1997); Richard N. Lebow and Janice G. Stein, *We All Lost the Cold War* (Princeton, 1994).

2 Dean Acheson, *Present at the Creation* (New York, 1969), esp. 726–728, 737. See also Vladislav M. Zubok and Constantine Pleshakov, *Inside the Kremlin's Cold War* (Cambridge, MA, 1996), esp. 2–7, 182–185.

3 Havery Klehr, et al., *The Secret World of American Communism* (New Haven, 1995). Membership in Dorothy Healey UCLA OH, 1:281, 2:646. Informants in Carey McWilliams UCLA OH, 352. See also Richard G. Powers, *Not without Honor* (New York, 1995), esp. 195–282.

4 (Hiss) Sam Tanenhaus, *Whittaker Chambers* (New York, 1997); Allen Weinstein, *Perjury* (New York, 1983); (FBI) Curt Gentry, *J. Edgar Hoover* (New York, 1991), 281, 417, 457–458, 474, 479; Athan G. Theoharis and John S. Cox, *The Boss* (Philadelphia, 1988), 6, 8, 227–229, 233–234; (files) John J. Abt with Michael Myerson, *Advocate and Activist* (Urbana, 1993), 282. See also Richard M. Fried, *Nightmare in Red* (New York, 1990).

5 (Stone) Robert C. Cottrell, *Izzy* (New Brunswick, NJ, 1992), 159, 228; (Bethe) *WP*, Feb. 10, 1962; (Lattimore) Robert P. Newman, *Owen Lattimore and the 'Loss' of China* (Berkeley, 1992), 53, 500–501; Barnes Riznick to Owen Lattimore, May 10, 1961 (quote), Box 16:2, OL Papers.

6 (Braden and Wilkinson) 365 U.S. 431 (1961); Richard Criley, *The FBI v. The First Amendment* (Los Angeles, 1990), 32–66; Griffin Fariello, *Red Scare* (New York, 1995), 528–537; Bud Schultz and Ruth Schultz, eds., *It Did Happen Here* (Berkeley, 1989), 265, 270–271; (Green) Gil Green, *Cold War Fugitive* (New York, 1984), 163–264; (Braden pardon) Jim Dombrowski to Carl Braden, Aug. 18, 1961, Box 11:8; Anne Braden to CB, Dec. 30, 1961, Box 11:9; Aubrey Williams to JD, Dec. 14, 1961 (1st quote), Box 21:7, all in Braden Papers; Harris Wofford to Lee White, Aug. 22, 1961, Box 11, Wofford Papers; (residues) William Peters to Joseph L. Rauh, Oct. 18, 1961 (2nd quote), Box 10:4, JLR Papers.

7 Melvin Arnold to Homer Jack, Dec. 18, 1961 (1st quote); HJ to Samuel J. Arnold, Apr. 26, 1962, both in Box B33, SANE Records; letter to Allan Forbes, Jr., Aug. 13 [1963] (2nd quote), Box 9:1, Joseph L. Rauh Papers.

8 (dinner) *NYT*, Apr. 29, 30, 1962; *WP*, Apr. 30, 1962; *San Francisco Chronicle*, May 1, 1962, p. 36 (1st quote); (Pauling) Letitia Baldrige, *Of Diamonds and Diplomats* (Boston, 1968), 209–210; Fariello, *Red Scare*, 426–428, 509–515; (Fermi Award) Adolf Berle to J. Robert Oppenheimer, Apr. 16, 1963 (2nd quote), Box 19:16, JRO Papers. McGeorge Bundy was probably most responsible for JRO's restoration. See letters, Box 23:11, JRO Papers.

9 Standard is Peter Wyden, *Bay of Pigs* (New York, 1979). Samuel F. Bemis to William F. Buckley, Jr., June 17, 1961, Box 13:31, WFB Papers. Quotes from Walfred A. Mattson to *SEP*, Sept. 21, 1961, Box 30, Alsop Papers; George Abell to Clare B. Luce, May 2 [1961], Box 213:9, CBL Papers; John B. Martin to Arthur M. Schlesinger, Jr., June 1, 1961, Box 44:6, JBM Papers; Wesley L. Gould to Hans J. Morgenthau, Sept. 6, 1962, Box 24:12, HJM Papers. See also Richard M. Bissell, Jr., with Jonathan E. Lewis

and Frances T. Pudlo, *Reflections of a Cold Warrior* (New Haven, 1996), 152–199.

10 Bill Lawrence, *Six Presidents, Too Many Wars* (New York, 1972), 261; Arthur M. Schlesinger, Jr., 2nd draft book MS, 468, Box W18, AMS Papers; Michael R. Beschloss, *The Crisis Years* (New York, 1991), 130; Wyden, *Bay of Pigs*, 294, 302.

11 Robert Lovett KOH, 36, 38; Dean Acheson to Harry S Truman, May 3, 1961, DA, *Among Friends*, ed. David S. McLellan and David C. Acheson (New York, 1980), 206–207; Barry M. Goldwater with Jack Casserly, *Goldwater* (New York, 1988), 137; Stephen E. Ambrose, *Nixon* (New York, 1987–1989), 1:633; John Kreuttner to William F. Buckley, Jr., Sept. 11, 1961, Box 15:22, WFB Papers; Philip Cortney to Clare B. Luce, June 7, 1961, Box 213:14, CBL Papers; David E. Lilienthal, *The Journals of David E. Lilienthal* (New York, 1972), 5:198.

12 Overton Harris to Arthur Krock, Apr. 22, 1961, Box 28, AK Papers, published with permission of Princeton Univ. Library; Stewart Alsop, *The Center* (New York, 1968), 228 (2nd quote), 211 (5th quote); Carey McWilliams Diary, Apr. 17, 21, 1961, CM Papers. See *Nation*, Nov. 19, 1960, p. 378; *NYT*, Nov. 20, 1960, p. 32; Jan. 10, 1961, pp. 1, 11.

13 Aleksandr Fursenko and Timothy Naftali, *One Hell of a Gamble* (New York, 1997), 9–10, 13–16, 19, 21, 29–30, 34–35, 42, 71–72; George H. Gallup, *The Gallup Poll* (New York, 1972), 3:1624, 1681. Quotes from Wechsler in Jeffrey Potter, *Men, Money & Magic* (New York, 1976), 246; Algren in Univ. of Chicago, *Phoenix* (1962), 4, copy in Box 15, Carey McWilliams Papers; Lawrence Ferlinghetti to Tram Combs, Dec. 17, 1960, LF Correspondence; Kerouac in LF to Allen Ginsberg, Jan. 25, 1961, Box 5, AG-CU; Gary Snyder to AG, Dec. 12, 1960, Box 59:16, AG-SU. See also Gaddis, *We Now Know*, 179–181.

14 Beschloss, *Crisis Years*, 134–140; Bissell, *Reflections*, 157–158, 200–203; Seymour M. Hersh, *The Dark Side of Camelot* (Boston, 1997), 162–167, 185–204, 211–214, 268–272, 342, 447–449; Trumbull Higgins, *The Perfect Failure* (New York, 1987), 88; *WP*, July 21, 1975, pp. A1, A3; Oct. 23, 1978, p. C27; Thomas Powers letter, *Times Literary Supplement*, Apr. 21, 1989, p. 423; Schlesinger–Moyers exchange, *WSJ*, July 5, 20, 27, 1977. Quotes from Lolita H. de Fernandez to Clare B. Luce, June 14, 1961, Box 213:15; Henry M. Cathles to CBL, June 6, 1961, Box 213:3, both in CBL Papers.

15 David Powers COH (1976), 52; Clifford in Hersh, *Dark Side*, 220; Dean Acheson KOH, 14; Sanford Gottlieb memo, May 3, 1961, Box 256, Norman Cousins Papers.

16 Notes of JFK on background in Chalmers Roberts KOH, 10–12. Quotes from Clarita L. Crosby to Clare B. Luce [ca. June 1961], Box 213:14, CBL Papers; Norman Jacobs to Hans J. Morgenthau, May 4, 1961, Box 43:5, HJM Papers. See also U.S. Dept. of State, *Foreign Relations of the United States, 1961–1963* (Washington, 1994), esp. 24:100–288.

17 Quotes from Gaddis, *We Now Know*, 146; Charles Bohlen KOH, 4; Llewellyn E. Thompson KOH, 3; Powers COH, 54; Beschloss, *Crisis Years*, 225. See also Richard Reeves, *President Kennedy* (New York, 1993), 136, 157–174; James Reston, *Deadline* (New York, 1991), 290–291; Zubok and Pleshakov, *Inside*, 243–248.

18 Gallup, *Gallup Poll*, 3:1729. Quotes from Khrushchev in Hubert H. Humphrey, *The Education of a Public Man* (New York, 1976), 145; Stewart Alsop to Martin Sommers, Sept. 15, 1961 (one word corrected), Box 30, Alsop Papers. Standard but dated is Honoré M. Catudal, *Kennedy and the Berlin Wall Crisis* (Berlin, 1980). See also Gaddis, *We Now Know*, 138–149; LaFeber, *America*, 199–202; Zubok and Pleshakov, *Inside*, 194–199, 247–251.

19 Beschloss, *Crisis Years*, 101, 264–283, 321; Reeves, *President Kennedy*, 186–190, 195–196, 201–216; Zubok and Pleshakov, *Inside*, 251–257. Quotes from Gerry McCauley to Hans J. Morgenthau, Oct. 16, 1962, Box 37:12, HJM Papers; Stewart Alsop to Martin Sommers, Sept. 7, 1961, Box 30, Alsop Papers; Marcus Raskin to Hans J. Morgenthau, June 22, 1961, Box 49:5, HJM Papers; SA to MS, July 5, 1961, Box 30, Alsop Papers; HJM to Frank Altschul, Sept. 21, 1961, Box 3:7, HJM Papers.

20 Quotes from George Brown to Joseph W. Alsop, Dec. 4, 1961, Box 17, Alsop Papers; George F. Kennan to J. Robert Oppenheimer, Sept. 21, 1961, Box 43:10, JRO Papers; James M. Gavin to JWA, Dec. 4, 1961, Box 17; Stewart Alsop to Martin Sommers, Oct. 27, 1961, Box 30; Joseph W. Alsop VI to JWA [June 1963], Box 19, all in Alsop Papers. On JFK in Berlin see Beschloss, *Crisis Years*, 605–608.

21 Gallup, *Gallup Poll*, 3:1654. Quotes from JFK, "Inaugural Address," *Public Papers of the Presidents: John F. Kennedy, 1961* (Washington, 1962), 1, 2; Donald [Tyerman] to Joseph W. Alsop, Dec. 18, 1961, Box 17; Louis J. Halle to JWA, May 16, 1962, Box 18, both in Alsop Papers.

22 Zubok and Pleshakov, *Inside*, 174–175, 178–182, 244–246; Elizabeth Bishop to Robert Lowell, Sept. 25 [1961], RL Papers; Victor Lasky to Arthur Krock, Dec. 17 [1961], Box 38, AK Papers; Gallup, *Gallup Poll*, 3:1738. Quotes from Nguyen C. Thanh, *Who Will Win in South Viet Nam?* (Peking, 1963), 4, copy in Box 123:36, Healey Coll.; Arthur M. Schlesinger, Jr., to Isaiah Berlin, Sept. 9, 1961, Box P30, AMS Papers; Helen Bevington, *Along Came the Witch* (New York, 1976), 34; Leo Szilard, "Are We on the Road to War?" (Nov. 14, 1961), speech, Box 10, Harris Wofford

Papers; Gaston [Coblentz] to Joseph W. Alsop, Dec. 14, 1961, Box 17, Alsop Papers.

23 Megadeath in Tom Engelhardt, *The End of Victory Culture* (New York, 1995), 156. Quotes from Lilienthal, *Journals*, 5:357; Thomas Merton to Maynard Shelly, Dec. 1961, TM, *Witness to Freedom*, ed. William H. Shannon (New York, 1994), 23; Gregory Corso to Allen Ginsberg, May 18, 1962, Box 3, AG-CU. One word corrected. See also Gaddis, *We Now Know*, 223–244.

24 Gallup, *Gallup Poll*, 3:1726, 1741; Perkins Harnly to Margie King and Alexander King, Apr. 15, 1961, Box 1:38, AK Papers. Quotes from Hoover in *Human Events*, Dec. 29, 1961; Taylor Caldwell to AK, June 23, 1959, Box 1:13, AK Papers.

25 Acheson, *Present*, 113; Allen Ginsberg to Louis Ginsberg, Sept. 10, 25, 1962, AG–LG, *Family Business*, ed. Michael Schumacher (New York, 2001), 183 (quote), 186; Daniel Berrigan to Karl Meyer, Mar. 3, 1961; June 17, 1961, Box 89; Thomas Merton to DB, Nov. 10, 1961, Box 136, all in Berrigan Coll.

26 Annie Gottlieb, *Do You Believe in Magic?* (New York, 1987), 21–22, 25; Sally Belfrage, *Un-American Activities* (New York, 1994), 29. Quotes from Istvan Botund to Henry R. Luce, Oct. 21, 1961, Box 16, Clare B. Luce Papers; Elaine W. Schwartz testimony to Calif. Assembly, Nov. 7, 1961, Box B34, SANE Papers; Jim Braden to Carl Braden, Sept. 19, 1961, Box 11:8, Braden Papers.

27 Quotes from Clare B. Luce to Chester B. Vernon, Dec. 22, 1961, Box 215:3, CBL Papers; Phil [Cortney] to CBL, Feb. 21, 1963, Box 217:6, CBL Papers. JFK and McNamara in Carl Kaysen KOH, 14. On JFK see also Zubok and Pleshakov, *Inside*, 245–246.

28 Gallup, *Gallup Poll*, 3:1808; Stewart Alsop to Martin Sommers, Sept. 20, 1961, Box 30, Alsop Papers; The Weavers, "I'm Standing on the Outside of Your Shelter," *Reunion at Carnegie Hall, Part 2* (1965 album), performed May 2–3, 1963. Quotes from Joseph H. Berke to Homer Jack, Nov. 1, 1961, Box B34, SANE Records; Gary Snyder to Allen Ginsberg, Nov. 15, 1962, Box 59:18, AG-SU. See also Kenneth D. Rose, *One Nation Underground* (New York, 2001). On the West Virginia shelter see *WP*, May 30, 1992, p. A1; *WP Magazine*, May 31, 1992, p. 10ff.

29 (Ike) Mary C. Brennan, *Turning Right in the Sixties* (Chapel Hill, 1995), 24 (quote); *New Republic*, Mar. 28, 1960, p. 2; (Birch Society) Brennan, *Turning Right*, 54–55, 62–63; Gallup, *Gallup Poll*, 3:1756; Stephen J. Whitfield, *The Culture of the Cold War* (Baltimore, 1991), 42; Clare B. Luce to Mrs. R. J. Evans, Oct. 1, 1962, Box 215:15, CBL Papers; (Congress) Joseph L. Rauh press release, Jan. 25, 1962, Box 12:1, JLR Papers; (Walker) *NYT*, Sept. 28, 1962, p. 23. See also Godfrey Hodgson, *The World Turned Right*

Side Up (Boston, 1996); Rebecca Klatch, *A Generation Divided* (Berkeley, 1999); Lisa McGirr, *Suburban Warriors* (Princeton, 2001).

30 (unity) William F. Buckley, Jr., to Robert Wagner, July 28, 1961, Box 17:47; WFB to Max Eastman, Aug. 21, 1962, Box 19:137; John Wisner to WFB, Sept. 21, 1962, Box 23:50; (liberals) Taylor Caldwell to WFB, July 23, 1962 (1st quote), Box 19:69; WFB to Fr. Alban, July 11, 1961 (2nd quote), Box 13:2, all in WFB Papers. See also John B. Judis, *William F. Buckley, Jr.* (New York, 1988).

31 (radio) Irwin Suall, *The American Ultras* (n.p., 1962), 47–48, copy in Box 6:2, Healey Coll.; (Hargis) *Cincinnati Enquirer*, June 1, 1962 (edit.); (Schwarz) Suall, *American Ultras*, 33, 46; (fluoride) Oliver K. Goff affidavit, June 22, 1957 (quote); National Commission against Fluoridation, Inc., mimeo, Apr. 20, 1963; letters, all in Box 1:26, Kathryn F. Dunaway Papers; (Lowman) Suall, *American Ultras*, 42–43.

32 *WP*, Dec. 28, 1960, p. 15; Anne Braden to Carl Braden, July 22, 1961, Box 11:7; replies, July 25, Aug. 5, Sept. 3, 1961, Box 11:10; Aubrey Williams to Ralph McGill, Jan. 5, 1962 (quote), Box 21:7, all in Braden Papers; Gale McGee to John Bailey, Aug. 24, 1961, Box 36, Theodore C. Sorensen Papers.

33 Robert C. Fiske to Averell Harriman [circa 1961–1962 school year], Box 1:8, AH Papers. On me-tooism see Robert A. Goldberg, *Barry Goldwater* (New Haven, 1995), 147.

34 Quotes from Goldwater, *Goldwater*, 119; Elizabeth C. Brown to Francesca Rhee, Nov. 9, 1963 (signs), Box 3:9, ECB Papers; Ducky [?] to Joseph W. Alsop, July 10, 1963, Box 19; Stewart Alsop to Martin Sommers, June 20, 1961, Box 30; SA to William A. Emerson, Jr., June 20, 1963, Box 31, all in Alsop Papers. See also Goldberg, *Goldwater*, 138–139; Gore Vidal, "A Liberal Meets Mr. Conservative," *Life*, June 9, 1961, p. 106ff.

35 William F. Buckley, Jr., to William H. Brady, Jr., Apr. 14, 1961, Box 13:51; Richard Viguerie to WFB, Apr. 19, 1962 (mimeo), Box 23:62, both in WFB Papers; *New York World Telegram and Sun*, Mar. 8, 1962; *Akron Beacon-Journal*, Mar. 8, 1962; *New York Herald Tribune*, Mar. 8, 1962, pp. 1, 19; *Washington Star*, Mar. 8, 1962 (quote). See also John A. Andrew, *The Other Side of the Sixties* (New Brunswick, NJ, 1997); Gregory L. Schneider, *Cadres for Conservatism* (New York, 1999), 7–71.

36 Donald Hall to Charles P. Taft, Aug. 2, 1961 (1st, 4th quotes), Box 12:8, CPT Papers; Constance Brown to William F. Knowland, June 13, 1960, Box 2:18, Elizabeth C. Brown Papers; W. A. Kilroy to Frank O. Williams, Feb. 10, 1961 (copy), Box 15:10, William F. Buckley, Jr. Papers; DH to CPT, Jan. 9, 1963, Box 12:9, CPT Papers.

37 Quotes from Carleton Smith to Martha E. Dodd, Dec. 25, 1962, Box 9:4, MED Papers; Ralph [Gilman] to Allard K. Lowenstein, Aug. 30, 1962,

Box 8:258; Michael A. Samuels to AKL, Jan. 21, 1961, Box 7:226, both in AKL Papers; Sheldon Gerry to Averell Harriman, Apr. 12, 1961, Box 1:12, AH Papers. (Peace Corps) *NYT*, Mar. 2, 1961, pp. 1, 13; Myer Feldman KOH, Pt. 2, pp. 38–39; Peter Lisagor KOH, 58. See also Thomas Hayden, "Who Are the Student Boat-Rockers?" *Mademoiselle*, Aug. 1961, p. 236ff; Steven Roberts and Carey McWilliams, Jr., "Student Leaders and Campus Apathy," *Nation*, Sept. 16, 1961, pp. 155–157.

38 The current best study of the Missile Crisis is James G. Blight, et al., *Cuba on the Brink* (New York, 1993), esp. 77–85, 205–208. This book is based on a conference held in Havana in 1992. Both McNamara and Castro participated. For Soviet sources, see Fursenko and Naftali, *One Hell*, 179–180, 182, 186. Quote from Ernest R. May and Philip D. Zelikow, eds., *The Kennedy Tapes* (Cambridge, MA, 1997), 113. See also Gaddis, *We Now Know*, 260–280; Gallup, *Gallup Poll*, 3:1787; Lebow and Stein, *We All Lost*, 19–145, esp. 97–101. Important documents are in Central Intelligence Agency, *The Secret Cuban Missile Crisis Documents* (Washington, 1992), and Laurence Chang and Peter Kornbluh, eds., *Cuban Missile Crisis, 1962* (New York, 1992).

39 (odds) Oleg Cassini, *In My Own Fashion* (New York, 1987), 323; (Jackie) Beschloss, *Crisis Years*, 476; C. David Heymann, *A Woman Named Jackie* (New York, 1994), 702; (troops and warheads) Fursenko and Naftali, *One Hell*, 188–189, 217, 236, 242–243, 246, 256, 272–273, 276, 312, 315; Gaddis, *We Now Know*, 274–276; Lebow and Stein, *We All Lost*, 293–296, 496n26, 497n32; Robert S. McNamara with Brian VanDeMark, *In Retrospect* (New York, 1995), 340–341; (arsenal) Blight, *Cuba*, 126–127, 131–134, 213, 254. On U.S. superiority see ibid., x–xii, 22, 55, 61–62, 67, 73–74, 111, 250–252. On Soviet policy see Zubok and Pleshakov, *Inside*, 258–269.

40 Bevington, *Witch*, 71 (1st, 3rd quotes); Richard Neustadt in May and Zelikow, *Kennedy Tapes*, 288 (2nd quote); "Crisis" [Oct 1962], memo, Ser. A3, Box 7, WSP Records; *Daily Texan* clipping, Oct. 1962 (signs); Jim [Monsonis] to Betty Garman, Nov. 12, 1962; Robb Burlage to Tom and Casey [Hayden], Dec. 14 [1962] (4th quote), all on reel 3, SDS Papers.

41 Gallup, *Gallup Poll*, 3:1793; Owen Lattimore to Arnold Bernhard, Oct. 26, 1962, Box 1:12, OL Papers.

42 Hersh, *Dark Side*, 341; Beschloss, *Crisis Years*, 543 (2nd, 5th quotes), 551 (6th quote); *NYT Magazine*, Aug. 30, 1987, p. 51; *Esquire*, Feb. 1969, p. 76; Richard N. Goodwin, *Remembering America* (Boston, 1988), 218; Reeves, *President Kennedy*, 512.

43 Stewart Alsop to Otto Friedrich, Feb. 20, 1963 (one word corrected), Box 31, Alsop Papers; D. N. Pritt to Martha E. Dodd and Alfred K. Stern, Jan. 10, 1963, Box 8:10, MED Papers; Roger N. Saleeby to Clare B. Luce,

May 22, 1963, Box 217:12; Marquise Dedons de Pierrefeu to CBL, Feb. 12, 1963, Box 218:10; CBL to Daniel James, July 24, 1963, Box 218:1; Henry A. Wise to CBL, Oct. 24, 1963, Box 219:6, all in CBL Papers.

44 (Turkey trade) *WP*, Aug. 29, 1987, pp. A1, A9; Lebow and Stein, *We All Lost*, 120–124, 133–134, 442n158. See also Barton J. Bernstein, "The Cuban Missile Crisis: Trading the Jupiters in Turkey?" *Political Science Quarterly*, 95:1 (Spring 1980), 97–125; (Mongoose) Beschloss, *Crisis Years*, 376–377, 411, 418, 594, 639–640, 659, 667, 683; John H. Davis, *The Kennedys* (New York, 1984), 442, 494–498, 513–514, 548, 550, 577; Taylor Branch and George Crile III, "The Kennedy Vendetta," *Harper's Magazine*, Aug. 1975, pp. 49–63; notes on background with Rusk in Roberts KOH, 20 (quote).

45 A good summary is Michael Harrington, "The New Peace Movement," *New Leader*, Aug. 20, 1962, pp. 6–8. (NY drills) *Village Voice*, May 11, 1960, pp. 1, 13; *New University Thought*, 1:3 (Spring 1961), 81–83; Maurice Isserman, *If I Had a Hammer* (New York, 1987), 145–147; Andrew Jamison and Ron Eyerman, *Seeds of the Sixties* (Berkeley, 1994), 198–199.

46 Quote from J. Robert Oppenheimer to D. G. Brennan, Apr. 26, 1963, Box 22:15, JRO Papers. On Pugwash see Lilienthal, *Journals*, 5:239; Joseph Rotblat, *Scientists in the Quest for Peace* (Cambridge, MA, 1972); Walt Rostow KOH, 29–30; *Toronto Financial Post*, June 3, 1961. On tests see Zubok and Pleshakov, *Inside*, 188–193, 253, 257.

47 Milton S. Katz, *Ban the Bomb* (Westport, CT, 1986); (CP) Barbara Deming, "The Ordeal of SANE," *Nation*, Mar. 11, 1961, pp. 200–205; Norman Cousins to Edmund Berkeley, June 1, 30, 1960, Box 231; SANE Wash. Office to NC, Oct. 18, 1960, Box 253, all in NC Papers; (students) National SANE, "Staff Conclusions and Recommendations about National Student SANE" (Jan. 10, 1962), Box 306, NC Papers; (autocratic) Gerard A. Bertin to Homer Jack, Jan. 27, 1961, Box B34, SANE Records; (Spock) Neil Litvak to Benjamin Spock, May 1, 1962; Donald [Keys] to NC [ca. June 1962]; National SANE board, July 25, 1962, minutes, all in Box 306, NC Papers; Homer Jack to BS, Jan. 15, 29, 1962; replies, Jan. 17, 1962; Feb. 28, 1962, all in Box B33, SANE Records.

48 Standard is Amy Swerdlow, *Women Strike for Peace* (Chicago, 1993). See also Midge Dector, "The Peace Ladies," *Harper's Magazine*, Mar. 1963, pp. 48–53; *NYT*, Nov. 22, 1961, p. 4; *WP*, Nov. 2, 1961, pp. D1, D5; Nov. 15, 1961, pp. A1, D1; Janet Stevenson to [Margaret] Russell, Oct. 12, 1961; Dagmar Wilson to Mrs. John F. Kennedy, Oct. 26, 1961; Nov. 27, 1961; reply, Nov. 13, 1961; L.F.K. to Annalee Stewart, Nov. 14, 1961; Philip S. Rowen to DW, Feb. 26, 1962; DW to Mrs. Harry Cooper,

Mar. 26, 1962, all in Ser. A3, Box 6; DW to Mary Weik, Nov. 26, 1962, Ser. A3, Box 7, WSP Records.

49 Jeanne S. Bagby to Mrs. Margaret Gowan, Dec. 11, 1961; Ruth G. Colby Christmas letter, Dec. 12, 1961, both in Ser. A3, Box 6, WSP Records; (pickets) *NYT*, Jan. 16, 1962, pp. 1, 18; (HUAC) *NYT*, Dec. 7, 1962, p. 3; *WP*, Dec. 6, 1962, p. A30; Harold J. Bass to Dagmar Wilson, Dec. 14, 1962 (1st quote), Sec. A4, Box 1, WSP Records; (Geneva) *NYT*, Apr. 2, 1962, p. 3; *San Francisco Examiner*, May 21, 1962; *New York Post* clipping, May 1963, Box 313, Norman Cousins Papers; *Nation*, May 5, 1962, pp. 395–397; *National Guardian*, Apr. 16, 1962; (women) Belle W. Schulz to Rosa J. de Hardy, Apr. 30, 1962 (2nd quote), Ser. A3, Box 6, WSP Records.

50 Agnes Meyer to J. Robert Oppenheimer, Nov. 11, 1961 (quote), Box 51:1, JRO Papers; AM to Adlai E. Stevenson, Jan. 2, 14, 22, 1963; Feb. 5, 11, 1963, Box 62, AES Papers.

51 The best summary is Sanford Gottlieb, "The Peace Candidates and the 1962 Election" (Nov. 1962), Box 306, Norman Cousins Papers. (Hughes) H. Stuart Hughes, *Gentleman Rebel* (New York, 1990), 250–260; Artists and Writers for Stuart Hughes Papers.

52 (SPU) Isserman, *Hammer*, 195–200; SPU Program Statement (1961), reel 9, SDS Papers; (symbol) David Golden to Kenneth Rexroth, July 28, 1961, Box 181, KR Papers; (picket) *NYT*, Feb. 17, 1962, pp. 1, 3; Feb. 18, 1962, p. 51; *WP*, Feb. 17, 1962, pp. A7, A10; *Washington Star*, Feb. 18, 1962, p. B1; *National Guardian*, Feb. 26, 1962, pp. 1, 10; *Dissent*, 9 (Spring 1962), 179–182; *Nation*, Mar. 3, 1962, pp. 187–190; handouts on reel 2, SDS Papers; Hannah Arendt to Gertrud and Karl Jaspers, Feb. 19, 1962, Arendt–Jaspers, *Hannah Arendt–Karl Jaspers*, ed. Lotte Kohler and Hans Saner (New York, 1992), 471 (quote); (decline) Philip Altbach, "The Quiet Campus," *New Leader*, Aug. 5, 1963, pp. 12–14.

53 Fursenko and Naftali, *One Hell*, 9–11; Van Gosse, *Where the Boys Are* (New York, 1993), 1–6, 116, 128–129, 198–199; James Miller, *Democracy Is in the Streets* (New York, 1987), 86–87; *NYT*, Apr. 26, 1959, p. 3; Ginsberg–Ginsberg, *Family Business*, 192–193, 211–212; Steve Max to SDS Chapter Officers, Sept. 30, 1963, reel 6; Mike [?] to Tom [Hayden?], Mar. 15, 1963, reel 18, both in SDS Papers.

54 Standard is Kirkpatrick Sale, *SDS* (New York, 1973). (members) Al Haber memo, May 20, 1961; League for Industrial Democracy Exec. Comm. meeting, Sept. 21, 1961, both on reel 1, SDS Papers; (colleges) Paul Buhle, ed., *History and the New Left* (Philadelphia, 1990), 24, 73, 76, 111, 138–139; Todd Gitlin, *The Sixties* (New York, 1987), 87–101; W. J. Rorabaugh, *Berkeley at War* (New York, 1989), 15–16; Tom Hayden, *Reunion* (New York, 1988), 30–33, 48–52.

55 (CP) SDS Constitution (1962), reel 1; Jim Monsonis Report to National Council (1962), reel 2, both in SDS Papers; Thomas Hayden and Richard Flacks, "End of the Cold War," *Liberation*, Nov. 1963, pp. 14–19. Quotes from SDS, "The Port Huron Statement," in Miller, *Democracy*, 329; SDS, "What is the S.D.S.?" (1962), mimeo (2nd, 3rd quotes), reel 1; Tom [Hayden] to Steve Johnson, May 10 [1962?], reel 4; Steve Max, "Thoughts of Sorts" (ca. 1962–1963), reel 4; Don McKelvey to Mark Manis, Aug. 22, 1963, reel 4, all in SDS Papers.

56 Gallup, *Gallup Poll*, 3:1753, 1837; Reeves, *President Kennedy*, 226–228, 251, 514, 545–548, 551, 553, 556; Theodore Sorensen KOH, 75, 79–80; Arthur Krock int. with JFK, May 5, 1961, Memo Book III, #342, AK Papers; Frederick Seidel to Robert Lowell, May 6, 1962, RL Papers; (picket) *NYT*, Nov. 24, 1961, pp. 1, 35; *Amherst Student*, Nov. 30, 1961, copy in Box B33, SANE Records. Quotes from Homer A. Jack to Norman Cousins, Nov. 1, 1961, Box 256, NC Papers; JFK, *Public Papers, 1963*, 462.

57 Useful studies include William J. Rust, *Kennedy in Vietnam* (New York, 1985); John M. Newman, *JFK and Vietnam* (New York, 1992); David Kaiser, *American Tragedy* (Cambridge, MA, 2000); and Francis X. Winters, *The Year of the Hare* (Athens, GA, 1997). Quotes from Davis, *Kennedys*, 446; Averell Harriman to Mr. [Walt?] Rostow, Apr. 5, 1962, Box 519:6, AH Papers. See also [Pentagon Papers] U.S. Dept. of Defense, *United States–Vietnam Relations, 1945–1967* (12 vols., Washington, 1971); U.S. Dept of State, *Foreign Relations of the United States, 1961–1963* (Washington, 1988–1991), vols. 1–4.

58 (counterguerrillas) Arthur M. Schlesinger, Jr., *A Thousand Days* (Boston, 1965), 540–541, 985–986; *Life*, Jan. 25, 1963, pp. 31–32; *Reporter*, Aug. 17, 1961, pp. 28–30; Roger Hilsman COH, 7, 63–65; Hilsman KOH, 18–20; (hamlets) U.S. Dept. of State, *Foreign Relations*, 2:597–598, 700–701, 704, 727–729, 736–737; 3:551; Schlesinger, *Thousand Days*, 549, 982–983, 986; *SEP*, Jan. 6, 1962, p. 20; Sept. 28, 1963, p. 34; Hilsman KOH, 27–28.

59 (Buddhists) U.S. Dept. of State, *Foreign Relations*, 1:150, 152, 702; 3:528, 551, 553, 555, 558–560 (1st quote at 559n6); 4:400, 416; *Reporter*, Oct. 10, 1963, pp. 39–42; (Lodge) The crucial wire was State to Lodge, Aug. 24, 1963, Box 198, JFK NSF. See also James A. Bill, *George Ball* (New Haven, 1997), 154–157; David L. DiLeo, *George Ball, Vietnam, and the Rethinking of Containment* (Chapel Hill, 1991), 60–61; U.S. Dept. of State, *Foreign Relations*, 2:600; 3:555, 583, 595–675; 4:282; Hilsman KOH, 34–35; Michael Forrestal to McHugh for JFK, Aug. 24, 25 (2nd quote), 1963; Lodge to Rusk, Aug. 26, 29 (3rd quote), 31, 1963; reply, Aug. 28,

30, 31, 1963; CIA to McGeorge Bundy, Aug. 28, 1963; JFK to Lodge, Aug. 29, 1963, all in Box 198; Chester Cooper memo, Sept. 19, 1963, Box 200; JFK to Lodge, Aug. 29, 1963, Box 316; Memoranda of Conferences with the President, Aug. 27–29, 1963, Box 316, all in JFK NSF.

60 JFK int. with Walter Cronkite, Sept. 2, 1963, Box 519:8, Averell Harriman Papers; Rusk at Meeting in the Situation Room, Sept. 11, 1963, Box 316, JFK NSF; Rusk to Lodge, Sept. 12, 14, 1963, both in Box 519:8, AH Papers; JFK in Schlesinger, *Thousand Days*, 993.

61 Quotes from JFK in Memorandum of Conference with the President, Oct. 29, 1963, Box 317, JFK NSF; LBJ in Humphrey, *Education*, 196; Nolting in *U.S. News*, July 26, 1971, p. 67. See also Anne E. Blair, *Lodge in Vietnam* (New Haven, 1995), esp. 14, 42, 45, 72–73; Hersh, *Dark Side*, 412–435; Reeves, *President Kennedy*, 638–651; Rust, *Kennedy*, 112–178; U.S. Dept. of State, *Foreign Relations*, 4:394, 427–537; William Bundy JOH, 1:6–7; Chester Cooper KOH, 53–57; Roswell Gilpatric KOH, 30–33; Hilsman KOH, Pt. 2, pp. 34–35; William H. Sullivan KOH, 41–42, 45–46.

62 Joseph W. Alsop to Viscount [Tony] Lambton, Oct. 15, 1963, Box 19, Alsop Papers; Hans J. Morgenthau to Luther A. Allen, Sept. 24, 1963; Feb. 29, 1964, both in Box 3:3, HJM Papers; Thomas J. Dodd to Clare B. Luce, Dec. 12, 1963, Box 217:8; CBL to John H. Wilkens, Nov. 3, 1963, Box 219:6, both in CBL Papers.

63 Thomas Brown, *JFK* (Bloomington, IN, 1988), 34–35, 39–40; Newman, *JFK*, xiii–xiv, 323; Rust, *Kennedy*, ix–x; Arthur Krock int. with JFK, Oct. 11, 1961, Memo Book III, #343, AK Papers; Charles Bartlett KOH, 30; Chester Bowles KOH (1970), 99; William Bundy JOH, 1:10; Gilpatric KOH, 97; Hilsman COH, 40–42, 63–64; Hilsman KOH, Pt. 2, pp. 20–21, 64–65; Roberts KOH, 14–16, 35; Sorensen KOH, 96–98.

Chapter Three

1 (North) Marvin Caplan to Edward R. Murrow, Dec. 20, 1960, Box 26:122, ERM Papers; Parry W. Jones to Caroline K. Simon, Feb. 20, 25, 1963; *Louis Lefkowitz v. Mell Farrell*, summary, both in reel 5, CORE Papers; (South) Fred Powledge, *Free at Last?* (Boston, 1991), 241; James G. Cook, *The Segregationists* (New York, 1962), 3.

2 (31 percent) *Fortune*, Mar. 1962, p. 88; (1 percent) *Commentary*, Sept. 1961, p. 212; (Cleveland) Jean M. Capers to A. Philip Randolph, Aug. 1, 1963, Box 28:2, Bayard Rustin Papers; (6/13) Iota Phi Lambda to Harris Wofford, Aug. 4, 1961, Box 3, HW Papers; (98 percent) Cook Co. data, 1958, in *Look*, Apr. 10, 1962, p. 28. See also *Commentary*, Dec. 1959, pp. 479–488; Apr. 1960, p. 349; *Midwest Quarterly*, Winter 1964,

pp. 106–107; *LAT*, Sept. 1, 1963, p. C7 (Lippmann); *NYT Magazine*, Feb. 14, 1960, p. 80; Nov. 19, 1961, p. 26; *Village Voice*, June 6, 1963, p. 9; *WSJ*, May 10, 1963, p. 17.

3 Michael Harrington, "Harlem Today," *Dissent*, 8:3 (Summer 1961), 374; David Koff to Allard K. Lowenstein, July 3, 1961, Box 7:226, AKL Papers; (Little Rock) Daisy Bates, *The Long Shadow of Little Rock* (New York, 1962); Elizabeth Huckaby, *Crisis at Central High, Little Rock, 1957–58* (Baton Rouge, 1980). Eastland quoted in Cook, *Segregationists*, 5.

4 James Forman, *The Making of Black Revolutionaries* (2nd ed., Washington, 1985; orig. 1972), 85, 100; David J. Garrow, *Bearing the Cross* (New York, 1986), 32, 42–43, 71; Pat Watters, *Down to Now* (2nd ed., Athens, GA, 1993; orig. 1971), xii–xiii, xvi; James Baldwin, "Letter from a Region in My Mind," *New Yorker*, Nov. 17, 1962, p. 60. Quotes from *Afro-American*, Apr. 21, 1962, p. 8; *Chicago Daily News*, July 20, 1963.

5 David L. Lewis, *King: A Biography* (2nd ed., Urbana, 1978; orig. 1970), 35–37, 56, 81, 85–86, 98, 103, 108; Ralph D. Abernathy, *And the Walls Came Tumbling Down* (New York, 1990), 150–185; Garrow, *Bearing*, 11–32, 51–82, 85, 97; Virginia F. Durr, *Outside the Magic Circle*, ed. Hollinger F. Barnard (Tuscaloosa, 1985), 280, 293; Cleveland Sellers with Robert Terrell, *The River of No Return* (New York, 1973), 16–17; Adam Fairclough, *To Redeem the Soul of America* (Athens, GA, 1987), 13, 38; Watters, *Down*, 45; *Jet*, June 22, 1961, p. 8; Reese Cleghorn, "Apostle of Crisis," *SEP*, June 15, 1963, p. 17. Quotes from *Afro-American*, Oct. 29, 1960, p. 1; Taylor Branch, *Parting the Waters* (New York, 1988), 203. On Montgomery see MLK, *Stride toward Freedom* (New York, 1958); Jo Ann G. Robinson, *The Montgomery Bus Boycott and the Women Who Started It* (Knoxville, 1987).

6 Garrow, *Bearing*, 90–91; *NYT*, Oct. 14, 1962, p. 20; Nov. 24, 1962, p. 2; John Lewis in Juan Williams, *Eyes on the Prize* (New York, 1987), 139; David Koff to Allard K. Lowenstein, July 3, 1961, Box 7:226; Tom Boysen to AKL, Oct. 22, 1963, Box 9:299, both in AKL Papers; Alice Cobb to Anne Braden, May 31, 1961, Box 11:7, Braden Papers. See also Thomas Borstelmann, *The Cold War and the Color Line* (Cambridge, MA, 2001). Quotes from Mitchell JOH, 1:23; Bayard Rustin to Bernice Wilds and Miss Rodwell, Feb. 17, 1963, Box 1:9, BR Papers; Daniel Berrigan to John Heidbrink, June 18, 1961, Box 89, Berrigan Coll.; Harris Wofford to JFK, Jan. 23, 1962, Box 9, HW Papers; RFK in Branch, *Parting*, 566; Gordon R. Carey to T. M. H. Wallace, July 22, 1960, reel 1; Stephen D. Pfeiffer to CORE, May 17, 1961, reel 25, both in CORE Papers.

7 August Meier and Elliott Rudwick, *CORE* (New York, 1973), 162–163; Hope R. Miller, *Embassy Row* (New York, 1969), 127–130, 263; Renee

Romano, "No Diplomatic Immunity," *Journal of American History*, 87:2 (Sept. 2000), 546–579; *Afro-American*, Sept. 2, 1961, p. 1; *NYT*, May 26, 1961, p. 21; July 12, 1961, p. 13; *Washington Star*, Nov. 8, 1961, p. A24; *America*, Sept. 23, 1961, pp. 795–796; *Life*, Nov. 17, 1961, p. 6; *Nation*, Jan. 27, 1962, pp. 71–73; *Reporter*, Oct. 26, 1961, p. 41; Wofford KOH, 61; Theodore M. Berry to Joseph L. Rauh, Mar. 7, 1961, Box 8:4, JLR Papers; file 496, reel 46, CORE Papers; LBJ call to Porter Parrish, June 15, 1961, Box 61, LBJ-VP Papers. Quotes from Virginia Durr to LBJ, Dec. 13, 1960, Box 61, LBJ-VP Papers; Kris [Kleinbauer] to Allard K. Lowenstein, Sept. 8, 1963, Box 8:296, AKL Papers; Stewart Alsop to [Robert Sherrod], July 30, 1963, Box 31, Alsop Papers.

8 William H. Chafe, *Civilities and Civil Rights* (New York, 1980); Miles Wolff, *Lunch at the 5 & 10* (rev. ed., Chicago, 1990; orig. 1970). Quote in Numan V. Bartley, *The New South, 1945–1980* (Baton Rouge, 1995), 298.

9 (early sit-ins) James Farmer, *Freedom-When?* (New York, 1965), 61; Henry Hampton and Steve Fayer, eds., *Voices of Freedom* (New York, 1990), 53; James Peck, *Freedom Ride* (New York, 1962), 42, 68; Watters, *Down*, 51; Howard Zinn, *You Can't Be Neutral on a Moving Train* (Boston, 1994), 26; Carl R. Graves, "The Right To Be Served," *Chronicles of Oklahoma*, 59 (Summer 1981), 152–166; *NYT* letters, Mar. 15, 1990; Apr. 5, 1990; *Nation*, Aug. 12, 1961, pp. 78–81; (publicity) Bartley, *New South*, 298–299; Clayborne Carson, *In Struggle* (Cambridge, MA, 1981), 9–18; Powledge, *Free*, 224; Sellers, *River*, 18–24; Nancy J. Weiss, *Whitney M. Young, Jr., and the Struggle for Civil Rights* (Princeton, 1989), 65–66; (North) Sara Evans, *Personal Politics* (New York, 1979), 106; Meier and Rudwick, *CORE*, 109–110. Statistics in Meier and Rudwick, *CORE*, 101; Charles M. Payne, *I've Got the Light of Freedom* (Berkeley, 1995), 78. Quotes from Tom Gaither to James Farmer, Feb. 7, 1961, reel 24, CORE Papers; MLK in Branch, *Parting*, 276.

10 Hampton and Fayer, *Voices*, 67; Meier and Rudwick, *CORE*, 112; Powledge, *Free*, 204–213, 227, 232; Wolff, *Lunch*, 149, 167, 179. Quotes from *Business Mood Survey*, Nov. 1961, Box 2:13, Thurgood Marshall Papers; Jim Dombrowski to Eleanor Roosevelt, Mar. 16, 1961, Box 20:11, Carl and Anne Braden Papers.

11 Carson, *In Struggle*, 19–21; Mary King, *Freedom Song* (New York, 1987), 43, 46; Eric Burner, *And Gently He Shall Lead Them* (New York, 1994), 21; Forman, *Making*, 216–218, 236–239; Payne, *I've Got*, 5, 79–82, 96; Carol Mueller, "Ella Baker and the Origins of 'Participatory Democracy,'" in Vicki L. Crawford, Jacqueline A. Rouse, and Barbara Woods, eds., *Women in the Civil Rights Movement* (Brooklyn, 1990), 51–70; Fairclough, *Redeem*, 62; Sellers, *River*, 33–38.

12 Carson, *In Struggle*, 21–23; *Harper's Magazine*, Oct. 1961, pp. 133 (1st quote), 135 (2nd quote); King, *Freedom Song*, 8 (3rd quote), 272–276; Powledge, *Free*, 234–237; Watters, *Down*, 127–129; *Dissent*, 7 (Spring 1960), 142; *Look*, Apr. 10, 1962, p. 34; *New Leader*, Sept. 12, 1960.

13 Quotes from *Harper's Magazine*, Oct. 1961, p. 134; Phil Berrigan to Dan Berrigan [ca. Jan. 1962], Box 101, Berrigan Coll.; Paula Giddings, *When and Where I Enter* (New York, 1984), 286; *NYT Magazine*, Sept. 10, 1961, p. 119; Bartley, *New South*, 304.

14 John M. Orbell, "Protest Participation among Southern Negro College Students," *American Political Science Review*, 61 (June 1967), 446–456; Ruth Searles and J. Allen Williams, Jr., "Negro College Students' Participation in Sit-Ins," *Social Forces*, 40:3 (March 1962), 215–220; Bartley, *New South*, 300; King, *Freedom Song*, 163, 298; Simeon Booker, *Black Man's America* (Englewood Cliffs, NJ, 1964), 88; Payne, *I've Got*, 237; Wolff, *Lunch*, 69; James Baldwin, "The Dangerous Road before Martin Luther King," *Harper's Magazine*, Feb. 1961, p. 41 (quote); *SEP*, Sept. 8, 1962, p. 8; Robert Weaver KOH, 191–192.

15 John Dittmer, *Local People* (Urbana, 1994), 34; James Meredith, *Three Years in Mississippi* (Bloomington, IN, 1966), 15; Erle Johnston, *Mississippi's Defiant Years, 1953–1973* (Forest, MS, 1990), 11; Marvin Rich to James Farmer, Sept. 10, 1963; SNCC, "The General Condition of the Mississippi Negro" (ca. 1963), both on reel 25, CORE Papers. Quotes from Boyd Campbell in Benjamin Muse memo, Apr. 30, 1962, Box 8, Burke Marshall Papers; John R. Salter, Jr., *Jackson, Mississippi* (2nd ed., Malabar, FL, 1987), 28. For an overview, see David R. Goldfield, *Black, White, and Southern* (Baton Rouge, 1990).

16 Hampton and Fayer, *Voices*, xxiv; Carl T. Rowan, *Breaking Barriers* (Boston, 1991); Weiss, *Young*, 31–34; Myrlie Evers with William Peters, *For Us, the Living* (Garden City, NY, 1967), 24–25; Louis Lomax, "The Negro's New Comedy Act," *Harper's Magazine*, June 1961, p. 42; James Farmer, WINS radio transcript, Apr. 21, 1963, reel 5, CORE Papers; Charlayne Hunter-Gault, *In My Place* (New York, 1992), 140. Quotes from Joseph G. Goulden, *The Best Years, 1945–1950* (New York, 1976), 353; Watters, *Down*, 118.

17 Evers, *For Us*, 53–54; Hunter-Gault, *In My Place*, 93–94, 130–138, 172–191; Helen Fuller in *New Republic*, Apr. 25, 1960; Evers quoted in *SEP*, Nov. 10, 1962, p. 22.

18 Carson, *In Struggle*, 1–4; Julian Bond, "The Southern Youth Movement," *Freedomways*, 2:3 (Summer 1962), 308–310; Payne, *I've Got*, 100–101. Quotes from Ella Baker int., 4; Hamer int., 2, both in Romaine Papers.

19 King, *Freedom Song*, 283–290; Forman, *Making*, 220, 240, 293–294; *Atlanta Journal-Constitution*, Feb. 2, 1964, p. 7. Quotes from Payne,

I've Got, 103; Clarice T. Campbell, *Civil Rights Chronicle* (Jackson, MS, 1997), 102; Howard Zinn notes of Sherrod, Dec. 1963, Box 3:4, HZ Papers.

20 King, *Freedom Song*, 281; Al Lowenstein int., 12, Romaine Papers.

21 "Freedom Now" in Aaron E. Henry memo [1960], Box 6:1, Amzie Moore Papers; *Gandhi Marg*, 7:4 (Oct. 1963), 299; *Life*, Nov. 29, 1963, p. 78; *New Politics*, 2:3 (Summer 1963), 7.

22 Payne, *I've Got*, 78; Lewis, *King*, 119; Alan Draper, *Conflict of Interests* (Ithaca, 1994), 86; George H. Gallup, *The Gallup Poll* (New York, 1972), 3:1724; *NYT*, Jan. 29, 1961, p. 64.

23 (1947) Jervis Anderson, *Bayard Rustin* (New York, 1997), 113–122; (1961) James Farmer, *Lay Bare the Heart* (New York, 1985), 197; Peck, *Freedom*, 115–116; *Jet*, June 8, 1961, p. 18; *U.S. News*, Oct. 23, 1961, p. 78; Oct. 30, 1961, p. 70; James Farmer to Ormond Drake, May 10, 1962 (quote), reel 3; JF to Mr. and Mrs. Charles Larsen, Apr. 26, 1962, reel 4; John R. Lewis application, 1961, reel 44, all in CORE Papers.

24 Branch, *Parting*, 416–420 (1st quote at 417); Curt Gentry, *J. Edgar Hoover* (New York, 1991), 483–484; Booker, *Black*, 1–3, 5, 200; William A. Nunnelley, *Bull Connor* (Tuscaloosa, 1991), 97–99; Peck, *Freedom*, 14, 116–128; Powledge, *Free*, 273–274; *Birmingham Post-Herald*, May 15, 1961, pp. 1–2, 4; *NYT*, May 15, 1961, pp. 1, 22; May 17, 1961, p. 23; *Jet*, May 25, 1961, pp. 10–15; June 1, 1961, pp. 13–15; Thomas in *Harper's Magazine*, Oct. 1961, p. 138 (2nd quote); Burke Marshall KOH, 11, 14; John Boardman to Marv [Rich], May 20, 1961, reel 25, CORE Papers; Tom Kahn statement [May 1962], reel 1, SDS Papers.

25 Branch, *Parting*, 444–451; Edwin Guthman, *We Band of Brothers* (New York, 1971), 171–173; Powledge, *Free*, 394n; Watters, *Down*, 105–106; *NYT*, May 21, 1961, pp. 1, 78; *Life*, May 26, 1961, pp. 22–25; *Newsweek*, May 29, 1961, p. 21; Burke Marshall KOH, 8, 14–34; Clarence Mitchell KOH, 15; John Patterson KOH, 34–35, 38, 41, 43; Virginia Durr COH, 306–317. Quotes from Kenneth O'Reilly, *Black Americans* (New York, 1994), 27; Durr, *Outside*, 297. On marshals see Helen Fuller, *Year of Trial* (New York, 1962), 136; Robert F. Kennedy, *Robert Kennedy in His Own Words* (New York, 1988), 87, 90; Katzenbach KOH, 12–15; RFK memo, May 20, 1961, Box 10, RFK Papers. Gallup, *Gallup Poll*, 3:1723.

26 Bartley, *New South*, 311; Jack Bass, *Unlikely Heroes* (New York, 1981), 143–146; Branch, *Parting*, 470; Dittmer, *Local People*, 90–91; RFK, *Robert Kennedy*, 96–97; Burke Marshall KOH, 37–40; Telephone calls, Box 10, RFK Papers. Quotes from Farmer, *Lay Bare*, 205; *Atlanta Constitution*, May 24, 1961, p. 1; *Ebony*, Aug. 1961, pp. 22, 23; *Newsweek*, June 5, 1961, p. 20.

27 Farmer, *Lay Bare*, 6, 8 (1st quote), 9, 18 (3rd quote); Dittmer, *Local People*, 97 (2nd quote); Hampton and Fayer, *Voices*, 94; *Boston Globe*, July 2, 1961, p. 1; *Chicago Defender*, May 27, 1961, p. 1 (slogan); *NYT*, May 25, 1961, pp. 1, 24; May 27, 1961, pp. 1, 8; *Jet*, June 15, 1961, pp. 12–13; June 22, 1961, p. 8 (poll); William Mahoney, "In Pursuit of Freedom," *Liberation*, Sept. 1961, pp. 7–11; Frank Holloway, "Travel Notes from a Deep South Tourist," *New South*, 16:7 (July–Aug. 1961), 3–8; Tom Kahn statement [May 1962] (4th quote), reel 1, SDS Papers; Bernard LaFayette, Jr., to Jim [Farmer], Apr. 9, 1962 (5th quote), reel 4, CORE Papers; Carl Braden to Anne Braden, May 27, 1961 (6th quote), Box 11:8, Braden Papers.

28 Guy Carawan and Candie Carawan, comps., *We Shall Overcome!* (New York, 1963), 111; Farmer, *Lay Bare*, 27–28; Peck, *Freedom*, 146–152; *Militant*, Feb. 26, 1962, p. 1. Quotes from James Dombrowski to Carl Braden, Aug. 15, 1961, Box 11:8, Braden Papers; Jim [Farmer] to Marv [Rich], June 14, 1961; JF to [CORE], June 1, 1961, both on reel 25, CORE Papers; *Jubilee*, Nov. 1961; Pete Seeger and Bob Reiser, *Everybody Says Freedom* (New York, 1989), 63, 82; Watters, *Down*, 109.

29 Dittmer, *Local People*, 95; Farmer, *Freedom*, 72; Jack Greenberg, *Crusaders in the Courts* (New York, 1994), 288; Hampton and Fayer, *Voices*, 94; King, *Freedom Song*, 317, 402; William M. Kunstler with Sheila Isenberg, *My Life as a Radical Lawyer* (New York, 1994), 106; Powledge, *Free*, 289; Williams, *Eyes*, 160; *Afro-American*, Mar. 2, 1963, p. 1; May 4, 1963, p. 1; Justice Dept. survey, June 1961, Box 22:7, Thurgood Marshall Papers; Cyril Simon to Margaret Ihra, Nov. 28, 1961, reel 43; Arthur L. Williams report, June 16, 1962, reel 46, both in CORE Papers; "Dear Freedom Fighter" (ca. June 13, 1963), leaflet, Box E9:8, NAACP Papers. Quotes from George J. Leake to CORE, July 6, 1961, reel 36, CORE Papers; Farmer, *Lay Bare*, 211; Burke Marshall to James Farmer, rec'd July 16, 1962, reel 2, CORE Papers.

30 (data) *Jackson Daily News*, Mar. 22, 1962; Meredith, *Three Years*, 7–8; Williams, *Eyes*, 208; *NYT Magazine*, Apr. 28, 1963, p. 104; (Delta) King, *Freedom Song*, 130; Payne, *I've Got*, 17, 134; Robert Sherrill, *Gothic Politics in the Deep South* (New York, 1968), 189. Quotes from Howard Zinn notes of Bob Moses at Miss. Staff Meeting [Nov. 1963], Box 2:10, HZ Papers; James C. Cobb, *The Most Southern Place on Earth* (New York, 1992), 231. See also David L. Cohn, *The Mississippi Delta and the World* (Baton Rouge, 1995).

31 Frances B. Rankin to James W. Silver, Nov. 12, 1962, Box 21:4; Henry A. Fly to JWS, Sept. 17, 1963, Box 5:10, both in JWS Coll.; Mississippi Education fact sheet, Apr. 7, 1961, Box A232:8, NAACP Papers; *New*

NOTES TO PAGES 87–89

South, 16:4 (Apr. 1961), 13; Walter Lord, *The Past That Would Not Die* (New York, 1967; orig. 1965), 78; Campbell, *Chronicle*, 83; SNCC, "The General Condition of the Mississippi Negro" (ca. 1963), reel 25, CORE Papers; Sandy Leigh int., 14, Romaine Papers.

32 (votes) Dittmer, *Local People*, 70; Payne, *I've Got*, 1; W. F. Minor to Jack Minnis [Dec. 26, 1963], reel 176, SRC VEP Papers; (Jackson) VEP, "Participatory Programs," Nov. 1, 1962, reel 21, CORE Add. Papers; (police) Frederick P. Huey to Amzie Moore, Feb. 16, 1960, Box 1:4, AM Papers; Meredith, *Three Years*, 38; (mail) Payne, *I've Got*, 137–138; Bob Moses note on Anne Braden to BM, Oct. 24, 1962 (quote), Box 55:13, Braden Papers; John R. Salter, Jr., to 'Dear Folks' [early Apr. 1963], reel 3, JRS Papers; (phones) Payne, *I've Got*, 248; Calia [?] to Bob [Moses?], Sept. 26, 1962, Box 2:3, AM Papers; (boycotts) Campbell, *Chronicle*, 72; (Dixie Week) Seeger and Reiser, *Everybody*, 141.

33 (Eastland) Carl Braden to Amzie Moore, May 29, 1963 (1st quote), Box 1:5, AM Papers; Sherrill, *Gothic Politics*, 192; (lynching) Kay Mills, *This Little Light of Mine* (New York, 1994; orig. 1993), 29–31; (Citizens' Council) Sherrill, *Gothic Politics*, 213; E. Culpepper Clark, *The Schoolhouse Door* (New York, 1993), 92; (Cox) Bass, *Unlikely Heroes*, 86, 164–167; RFK, *Robert Kennedy*, 109–112; Arthur M. Schlesinger, Jr., *Robert Kennedy and His Times* (Boston, 1978), 307–308; Sherrill, *Gothic Politics*, 195 (2nd–3rd quotes); Pat Watters and Reese Cleghorn, *Climbing Jacob's Ladder* (New York, 1967), 216–218; Katzenbach KOH (1964), 88–89; Burke Marshall KOH, 93–94; Wilkins KOH, 24; W. F. Minor dispatch, 1961, and David W. Clark, "The Civil Rights Record of Federal District Judge William Harold Cox" (1970), both in Box 2 (1993 acc.), WFM Papers; Roy Wilkins wire to JFK, June 22, 1961, Box A176:7, NAACP Papers.

34 Standard is Neil R. McMillen, *The Citizens' Council* (2nd ed., Urbana, 1994; orig. 1971), esp. 19, 27, 122–132. See also Cook, *Segregationists*, 62, 67; John B. Martin, *The Deep South Says Never* (New York, 1957), 140; Powledge, *Free*, 184; Minor MOH, 4; Jane Schutt MOH, 4–5; Simmons biography in *NYT*, Sept. 28, 1962, p. 23; *Esquire*, Jan. 1964, pp. 135–136 (1st quote at 136); items, Box 2, Minor Papers; William J. Simmons to John B. Martin, May 18, 1962, Box 45:2, JBM Papers. (conformity) *NYT*, Mar. 30, 1961, p. 18; Dittmer, *Local People*, 63; Johnston, *Mississippi's Defiant Years*, 188; McMillen, *Citizens' Council*, 161, 174, 179 (2nd quote), 200, 239; Martin, *Deep South*, 127; Memphis *Press-Scimitar*, Dec. 4, 1962, p. 1; Schutt MOH, 18, 36–37; [?] to David and Sandy [Burner], Dec. 4, 1963, Box 15:17, James W. Silver Coll.

35 William M. Kunstler, *Deep in My Heart* (New York, 1966), 147; Wiesenberg MOH, 30, 32; *NYT*, Sept. 28, 1962, p. 23; Adam Nossiter, *Of Long*

Memory (Reading, MA, 1994), 68 (quote); Frank E. Smith, *Congressman from Mississippi* (New York, 1964), 281, 292, 298. Song in McNamara memo, ca. 1962, Box G239, 2 of 3, Drew Pearson Papers.

36 (papers) Dittmer, *Local People*, 64–65; Maryanne Vollers, *Ghosts of Mississippi* (Boston, 1995), 262; P. J. Ford to James W. Silver, Nov. 3, 1962, Box 21:5, JWS Coll. Quotes from *Jackson Daily News*, June 22, 1963; Nossiter, *Of Long Memory*, 83; Henry A. Fly to JWS, Nov. 5, 1962, Box 21:5, JWS Coll. (tv) Burner, *Gently*, 67–68; Cook, *Segregationists*, 82; Dittmer, *Local People*, 65 (tv message), 451n63; McMillen, *Citizens' Council*, 38–39; *Reporter*, Jan. 17, 1963, p. 24; Bill Higgs int., pp. 4–5, Dec. 19, 1965; R. L. T. Smith int., pp. 2–4, Dec. 30, 1965, both in Box 3:10, Howard Zinn Papers; Arthur D. Morse to Burke Marshall, Nov. 2, 1962, Box 5, BM Papers; R. L. T. Smith to FCC, Jan. 16, 1962 (copy); reply, Feb. 21, 1962, both in Box 8, Wofford Papers.

37 Vollers, *Ghosts*, 69–70; "Mississippi: Determined Lady," *Columbia Journalism Review*, 2:3 (Fall 1963), 37–38; Smith in *St. Louis Post-Dispatch*, Nov. 26, 1961, pp. H1, 7; Hazel B. Smith to Stephen W. Burks, July 28, 1963, Box 32:352, Allard K. Lowenstein Papers; Ira B. Harkey, Jr., *The Smell of Burning Crosses* (Jacksonville, IL, 1967); *The Petal Paper*, Over-sized, W. F. Minor Papers. Quotes from Wiesenberg MOH, 34; Hodding Carter to Rebecca J. Bell, Jan. 10, 1961, Box 20, HC Papers; Cook, *Segregationists*, 90n.

38 Dittmer, *Local People*, 157–158; Austin Moore III to 'Hello Folks,' May 21, 1963, reel 1; FBI Report, Dec. 1, 1960, reel 3; John R. Salter, Jr., to 'Dear Folks,' Oct. 27, 1961, reel 3, all in JRS Papers; [?] to David and Sandy [Burner], Dec. 4, 1963, Box 5:17, James W. Silver Coll. Quotes from James Symington notes, Oct. 10, 1962, Box 11, RFK Papers; Carl Braden to Joanne [?], Nov. 5, 1962, Box 55:13, Braden Papers; Salter in Salter-King MOH, 15, 16, 17, 16.

39 Jack Bass, *Taming the Storm* (New York, 1993), 104; Dan T. Carter, *The Politics of Rage* (New York, 1995), 84; Cook, *Segregationists*, 201; Watters and Cleghorn, *Climbing*, 151; Joe T. Patterson address, May 11, 1963, Box 11, W. F. Minor Papers.

40 (pressure) Cook, *Segregationists*, 56, 75; Dittmer, *Local People*, 47; McMillen, *Citizens' Council*, 209–210; Bayard Rustin, *Down the Line* (Chicago, 1971), 69; Watters and Cleghorn, *Climbing*, 129 (quote); Amzie Moore in Rev. Malcolm Boyd, "Survival of a Negro Leader," *Ave Maria*, Feb. 27, 1965, pp. 9–10, copy in Box 8:10, AM Papers; (Sovereignty Commission) Booker, *Black*, 170; Cook, *Segregationists*, 85; Dittmer, *Local People*, 60; Erle Johnston, *I Rolled with Ross* (Baton Rouge, 1980),

26–28, 47; McMillen, *Citizens' Council*, 336–337; Nossiter, *Of Long Memory*, 67–68, 96–97, 101–102, 236; Rustin, *Down the Line*, 70.

41 Cook, *Segregationists*, 20, 55; McMillen, *Citizens' Council*, 22–23; Jack Nelson, *Terror in the Night* (New York, 1993), 43–44; Powledge, *Free*, 184; Watters and Cleghorn, *Climbing*, 151; *New Republic*, June 11, 1962, p. 13; Informant report, Oct. 10, 1960, Box A282:6, NAACP Papers. Quotes from Carter, *Politics*, 95; *New South*, 17:10 (Oct. 1962), 16. On the mid-1960s see Nelson, *Terror*.

42 Evers, *For Us*, 24–27, 72, 76, 78–79, 100, 102, 133; Nossiter, *Of Long Memory*, 28, 36, 42; Payne, *I've Got*, 47; Vollers, *Ghosts*, 31–33, 43, 45, 116 (quote); *Ebony*, Sept. 1963, pp. 143–148 (orig. Nov. 1958).

43 (murders) Evers, *For Us*, 159, 173, 205–214; Nossiter, *Of Long Memory*, 29, 42; Payne, *I've Got*, 37; Salter in Salter-King MOH, 31, 38; Ed King in Salter-King MOH, 85; Lawrence Guyot int., 2, Romaine Papers; (Till) Dittmer, *Local People*, 55–58; Martin, *Deep South*, 32–33; Anne Moody, *Coming of Age in Mississippi* (New York, 1968), 103–110; Payne, *I've Got*, 54, 142; Vollers, *Ghosts*, 65–67; Stephen J. Whitfield, *A Death in the Delta* (Baltimore, 1991; orig. 1988), esp. viii, 23, 61, 90; Joe Sinsheimer, "Never Turn Back," *Southern Exposure*, 15:2 (Summer 1987), 42; Jimmy Wechsler to Arthur M. Schlesinger, Jr., Nov. 23, 1955 (copy), Box 131:7, Joseph L. Rauh Papers; Barrett Strong, "Money (That's What I Want)" (1960 record).

44 (summary) Louis E. Lomax, "The Kennedys Move In on Dixie," *Harper's Magazine*, May 1962, pp. 27–33. Bartley, *New South*, 172; Booker, *Black*, 199; RFK, *Robert Kennedy*, 102–103; Humphrey JOH (1977), 3:11–12; Katzenbach KOH (1964), 20; Clarence Mitchell KOH, 34; Ed King in Salter-King MOH, 98; Tom Kahn statement [May 1962], reel 1, SDS Papers. Quotes from Eugene V. Rostow to Berl I. Bernhard, May 31, 1961, Box 3, BIB Papers; Elizabeth C. Brown to Francesca Rhee, May 26, 1963, Box 3:9, ECB Papers.

45 (VEP) Branch, *Parting*, 479–480; Burner, *Gently*, 34, 77, 103; Carson, *In Struggle*, 38–39; Forman, *Making*, 221–222, 235, 264–266; RFK, *Robert Kennedy*, 104; Meier and Rudwick, *CORE*, 172–175; Payne, *I've Got*, 108–109; Powledge, *Free*, 370; Mark Stern, *Calculating Visions* (New Brunswick, NJ, 1992), 63–67; Ed King in Salter-King MOH, 99; Ella Baker int., 5–6, Romaine Papers; (miscalculated) VEP *Newsletter*, 1:2 (Mar. 1964), 4; Ella Baker int., 2, Romaine Papers.

46 Sally Belfrage, *Freedom Summer* (New York, 1965), 11, 25; Branch, *Parting*, 325–326; Elizabeth Sutherland, ed., *Letters from Mississippi* (New York, 1965), 38. Quotes from *SEP*, Sept. 8, 1962, p. 15; Payne,

I've Got, 104; Hamer int., 1, Romaine Papers. On COFO see Moses int., pt. II, pp. 2–3, Romaine Papers. In general see Burner, *Gently.*

47 (summary) *WP*, Sept. 10, 1962. Branch, *Parting*, 635; Burner, *Gently*, 71; Carson, *In Struggle*, 77–80; Payne, *I've Got*, 105; Wiley Branton-Sam Block call, Aug. 17, 1962, reel 176, SRC VEP Papers; SB reports, July 26, 1962; Aug. 12, 1962, both in Box 8:7, Amzie Moore Papers; SB press release, Aug. 11, 1962 (quotes), Box 55:13, Braden Papers.

48 Dittmer, *Local People*, 138–142; Seeger and Reiser, *Everybody*, 157n; *NYT*, Oct. 21, 1965, p. 65. Quotes from Meredith, *Three Years*, 3; *Chicago Defender*, Oct. 27, 1962, p. 10.

49 (Meredith) Ed King in Salter-King MOH, 88–89 (1st quote at 88); Bass, *Unlikely Heroes*, 174–182; Greenberg, *Crusaders*, 325; Johnston, *Rolled*, 89–93; Irving Engel file, Box 26:6, Hugo Black Papers; items, Boxes 19–20, Burke Marshall Papers; (murder) Russell H. Barrett, *Integration at Ole Miss* (Chicago, 1965), 71; Meredith, *Three Years*, 79–80; Steve Whitaker to Russell Barrett, Dec. 17, 1962 (2nd quote), Box 5:10, James W. Silver Coll.; anon. to Roy Wilkins, Oct. 10, 1962, Box A151:6, NAACP Papers.

50 (calls) Bass, *Unlikely Heroes*, 192–193; RFK, *Robert Kennedy*, 160; Victor S. Navasky, *Kennedy Justice* (New York, 1971), 189–190, 209–217; Schlesinger, *Robert Kennedy*, 318; Katzenbach KOH (1964), 94; (Barnett) Burke Marshall JOH, 20; (Simmons) McMillen, *Citizens' Council*, 334–335, 343, 344n; Nossiter, *Of Long Memory*, 93; Memphis *Press-Scimitar*, Dec. 4, 1962, p. 1; William J. Simmons biography, Box 2, W. F. Minor Papers. Quotes from Telephone transcript, Sept. 25, 1962, 12:20 p.m., Box 20, Burke Marshall Papers; Schlesinger, *Robert Kennedy*, 318; James W. Silver to Paul [?], Jan. 6, 1961, Box 6:8, JWS Coll.

51 (negotiations) Guthman, *We Band*, 193–194, 200 (quote at 194); Lord, *Past*, 161; McMillen, *Citizens' Council*, 345; Schlesinger, *Robert Kennedy*, 321; Burke Marshall JOH, 20; Burke Marshall KOH, 75–77; Telephone transcript, Sept. 30, 1962, 12:45 p.m., Box 20, Burke Marshall Papers; (Meredith) Johnston, *Rolled*, 105; Meredith, *Three Years*, 211; Katzenbach KOH (1964), 106.

52 Guthman, *We Band*, 99–100; Johnston, *Rolled*, 104–105; RFK, *Robert Kennedy*, 163; Katzenbach KOH (1964), 97, 99, 104, 108, 115; Dean Markham notes, 1962, Box 11, RFK Papers; James J. P. McShane deposition, Dec. 11, 1962, Box 2, JJPM Papers; John Doar to Nicholas Katzenbach, Nov. 21, 1962, Box 5, Burke Marshall Papers. For a lively narrative see William Doyle, *An American Insurrection* (New York, 2001).

53 (marshals) Johnston, *Mississippi's Defiant Years*, 155; Lord, *Past*, 170; *NYT*, Oct. 1, 1962, p. 23; *Jackson Daily News*, Oct. 1, 1962, p. 7C;

Charles Vanderburgh, "A Draftee's Diary from the Mississippi Front," *Harper's Magazine*, Feb. 1964, p. 39; McShane deposition, Dec. 11, 1962, Box 2, McShane Papers; (jeers) Guthman, *We Band*, 201 (1st, 3rd quotes); Barrett, *Integration*, 139 (2nd quote).

54 (crowd) Barrett, *Integration*, 173; Robert Massie, "What Next in Mississippi?" *SEP*, Nov. 10, 1962, p. 18; Mayor Hartsfield call to Burke Marshall, Oct. 1, 1962, Box 19, BM Papers; (Walker) Johnston, *Rolled*, 103. Quotes from Nossiter, *Of Long Memory*, 65; *NYT*, Sept. 28, 1962, p. 23; Walker address, Dec. 29, 1961, Box 14, W. F. Minor Papers.

55 (gas) Barrett, *Integration*, 148, 155; Lord, *Past*, 183–184; Massie in *SEP*, 18; Katzenbach KOH (1964), 104, 107; Burke Marshall KOH, 79; (riot) Guthman, *We Band*, 201–203; Massie in *SEP*, 18–23 (quote at 18); Memphis *Commercial Appeal* and *NYT*, Oct. 1–3, 1962; Greenville *Delta Democrat-Times*, Oct. 3, 1962; New Orleans *Times-Picayune*, Oct. 2, 1962; Jackson *Clarion-Ledger*, Oct. 2–3, 1962; *U.S. News*, Oct. 15, 1962, pp. 43–47; Katzenbach KOH (1964), 105; Silver MOH, 45–51, 87; James W. Silver to his daughter Betty, Oct. 2, 1962, Box 7:3, JWS Coll.; McShane statement, n.d., Box 2, McShane Papers.

56 Barrett, *Integration*, 145, 156; Lord, *Past*, 188–191, 197; Powledge, *Free*, 439; Massie in *SEP*, 18; Memphis *Commerical Appeal*, Oct. 1, 1962, p. 1; Oct. 2, 1962, pp. 15, 22; *Jackson Daily News*, Oct. 2, 1962, p. 17A; Jackson *Clarion-Ledger*, Oct. 2, 1962, p. 1; Greenville *Delta Democrat-Times*, Oct. 3, 1962, p. 1; *National Guardian*, Oct. 8, 1962, p. 3; Oct. 22, 1962, p. 5; Silver MOH, 46; W. F. Minor draft, n.d., Box 9, WFM Papers; J. Robertshaw to Amon G. Carter, Jr., Oct. 18, 1963, Box 23, Hodding Carter Papers; WMPS radio news release, Oct. 3, 1962, Box 125, LBJ-VP Papers; Joan [Trumpauer] to Anne [Braden], Oct. 2, 1962, Box 55:13, Braden Papers; James W. Silver to his daughter Betty, Oct. 2, 1962, Box 7:3, JWS Coll. Silver wrote as W. J. Weatherby in *Manchester Guardian*, Oct. 3–5, 8–10, 1962.

57 Dittmer, *Local People*, 141; Guthman, *We Band*, 203–204 (quotes at 204); Lord, *Past*, 194, 201–203; Katzenbach KOH (1964), 17, 111–114; Burke Marshall KOH, 80, 82; Schlei KOH, 18–19; *NYT*, Oct. 2, 1962, p. 24; John Faulkner in *SEP*, Nov. 10, 1962, pp. 24–25; Vanderburgh in *Harper's Magazine*, 39; Adelaide, Australia *Advertiser*, Oct. 2, 1962, p. 1, copy in Box 5:17, James W. Silver Coll.

58 (aftermath) Barrett, *Integration*, 162, 167; Dittmer, *Local People*, 141–142; RFK, *Robert Kennedy*, 161; *NYT*, Oct. 2, 1962, pp. 1, 24, 27; Oct. 4, 1962, p. 30; Adelaide, Australia *Advertiser*, Oct. 2, 1962, p. 1; *Look*, Dec. 31, 1962, p. 34; Burke Marshall to Lawrence W. Rabb, Nov. 9, 1962, Box 5, BM Papers; (Meredith) Jackson *Clarion-Ledger*, Oct. 5,

1962, p. 1; Barrett, *Integration*, 190, 202; Meredith, *Three Years*, 212, 226, 244–245, 247, 283; Nossiter, *Of Long Memory*, 72–75; *Progressive*, June 1964, pp. 35–38. Quotes from Memphis *Commercial Appeal*, Oct. 2, 1962, p. 8; *Jackson Daily News*, Oct. 3, 1962, p. 11A; Greenville *Delta Democrat-Times*, Oct. 9, 1962, p. 1; Vanderburgh in *Harper's Magazine*, 42 (sign, last quote).

59 New Orleans *Times-Picayune*, Sept. 17, 1972, Sec. III, p. 6; *NYT*, Oct. 3, 1962, pp. 1, 28; Nelson Rockefeller statement, Oct. 2, 1962, reel 5, CORE Papers; Benjamin Muse memo, Jan. 1964, Box 8, Burke Marshall Papers; Joseph F. Dolan to Nicholas Katzenbach, Apr. 19, 1963, Box 11, RFK Papers. Quotes from *WSJ*, Oct. 4, 1962, p. 18; Hodding Carter to Bill Howland, Oct. 13, 1962, Box 21, HC Papers; *The Citizen*, Sept. 1962.

60 Quotes from Paul B. Johnson press release, Oct. 14, 1963, Box 4, W. F. Minor Papers; Mrs. Norma V. Green to LBJ, Oct. 1, 1962; E. E. Payne to LBJ, Sept. 29, 1962, both in Box 125, LBJ-VP Papers; noble quoted by Taylor Caldwell to William F. Buckley, Jr., Oct. 14–19, 1962, Box 19:69, WFB Papers; RFK, *Robert Kennedy*, 159; Stephan Lesher, *George Wallace* (Reading, MA, 1993), 171.

61 Abernathy, *Walls*, 201, 206, 217, 226–227; Branch, *Parting*, 524–561 (1st quote at 558); David L. Chappell, *Inside Agitators* (Baltimore, 1994), 122–143; Forman, *Making*, 247–262; Garrow, *Bearing*, 173–230; Lewis, *King*, 151, 160–170 (2nd quote at 162); Powledge, *Free*, 379, 415–416; Watters, *Down*, 161–215, 233; Andrew Young, *An Easy Burden* (New York, 1996), 178, 181; *Atlanta Constitution*, Dec. 13–22, 1961; July 11–Aug. 11, 1962; *NYT*, Dec. 13–19, 1961; July 11–Aug. 16, 18, 29, 1962; Nov. 15, 19, 1962; June 23, 1963; July 5, 1963; *LAT*, Aug. 6, 1962, pt. I, pp. 3, 7.

62 Watters, *Down*, 14; Young, *Easy*, 193; Zinn, *You*, 54–55; *Afro-American*, Aug. 18, 1962, p. 2 (quote); MLK, "Bold Design for a New South," *Nation*, Mar. 30, 1963, pp. 259–262.

63 Abernathy, *Walls*, 231, 234; Bartley, *New South*, 330–331; Jack M. Bloom, *Class, Race, and the Civil Rights Movement* (Bloomington, IN, 1987), 174–175; Branch, *Parting*, 690–691; Angela Y. Davis, *Angela Davis-an Autobiography* (New York, 1974), 77–102; Hampton and Fayer, *Voices*, 124 (quote); Lewis, *King*, 172–173; Nunnelley, *Connor*, 185; Watters, *Down*, 236–237; August Meier in *New Politics*, 2:4 (Summer 1963), 26; *SEP*, Mar. 2, 1963, pp. 11–18; Virginia Durr to Burke Marshall, Nov. 16, 1961, Box 4, BM Papers; Irving M. Engel to Charles Morgan, Jr., Sept. 17, 1963, Box 26:6, Hugo Black Papers. On unions see file, Box 23:11; A. Philip Randolph to George Meany [ca. June 1961], Box 23:12, both in APR Papers.

64 (Connor) Hugo Black, Jr., *My Father* (New York, 1975), 214, 218–221; Carter, *Politics*, 115, 166; Durr, *Outside*, 109–110, 121; Nunnelley,

Connor, 114–115, 118, 181–184; Young, *Easy*, 199; *Nation*, May 5, 1962, pp. 397–401; Virginia Durr COH, 115; Hugo Black, Jr., to HB, Apr. 10, 1960, 4:2; Virginia Durr to HB, Mar. 9, 1962, Box 7:3, both in HB Papers; SAC NY to Dir. FBI, Sept. 23, 1963, reel 2, MLK FBI File; Informant report, Oct. 10, 1960, Box A282:6, NAACP Papers; (Shelton) Carter, *Politics*, 94–95, 167; Cook, *Segregationists*, 128–133.

65 (summary) *Atlanta Constitution*, July 17, 1963, pp. C1, C14. Bloom, *Class*, 174–175; Forman, *Making*, 311; Lewis, *King*, 177, 182–191; Coretta S. King, *My Life with Martin Luther King, Jr.* (New York, 1969), 233 (quote); Young, *Easy*, 225–226; *NYT*, Apr. 13, 1963, pp. 1, 15; Apr. 14, 1963, pp. 1, 46; Apr. 16, 1963, p. 17; VEP, "Participatory Programs," Nov. 1, 1962 (voting statistics), reel 21, CORE Add. Papers.

66 "Letter from Birmingham Jail" is in King, *Why We Can't Wait* (New York, 1964), ch. 5. Abernathy, *Walls*, 255; Daniel Berrigan to Rev. James J. Shanahan, July 21, 1963 (quote), Box 89, Berrigan Coll.

67 Abernathy, *Walls*, 262–263; Branch, *Parting*, 754–764, 775; Carter, *Politics*, 124; Forman, *Making*, 312; Lewis, *King*, 192–201; Young, *Easy*, 246; *Life*, May 17, 1963, p. 29ff; Virginia Durr COH, 294; Burke Marshall KOH, 95–102; Burke Marshall KOH (Hackman), 24; James Farmer to Leo Zacharow, June 7, 1963, reel 3, CORE Papers. Quotes from *NYT*, May 11, 1963, p. 9; Nubar Esaian to James Farmer, May 8, 1963, reel 3, CORE Papers; *NYT*, May 8, 1963, p. 28.

68 Carter, *Politics*, 175, 188–193; Davis, *Davis*, 128–130; Hampton and Fayer, *Voices*, 171–176; *NYT*, Sept. 16, 1963, pp. 1, 26; J. Edgar Hoover to RFK, Sept. 30, 1963, Box 3, Scott Rafferty Papers. Quotes from Booker, *Black*, 55; Lillian Smith to Marv [Rich], Sept. 23, 1963, reel 11, CORE Add. Papers; A. Philip Randolph wire to JFK, Sept. 16, 1963, Box 2:9, APR Papers.

69 Quotes from Forman, *Making*, 312; *Liberation*, June 1963, p. 31; G. Mennen Williams to JFK, June 15, 1963, Box 9, RFK Papers; Ralph J. Gleason to Alexander P. Hoffman, June 1, 1963, RJG Letters; Aubrey Williams to Jim Dombrowski, June 6 [1963], Box 21:7, Braden Papers; Mrs. W. R. Broadgus to LBJ, May 26, 1963, Box 189, LBJ-VP Papers; *Houston Press*, May 20, 1963, p. 2; Wilkins and Young in *NYT*, Apr. 23, 1963; RFK in Fairclough, *Redeem*, 136; MLK-Stanley Levison conversation, NY FBI memo, June 4, 1963, reel 1, MLK FBI File. Statistics in Booker, *Black*, 56.

70 Booker, *Black*, 53–55; RFK, *Robert Kennedy*, 171–172; Lewis, *King*, 208; *WP*, June 7, 1963, p. A17 (Joe Alsop); *Nation*, Mar. 30, 1963, p. 262; Burke Marshall KOH, 61; Ralph J. Gleason to Alexander P. Hoffman, June 24, 1963 (quote), RJG Letters.

71 Carter, *Politics*, 142–151; Clark, *Schoolhouse*, 179–180, 203–206, 222–231; Guthman, *We Band*, 215–218; Bill Jones, *The Wallace Story* (Northport, AL, 1966), 37 (quote), 84–85, 90–105; RFK, *Robert Kennedy*, 187–195; Lesher, *Wallace*, 201–204, 228–234; *NYT*, June 12, 1963, pp. 1, 20; Burke Marshall KOH, 107–108; Salter in Salter-King MOH, 18; Grover C. Hall, Jr., to Hugo Black, Oct. 21, 1963, Box 33:8, HB Papers.

72 JFK, *Public Papers of the Presidents of the United States: John F. Kennedy, 1963* (Washington, 1964), 468–471 (quotes at 469, 468–469). RFK, *Robert Kennedy*, 175–177, 199–200; *NYT*, June 10, 1963, p. 20; June 12, 1963, pp. 1, 20; *Nation*, Feb. 4, 1961, pp. 91–95; Burke Marshall KOH, 109–110; Burke Marshall KOH (Hackman), 30; MLK-Levison talk, NY FBI memo, June 12, 1963 (3rd quote), reel 1, MLK FBI File.

73 (summary) Branch, *Parting*, 715, 718, 725; Lawrence Guyot int., 4–5, 9, Romaine Papers. *NYT*, Apr. 1, 1963, p. 15; *WP*, Apr. 1, 1963; Robert Moses, "Mississippi: 1961–62," *Liberation*, Jan. 1970, pp. 15–17; *Nation*, Oct. 5, 1963, pp. 193–196; Sam Block in *Southern Exposure*, 15:2 (Summer 1987), 37–50. Quotes from *New York Post*, Mar. 19, 1963, p. 34; *Look*, May 21, 1963, p. 41. Statistics in *WP*, Apr. 5, 1963, p. 2A. In general see Payne, *I've Got*.

74 Branch, *Parting*, 713–722; Dick Gregory with Robert Lipsyte, *Nigger* (New York, 1964), 176, 183–193; (food) *Greenwood Commonwealth*, Mar. 20, 1963, p. 1; *Mississippi Newsletter*, Feb. 28, 1963 (mimeo), Box 55:14, Braden Papers; Rev. D. L. Tucker to Alfred B. Lewis, Nov. 15, 1963, Box C74:8, NAACP Papers; (Travis) *NYT*, Mar. 2, 1963, p. 4; *Atlanta Journal-Constitution*, Mar. 3, 1963; Greenville *Delta Democrat-Times*, Mar. 1, 1963; SNCC press release, Mar. 1, 1963; SNCC memo [Mar. 1963], both in Box 46, Social Action Vertical File; Bob Moses int., Pt. II, pp. 8–9, Romaine Papers; (Branton) Watters and Cleghorn, *Climbing*, 59–60; David Dennis to James McCain, Mar. 25, 1963, reel 6, CORE Papers; (Tucker) *NYT*, Mar. 29, 1963, p. 1; (festival) Seeger and Reiser, *Everybody*, 167; *NYT*, July 6, 1963, p. 7; *Greenwood Commonwealth*, July 8, 1963; SNCC press release, July 8, 1963, Box 46, Social Action Vertical File. Quotes from John Morsell memo, Mar. 29, 1963 (1st–3rd quotes), Box A231:9, NAACP Papers; Young in *New York Herald Tribune*, May 3, 1963, p. 8; *Southern Exposure*, 15:2 (Summer 1987), 41.

75 (Evers) Evers address, May 20, 1963 (1st quote), reel 2, John R. Salter, Jr. Papers; (protests) Moody, *Coming of Age*, 236–240; Salter, *Jackson*, 132–139; NAACP press release, June 1, 1963 (2nd quote), Box A232:2, NAACP Papers; Vollers, *Ghosts*, 109–114 (3rd quote at 114); *NYT*, May 29, 1963, p. 1; June 1, 1963, pp. 1, 8; June 2, 1963, p. 70; *Jet*, June 20, 1963, p. 8; *New Politics*, 2:3 (Summer 1963), 14; Mrs. Bradshaw Speller

to Roy Wilkins, June 3, 1963; Percy E. Sutton to RW, June 3, 1963, both in Box A233:7, NAACP Papers.

76 Branch, *Parting*, 829; Reed Massengill, *Portrait of a Racist* (New York, 1994), 135 (sweatshirts); Moody, *Coming of Age*, 247–248; Nossiter, *Of Long Memory*, 60–63; Salter in Salter-King MOH, 93; King in Salter-King MOH, 100; Mendy Samstein int., 2:19, Romaine Papers; items in Box A114:8, NAACP Papers; Roy Wilkins wire to A. Philip Randolph, June 13, 1963, Box 2:9, APR Papers. Quotes from *Christian Science Monitor*, June 13, 1963, p. 5; Johnston, *Mississippi's Defiant Years*, 180; *NYT Magazine*, June 23, 1963, p. 11; *NYT*, June 16, 1963, p. 58; *Chicago Defender*, June 15, 1963, p. 2; Anderson, *Rustin*, 243.

77 Evers, *For Us*, 333, 335, 358, 368–369; Massengill, *Portrait*, 41, 105, 150–155, 163, 201, 206, 215, 338–339, 343; Nossiter, *Of Long Memory*, xiv, 27, 90, 105–109, 117–118, 129–131, 238, 248; Powledge, *Free*, 190; Vollers, *Ghosts*, 28–30, 377–378; *NYT*, June 13, 1963, pp. 1, 12; June 23, 1963, pp. 1, 63; *WP*, June 24, 1963, pp. A1, A6; *SEP*, Mar. 14, 1964, pp. 77–81; Beckwith biography in *Jackson Daily News*, June 24, 1963, pp. 1–2. Quotes from Burke Marshall to RFK, Nov. 4, 1963, Box 8, BM Papers; *Jackson Daily News*, June 12, 1963, p. 1A.

78 Dittmer, *Local People*, 169, 178; Moody, *Coming of Age*, 253; Nossiter, *Of Long Memory*, 177; Joan Trumpauer to Mr. and Mrs. John R. Salter, Jr., Dec. 12, 1963; Bette A. Poole to Mr. and Mrs. JRS, Dec. [1963], both on reel 3, JRS Papers; Florence La Fontaine to Amzie Moore, June 20, 1963 (quote), Box 1:5, AM Papers; Gloster B. Current phone call memo to Roy Wilkins, June 17, 1963, Box A114:4; Calvin D. Banks memo to RW, Aug. 2, 1963 (memorials), Box A114:13, both in NAACP Papers.

79 Michael R. Beschloss, *Taking Charge* (New York, 1997), 163–165; Stern, *Calculating*, 46; *NYT*, June 3, 1963, pp. 1, 19; June 7, 1963, p. 30 (Reston); June 23, 1963, p. E3; *WSJ*, Aug. 28, 1963, p. 24; Theodore Hesburgh JOH, 5–7, 11; Katzenbach KOH (1964), 128–140; Burke Marshall KOH, 106; Clarence Mitchell KOH, 36; Rauh KOH, 102–109; Smathers KOH, 8F; Hobart Taylor, Jr. KOH, 34; Wofford KOH, 57; LBJ–Sorensen phone call, June 3, 1963 (quote), Box 30, Sorensen Papers (orig. at LBJ Library); Mike Mansfield to JFK, June 18, 1963, Box 30, Sorensen Papers; Norbert A. Schlei memo, June 4, 1963; Nicholas Katzenbach to RFK, June 29, 1963, both in Box 11, RFK Papers; James Farmer to Harry Golden, Oct. 24, 1963, reel 3, CORE Papers; Joseph L. Rauh to Clinton Anderson, Aug. 8, 1963, Box 24:8, JLR Papers; items in Box 11, RFK Papers.

80 Anderson, *Rustin*, 178, 208; Branch, *Parting*, 564–565; Michael Friedly with David Gallen, *Martin Luther King, Jr.* (New York, 1993), 23–28;

David J. Garrow, *The FBI and Martin Luther King, Jr.* (New York, 1981), 14, 26–29, 33–48, 65, 70, 85–86, 98; Garrow, *Bearing*, 117, 168, 195, 200, 235; Gentry, *Hoover*, 497–503; a deceptive account is in Navasky, *Kennedy Justice*, 81, 86–87, 136–138, 150; O'Reilly, *Black Americans*, 29; Schlesinger, *Robert Kennedy*, 353–357; Athan G. Theoharis and John S. Cox, *The Boss* (Philadelphia, 1988), 333n; Katzenbach KOH (1969), 60–64; Burke Marshall KOH (Hackman), 42–43; FBI memos, Apr. 12, 1962, June 11, 1963; J. Edgar Hoover to Kenneth O'Donnell, Apr. 20, 1962; JEH to RFK, June 3, Aug. 2, 1963, all on reel 1, MLK FBI File; Karl Prussion affidavit, Sept. 28, 1963, Box 8, Burke Marshall Papers. Quotes from G. H. Scatterday to A. Rosen, May 22, 1961, reel 1; Sullivan to Belmont, Aug. 30, 1963, reel 2, both in MLK FBI File.

81 Branch, *Parting*, 692, 835–838; Friedly, *King*, 30–38, 148, 162–165, 168; Garrow, *FBI and King*, 44, 49, 55, 59–63 (quote at 61), 79; Garrow, *Bearing*, 195, 222–223, 272; Gentry, *Hoover*, 504–509; RFK, *Robert Kennedy*, 141–147; O'Reilly, *Black Americans*, 30; Schlesinger, *Robert Kennedy*, 357–360; Young, *Easy*, 201, 265–266, 269; *Afro-American*, Aug. 3, 1963, pp. 1–2; Burke Marshall KOH (Hackman), 43–45; Wofford KOH, 140–144; J. Edgar Hoover memo, June 17, 1963, reel 1, MLK FBI File.

82 Branch, *Parting*, 573–574, 675–678, 904; Friedly, *King*, 25–30, 34–35, 39, 128, 133; Garrow, *FBI and King*, 29, 46, 50–54, 57, 62, 66–67, 73–74, 77, 81, 86–87; Garrow, *Bearing*, 200–201, 222, 275, 279; Gentry, *Hoover*, 506–508, 527–528; Young, *Easy*, 264; *Long Island Star-Journal*, Nov. 2, 1962; *Atlanta Constitution*, July 25, 1963, pp. 1, 17; July 26, 1963, pp. 1, 6–7; Burke Marshall KOH (Hackman), 45; SAC NY to J. Edgar Hoover, May 29, Sept. 28, Dec. 3, 1962; JEH to RFK, June 25, 1962; June 7, 1963; FBI memo, Nov. 15, 1962; SAC NO to JEH, Nov. 20, 1962; DeLoach to Mohr, Jan. 15, 1963 (quote), annotated "I concur" by JEH; NY FBI memo, June 10, 1963, all on reel 1; JEH to RFK, July 23, 1963; FBI memos, July 22, 1963; Oct. 22, 1963; Evans to Belmont, June 25, 1963; JEH to SAC Atlanta and NY, Sept. 4, 1963; Bland to Sullivan, Sept. 6, 1963; JEH to SAC NY, Oct. 14, 1963, all on reel 2, MLK FBI File. On O'Dell/Kilgore see NY FBI memo, Aug. 14, 1963, reel 1; FBI reports, Nov. 14, 1962; Sept. 30, 1963, both on reel 2, MLK FBI File; *Nation*, Sept. 7, 1963, p. 104.

83 (MLK) Fairclough, *Redeem*, 150–151; NY FBI memos, June 4, 7, 10, 1963, all on reel 1, MLK FBI File; (Randolph) Anderson, *Rustin*, 60, 239–242; Lewis, *King*, 214–215; Paula E. Pfeffer, *A. Philip Randolph* (Baton Rouge, 1990), 240–270; Rustin JOH, 1:4–6; [Lilly Whitney] to A. Philip Randolph, June 4, 1963, Box 2:9, APR Papers; APR to Roy Wilkins, Mar. 25, 1963 (copy), Box 27:10; Negro American Labor Council minutes, Apr. 4, 1963, Box 30:14, both in Bayard Rustin Papers; (jobs) John Brophy

notes, 1962, Box 23, JB Papers; Seymour Kahan to John B. Martin, Oct. 12, 1960, Box 74:1, JBM Papers; Booker, *Black*, 69, 71. Quotes from FBI memo, June 6, 1963, reel 1, MLK FBI File; *NYT*, June 23, 1963, p. 1; A. Philip Randolph to Louis Simon, July 18, 1963, Box 30:18, Bayard Rustin Papers.

84 (general) Garrow, *Bearing*, 265–268, 272, 278; *LAT*, Aug. 25, 1963, p. B1 (quote); "Proposed Plans for March," July 2, 1963, Box A229:4, NAACP Papers; items, Box 27:10, Bayard Rustin Papers; FBI reports, June 6, 10, 1963, both on reel 4, MLK-SL FBI File; (Young) Weiss, *Young*, esp. 102–104; (Wilkins) Roy Wilkins to James K. Baker, July 17, 1963; John A. Morsell to S. N. Tammany, Aug. 7, 1963, both in Box A228:2, NAACP Papers; (Randolph) Jervis Anderson, *A. Philip Randolph* (New York, 1972), 322–324; (unions) Forman, *Making*, 333; *NYT*, Aug. 13, 1963, p. 22; Aug. 14, 1963, p. 21; Bayard Rustin to David Dubinsky, Aug. 5, 1963, Box 28:3, BR Papers; (religion) Dan Berrigan to Rev. James J. Shanahan, July 21, 1963; DB to Karl and Jean Meyer, Aug. 24, 1963, both in Box 89; Phil Berrigan to DB [ca. Aug. 1963], Box 101; John Harmon to DB, Aug. 2, 1963, Box 154, all in Berrigan Papers.

85 (goal) *WP*, June 24, 1963, p. B3 (quote); DC Coordinating Committee for March on Washington memo, July 17, 1963, Box A228:1; Barbara W. Moffett to A. Philip Randolph, Aug. 2, 1963 (copy), Box A228:2, both in NAACP Papers; Bayard Rustin to Hamish Sinclair, Aug. 1, 1963, Box 28:2, BR Papers; NY FBI memo, Aug. 14, 1963, reel 1, MLK FBI File; (minorities) LBJ to Antonio J. Taylor, Nov. 30, 1962, Box 139, LBJ-VP Papers; Sandy Leigh memo to Bayard Rustin [ca. Aug. 29, 1963], Box 28:15, BR Papers; (JACL) APR to Mike Masaoka, Aug. 1, 1963, Box 28:2, BR Papers; (unions) Draper, *Conflict*, 4; BR to Bill Becker, Aug. 7, 1963, Box 28:4, BR Papers; (numbers) Anderson, *Rustin*, 256; Booker, *Black*, 57; Hubert H. Humphrey, *The Education of a Public Man* (New York, 1976), 201; King, *My Life*, 237; Lewis, *King*, 224; Doris E. Saunders, ed., *The Day They Marched* (Chicago, 1963), 3; Williams, *Eyes*, 199.

86 Booker, *Black*, 32; Farmer, *Lay Bare*, 243; Humphrey, *Education*, 202; RFK, *Robert Kennedy*, 226–227; Lewis, *King*, 216–219; Pfeffer, *Randolph*, 244–245, 250; *NYT*, July 18, 1963, p. 1; Aug. 29, 1963, p. 1; *WP*, Aug. 29, 1963, p. D14; *LAT*, Sept. 1, 1963, p. C7 (Lippmann); Booker KOH, 37; Clarence Mitchell KOH, 37, 40 (quote); Carl Murphy to APR, Sept. 25, 1963, 29:4, BR Papers. On women, see Pauli Murray, *Song in a Weary Throat* (New York, 1987), 353; *WP*, Nov. 15, 1963, p. C2.

87 Anderson, *Randolph*, 332; Carawan and Carawan, *We Shall Overcome*, 101; Forman, *Making*, 331–337; Garrow, *Bearing*, 281–283; Hampton and Fayer, *Voices*, 166–167; Saunders, *Day*, 12, 36–37 (signs at 36, 36,

37), 43, 45, 66–68; *NYT*, Aug. 29, 1963, pp. 1, 16–17, 19–21; *WP*, Aug. 29, 1963, pp. A1 (1st quote), A12–14, A20–23, A26–27; Booker, *Black*, 50 (2nd quote); *Ebony*, Nov. 1963, p. 29ff; *Gandhi Marg*, 7:4 (Oct. 1963), 299 (3rd quote); Archbishop Patrick A. O'Boyle to Bayard Rustin, Aug. 20, 1963, Box A228:3, NAACP Papers.

88 (tv) Pfeffer, *Randolph*, 252; Saunders, *Day*, 3; *NYT*, Aug. 29, 1963, p. 19; *WP*, Aug. 25, 1963, p. A19; Aug. 29, 1963, pp. D16, E3; *Christian Science Monitor*, Aug. 30, 1963, p. 1; *LAT*, Sept. 1, 1963, p. C4; Sen. Harrison Williams to Bayard Rustin, Sept. 4, 1963, Box 29:2, BR Papers; Chester Bowles to Roy Wilkins, Sept. 3, 1963, Box A229:1, NAACP Papers; (Malcolm X) *Jet*, Sept. 12, 1963, pp. 22–23; *New Republic*, Sept. 14, 1963, p. 19. Quotes from Gentry, *Hoover*, 527; King, *My Life*, 242; Forman, *Making*, 333; Anderson, *Rustin*, 262.

89 Abernathy, *Walls*, 280; Farmer, *Lay Bare*, 245; Sellers, *River*, 66; Clarence Mitchell KOH, 41; Mrs. C. M. Gray to NAACP, Sept. 1, 1963, Box A228:1; Roy L. Reuther to Roy Wilkins, Aug. 30, 1963, Box A228:5; B. E. Murph to Roy Wilkins, Aug. 31, 1963, Box A228:6, all in NAACP Papers. Quotes from Elta Brazier to Richard Haley, Aug. 15, 1963, reel 6, CORE Papers; *Chicago Defender*, Aug. 31, 1963, pp. 1–2; *Framingham News*, Sept. 3, 1963; Humphrey, *Education*, 202; Hampton and Fayer, *Voices*, 161; Booker, *Black*, 57.

90 *WP*, Aug. 30, 1963, p. A1; *NYT Magazine*, Aug. 25, 1963, p. 7ff (quotes at 8, 9); Charles Evers to Gloster Current, Dec. 18, 1963, Box C73:7, NAACP Papers.

91 *Commonweal*, Sept. 20, 1963, p. 553 (quote); Rev. Frederick J. Warnecke report, Aug. 12, 1963, Box 23:6, Thurgood Marshall Papers; Harry H. Purvis to [James] Baldwin, Sept. 26, 1963 (copy), Box 1:10; Bayard Rustin interview transcript, after Aug. 28, 1963, Box 29:14, both in BR Papers.

92 Quotes from James Baldwin, "The Dangerous Road before Martin Luther King," *Harper's Magazine*, Feb. 1961, p. 42; Daniel Berrigan to Catherine Quigley, Apr. 28 [1962?], Box 89, Berrigan Coll.

93 Quotes from John Newman to James Farmer, Oct. 25, 1963, reel 3, CORE Papers; [Marvin Rich] to Lillian Smith, Nov. 5, 1963, reel 11, CORE Add. Papers; King, *Freedom Song*, 34.

Chapter Four

1 *The First Family* (1962 album). *Life*, Dec. 14, 1962, p. 83ff; Benjamin F. Bradlee, *Conversations with Kennedy* (New York, 1975), 123; Daisy [and Mark] to [Constance and Elizabeth C. Brown], [ca. Dec. 1962], Box 2:2, ECB Papers.

2 (royalty) Mary McCarthy to Hannah Arendt, Sept. 28, 1962, Arendt–McCarthy, *Between Friends*, ed. Carol Brightman (New York, 1995), 140; Richard S. Wheeler to William F. Buckley, Jr., Sept. 27, 1962, Box 23:40, WFB Papers; Elizabeth Bishop to Robert Lowell, Mar. 1, 1961, RL Papers; Stewart Alsop to Martin Sommers, Dec. 21, 1961, Box 30, Alsop Papers; (charity) Gertrude Ball to Miss Farmer, Aug. 30, 1962, Box 215:9, Clare B. Luce Papers; (rat pack) *Cosmopolitan*, Oct. 1961, pp. 56–60; (family) Arthur M. Schlesinger, Jr., *Robert Kennedy and His Times* (Boston, 1978), 585 (quote), 592; *NYT Magazine*, May 26, 1963, p. 30ff; Gore Vidal, "The Holy Family," *Esquire*, Apr. 1967, p. 99ff; (pool) David Brinkley, *Memoirs* (New York, 1995), 152; Warren Rogers, *When I Think of Bobby* (New York, 1993), 83–86; Irenee and Marie [?] to Constance and Elizabeth C. Brown, Aug. 27, 1962, Box 2:1, ECB Papers.

3 Bradlee, *Conversations*, 159; John H. Davis, *The Kennedys* (New York, 1984), 323, 340–341; Jacques Lowe, *Kennedy, a Time Remembered* (New York, 1983); Tom Wicker, *Kennedy without Tears* (New York, 1964), 46–47; *Good Housekeeping*, Sept. 1962, p. 68ff. Quotes from Clare B. Luce to James Keough, Oct. 24, 1963, Box 218:2, CBL Papers; Stewart Alsop to Clay Blair, Jr., Apr. 5, 1963, Box 31, Alsop Papers.

4 Brinkley, *Memoirs*, 153–155; Oleg Cassini, *In My Own Fashion* (New York, 1987), 303–311, 319; C. David Heymann, *A Woman Named Jackie* (New York, 1994), 202, 204, 210 (1st quote), 220, 250; *NYT*, Jan. 20, 1962, p. 14 (2nd quote); Elizabeth Gatov KOH, 20–21; George H. Gallup, *The Gallup Poll* (New York, 1972), 3:1728; (redecorating) Maxine Cheshire with John Greenya, *Maxine Cheshire, Reporter* (Boston, 1978), 50–54; Davis, *Kennedys*, 477; Heymann, *Jackie*, 263n, 323.

5 Letitia Baldrige, *Of Diamonds and Diplomats* (Boston, 1968), 160–162; Cheshire, *Cheshire*, 41; Davis, *Kennedys*, 182 (quote), 194–195, 199, 207, 211, 285, 326; Diana DuBois, *In Her Sister's Shadow* (Boston, 1995), 5–8, 142; Heymann, *Jackie*, 52, 78, 223, 349n; Pierre Salinger, *P.S., a Memoir* (New York, 1995), 103; *Life*, Apr. 26, 1963, pp. 26–31.

6 Daniel Horowitz, *Betty Friedan and the Making of the Feminine Mystique* (Amherst, MA, 1998), 125; Elaine T. May, *Homeward Bound* (New York, 1988), 76; Susan E. Riley, "Caring for Rosie's Children: Federal Child Care Policies in the World War II Era," *Polity*, 26:4 (Summer 1994), 655–675. On Friedan and Peck see Judith Hennessee, *Betty Friedan* (New York, 1999), 42; Horowitz, *Friedan*, 120.

7 Jo Freeman, *The Politics of Women's Liberation* (New York, 1975), 31; Betty Friedan, *The Feminine Mystique* (New York, 1964; orig. 1963), 13; May, *Homeward*, 77, 81–83, 87–88; Susan Hartmann in Joanne Meyerowitz, ed., *Not June Cleaver* (Philadelphia, 1994), 86. Statistics from

U.S. Bureau of the Census, *Historical Statistics of the United States, Colonial Times to 1970* (Washington, 1975), 131–133, 164, 177.

8 Joseph W. Alsop with Adam Platt, *I've Seen the Best of It* (New York, 1992), 17–39; Richard J. Whalen, *The Founding Father* (New York, 1964), 184.

9 (veterans) Igor Cassini with Jeanne Molli, *I'd Do It All Over Again* (New York, 1977), 132; Cassini, *Fashion*, 148; Hank Greenspun with Alex Pelle, *Where I Stand* (New York, 1966), 28, 43, 65, 180, 185; Richard Reeves, *President Kennedy* (New York, 1993), 15; Michael Novak to John Kenneth Galbraith, May 2, 1961, Box 16, JKG Papers; (marriage) Robert S. Ellwood, *The Sixties Spiritual Awakening* (New Brunswick, NJ, 1994), 39; Annie Gottlieb, *Do You Believe in Magic?* (New York, 1987), 218; Will Herberg, *Protestant, Catholic, Jew* (New York, 1955); Denise [B?] to Allard K. Lowenstein, Apr. 10, 1961, Box 7:233; George H. Hazelrigg to AKL [1961?], Box 7:243, both in AKL Papers; (fraternities) [Emory] Bundy to AKL, Oct. 6, 1961, Box 7:239, AKL Papers.

10 Patrick Allitt, *Catholic Intellectuals and Conservative Politics in America, 1950–1985* (Ithaca, 1993), 18–20, 78; Ellwood, *Sixties*, 39–40; John Gruen, *The Party's Over Now* (Wainscott, NY, 1989; orig. 1972), 68; George F. Kennan, *Sketches from a Life* (New York, 1989), 183; Dan A. Oren, *Joining the Club* (New Haven, 1985); W. J. Rorabaugh, *Berkeley at War* (New York, 1989), 25; Carl Bridenbaugh, "The Great Mutation," *American Historical Review*, 68:2 (Jan. 1963), esp. 322–323, 328–329; Jeffrey Hart in *Columbia Magazine*, ca. June 1962, pp. 26–27, copy in Box 20:55; Douglas Stewart to William F. Buckley, Jr., rec'd Apr. 16, 1962, Box 22:81; John Wisner to WFB, May 1, 1962, Box 23:50, all in WFB Papers.

11 *Quiz Show* (1994 film). Ethnicity is more important in the film, which Goodwin helped script, than in his earlier book. Richard N. Goodwin, *Remembering America* (Boston, 1988), 16, 24, 32, 42, 44–45, 55, 69–71, 74, 81; David Halberstam, *The Fifties* (New York, 1993), 648–666.

12 Stephen E. Ambrose, *Nixon* (New York, 1987–1989), 1:513–514; 2:34–35; David Burner and Thomas R. West, *The Torch Is Passed* (New York, 1984), 204; Cassini, *I'd Do It*, 160; Goodwin, *Remembering*, 135; Wicker, *Kennedy*, 35–38, 45; Peter Lisagor KOH, 61; Esther Peterson KOH, 13; Mary Bakshian to Elizabeth C. Brown, Apr. 13, 1962, Box 1:7, ECB Papers; John Wisner to William F. Buckley, Jr., Mar. 15, 1962; Sept. 21, 1962, both in Box 23:50, WFB Papers; Isador Lubin to John K. Galbraith, Mar. 30, 1960 [actually 1961]; reply, Apr. 7, 1961, both in Box 39; JKG to James G. Patton, Mar. 15, 1961 (quote), Box 49, all in JKG Papers; letters to

Charles P. Taft, Apr. 3, 1969; July 28 [1969], Box 13:3; CPT to 'Robins,' Sept. 25, 1962, Box 33:1, all in CPT Papers.

13 Michael R. Beschloss, *The Crisis Years* (New York, 1991), 250, 312, 404; Bradlee, *Conversations*, 75, 102n; Reeves, *President Kennedy*, 303; Arthur M. Schlesinger, Jr., *A Life in the Twentieth Century: Innocent Beginnings, 1917–1950* (Boston, 2000), 1, 5, 15, 58; Theodore Sorensen, *Kennedy* (New York, 1965), 19, 253; *Harper's Magazine*, Dec. 1962, pp. 29–36; Stewart Alsop to Martin Sommers, Jan. 8, 1962, Box 31, Alsop Papers; Schlesinger conversation in John B. Martin Diary, Jan. 20, 1961, Box 1:6, JBM Papers; Richard E. Neustadt to Lee White, Feb. 22, 1962; James Rowe to REN, June 12, 1962, both in Box 1; 'H' to REN, May 12, 1962, Box 13, all in REN Papers; Theodore C. Sorensen to Earl Latham, Oct. 17, 1961, Box 85, TCS Papers.

14 Stewart Alsop, *The Center* (New York, 1968), 19; Beschloss, *Crisis Years*, 248–249, 591; Chester Bowles, *Promises to Keep* (New York, 1971), 305, 307, 316–317, 353, 628–630; Goodwin, *Remembering*, 209, 213; Howard B. Schaffer, *Chester Bowles* (Cambridge, MA, 1993), 188–192, 228; Schlesinger, *Robert Kennedy*, 437–441; Sorensen, *Kennedy*, 287–290; George McGovern in Kenneth W. Thompson, ed., *The Kennedy Presidency* (Lanham, MD, 1985), 44; Lisagor KOH, 47; Joseph W. Alsop to JFK, Oct. 3, 1962, Box 18, Alsop Papers; [Elizabeth C. Brown] to [Thomas Dodd], Mar. 8, 1963, Box 1:25, ECB Papers; William O. Douglas to Ruth S. Roberts, Aug. 14, 1961, Box 280:2; WOD to Dan F. Barr, Mar. 9, 1962, Box 281:7, both in WOD Papers; Wharton [Hubbard?] to Clare B. Luce, Apr. 4, 1961, Box 214:5; Elizabeth C. Brown to CBL, Mar. 11, 1963, Box 217:1, both in CBL Papers; Frederick G. Dutton to Richard E. Neustadt, Dec. 28, 1961, Box 1; REN to Amb. Kenneth T. Young, Dec. 8, 1962, Box 12, both in REN Papers.

15 (prewar) Virginia F. Durr, *Outside the Magic Circle*, ed. Hollinger F. Barnard (Tuscaloosa, 1985), 45, 60; (war) D'Ann Campbell, *Women at War with America* (Cambridge, MA, 1984); John D'Emilio, *Sexual Politics, Sexual Communities* (Chicago, 1983), 23–24; Regina Kunzel in Meyerowitz, *Not June Cleaver*, 307, 315; (sixties) Hope R. Miller, *Scandals in the Highest Office* (New York, 1973), 250 (1st quote); Laura Kalman, *Abe Fortas* (New Haven, 1990), 196; William D. Rogers to Owen and Eleanor Lattimore, July 3, 1963, Box 17:6, OL Papers; John B. Martin Diary, Jan. 21, 1961 (2nd quote), Box 1:6, JBM Papers.

16 Hugh M. Hefner, "The Playboy Philosophy," *Playboy*, Dec. 1962–Feb. 1963; Halberstam, *Fifties*, 578–580; Beth Bailey in David Farber, ed., *The Sixties* (Chapel Hill, 1994), 247–249; *One, Two, Three* (1961 film)

(1st quote); Groucho Marx to Goodman Ace, Jan. 23, 1962 (2nd quote), Box 1:1, GM Papers; Brinkley, *Memoirs*, 141–142; William A. Emerson, Jr., to Stewart Alsop, June 3, 1963; SA to Otto Friedrich, Dec. 8, 1963 (3rd quote), both in Box 31, Alsop Papers.

17 (Ferlinghetti) Barry Silesky, *Ferlinghetti* (New York, 1990), 70–79; *Life*, Sept. 9, 1957, pp. 105–108; (Miller) Morrie Ryskind in *LAT*, Mar. 23, 1962; Henry Miller–James Laughlin, *Henry Miller and James Laughlin*, ed. George Wickes (New York, 1996), 174 (JL to HM, Jan. 27, 1960, quote), 195–196, 204n, 216; Ted Wilentz to Allen Ginsberg, May 21, 1961, Box 67:26, AG–SU; (Burroughs) William S. Burroughs, *The Letters of William S. Burroughs, 1945–1959*, ed. Oliver Harris (New York, 1993), 418; Barry Miles, *William Burroughs* (New York, 1993), 84, 95, 106; Steven Watson, *The Birth of the Beat Generation* (New York, 1995), 282–284; Paul Bowles to Allen Ginsberg, Oct. 30, 1962; William S. Burroughs to AG, Dec. 2, 1962, both in Box 1, AG-CU; (*CLJ*) Lawrence Ferlinghetti to AG, Oct. 7, 1961, Box 5, AG-CU; (*FY*) John Gruen, *The New Bohemia* (New York, 1966), 65–69; Gregory Corso to AG, Mar. 31, 1963, Box 3, AG-CU; (Bruce) LF to AG, Mar. 10, 1962, Box 5, AG-CU; Ralph J. Gleason to Alexander P. Hoffman, June 1, 1963, RJG Letters.

18 Tom Engelhardt, *The End of Victory Culture* (New York, 1995), 140–144; Halberstam, *Fifties*, 479; *SEP*, Dec. 23, 1961, p. 102; Stewart Alsop to Martin Sommers, July 16, 1962, Box 31, Alsop Papers; (teen market) *Life*, Aug. 13, 1959, pp. 78–83; *New Yorker*, Nov. 22, 1958, p. 57ff. In general see James B. Gilbert, *A Cycle of Outrage* (New York, 1986). Statistics from Gallup, *Gallup Poll*, 3:1654, 1817; Beth Bailey, *From Front Porch to Back Seat* (Baltimore, 1988), 50.

19 Dorothy Day, *On Pilgrimage: The Sixties* (New York, 1972), 90; Gottlieb, *Do You Believe*, 239; Bailey in Farber, *Sixties*, 244; *Life*, Dec. 14, 1962, pp. 90A, 92; Norman L. Corwin to Edelaine Harburg, May 15, 1961 (quote), NLC, *Norman Corwin's Letters*, ed. A. J. Langguth (New York, 1994), 202.

20 Ellwood, *Sixties*, 92–93; Halberstam, *Fifties*, 605; *NYT*, May 10, 1960, p. 75; Dr. John Rock to John K. Galbraith, Dec. 6, 1963, Box 52, JKG Papers; Gloria B. Sessler to Mrs. Holloran, Nov. 14, 1963, Box 218:13; Bishop John Wright to Clare B. Luce, Sept. 21, 1963, Box 219:6, both in CBL Papers; Mrs. William L. Ransom, Jr., to John B. Martin, July 26, 1961; reply, Oct. 29, 1961, both in Box 32:7, JBM Papers; (statistics) May, *Homeward*, 137, 155; U.S. Census, *Historical Statistics*, 19. See also Donald T. Critchlow, *Intended Consequences* (New York, 1999); David M. Kennedy, *Birth Control in America* (New Haven, 1970).

21 Sally Belfrage, *Un-American Activities* (New York, 1994), 202, 205, 218–220; Rickie Solinger in Meyerowitz, *Not June Cleaver*, 335, 348; *SEP*, May 20, 27; June 3, 1961; letters, June 24; July 8, 29, 1961. Quote from Edward E. Miller to John B. Martin, May 18, 1961, Box 32:3; other letters in Box 32, folders 3, 8–9, JBM Papers. See also E. Wayne Carp, *Family Matters* (Cambridge, MA, 1998); Leslie J. Reagan, *When Abortion Was a Crime* (Berkeley, 1997).

22 (homosexuals) D'Emilio, *Sexual Politics*, 9, 18–19, 31–32, 44, 49, 62, 132–133, 137–139, 158–159; *NYT*, July 16, 1962, pp. 47, 48; Dec. 17, 1963, pp. 1, 33; *Harper's Magazine*, Mar. 1963, pp. 85–92; *Newsweek*, July 30, 1962, p. 48; Dec. 17, 1963, p. 42; *Village Voice*, Sept. 27, Oct. 11, 1962; (Vidal) Muriel Gamadge to Gore Vidal [1960?], Box 7:2, GV Papers; Frederick W. Dupee to Robert Lowell [n.d.], RL Papers; (marriage) Ralph [Menapace] to Allard K. Lowenstein, Apr. 30, 1961, Box 7:233, AKL Papers.

23 William H. Chafe, *Never Stop Running* (New York, 1993), 117–122, 128–130, 151–154; Lindy Boggs, *Washington through a Purple Veil* (New York, 1994), 64, 72, 97, 107, 156; Libby [McCord?] to Allard K. Lowenstein [Feb. 9, 1961?] (quote), Box 7:247; Mrs. Gerald Lowenstein to AKL, Aug. 7, 1961, Box 7:237; Barbara Boggs to AKL, Jan. 10, 1961, Box 7:224; Nov. 1, 1961, Box 7:240; Cokie [Boggs] to AKL, Oct. 24, 1961, Box 7:239, all in AKL Papers; Geoff Cowan to Paul and Rachel Cowan, July 2, 1966, Box 1:1, PC Papers; Ralph McCabe to James Burnham, Dec. 30, 1963, Box 6:60, JB Papers.

24 Chafe, *Never*, 4, 16, 61, 154–158; Boggs, *Washington*, 165–166; BB to AKL, June 10, 1961, Box 7:235; July 27, 1961, Box 7:236; Nov. 12, 1961, Box 7:240; Dec. 28, 1961, Box 7:241; Feb. 18, 1962, Box 7:248; Sept. 9, 1962, Box 8:259; reply, Aug. 9, 1962, Box 16:562, all in AKL Papers.

25 Robert J. Eisenkopf to Daniel Berrigan, Jan. 11, 1963; Tom Giering statement, Apr. 6, 1963; John Harmon to DB, Aug. 2, 1963 (quote), all in Box 154, Berrigan Coll.; Marie Eichelberger to Margaret Mead, Aug. 18, 1963, Box B14:3; MM to Geoffrey Gorer, June 16, 1960, Box B16:1, both in MM Papers. See also Allitt, *Catholic Intellectuals*, 12, 123, 132, 137.

26 Chafe, *Never*, 233–237, 267–272, 311, 417, 426, 458–459; Boggs, *Washington*, 165, 183, 206, 363, 365; *NYT*, Oct. 11, 1990, p. D21; BB to AKL, Oct. 28, 1963, Box 9:299; Ilene Strelitz to 'Beep,' Sept. 10, 1964, Box 32:352, both in AKL Papers; 'H' to Paul and Rachel Cowan, Oct. 2, 1966, Box 1:1, PC Papers.

27 Chafe, *Never*, 22–23, 82–83, 122–123, 127–128, 221–227, 407–410, 445–446; David Harris, *Dreams Die Hard* (New York, 1982), 49–50, 108–110, 192, 259, 307, 316–318, 321–322, 328–335.

278   NOTES TO PAGES 146–150

28 (Wesleyan) Rosalie Colie to Hannah Arendt, Apr. 28, 1963, Box 8:4, HA
   Papers; (Lawford) James Spada, *Peter Lawford* (New York, 1991), 333–
   334, 355, 366. Divorce statistics in *World Almanac, 1965* (New York,
   1965), 342.
29 Anthony Summers, *Goddess* (New York, 1985). Belfrage, *Un-American*,
   92; Friedan, *Feminine Mystique*, 13; Hennessee, *Friedan*, 75. See also *Kiss
   Me Kate* (1953 film), a Cole Porter musical with an all-white cast, including
   a jazz band, pastel colors, and a character named Bianca. The movie opens
   with the star Kathryn Grayson having Monroe–like blonde hair and red
   lips.
30 Summers, *Goddess*, 148, 160, 198, 206, 215, 217–229, 243, 250, 260–
   266, 270–272, 281, 283–290, 308–312; Seymour M. Hersh, *The Dark
   Side of Camelot* (Boston, 1997), 102–106; Patricia S. Lawford with Ted
   Schwarz, *The Peter Lawford Story* (New York, 1988), 153–199; Reeves,
   President Kennedy, 315 (1st quote); Schlesinger, *Robert Kennedy*, 590;
   Spada, *Lawford*, 4–5, 229, 297–332; Adlai E. Stevenson to Mrs. Albert
   Lasker, May 21, 1962 (2nd quote), AES, *The Papers of Adlai E. Stevenson*,
   ed. Walter Johnson (Boston, 1979), 8:247; *NYT*, Jan. 20, 1962, p. 14; Ted
   Wilentz to Peter Orlovsky and Allen Ginsberg, Aug. 10 [1962], Box 67:27,
   AG-SU.
31 Letter to Clare B. Luce, Aug. 4 [1963?], Box 216:14, CBL Papers; letters
   to Margaret Mead, Box A2:2, MM Papers; Marthe Rexroth to Kenneth
   Rexroth, July 7 [1960], Box 18; letter to KR, Apr. 25, 1961, Box 180, both
   in KR Papers; Curtis P. Freshel to CBL, Feb. 8, 1961, Box 213, CBL Papers.
32 Alfred C. Kinsey et al., *Sexual Behavior in the Human Male* and *Sexual Behavior in the Human Female* (Philadelphia, 1948 and 1953); Barnes Riznik
   to Owen and Eleanor Lattimore, Nov. 4, 1962, Box 16:2, OL Papers. See
   also James H. Jones, *Alfred C. Kinsey* (New York, 1997).
33 William O. Douglas, *Go East, Young Man* (New York, 1974), 144; William
   O. Douglas, *The Court Years, 1939–1975* (New York, 1980), 85; James
   F. Simon, *Independent Journey* (New York, 1980), 1–2, 221, 354; (scotch)
   William O. Douglas to Mrs. Robert Eichholz, Oct. 7, 1963, Box 243:1;
   WOD to Joseph P. Kennedy, Jan. 2, 1962, Box 281:3, both in WOD Papers.
34 Douglas, *Go East*, 416; Simon, *Independent*, 60–61, 235–240, 275;
   William O. Douglas, *The Douglas Letters* (Bethesda, MD, 1987), 309;
   WOD to Sheldon S. Cohen, Apr. 17, 1962, Box 282:2; WOD to WOD,
   Jr., May 18, 1962, Box 282:4; WOD to Helen Strauss, June 7, 1962,
   Box 282:5, all in WOD Papers; WOD and Mildred R. Douglas agree-
   ment, 1953; amendment, 1955, both in Box 64:6, Joseph L. Rauh Papers;
   (Stevenson) Katie Louchheim COH, 19; Mike Monroney COH, 104.
35 Simon, *Independent*, 370–374; Bradlee, *Conversations*, 185 (1st quote);
   WOD to Martha D. Bost, Apr. 16, 1963, Box 238:3, WOD Papers;

W. R. Walters to Hugo Black, posted Aug. 23, 1963; W. A. Flowers wire to HB, Aug. 7, 1963; Mrs. H. Disney to HB, Aug. 19, 1963, all in Box 59:2, HB Papers; Mary Bakshian to Elizabeth C. Brown, Apr. 13, 1962 (2nd quote), Box 1:7, ECB Papers; (Rockefeller) Robert A. Goldberg, *Barry Goldwater* (New Haven, 1995), 170–172, 176; Barry M. Goldwater with Jack Casserly, *Goldwater* (New York, 1988), 141; Martin Sommers to Stewart Alsop, Mar. 19, 1962, Box 31, Alsop Papers; Peter R. Taft to Charles P. Taft, Apr. 14 [1962], Box 24:7, CPT Papers.

36 *Washington Star*, Apr. 11, 1963, p. 1; Martha D. Bost to WOD, Feb. 26, 1963; [1963]; May 17, 1963, all in Box 238:3, WOD Papers; Joseph L. Rauh press release, Apr. 11, 1963, and other items, all in Box 64:6, JLR Papers. See also Simon, *Independent*, 374–388; Douglas, *Letters*, 342, 344–345. First Bost letter published with permission of WOD Estate.

37 Deborah Davis, *Katharine the Great* (New York, 1979), 40, 77–83, 118, 122–123, 142, 151, 156; Carol Felsenthal, *Power, Privilege, and the Post* (New York, 1993), 28, 34, 43, 51, 87–101, 106, 110, 117, 119, 130–134, 149, 174–180, 198. See also Katharine Graham, *Personal History* (New York, 1997).

38 Davis, *Katharine*, 126–127, 144–146, 149–157, 160–163; Felsenthal, *Power*, 156 (3rd quote), 165, 178 (1st quote), 183, 190, 195, 197, 202–207; Graham, *Personal History*, 243–246, 288, 300–301, 306–308; *Washingtonian*, Aug. 1992, p. 168; Agnes Meyer to Adlai E. Stevenson, Jan. 22, 1963; Feb. 5, 1963; May 4, 1963 (2nd quote; published with permission of Princeton Univ. Library), all in Box 62, AES Papers.

39 Davis, *Katharine*, 163–165; Felsenthal, *Power*, 198, 208, 215–217; Graham, *Personal History*, 309–311; Laurence Leamer, *Playing for Keeps* (New York, 1977), 17; (Mary Meyer) Nina Burleigh, *A Very Private Woman* (New York, 1998), esp. 169–171, 187–197, 211–212, 216, 246–248, 290, 300; Felsenthal, *Power*, 188, 198; Summers, *Goddess*, 279; "Ben Bradlee Interview," *American Journalism Review*, Mar. 1995, p. 40; *Washingtonian*, Oct. 1990, p. 201.

40 Felsenthal, *Power*, 212–214, 243; Graham, *Personal History*, 322–323; (Profumo) Phillip Knightley and Caroline Kennedy, *An Affair of State* (New York, 1987), esp. xiii, 4–9, 97–99, 126, 133–137, 157–158, 201–203, 206; Bradlee, *Conversations*, 203, 230; Hersh, *Dark Side*, 391–396; Isaiah Berlin to Arthur M. Schlesinger, Jr., June 13, 1963 (quote); Lady Pamela Berry to AMS, June 11 [1963] (2 pages of this letter are closed), both in Box P30; AMS to Charles Wintour, June 20, 1963; AMS to Mr. and Mrs. CW, July 1, 1963, both in Box P40, all in AMS Papers; Stewart Alsop to William A. Emerson, Jr., May 16, 1963, Box 31, Alsop Papers.

41 Davis, *Katharine*, 168–169, 176; Graham, *Personal History*, 325–330; David Richards, *Played Out* (New York, 1981), 73, 98, 115, 123–124, 135,

138–140 (1st quote at 139); Felsenthal, *Power*, 217–218, 223 (2nd quote); *WP*, Aug. 4, 1963, p. 1; Agnes Meyer to Adlai E. Stevenson, Sept. 23, 1963, Box 62, AES Papers; (Ward) Knightley and Kennedy, *Affair*, 126–127, 164, 245–247; (Rometsch) Robert G. Baker with Larry L. King, *Wheeling and Dealing* (New York, 1978), 79–80; Bradlee, *Conversations*, 228; Hersh, *Dark Side*, 387–390, 398–406; [Stewart Alsop] to Otto [Friedrich], Oct. 29, 1963, Box 31, Alsop Papers.

42 On stress see Evan Thomas, *The Very Best Men* (New York, 1995), 313, 315, 317, 320, 332–333; Burleigh, *Very Private*, 125–129, 132–135; Davis, *Katharine*, 139–140.

43 Friedan, *Feminine Mystique*, 12, 24–25, 29–35, 42–44, 48, 53, 154, 176, 232 (quote), 282, 345–347; Hennessee, *Friedan*, 71. U.S. Census, *Historical Statistics*, 19, 49. Friedan was not alone. See also Marion K. Sanders, "A Proposition for Women," *Harper's Magazine*, Sept. 1960, pp. 41–48. For a different view see Joanne Meyerowitz in Meyerowitz, *Not June Cleaver*, 229–262.

44 Friedan, *Feminine Mystique*, 49–50, 63, 67, 69, 144–146; Horowitz, *Friedan*, 100, 180, 182; BF quoted in unidentified news clipping, Feb. 23, 1961, Box 1:89f, BF Papers, Schlesinger Library, Radcliffe Institute, Harvard Univ.

45 Friedan, *Feminine Mystique*, 65, 67, 71, 179 (quotes at 15, 64); Horowitz, *Friedan*, 161–163.

46 Friedan, *Feminine Mystique*, 14 (quote), 16, 28, 233–234, 253; Horowitz, *Friedan*, 165, 170–171. See also Kenneth T. Jackson, *Crabgrass Frontier* (New York, 1985); Peter Wyden, *Suburbia's Coddled Kids* (Garden City, NY, 1962).

47 *McCall's* letters are in Box 21:741–742, BF Papers. The magazine ran a symposium in August 1963. BF also published extracts in *Mademoiselle*, May 1962; *Ladies Home Journal*, Jan.–Feb. 1963; and *Smith Alumnae Quarterly*, Winter 1963. Her first essay on the subject was in *Good Housekeeping*, Sept. 1960.

48 *Dallas Morning News*, Oct 30, 1963 (1st quote); Friedan, *Feminine Mystique*, 34 (2nd quote), 63–65, 67, 71, 93, 260, 296, 298, 327, 344; Hennessee, *Friedan*, 31; Horowitz, *Friedan*, 177; Freeman, *Politics*, 9; Cynthia Harrison, *On Account of Sex* (Berkeley, 1988), ix; *Saturday Review*, May 18, 1963, pp. 66–70, 82–83. Statistics from Gottlieb, *Do You Believe*, 253.

49 Hennessee, *Friedan*, 39–42, 52, 61, 63, 83–84, 131, 217, 231; Horowitz, *Friedan*, 5, 7, 10–11, 102–104, 121, 133–134, 141, 150, 153, 155, 191, 212–213; Meyerowitz, *Not June Cleaver*, esp. 1–9.

50 Hennessee, *Friedan*, 77–79; Halberstam, *Fifties*, 598; *Life*, Nov. 1, 1963, p. 84ff.

51 Leila J. Rupp and Verta Taylor, *Survival in the Doldrums* (New York, 1987), 166–168; Mary C. Kennedy, National Woman's Party, to Congressional nominees, Oct. 18, 1960, Box 10:1; NWP fact sheet, 1960, Box 11:5, both in Gore Vidal Papers. The fake letter is JFK to Emma G. Miller, Oct. 7, 1960. Miller was the fabricator. A copy is in Box 10:1, GV Papers. See also Christine A. Lunardini, *From Equal Suffrage to Equal Rights* (New York, 1986); Susan D. Becker, *The Origins of the Equal Rights Amendment* (Westport, CT, 1981).

52 Freeman, *Politics*, 52; Harrison, *On Account*, 74–77, 85, 87, 109, 112, 115, 118, 120, 126, 138–165, 171; Rupp and Taylor, *Survival*, 168–172; Pauli Murray, *Song in a Weary Throat* (New York, 1987), 347, 351–352; Dorothy Cobble in Meyerowitz, *Not June Cleaver*, 70; Esther Peterson COH, 72, 89, 96, 288; Peterson KOH, 23, 32–34, 43, 55; President's Commission on the Status of Women, "Draft Report" (Apr. 29, 1963), Box 6, Myer Feldman Papers; Roger Kent to Stanley Mosk and William A. Munnell, May 8, 1961, Box 4; NBC radio transcript, Dec. 25, 1960, Box 13, both in Elizabeth Smith Gatov Papers; Gladys Tillett to Allard K. Lowenstein, Feb. 17, 1961, Box 7:228, AKL Papers.

53 Freeman, *Politics*, 175; Friedan, *Feminine Mystique*, 177; Harrison, *On Account*, 89, 91, 188, 203–204; Judith Sealander, *As Minority Becomes Majority* (Westport, CT, 1983), 9; Cobble in Meyerowitz, *Not June Cleaver*, 61–62, 66, 68; Peterson COH, 288–289, 310; Peterson KOH, 31–32, 46–47, 51, 57–65, 75; Joan Kilroy to Clare B. Luce, June 28, 1963, Box 218:2, CBL Papers.

54 Meyerowitz in Meyerowitz, *Not June Cleaver*, 251–252; Horowitz, *Friedan*, 221.

Chapter Five

1 Lionel Abel, *The Intellectual Follies* (New York, 1984), 150, 157; Joseph C. Goulden, *The Best Years, 1945–1950* (New York, 1976), 7, 9; Serge Guilbaut, *How New York Stole the Idea of Modern Art*, tr. Arthur Goldhammer (Chicago, 1983), 107–108; Julian Huxley, ed., *Aldous Huxley, 1894–1963* (New York, 1965), 80; George Lipsitz, *Rainbow at Midnight* (Urbana, 1994; orig. 1981), 261 (membership); Michael McClure, *Scratching the Beat Surface* (New York, 1994; orig. 1982), 50; Henry F. May, *The Divided Heart* (New York, 1991), 21–24; *Look*, Jan. 5, 1960, p. 14 (poll).

2 Patrick Allitt, *Catholic Intellectuals and Conservative Politics in America, 1950–1985* (Ithaca, 1993), 23, 29, 31, 60; Robert S. Ellwood, *The Sixties Spiritual Awakening* (New Brunswick, NJ, 1994), 26, 36–39, 41, 56, 62, 65; Lipsitz, *Rainbow*, 262.

3 Gerald Nicosia, *Memory Babe* (New York, 1983), 430 (1st quote); Janet
Flanner, *Darlinghissima*, ed. Natalia D. Murray (New York, 1985), 323
(2nd quote), 346; Ellwood, *Sixties*, 5; Goulden, *Best Years*, 430; Guilbaut,
New York, 6; Arthur Knight and Kit Knight, eds., *Kerouac and the Beats*
(New York, 1988), 161.
4 Ellwood, *Sixties*, 19, 65, 85; Joanne Meyerowitz, ed., *Not June Cleaver*
(Philadelphia, 1994), esp. 5, 232–233; Ronald Sukenick, *Down and In*
(New York, 1987), 77–79; Dan Wakefield, *New York in the Fifties* (Boston,
1992), 3–7; Andy Warhol and Pat Hackett, *Popism* (New York, 1980), 43;
Lew Welch, *I Remain* (Berkeley, 1980), 1:11; Ochs quoted in *Broadside*,
#63 (Oct. 15, 1965), 5.
5 Allitt, *Catholic Intellectuals*, 1–14, 101–105; Guilbaut, *New York*, 102;
John B. Judis, *William F. Buckley, Jr.* (New York, 1988), 14, 18, 45, 116,
137, 147, 169–170; Wakefield, *New York*, 6, 263.
6 (analysis) Abel, *Intellectual*, 221; Nina Burleigh, *A Very Private Woman*
(New York, 1998), 134, 138; William S. Burroughs, *The Letters of William
S. Burroughs, 1945–1959*, ed. Oliver Harris (New York, 1993), 321–
322; Allen Ginsberg–Neal Cassady, *As Ever*, ed. Barry Gifford (Berkeley,
1977), 84; John Gruen, *The Party's Over Now* (Wainscott, NY, 1989;
orig. 1972), 82, 108; Guilbaut, *New York*, 165; Joyce Johnson, *Minor
Characters* (Boston, 1983), 67, 94; Anaïs Nin, *The Diary of Anaïs Nin*, ed.
Gunther Stuhlmann (New York, 1974), 5:252; Sukenick, *Down and In*, 32;
Wakefield, *New York*, 6, 135, 152, 210, 215–221, 321; Welch, *I Remain*,
1:48, 52, 77, 162; Edmund Wilson, *The Sixties*, ed. Lewis M. Dabney (New
York, 1993), 42, 174, 233; (corporal punishment) George H. Gallup, *The
Gallup Poll* (New York, 1972), 3:1587.
7 (early) Victor Bockris, *With William Burroughs* (New York, 1981), xiv;
Allen Ginsberg, *Composed on the Tongue* (San Francisco, 1980), 69–74,
83; Jack Kerouac, *Selected Letters, 1940–1956*, ed. Ann Charters (New
York, 1995), 52–64, 76, 390; WSB int. by Tytell in Arthur Knight and
Kit Knight, eds., *The Beat Diary* (California, PA, 1977), 36, 43; Nicosia,
Memory Babe, 103–106; Michael Schumacher, *Dharma Lion* (New York,
1992), 53–55, 58–59; Steven Watson, *The Birth of the Beat Generation*
(New York, 1995), 35–53; (sex) Burroughs, *Letters*, 45, 88, 369; Ginsberg,
Composed, 81, 85; Allen Ginsberg, *Journals Mid-Fifties, 1954–1958*, ed.
Gordon Ball (New York, 1995), 4–6; AG to NC, Sept. 4, 1953, Ginsberg–
Cassady, *As Ever*, 154; Corso in Knight and Knight, *Beat Diary*, 13; WSB
int. by Tytell, 36, 39; AG in Knight and Knight, *Kerouac and the Beats*,
250, 259–260; Nicosia, *Memory Babe*, 117, 121–122, 620; (Ginsberg's
mother) Louis Ginsberg to Selden Rodman, Nov. 23, 1962, Box 7,
AG–CU.

8 (general) Ginsberg, *Composed*, 69, 72; Arthur Knight and Kit Knight, eds., *Beat Angels* (California, PA, 1982), 108, 110, 124; Sukenick, *Down and In*, 13–14, 17, 21; (quest) Stephen Prothero, "On the Holy Road: The Beat Movement as Spiritual Protest," *Harvard Theological Review*, 84:2 (Apr. 1991), 205–222; Wakefield, *New York*, 180–181, 183; Kerouac, *Letters*, 193 (1st quote); Burroughs, *Letters*, 61, 79, 125 (2nd quote), 398; (Beat) Tom Clark, *Jack Kerouac* (San Diego, 1984), 168–169; Kerouac in *Playboy*, June 1959, pp. 42, 79; Kerouac, *Letters*, 433; Jack Kerouac, *Safe in Heaven Dead*, ed. Michael White (Madras, India, and New York, 1990), 28, 32; Nicosia, *Memory Babe*, 252, 273, 468.

9 (French) Jane Kramer, *Allen Ginsberg in America* (New York, 1969), 120; (jazz) Lewis Erenberg in Lary May, ed., *Recasting America* (Chicago, 1989), 237, 240; Knight and Knight, *Beat Diary*, 121, 138 (quote); Nicosia, *Memory Babe*, 125; John C. Holmes COH, 106; (religion) Edward H. Foster, *Understanding the Beats* (Columbia, SC, 1992), 61–62, 75, 118–119; Allen Ginsberg, *Journals: Early Fifties, Early Sixties*, ed. Gordon Ball (New York, 1995), 269; Allen Ginsberg–Peter Orlovsky, *Straight Hearts' Delight*, ed. Winston Leyland (San Francisco, 1980), 131; Kerouac, *Letters*, 408, 419, 426–427, 439–440, 444, 462, 496, 547; Kerouac, *Safe*, 92–93, 104, 107; (drugs) Ginsberg–Cassady, *As Ever*, 40, 88, 133–134, 151; Ginsberg, *Journals Mid-Fifties*, 216; Ginsberg, *Composed*, 76–77; Herbert Huncke, *Guilty of Everything* (New York, 1990), 72; Kerouac, *Letters*, 365, 369–371; (Burroughs habit) Daniel Odier, *The Job* (rev. ed., New York, 1970; orig. 1969), 143–147.

10 Carolyn Cassady, *Off the Road* (New York, 1990), 185; Neeli Cherkovsky, *Ferlinghetti* (Garden City, NY, 1979), 113 (sales); Allen Ginsberg, *Howl: Original Draft Facsimile ...*, ed. Barry Miles (rev. ed., New York, 1986; orig. 1956), 165–166; Ginsberg, *Journals Mid-Fifties*, 78, 441–442; Ginsberg–Cassady, *As Ever*, 58–59, 84; Huncke, *Guilty*, 105–107; Kerouac, *Letters*, 563; Kramer, *Ginsberg*, 42; McClure, *Scratching*, 11–24 (quote at 13); Barry Miles, *Ginsberg* (New York, 1989), 125; Watson, *Beat Generation*, 186–187 (JK quote); *NYT Book Review*, Sept. 2, 1956, pp. 7, 18.

11 *NYT*, Sept. 5, 1957, p. 27; Clark, *Kerouac*, 161, 164–166, 173 (sales); Foster, *Beats*, 39 (1st quote), 44–45; Ginsberg–Cassady, *As Ever*, 106; Lawrence Grobel, *Conversations with Truman Capote* (New York, 1985), 32 (2nd quote); Kerouac, *Letters*, 248 (3rd quote), 315–316, 318; John C. Holmes in Knight and Knight, *Kerouac and the Beats*, 153; Nicosia, *Memory Babe*, 556–557; Wakefield, *New York*, 161, 165.

12 (general) Nicosia, *Memory Babe*, 343–347; Wakefield, *New York*, 116, 121, 124–127; (Kesey) *Crawdaddy*, #19 (Dec. 1972), 37; (Hayden) Tom

Hayden, *Reunion* (New York, 1988), 18–19, 33, 35; Milton Viorst, *Fire in the Streets* (New York, 1979), 167; (Nolte) William Plummer, *The Holy Goof* (New York, 1990; orig. 1981), 55. Quotes in Wini Breines in Meyerowitz, *Not June Cleaver*, 392; Steve Turner, *Angelheaded Hipster* (London, 1996), viii, 17.

13 Diane di Prima, *Memoirs of a Beatnik* (2nd ed., San Francisco, 1988; orig. 1969), 126–127; (Beatnik) *San Francisco Chronicle*, Apr. 2, 1958, p. 15; Johnson, *Minor*, 188; Nicosia, *Memory Babe*, 574; (danger) Ned Polsky, "The Village Beat Scene: Summer 1960," *Dissent*, 8:3 (Summer 1961), 339–359; Norman Podhoretz, "The Know-Nothing Bohemians," *Partisan Review*, 25:2 (Spring 1958), 305–318; *Life*, Nov. 30, 1959, p. 115ff. On Beat women see Wini Breines in Meyerowitz, *Not June Cleaver*, 382–408; Brenda Knight, *Women of the Beat Generation* (Berkeley, 1996).

14 Nicosia, *Memory Babe*, 565, 604; Lisa Phillips, ed., *Beat Culture and the New America, 1950–1965* (New York, 1995), 169; Vincent Terrace, *Encyclopedia of Television* (New York, 1986), 1:126–127, 391; *Life*, Nov. 30, 1959. Excerpts of Kerouac on television are in *The Source* (1999 film).

15 Daniel Belgrad, *The Culture of Spontaneity* (Chicago, 1998), 247; Kerouac, *Safe*, 37; Fred W. McDarrah and Gloria S. McDarrah, *Beat Generation* (New York, 1996), 1–7; Miles, *Ginsberg*, 263; Sukenick, *Down and In*, 137; Lawrence Ferlinghetti to Allen Ginsberg, Feb. 28, 1963, Box 4, AG-CU; (dress) Jaharana Romney in John Bauldie, ed., *Wanted Man* (New York, 1991; orig. 1990), 19; John Calmann, *The Letters of John Calmann* (London, 1986), 47; James J. Farrell, *The Spirit of the Sixties* (New York, 1997), 71; McDarrah and McDarrah, *Beat Generation*, 213; Sukenick, *Down and In*, 41, 57; Watson, *Beat Generation*, 258–259; Diana Trilling in *Partisan Review*, 26:2 (Spring 1959), 224.

16 (visions) Foster, *Beats*, 91–92; Ginsberg, *Journals: Early Fifties, Early Sixties*, xiv; Allen Ginsberg–Louis Ginsberg, *Family Business*, ed. Michael Schumacher (New York, 2001), 182; Miles, *Ginsberg*, 103–104, 326–327; Schumacher, *Dharma Lion*, 94–99; (drugs) William S. Burroughs–Allen Ginsberg, *The Yage Letters* (3rd ed., San Francisco, 1988; orig. 1963), 49–55, 64 (quote at 51); Ginsberg–Ginsberg, *Family Business*, 163; Barry Miles, *William Burroughs* (New York, 1993), 64–65; Miles, *Ginsberg*, 141; Schumacher, *Dharma Lion*, 205.

17 Ginsberg, *Indian Journals, March 1962–May 1963* (San Francisco, 1970), esp. 4, 37, 39, 111, 149–150, 171; Ginsberg–Ginsberg, *Family Business*, 175–177, 203–205, 210–215; Miles, *Ginsberg*, 301, 304, 308, 326–328 (quote at 327), 331; Carol Polsgrove, *It Wasn't Pretty, Folks, but Didn't We Have Fun?* (New York, 1995), 78–80; (Dylan) Raymond Foye in Bauldie,

Wanted Man, 144; Ginsberg, *Composed,* 58, 93; Knight and Knight, *Kerouac and the Beats,* 242; Miles, *Ginsberg,* 333; Robert Shelton, *No Direction Home* (New York, 1987; orig. 1986), 313, 385–386, 389, 400, 427; Richard Williams, *Dylan* (New York, 1992), 91, 107; Ginsberg–Orlovsky, *Straight,* 229.

18 Bruce Cook, *The Beat Generation* (2nd ed., New York, 1994; orig. 1971), 117; Ginsberg, *Journals: Early Fifties, Early Sixties,* 112, 138, 146, 154–156, 163; Ginsberg–Ginsberg, *Family Business,* 164, 167; Ginsberg–Orlovsky, *Straight,* 157–158; Kerouac, *Safe,* 26, 31; Kerouac, *Letters,* 82, 98, 167, 523; Gary Snyder in Knight and Knight, *Beat Diary,* 144–146; Gregory Corso to Allen Ginsberg, June 12, 1962 (1st quote); Mar. 7, 31, 1963, all in Box 3, AG-CU; Barry Silesky, *Ferlinghetti* (New York, 1990), 205 (2nd quote); William Manchester to Kay Boyle, Aug. 21, 1963, Box 20:11, KB Papers; Elizabeth Bishop to Robert Lowell, June 25, 1961; Apr. 26 [1962], RL Papers.

19 Belgrad, *Culture,* 167–169; Clark, *Kerouac,* 167; Foster, *Beats,* 71; Ginsberg, *Journals: Early Fifties, Early Sixties,* esp. 184, 192, 210, 268, 273–275; Ginsberg, *Journals Mid-Fifties,* 124; Kerouac, *Letters,* 94, 144–145, 324, 363–364, 390; Kramer, *Ginsberg,* 86; Nicosia, *Memory Babe,* 562–563, 576, 609.

20 (general) Belgrad, *Culture,* 1–2, 5–9; (jazz-poetry) Sally Banes, *Greenwich Village 1963* (Durham, NC, 1993), 25; (plays) Abel, *Intellectual,* 220, 228; Banes, *Greenwich,* 34; Gruen, *Party's Over,* 90, 114; (Living Theater) Banes, *Greenwich,* 40–43, 176, 179, 182, 184–187; Belgrad, *Culture,* 150–156; Gruen, *Party's Over,* 92–93, 98, 102; McDarrah and McDarrah, *Beat Generation,* 153; *The Brig* (1964 film), directed by Mekas.

21 (Happenings) Banes, *Greenwich,* 28, 51–52, 59, 86; Belgrad, *Culture,* 163; Thomas Crow, *The Rise of the Sixties* (New York, 1996), 11, 33–34; Barbara Haskell, *Blam!* (New York, 1984), 32–43; John Russell and Suzi Gablik, *Pop Art Redefined* (New York, 1969), 16; (Ono) Crow, *Rise,* 124; Haskell, *Blam!,* 51; Sukenick, *Down and In,* 137; (film) Banes, *Greenwich,* 74–75, 78; Miles, *Ginsberg,* 258; Nicosia, *Memory Babe,* 583, 585; Lawrence Ferlinghetti to Allen Ginsberg, Feb. 17, 1963, Box 4, AG-CU; (Judson) Banes, *Greenwich,* 29, 66–72; Crow, *Rise,* 126–128; Haskell, *Blam!,* 61, 64. Quote from Ralph McCabe to John Burnham, Apr. 13 [1961], Box 6:60, JB Papers.

22 Miles, *Ginsberg,* 285; Miles, *Burroughs,* 94, 111–112, 119, 130–131 (quote at 130), 168, 170; Odier, *Job,* 25, 51, 65.

23 Belgrad, *Culture,* 41–43, 142; Timothy F. Leary, *Flashbacks* (Los Angeles, 1983), 123–124; Michael Wreszin, *A Rebel in Defense of Tradition* (New York, 1994), 354–355, 357.

24 Michelle Phillips, *California Dreamin'* (New York, 1987; orig. 1986), 17–22, 51–54; Sukenick, *Down and In*, 89; Woliver, *Hoot!* (New York, 1994; orig. 1986), esp. ix–xi, 5–11; (Kingston Trio) Robert Cantwell, *When We Were Good* (Cambridge, MA, 1996), 2; Kingston Trio, *The Capitol Collector's Series* (1990 album), notes; chart positions in *Rolling Stone Rock Almanac* (New York, 1983).

25 (early) Cantwell, *When*, 313–315; Lipsitz, *Rainbow*, 314–320, 325–329; Greil Marcus, ed., *Rock and Roll Will Stand* (Boston, 1969), 12–13; Wilfred Mellers, *A Darker Shade of Pale* (New York, 1985; orig. 1984), 101–104; Sukenick, *Down and In*, 89; Woliver, *Hoot*, 119–120; (Twist) Jim Dawson, *The Twist* (Boston, 1995), esp. xi–xii, 16–17, 34, 43–44, 62–63, 65, 72, 89–90; Herbert O. Kubly to Kay Boyle, July 31, 1962 (quote), Box 16:2, KB Papers.

26 Cantwell, *When*, 21–22, 34, 81, 94, 118, 122, 126–130, 142, 145, 165–167, 245–254; Marcus, *Rock*, 125–127; Pete Seeger, *The Incompleat Folksinger*, ed. Jo M. Schwartz (Lincoln, NE, 1992; orig. 1972), 14–22, 27–29, 34; Jacques Vassal, *Electric Children*, tr. Paul Barnett (New York, 1976; orig. 1971), 89–99; *Chicago Tribune*, Jan. 5, 1943, p. 1; (Weavers) Cantwell, *When*, 179; Seeger, *Folksinger*, 22 (sales); Woliver, *Hoot*, 37; *Newsweek*, May 13, 1963, p. 95; *Sing Out!*, Sept.–Oct. 1980, pp. 2–7. See also Robbie Lieberman, *My Song Is My Weapon* (Urbana, 1989).

27 (Weavers) Cantwell, *When*, 15–19, 178–181, 186–187, 276, 325; Seeger, *Folksinger*, 22–26, 211–212, 216; Bert Spector, "The Weavers: A Case History in Show Business Blacklisting," *Journal of American Culture*, 5 (Fall 1982), 113–120; *NYT*, Jan. 6, 1962, p. 41; Nov. 24, 1962, p. 15; May 3, 1963, p. 34; *Variety*, May 1, 1963, pp. 65, 67; Seeger in Bud Schultz and Ruth Schultz, eds., *It Did Happen Here* (Berkeley, 1989), 18–20; (hoots) Cantwell, *When*, 257; Seeger, *Folksinger*, 244; Shelton, *No Direction*, 192–193; Terrace, *Encyclopedia of Television*, 1:207; Vassal, *Electric*, 111–112; *John Edwards Memorial Foundation Quarterly*, 16 (Summer 1980), 95–98.

28 Shelton, *No Direction*, 125, 183; Williams, *Dylan*, 53; Woliver, *Hoot*, 38, 58; Peter, Paul and Mary, *Ten Years Together* (1970 album), notes.

29 Cantwell, *When*, 8, 14–15, 19, 22, 40, 53–55, 285–286; Marcus, *Rock*, 90–92; Seeger, *Folksinger*, 215–217; Pete Seeger and Bob Reiser, *Everybody Says Freedom* (New York, 1989), 38. Quotes from Mary Travers at a concert in Boston, Aug. 22, 1996; Shelton, *No Direction*, 3.

30 Cantwell, *When*, 295–297, 305–308, 343; Vassal, *Electric*, 105, 170–175; Woliver, *Hoot*, 92–97. See also Joan Baez, *And a Voice to Sing with* (New York, 1987).

NOTES TO PAGES 187–191 287

31 Cantwell, *When*, 298, 300, 338–341, 344, 351–352; Farrell, *Spirit*, 74 (sales); Seeger, *Folksinger*, 233; Shelton, *No Direction*, 191 (quote), 197–200; Vassal, *Electric*, 126; Williams, *Dylan*, 53–54; *NYT*, July 27, 1963, p. 9; July 29, 1963, p. 15; Aug. 19, 1963, p. 21. "God" on Newport Folk Festival, 1963, *Newport Broadside* (1964 album); "Wind" and "Overcome" on NFF, 1963, *The Evening Concerts* (1964 album), notes.

32 (Dylan) Farrell, *Spirit*, 75; Shelton, *No Direction*, 7, 10, 13, 17, 23, 27, 44–45, 65–82, 87, 92, 101–102, 108, 212, 223–225; Wakefield, *New York*, 158; Williams, *Dylan*, 21, 25–27, 29, 38, 55–56; Woliver, *Hoot*, 62–74; *NYT*, Sept. 29, 1961; Jaharana Romney in Bauldie, *Wanted Man*, 18–20; Bauldie in Bauldie, *Wanted Man*, 31, 35–42; (Guthrie) Cantwell, *When*, 110, 135–137, 345; Mellers, *Darker Shade*, 118–119, 124; Tim Riley, *Hard Rain* (New York, 1992), 17–20; Seeger, *Folksinger*, 41–60; Vassal, *Electric*, 72–82, 120, 122; Richard A. Reuss, "Woody Guthrie and His Folk Tradition," *Journal of American Folklore*, 83 (July–Sept. 1970), 273–303; Pete Seeger in *Seeing Red* (1983 film).

33 (Dylan) Farrell, *Spirit*, 75 (quote); Mellers, *Darker Shade*, 130–131; Riley, *Hard Rain*, 69; Shelton, *No Direction*, 119; Woliver, *Hoot*, 74–78; (Ochs) Shelton, *No Direction*, 108, 156–160; Vassal, *Electric*, 156–160; Woliver, *Hoot*, 86–87, 120, 123–124; *Broadside*, #63 (Oct. 15, 1965), 4–5; *Esquire*, Oct. 1976, p. 110ff.; (songs) "Masters" and "Blowin'" on *Freewheelin'* (1963 album); "Hattie Carroll," "Pawn," and "Ship" on *The Times They Are A-Changin'* (1964 album); Dylan recorded "Redwing" in April 1963; it was issued on *The Bootleg Series, Vols. 1–3* (1991 album). Ochs's "The Ballad of Medgar Evers" is on *Newport Broadside* (1964 album); "I Ain't Marching Anymore" is on the album of the same title (1965); "Revolution" on *Phil Ochs in Concert* (1966 album).

34 "God" on *The Times They Are A-Changin'* (1964 album); "Blowin'" on *Freewheelin'* (1963 album).

35 ("Hard Rain") Mellers, *Darker Side*, 132–133; Riley, *Hard Rain*, 4–8, 16, 22, 59–61; Shelton, *No Direction*, 172; Vassal, *Electric*, 124; "Hard Rain" on *Freewheelin'* (1963), notes; ("Why Do You") Robert Cohen, *When the Old Left Was Young* (New York, 1993), 299–303, 412n67; Joe Klein, *Woody Guthrie* (New York, 1980), 144–145; *Sing Out!*, 23:5 (Nov.–Dec. 1974); *Sarah Ogan Gunning* (1965 album), notes.

36 Marcus, *Rock*, 22–24, 39–49; Mellers, *Darker Side*, 114, 117–118, 128; Milton "Mezz" Mezzrow and Bernard Wolfe, *Really the Blues* (New York, 1990; orig. 1946), 14, 31, 107; Riley, *Hard Rain*, 31–41; Shelton, *No Direction*, 31–34, 37, 41; Williams, *Dylan*, 46 (quote).

37 Mellers, *Darker Shade*, 137; Riley, *Hard Rain*, 13–15, 62; Shelton, *No Direction*, 313–314; Williams, *Dylan*, 66, 68, 72; Woliver, *Hoot*, 85; Elliott

Landy in Bauldie, *Wanted Man*, 76–77; *Broadside*, #93 (July–Aug. 1968), 5; *Biograph* (1985 album), song list insert. Both songs are on *Bringing It All Back Home* (1965 album).

38 Marcus, *Rock*, 20; D. A. Pennebaker, *Bob Dylan* (New York, 1968), 123; Sukenick, *Down and In*, 120–121; Turner, *Angelheaded*, 20–21; Williams, *Dylan*, 53, 64; Paul McCartney in Bauldie, *Wanted Man*, 72; Phil Ochs in *Broadside*, #63 (Oct. 15, 1965), 3–4. Quotes from Shelton, *No Direction*, 181; *Crawdaddy*, #19 (Dec. 1972), 35.

39 Pennebaker, *Dylan*, 124; Shelton, *No Direction*, 127, 140, 173–175; Vassal, *Electric*, 122–124, 135 (sales at 122); Williams, *Dylan*, 51–52; Woliver, *Hoot*, 78–83; *Biograph* (1985 album), booklet; (NFF) Cantwell, *When*, 309; Shelton, *No Direction*, 349; Williams, *Dylan*, 80, 82; Joe Boyd in Bauldie, *Wanted Man*, 64–66.

40 Cantwell, *When*, 15–16, 19, 51–55, 79, 325; Shelton, *No Direction*, 211, 219.

41 On the NEA see *The National Endowment for the Arts, 1965–1995* (Washington, 1995).

42 Banes, *Greenwich*, 81–82; Belgrad, *Culture*, 16; Cantwell, *When*, 102; Guilbaut, *New York*, 2–4, 12–13, 24–25, 30–32; Max Kozloff, "American Painting during the Cold War," *Artforum*, May 1973, pp. 43–54; William Hauptman, "The Suppression of Art in the McCarthy Decade," *Artforum*, Oct. 1973, pp. 48–52. See also Wanda M. Corn, *The Great American Thing* (Berkeley, 1999).

43 Abel, *Intellectual*, 95–96, 109, 112, 115; Gruen, *Party's Over*, 83, 129–130, 195, 265; Peggy Guggenheim, *Out of This Century* (2nd ed., London, 1983; orig. 1979), 227–228, 231, 245–246, 274–275; Guilbaut, *New York*, 5, 49, 59, 67, 81–82, 91, 110–111, 115, 125, 178; Huxley, *Aldous Huxley*, 94; Sidney Janis in Laura de Coppet and Alan Jones, *The Art Dealers* (New York, 1984), 33–34.

44 Belgrad, *Culture*, 17–20, 36–37, 78–79, 99, 106–115; Crow, *Rise*, 59–60; Emile de Antonio and Mitch Tuchman, *Painters Painting* (New York, 1984), 15–16, 43, 58–59; de Coppet and Jones, *Art Dealers*, 22–29, 68; Gruen, *Party's Over*, 130, 228–233 (quote at 232), 265; Guggenheim, *Out*, 295, 304, 314–316; Guilbaut, *New York*, 67, 85, 97, 110, 112, 157–159, 161, 176, 186; Sukenick, *Down and In*, 52; Eva Cockcroft, "Abstract Expressionism, Weapon of the Cold War," *Artforum*, June 1974, pp. 39–41.

45 (life) Abel, *Intellectual*, 211–213; de Antonio and Tuchman, *Painters*, 15–16; de Coppet and Jones, *Art Dealers*, 135; Gruen, *Party's Over*, 32, 128–129, 181, 218 (1st quote); McDarrah and McDarrah, *Beat Generation*, 25; Wakefield, *New York*, 130; Warhol and Hackett, *Popism*, 13; (success)

Sybille Bedford, *Aldous Huxley* (New York, 1985; orig. 1973–1974), 668 (2nd quote); Belgrad, *Culture*, 250; Gruen, *Party's Over*, 175–182, 214, 220; McClure, *Scratching*, 64, 75; (Johns) Crow, *Rise*, 18, 34; de Antonio and Tuchman, *Painters*, 95, 100–101; de Coppet and Jones, *Art Dealers*, 58–59; Lucy R. Lippard et al., *Pop Art* (New York, 1996; orig. 1966), 69; Steven H. Madoff, ed., *Pop Art* (Berkeley, 1997), 96; Russell and Gablik, *Pop Art*, 28.

46 Belgrad, *Culture*, 161, 163; Crow, *Rise*, 128; Haskell, *Blam!*, 17; John Rublowsky, *Pop Art* (New York, 1965), 28–29; Russell and Gablik, *Pop Art*, 14; de Antonio and Tuchman, *Painters*, 19 (quote).

47 Crow, *Rise*, 36, 91; Haskell, *Blam!*, 68, 70–71; Lippard, *Pop Art*, 96; Madoff, *Pop Art*, 27, 86; Rublowsky, *Pop Art*, 63, 66–67; Russell and Gablik, *Pop Art*, 14 (quote); Cécile Whiting, *A Taste for Pop* (Cambridge, U.K., 1997), 23; Glaser in *Artforum*, Feb. 1966, p. 22. For a different interpretation see Hilton Kramer, *The Age of the Avant-Garde* (New York, 1973). On postmodernism see Linda Hutcheon, *The Politics of Postmodernism* (New York, 1989), esp. 12–13.

48 Crow, *Rise*, 89; Haskell, *Blam!*, 77, 79, 81; Lippard, *Pop Art*, 95; Madoff, *Pop Art*, 30; Whiting, *Taste*, 101–105, 108–113, 117–119, 123–128, 130–132; Ivan Karp in de Coppet and Jones, *Art Dealers*, 139.

49 Haskell, *Blam!*, 81; Lippard, *Pop Art*, 86; Madoff, *Pop Art*, 30, 32.

50 (early) Victor Bockris, *The Life and Death of Andy Warhol* (New York, 1989), 59–60, 93; Andreas Brown, comp., *Andy Warhol* (New York, 1971); Bob Colacello, *Holy Terror* (New York, 1990), esp. 13, 19, 23–24, 26; Calvin Tomkins in John Coplans, *Andy Warhol* (New York, 1970), 9–12, 14; Crow, *Rise*, 84–85; de Antonio and Tuchman, *Painters*, 27–29; Grobel, *Capote*, 187; Haskell, *Blam!*, 77, 86–87; Madoff, *Pop Art*, xiv; Warhol and Hackett, *Popism*, 35; (soup) Bockris, *Warhol*, 106, 110, 115; de Coppett and Jones, *Art Dealers*, 155–156; Russell and Gablik, *Pop Art*, 117; Irving Sandler in *New York Post*, Dec. 2, 1962, p. 12. The Andy Warhol Museum, Pittsburgh, is worth a visit.

51 Bockris, *Warhol*, 112; Tomkins in Coplans, *Warhol*, 13; Crow, *Rise*, 86; Haskell, *Blam!*, 79, 81; Madoff, *Pop Art*, 267; Rublowsky, *Pop Art*, 113–116; Warhol and Hackett, *Popism*, 22; Whiting, *Taste*, 172–173; Mary Josephson, "Warhol: The Medium as Cultural Artifact," *Art in America*, 59:3 (May–June 1971), 41; *New York Review of Books*, Feb. 18, 1982, p. 8. Quotes from London *Observer Magazine*, June 12, 1966, p. 12; *Rolling Stone*, Apr. 9, 1987, p. 32.

52 Bockris, *Warhol*, 127–129; Crow, *Rise*, 86–87, 92, 105; de Antonio and Tuchman, *Painters*, 27; de Coppett and Jones, *Art Dealers*, 69–70,

95–96, 113; Haskell, *Blam!*, 84–85; Lippard, *Pop Art*, 98; Rublowsky, *Pop Art*, 110; Whiting, *Taste*, 91, 146–154, 160–166; Josephson, "Warhol," 41 (quote); "Andy Warhol, 1928–87," *Art in America*, 75:5 (May 1987), 140.

53 Banes, *Greenwich*, 84–85; Bockris, *Warhol*, 121; Lippard, *Pop Art*, 99; Madoff, *Pop Art*, 34; Henry Geldzahler, "Andy Warhol," *Art International*, Apr. 1964, pp. 34–35; John Richardson, "The Secret Warhol," *Vanity Fair*, July 1987, p. 127; London *Observer Magazine*, June 12, 1966, pp. 10–11; (Factory) Bockris, *Warhol*, 141, 147; Ultra Violet, *Famous for 15 Minutes* (San Diego, 1988), 16; Warhol and Hackett, *Popism*, 64–65; (films) Bockris, *Warhol*, 133, 142–143; Colacello, *Holy Terror*, 29; Crow, *Rise*, 92, 147; Haskell, *Blam!*, 133–134; Miles, *Ginsberg*, 335–336; Warhol and Hackett, *Popism*, 33; *NYT*, Sept. 12, 1964, p. 15; (Dylan) Shelton, *No Direction*, 389–390; Williams, *Dylan*, 64, 89–90; Gerard Malanga in Bauldie, *Wanted Man*, 67–71.

54 (Beats) Belgrad, *Culture*, 228–230; (Pop Art) Bockris, *Warhol*, 115; de Antonio and Tuchman, *Painters*, 119–120, 129; Lippard, *Pop Art*, 9–11; McClure, *Scratching*, 85; Madoff, *Pop Art*, xiii, 93; Thomas Merton, *The Courage for Truth*, ed. Christine M. Bochen (New York, 1993), 38 (quote).

55 Belgrad, *Culture*, 203; Huxley, *Aldous Huxley*, 13, 15, 18, 50, 101–102, 104, 150; Laura A. Huxley, *This Timeless Moment* (New York, 1968), 195–196; Nin, *Diary*, 6:331; Jay Stevens, *Storming Heaven* (New York, 1987), 33, 39–42; Robert Hughes, "The Rise of Andy Warhol," *New York Review of Books*, Feb. 18, 1982, p. 7 (quote).

56 David K. Dunaway, *Huxley in Hollywood* (London, 1989), 14–17, 22, 26, 28, 31, 61–62, 73, 89, 116, 312; Huxley, *Aldous Huxley*, 22, 42, 61, 90–91.

57 Dunaway, *Huxley*, 285–289, 293, 297; Huxley, *Aldous Huxley*, 114–115, 118; Huxley, *Timeless*, 138–139; Stevens, *Storming Heaven*, 79–80, 83; Dan Wakefield in *Playboy*, Nov. 1963, pp. 200–201.

58 Bedford, *Huxley*, 588–589; Dunaway, *Huxley*, 316, 324–326; Stevens, *Storming Heaven*, 55–57 (1st quote at 56); Aldous Huxley, *Letters of Aldous Huxley*, ed. Grover Smith (New York, 1969), 923–925, 938 (2nd quote); Huxley, *Aldous Huxley*, 105; Huxley, *Timeless*, 133–134, 144, 152; Nin, *Diary*, 6:44, 170. See also Martin A. Lee and Bruce Shlain, *Acid Dreams* (New York, 1985). Huxley's two books were combined as *The Doors of Perception, and Heaven and Hell* (New York, 1956).

59 (strategy) Dunaway, *Huxley*, 298, 300, 371; Huxley, *Letters*, 895, 902–903, 905; Huxley, *Aldous Huxley*, 120; Huxley, *Timeless*, 135; Michael Hollingshead, *The Man Who Turned on the World* (New York, 1974; orig. 1973), 7, 10–11, 31; (trippers) Ellwood, *Sixties*, 82; Nin, *Diary*, 5:256–262; 6:116, 132; Stevens, *Storming Heaven*, 63, 64, 69, 72; Peter O. Whitmer and Bruce VanWyngarden, *Aquarius Revisited* (New York, 1991;

orig. 1987), 92; (Luce) Laura M. Jenkins to Clare B. Luce, Sept. 18 [1962]; July, 26 [1960–62?], Box 213:8; Jay M. Barrie to CBL, [Oct. 1961], Box 213:10; Sid [Cohen] to CBL, Nov. 16, 1961, Box 213:14; Gerald [Heard] to CBL, Aug. 31, 1961, Box 214:5; CBL to Carlos Chavez, May 12, 1962, Box 215:12; to Phillip Cortney, Jan. 16, 1962, Box 215:13; Anne Ford to CBL, [1963], Box 217:10; Peggy Hitchcock to CBL, June 6, 1963; reply, July 31, 1963, both in Box 217:14, all in CBL Papers. See also *Vancouver Province*, Aug. 29–Sept. 5, 1959; Steven J. Novak, "LSD before Leary: Sidney Cohen's Critique of 1950s Psychedelic Drug Research," *ISIS*, 88:1 (March 1997), 87–110; Sidney Cohen, *The Beyond Within* (New York, 1965).

60 Burroughs, *Letters*, 322; Ginsberg, *Indian Journals*, 28; Ginsberg, *Journals: Early Fifties, Early Sixties*, xxii; Ginsberg–Orlovsky, *Straight*, 189; Kramer, *Ginsberg*, 186; Miles, *Ginsberg*, 260 (1st–3rd quotes), 262, 266, 269–274 (4th quote at 270); Schumacher, *Dharma Lion*, 311–313, 327–333; Whitmer and VanWyngarden, *Aquarius*, 157.

61 (mushrooms) Cook, *Beat Generation*, 187–188; Leary, *Flashbacks*, 29–35; Stevens, *Storming Heaven*, 123–125, 134; Whitmer and VanWyngarden, *Aquarius*, 16–17, 22, 25–30; Timothy Leary to Arthur Koestler, Jan. 4, 1961 (copy); TL to Allen Ginsberg, Jan. 7, 1961, both in Box 38:21, AG-SU; (Leary–Huxley) Dunaway, *Huxley*, 353–354; Huxley, *Letters*, 909, 929, 944; Stevens, *Storming Heaven*, 141–142; Whitmer and VanWyngarden, *Aquarius*, 32, 157; (Leary–Ginsberg) Kramer, *Ginsberg*, 187–188; Miles, *Ginsberg*, 276, 280; Schumacher, *Dharma Lion*, 344–346; Stevens, *Storming Heaven*, 144–146; Whitmer and VanWyngarden, *Aquarius*, 157–159; *Esquire*, July 1968, pp. 84–86, 116–117. Quotes from Leary, *Flashbacks*, 44; Ginsberg–Cassady, *As Ever*, 205.

62 (intellectuals) Leary, *Flashbacks*, 65–70; Miles, *Ginsberg*, 281; Schumacher, *Dharma Lion*, 347–348; Wakefield, *New York*, 172–174; Whitmer and VanWyngarden, *Aquarius*, 158; Wakefield in *Playboy*, Nov. 1963, p. 210; TL to WSB, Jan. 5, 1961 (copy), Box 38:21, AG-SU; (Kerouac) Clark, *Kerouac*, 193; Cook, *Beat Generation*, 183 (quote); Miles, *Ginsberg*, 281; Nicosia, *Memory Babe*, 621, 630; JK to TL, [early 1961] (copy), Box 38:21, AG-SU; (danger) Dunaway, *Huxley*, 355, 370–371; Huxley, *Letters*, 945; Miles, *Ginsberg*, 280; Whitmer and VanWyngarden, *Aquarius*, 28, 31, 33–35.

63 (Gysin) *Esquire*, July 1968, p. 87 (1st quote); (Tangier) Ginsberg–Orlovsky, *Straight*, 203–205, 207 (2nd quote); (Burroughs) Ginsberg–Orlovsky, *Straight*, 211; Whitmer and VanWyngarden, *Aquarius*, 125–126; *Esquire*, July 1968, p. 86; TL to AG, Oct. 21, 1961 (3rd–4th quotes), Box 38:21, AG-SU; (Harvard) TL to AG, Nov. 15, 1961 (5th–6th quotes), Box 38:21, AG-SU; (prison) Hollingshead, *Man*, 47–50, 52; Leary, *Flashbacks*, 79,

83–90; Stevens, *Storming Heaven*, 156–157; *Playboy*, Nov. 1963, pp. 202, 206; TL to AG, [ca. 1961], Box 38:21, AG-SU.

64 (Meyer) Burleigh, *Very Private*, 169–172, 174, 177, 212, 290, 299; Leary, *Flashbacks*, 128–130, 154–156, 194, 197–198, 224, 226–227; (set and setting) Dunaway, *Huxley*, 355; Hollingshead, *Man*, 20, 24, 31, 40, 44–45, 58, 67, 69; Nin, *Diary*, 6:331–333, 342; Stevens, *Storming Heaven*, 163, 165, 169, 184–203; Whitmer and VanWyngarden, *Aquarius*, 31, 36; *Playboy*, Nov. 1963, p. 206; WSB to Allen Ginsberg, Nov. 20, 1963 (quote), Box 1, AG-CU. See also *NYT*, Dec. 11, 1962, pp. 1, 3; *Reporter*, Aug. 15, 1963, pp. 35–43; Martin Mayer, "Getting Alienated with the Right Crowd at Harvard," *Esquire*, Sept. 1963, pp. 73, 141–144. On a bad trip see *Saturday Review*, June 1, 1963, pp. 39–43; (Millbrook) Huxley, *Letters*, 955; Leary, *Flashbacks*, 187–190, 193–198, 224–226, 243–244.

65 Plummer, *Holy Goof*, 116–119; Stevens, *Storming Heaven*, 222–227, 229; Stephen L. Tanner, *Ken Kesey* (Boston, 1983), 14, 21, 24; Whitmer and VanWyngarden, *Aquarius*, 200–203; *Crawdaddy*, #19 (Dec. 1972), 38–39; Vic Lovell in *The Free You*, 2:15 (Oct. 1968), 20; "Ken Kesey," *Genesis West*, 3:1–2 (Fall 1963), 20–21, 27; *San Francisco Chronicle*, July 21, 1963, p. 2.

66 (Pranksters) Plummer, *Holy Goof*, 122, 125–127; Stevens, *Storming Heaven*, 230–231; Tanner, *Kesey*, 90, 101; Whitmer and VanWyngarden, *Aquarius*, 99, 160, 204; Tom Wolfe, *The Electric Kool-Aid Acid Test* (New York, 1969; orig. 1968), 30–32, 36–48, 51–57, 60–92, 189, 210–221; (bus) Warren French, *Jack Kerouac* (Boston, 1986), 21; Leary, *Flashbacks*, 204–206; Nicosia, *Memory Babe*, 653; Plummer, *Holy Goof*, 123; Stevens, *Storming Heaven*, 232, 234–235; Tanner, *Kesey*, 89; Whitmer and VanWyngarden, *Aquarius*, 205; Wolfe, *Electric Kool-Aid*, 93–96. See also Paul Perry and Ken Babbs, *On the Bus* (New York, 1990); (Angels) Kramer, *Ginsberg*, 78–79; Stevens, *Storming Heaven*, 241; Whitmer and VanWyngarden, *Aquarius*, 87, 99. See also Hunter S. Thompson, *Hell's Angels* (New York, 1967).

67 (LSD) Gary Snyder in Knight and Knight, *Beat Diary*, 147; Dan Wakefield in *Playboy*, Nov. 1963, pp. 206, 208; (Huxley) Bedford, *Huxley*, 697, 699, 705–713, 740–741; Dunaway, *Huxley*, 348–352, 356–359, 364, 375, 384; Huxley, *Letters*, 890, 911; Huxley, *Aldous Huxley*, 120–121, 124–127, 160–162; Huxley, *Timeless*, 69–82, 96, 247–248, 263–264, 300–308.

Chapter Six

1 Stephen E. Ambrose, *Nixon* (New York, 1987–1989), 2:36; Ralph J. Gleason to Eric [?], Dec. 4, 1963 (copy), RJG Letters.

2 Adlai E. Stevenson, *The Papers of Adlai E. Stevenson*, ed. Walter Johnson (Boston, 1979), 8:460–463, 472 (quotes at 460, 461); *New York Post*, Nov. 22, 1964 (3rd quote).

3 (Graham) Carol Felsenthal, *Power, Privilege, and the Post* (New York, 1993), 232; Katharine Graham, *Personal History* (New York, 1997), 353; (Sorensen) Richard N. Goodwin, *Remembering America* (Boston, 1988), 231. Quotes from Goodwin, *Remembering*, 227; Michael R. Beschloss, *The Crisis Years* (New York, 1991), 676; George Reedy JOH, (1972), 3:25; Hale Boggs KOH, 34.

4 C. David Heymann, *A Woman Named Jackie* (New York, 1994), 408; Charles Bartlett JOH, 9. Quotes from Beschloss, *Crisis Years*, 675; Jacqueline Kennedy Onassis JOH, 15.

5 (Hoover) Curt Gentry, *J. Edgar Hoover* (New York, 1991), 537; Arthur M. Schlesinger, Jr., *Robert Kennedy and His Times* (Boston, 1978), 628–629; Nicholas Katzenbach KOH (1969), 73; (RFK) Merle Miller, *Lyndon* (New York, 1980), 321 (quote); (McNamara) Robert S. McNamara with Brian VanDeMark, *In Retrospect* (New York, 1995), 90–92; Schlesinger, *Robert Kennedy*, 611; (Arlington) John H. Davis, *The Kennedys* (New York, 1984), 534; Bartlett KOH, 149–150; (Salinger) Pierre Salinger, *P.S., a Memoir* (New York, 1995), 155–157.

6 (Rose) Charles Higham, *Rose* (New York, 1995), 378–379; (Lawford) Patricia S. Lawford with Ted Schwarz, *The Peter Lawford Story* (New York, 1988), 167; James Spada, *Peter Lawford* (New York, 1991), 346–348; (Vidal) Arthur M. Schlesinger, Jr., to Gore Vidal, Nov. 24, 1963, 37:5, GV Papers; (Radziwill) Diana DuBois, *In Her Sister's Shadow* (Boston, 1995), 150; (RFK) Schlesinger, *Robert Kennedy*, 611; Spada, *Lawford*, 349; (wake) Davis, *Kennedys*, 536; Spada, *Lawford*, 349; (JFK, Jr.) Maud Shaw, *White House Nannie* (New York, 1996; orig. 1965), 20–21; Davis, *Kennedys*, 542.

7 (LBJ) Robert G. Baker with Larry L. King, *Wheeling and Dealing* (New York, 1978), 152; (RFK) Seymour M. Hersh, *The Dark Side of Camelot* (Boston, 1997), 7, 9; (Salinger) Salinger, *P.S., a Memoir*, 158, 165; (Schlesinger) Goodwin, *Remembering*, 231; (staff) Joseph W. Alsop to Sir Isaiah Berlin, Dec. 11, 1963, Box 19, Alsop Papers; George Reedy JOH (1972), 5:43. Quotes from Miller, *Lyndon*, 324; Arthur M. Schlesinger, Jr., in Adolf A. Berle Diary, Dec. 28, 1963; Marian Schlesinger to Hans J. Morgenthau, after Nov. 22, 1963, Box 53:10, HJM Papers; Walt Rostow KOH, 140; *Newsweek*, Nov. 28, 1983, p. 65.

8 (image) Dan Wakefield, *New York in the Fifties* (Boston, 1992), 331; (Warhol) Andy Warhol and Pat Hackett, *Popism* (New York, 1980), 60; Thomas Crow, *The Rise of the Sixties* (New York, 1996), 87; (Stern)

Jackie: Behind the Myth (2000 film); (Menuhin) Julian Huxley, ed., *Aldous Huxley, 1894–1963* (New York, 1965), 9. Quotes from David E. Lilienthal, *The Journals of David E. Lilienthal* (New York, 1972), 5:522; Thomas Merton to Jacques Maritain, Dec. 2, 1963, TM, *The Courage for Truth*, ed. Christine M. Bochen (New York, 1993), 42, 43; Mailer in Carol Polsgrove, *It Wasn't Pretty, Folks, but Didn't We Have Fun?* (New York, 1995), 97; Victor Bockris, *The Life and Death of Andy Warhol* (New York, 1989), 140.

9 (Denmark) William Blair KOH, 31–36; (Sweden) J. Graham Parsons KOH, 34, 40.

10 (France) Daniel Berrigan to Jerry and Carol [?], Nov. 29, 1963 (1st quote), Box 88; DB to Brewster Kneen, Jan. 6, 1964, Box 89, both in Berrigan Coll.; François de Rose to J. Robert Oppenheimer, Dec. 3 [1963], Box 30:19, JRO Papers; (Soviet Union) Beschloss, *Crisis Years*, 676, 679; Ralph J. Gleason to Alexander P. Hoffman, Nov. 25, 1963, RJG Letters; (Hungary) Daniel Berrigan to Rev. James J. Shanahan, Jan. 7, 1964 (2nd quote), Box 89, Berrigan Coll.; (Czechoslovakia and Switzerland) [Sinclaire?] to Clare B. Luce, Dec. 19, 1963 (3rd quote), Box 219:1, CBL Papers.

11 (Japan) Harry McPherson, *A Political Education* (2nd ed., Boston, 1988), 213–214 (1st quote at 214); Keyes Beach to Joseph W. Alsop, Nov. 29, 1963, Box 19, Alsop Papers; (India) Chester Bowles, *Promises to Keep* (New York, 1971), 453–454; Benjamin C. Bradlee, *Conversations with Kennedy* (New York, 1975), 205; Jim F. Heath, *Decade of Disillusionment* (Bloomington, IN, 1975), 154; Richard Celeste in *Newsweek*, Nov. 28, 1983, p. 71; (Africa) James Farmer, *Freedom-When?* (New York, 1965), 136; Heath, *Decade*, 154 (2nd quote); (Dom. Rep.) Spencer M. King to John B. Martin, Dec. 2, 1963, Box 46:3, JBM Papers; (Brazil) Elizabeth Bishop to Frani B. Muser, Dec. 5, 1963, EB, *One Art*, ed. Robert Giroux (New York, 1994), 423; (Peru) Walt Rostow KOH, 144.

12 (Supreme Court) William O. Douglas, *The Court Years, 1939–1975* (New York, 1980), 305, 315; Roger K. Newman, *Hugo Black* (New York, 1994), 576; (theories) David Brinkley, *Memoirs* (New York, 1995), 158; Goodwin, *Remembering*, 227; Stan Levison in FBI report, Nov. 26, 1963, reel 3, MLK-SL FBI File; Jack H. Bell KOH, 71; (China bombing) William J. Gill, *The Ordeal of Otto Otepka* (New Rochelle, NY, 1969), 334; Hersh, *Dark Side*, 441–442; (Oswald attorney) John J. Abt with Michael Myerson, *Advocate and Activist* (Urbana, 1993), xi, 238, 251–252; William M. Kunstler with Sheila Isenberg, *My Life as a Radical Lawyer* (New York, 1994), 153–154, 158.

13 (Brown) Elizabeth C. Brown to Thomas Dodd, Dec. 2, 1963, Box 1:25, ECB Papers; (Luce) Letitia Baldrige to Arthur M. Schlesinger, Jr., June 3,

1964, Box P30, AMS Papers; (LBJ) Thomas Brown, *JFK* (Bloomington, IN, 1988), 127n11; Georgie A. Geyer, *Guerrilla Prince* (Boston, 1991), 300–301; Evan Thomas, *The Very Best Men* (New York, 1995), 330; (CIA plots) Brown, *JFK*, 75; Taylor Branch and George Crile III, "The Kennedy Vendetta," *Harper's Magazine*, Aug. 1975, p. 49ff; Thomas Powers in *Times Literary Supplement*, Apr. 21, 1989, p. 423; *NYT*, Apr. 30, 1975, p. 9; Oct. 4, 1975, p. 11; Nov. 21, 1975, pp. 1, 53; Mar. 2, 1976, p. 10; Mar. 12, 1976, p. 15; Feb. 25, 1977, pp. A1, A12; *WP*, Jan. 18, 1971, p. B7; Oct. 23, 1978, p. C27; Oct. 25, 1987, p. C5; *New York Post*, Aug. 23, 1976, p. 2; (other theories) Lawford, *Lawford*, 146; Schlesinger, *Robert Kennedy*, 615–616; Peter D. Scott, *Deep Politics and the Death of JFK* (Berkeley, 1993), 225. Quotes from Elizabeth C. Brown to Barry Goldwater, Dec. 8, 1963, Box 2:4, ECB Papers; Beschloss, *Crisis Years*, 676; ECB to Francesca Rhee, Feb. 15, 1964, Box 3:9, ECB Papers; Davis, *Kennedys*, 577.

14 (Warren Commission) *NYT*, Mar. 21, 1976, Sec. 1, p. 36; Charlotte Starr to Elizabeth C. Brown, Feb. 9, 1964, Box 3:18, ECB Papers; (Boggs) Lindy Boggs, *Washington through a Purple Veil* (New York, 1994), 182; (Black) Hugo Black to Perry Owen, Jan. 21, 1969, Box 37:7, HB Papers; (Baker) William R. Baker to David Ogilvy, Nov. 26, 1963, Box 2:10, DO Papers; (McCone) Schlesinger, *Robert Kennedy*, 609; (Krock) Arthur Krock private memoranda, Nov. 22 and Dec. 18, 1963, #340A and #346, Krock Memo Book III, Box 1, AK Papers; (Hoover) Michael R. Beschloss, *Taking Charge* (New York, 1997), 23 (tape).

15 Paul B. Sheatsley and Jacob J. Feldman, "The Assassination of President Kennedy," *Public Opinion Quarterly*, 28:2 (Summer 1964), 195, 201; Nancy Tuckerman and Pamela Turnure KOH, 44–46; Dean Acheson to Arthur J. Freund, Dec. 3, 1963, DA, *Among Friends*, ed. David S. McLellan and David C. Acheson (New York, 1980), 257; Janet Flanner, *Darlinghissima*, ed. Natalia D. Murray (New York, 1985), 345–346. Quotes from Joanne [?] to Gore Vidal and Howard Austin, Nov. 23 [1963], Box 91:2, GV Papers; Roger Hilsman KOH (O'Brien), 28; Kay Boyle to Fay Rappaport, Nov. 24, 1963, Box 1:7, Rappaport Coll.; Graham, *Personal History*, 353; Macdonald and Arendt in Hannah Arendt to Karl and Gertrud Jaspers, Dec. 1, 1963, Arendt–Jaspers, *Hannah Arendt–Karl Jaspers*, ed. Lotte Kohler and Hans Saner (New York, 1992), 537, 538; Helen Bevington, *Along Came the Witch* (New York, 1976), 120.

16 Sheatsley and Feldman in *Public Opinion Quarterly*, 197–198; Marshall Frady, *Wallace* (New York, 1968), vii. Quotes from Barbara Young to Eleanor Lattimore, Dec. 2, 1963, Box 22:9, Owen Lattimore Papers; Louis Ginsberg to Allen Ginsberg, Nov. 23, 1963, AG–LG, *Family Business*,

ed. Michael Schumacher (New York, 2001), 220; Hannah Arendt to Karl and Gertrud Jaspers, Nov. 24, 1963, Arendt–Jaspers, *Arendt–Jaspers*, 534.

17 Pamela Turnure in Tuckerman and Turnure KOH, 39; Bill Lawrence, *Six Presidents, Too Many Wars* (New York, 1972), 266. Quotes from Herbert O. Kubly to Kay Boyle, Nov. 26, 1963, Box 16:3, KB Papers; Rosie Waldeck to Clare B. Luce, Dec. 10, 1963, Box 219:5, CBL Papers.

18 (deified) Lilienthal, *Journals*, 5:535; Ralph J. Gleason to Alexander P. Hoffman, Nov. 25, 1963, RJG Letters; Shel Severinghaus to Henry R. Luce, Jan. 9, 1964, Box 19, Clare B. Luce Papers; (renaming) [?] to Constance and Elizabeth C. Brown, Nov. 29, 1963 (1st quote), Box 1:8, ECB Papers; (ratings) *Newsweek*, Nov. 28, 1983, p. 64; (Levison) Stanley Levison-Joan Daves conversation, FBI report, Nov. 26, 1963 (2nd quote), reel 3, MLK-SL FBI File.

19 George Herman, "The Elusive JFK," *New Leader*, Dec. 9, 1963, pp. 9–11; Constance Brown to Henry Regnery, Dec. 15, 1963, Box 2:37, Elizabeth C. Brown Papers. Quotes from *WP*, Sept. 9, 1963, p. A13; Edward R. Murrow to J. Robert Oppenheimer, Aug. 18, 1964, Box 5:22, JRO Papers; Charles Bohlen KOH, 28; Harry McPherson JOH, 2:32; Robert C. Cottrell, *Izzy* (New Brunswick, NJ, 1992), 215; Warren Weaver to JRO, Dec. 18, 1963, Box 77:1, JRO Papers; *Newsweek*, Nov. 28, 1983, p. 83.

20 Sheatsley and Feldman in *Public Opinion Quarterly*, 199; Andrew Young, *An Easy Burden* (New York, 1996), 279; Simeon Booker KOH, 39. Quotes from Bayard Rustin JOH, 2:16; Lewis in *Newsweek*, Nov. 28, 1983, p. 80; Coretta S. King, *My Life with Martin Luther King, Jr.* (New York, 1969), 244; Clayborne Carson, *Malcolm X* (New York, 1991), 245.

21 (Beckwith) Reed Massengill, *Portrait of a Racist* (New York, 1994), 177; (guilt) Joyce Ladner to Mr. and Mrs. John R. Salter, Jr., Dec. 5, 1963, reel 3, JRS Papers; (cheers) Clarice T. Campbell, *Civil Rights Chronicle* (Jackson, MS, 1997), 195; Charles Morgan, Jr., *A Time to Speak* (New York, 1964), 169; Frank E. Smith, *Congressman from Mississippi* (New York, 1964), 315; [?] to David and Sandy [Burner], Dec. 4, 1963 (copy), Box 5:17, James W. Silver Coll.; Virginia Durr to Hugo Black, Nov. 26, 1963, Box 7:3, HB Papers; (businessmen) Smith, *Congressman*, 315. Quotes from New Orleans *Times-Picayune*, Nov. 26, 1963; Adam Nossiter, *Of Long Memory* (Reading, MA, 1994), 253.

22 Quotes from Sheatsley and Feldman in *Public Opinion Quarterly*, 200; Susan M. Alsop, *To Marietta from Paris, 1945–1960* (Garden City, NY, 1975), 352; Sam Behrman to Arthur M. Schlesinger, Jr., Dec. 26, 1963, Box P30, AMS Papers; *Newsweek*, Nov. 28, 1983, p. 66.

23 On the Singing Nun, see *Time*, Nov. 15, 1963, p. 72; *Newsweek*, Dec. 23, 1963, p. 51.

24 Mike Mansfield to John K. Galbraith, Dec. 7, 1963 (quote), Box 42, JKG Papers; Pat Watters, *Down to Now* (2nd ed., Athens, GA, 1993; orig. 1971), 276–277.

25 Henry Graff in *Newsweek*, Nov. 28, 1983, p. 84; Hilsman KOH (O'Brien), 28 (quotes). See also Larry Berman, *Planning a Tragedy* (New York, 1982).

Manuscript Collections

Atlanta University, Atlanta, Georgia.
Southern Regional Council Papers, Voter Education Project Series. Film.

California State University, Long Beach.
Dorothy Healey Collection.

University of California, Berkeley. The Bancroft Library.
Lawrence Ferlinghetti Correspondence with Tram Combs. 88/131c.
Ralph J. Gleason Letters. 86/134c.

University of California, Los Angeles. Special Collections, Young Research Library.
Norman Cousins Papers.
Carey McWilliams Papers.
Kenneth Rexroth Papers.

Catholic University of America, Washington, D.C.
John Brophy Papers.

Columbia University, New York. Rare Book and Manuscript Library.
Allen Ginsberg Papers.

Cornell University, Ithaca, New York. Division of Rare and Manuscript Collections.
Daniel and Philip Berrigan Collection.

Emory University, Atlanta, Georgia. Special Collections.
Kathryn Fink Dunaway Papers.

Federal Bureau of Investigation, Washington, D.C.
    Martin Luther King, Jr. FBI File. Film.
    King-Levison FBI File. Film.

Harvard University, Cambridge, Massachusetts. Houghton Library.
    Artists and Writers for Stuart Hughes Papers.
    Robert Lowell Papers.

Hoover Institution, Stanford, California. Archives.
    Elizabeth Churchill Brown Papers.
    James Burnham Papers.

Lyndon B. Johnson Library, Austin, Texas.
    Lyndon B. Johnson Papers, Office Files of Walter Jenkins, Series 2.
    Lyndon B. Johnson Papers, U.S. Senate Papers.
    Lyndon B. Johnson Papers, Vice President.
    Drew Pearson Papers.

John F. Kennedy Library, Boston.
    Berl I. Bernhard Papers.
    Meyer Feldman Papers.
    John Kenneth Galbraith Papers.
    Elizabeth Smith Gatov Papers.
    John F. Kennedy Presidential Papers, National Security Files.
    Robert F. Kennedy's Attorney General's Papers.
    James J. P. McShane Papers.
    Burke Marshall Papers.
    Richard E. Neustadt Papers.
    Scott Rafferty Papers.
    Arthur M. Schlesinger, Jr. Papers.
    Theodore C. Sorensen Papers.
    Harris L. Wofford, Jr. Papers.

Martin Luther King, Jr. Center, Atlanta, Georgia.
    Congress of Racial Equality Papers, Addendum. Film.

Library of Congress, Washington, D.C. Manuscript Division.
    Joseph and Stewart Alsop Papers.
    Hannah Arendt Papers.
    Hugo L. Black Papers.
    Martha E. Dodd Papers.
    William O. Douglas Papers.
    W. Averell Harriman Papers.
    Alexander King Papers.

Owen Lattimore Papers.
Clare Boothe Luce Papers.
Thurgood Marshall Papers.
John Bartlow Martin Papers.
Groucho Marx Papers.
Margaret Mead Papers.
Hans J. Morgenthau Papers.
National Association for the Advancement of Colored People Papers,
    Group III.
David Ogilvy Papers.
J. Robert Oppenheimer Papers.
Asa Philip Randolph Papers.
Joseph L. Rauh, Jr. Papers.
Bayard T. Rustin Papers.
Charles Phelps Taft Papers.

Mississippi Department of Archives and History, Jackson.
John R. Salter, Jr. Papers.

Mississippi State University, Starkville. Special Collections.
Hodding and Betty Werlein Carter Papers.
Wilson F. Minor Papers.

University of Mississippi, Oxford. Special Collections.
James W. Silver Collection.

University of North Carolina, Chapel Hill. Southern Historical Collection.
Allard Kenneth Lowenstein Papers. #4340.

Princeton University, Princeton, New Jersey. Seeley G. Mudd Manuscript Library.
Arthur Krock Papers.
Adlai E. Stevenson Papers.

Radcliffe Institute, Harvard University, Cambridge, Massachusetts. Schlesinger Library.
Betty Friedan Papers.

Franklin D. Roosevelt Library, Hyde Park, New York.
Adolf A. Berle Diary. Film.

Southern Illinois University, Carbondale. Special Collections.
Kay Boyle Papers.
Herman and Fay Rappaport Collection of Kay Boyle Papers.

Stanford University, Stanford, California. Special Collections.
  Allen Ginsberg Papers.

Swarthmore College, Swarthmore, Pennsylvania. Peace Collection.
  SANE, a Citizens' Organization for a Sane World Records.
  Women Strike for Peace Records.

Tufts University, Medford, Massachusetts.
  Edward R. Murrow Papers.

State Historical Society of Wisconsin, Madison.
  Carl and Anne Braden Papers.
  Congress of Racial Equality Papers. Film.
  Paul Cowan Papers.
  Amzie Moore Papers.
  Anne Romaine Papers.
  Social Action Vertical File.
  Students for a Democratic Society Papers. Film.
  Gore Vidal Papers.
  Howard Zinn Papers.

Yale University, New Haven, Connecticut. Sterling Library, Manuscripts and Archives.
  William F. Buckley, Jr. Papers.

Oral Histories

University of California, Los Angeles.
Dorothy Healey   Carey McWilliams

Columbia University, New York. Oral History Office.
Virginia Durr   A. S. "Mike" Monroney
Roger Hilsman   Esther Peterson
John C. Holmes   David Powers
Katie Louchheim

Lyndon B. Johnson Library, Austin, Texas.
Charles Bartlett   Clarence Mitchell
William Bundy   Jacqueline Kennedy Onassis
Theodore Hesburgh   Thomas P. O'Neill
Hubert H. Humphrey (1977)   Joseph L. Rauh
Harry McPherson   George Reedy (1972)
Burke Marshall   Bayard Rustin

John F. Kennedy Library, Boston.
Dean Acheson   Burke Marshall (Hackman)
Robert Amory   Clarence Mitchell
Charles Bartlett   J. Graham Parsons
Jack Bell   John Patterson
William Blair   Esther Peterson
Hale Boggs   Joseph L. Rauh
Charles E. Bohlen   Chalmers Roberts
Simeon Booker   Walt Rostow

Chester Bowles (1970)
Chester Cooper
Myer Feldman
Elizabeth Smith Gatov
Roswell Gilpatric
Roger Hilsman
Roger Hilsman (O'Brien)
Nicholas Katzenbach (1964, 1969)
Carl Kaysen
Peter Lisagor
Robert Lovett
Burke Marshall

Norbert Schlei
George Smathers
Theodore C. Sorensen
William H. Sullivan
Hobart Taylor, Jr.
Llewellyn E. Thompson
Janet Travell
Nancy Tuckerman and
    Pamela Turnure
Robert Weaver
Roy Wilkins
Harris Wofford

Mississippi Department of Archives and History, Jackson.
Wilson F. Minor   James W. Silver
John R. Salter, Jr., and Rev. Edwin King
Mrs. Jane Schutt   Karl Wiesenberg

Index

WASPs, 132–5, 137, 144–5, 152, 163; blonde, 146–7; decline, xiv, 154; State Dept., 136–7
Watts, Alan, 207
Watts riot, xvii
Wayne, John, 43, 46
Weather Underground, xvii
Weavers, 41, 184
Webb, Robin, 152–3
Welch, Robert, 42
Wesleyan University, 146
West Virginia, 17, 41, 244 n19
White House, 3, 136–7, 219; protests, 54, 56–7, 59; redecoration, 129–30
Whitten, Jamie, 89
Wiesenberg, Karl, 89, 90
Wilkins, Roy, 75, 85, 110, 114, 119
Wilkinson, Frank, 26
Williams, Aubrey, 27, 44, 109–10
Williams, G. Mennen, 109
Williams, John Bell, 90
Wilson, Dagmar, 54
Winston-Salem, NC, 73
WLBT-TV, 90, 103
Wofford, Harris, 19, 71, 136
Wolfe, Tom, 202
Woman's party, 160

women, xv, 137, 154–63; jobs, 130–2, 162, 235; protests, 40, 52, 121
Women Strike for Peace, 54–5
women's movement, xv–xvi, 54, 162–3, 235, 236; feminism in, 158–9, 235, 237; and Friedan, 154–60
Woolworth's, 72, 113, 114
World Council of Churches, 27
World War II, 28, 32, 49, 64, 196, 215, 224, 235; Beats, 169–70; change, 133, 135, 137, 139–40, 165–7; Kennedy, 9–10, 233; veterans, xxi, 2, 15, 19, 77, 92–3, 99, 115, 133, 151; women, 130–1
Wroten, Joe, 89

X, Malcolm, 108, 110, 122, 228, 231

Yale University, 133–4
Yarrow, Peter, 185, 192
Young, Andrew, 113, 228
Young, Whitney, 77, 110, 119
Young Americans for Freedom (YAF), xix, 45–6
youth, xv, 4, 47, 59, 229, 235; culture, 139–40; folk music, 182, 186; rock and roll, 183, 190–1